After the Great Complacence

After the Great Complacence

Financial Crisis and the Politics of Reform

Ewald Engelen, Ismail Ertürk, Julie Froud,
Sukhdev Johal, Adam Leaver, Michael Moran,
Adriana Nilsson & Karel Williams

Centre for Research on Socio-Cultural Change, University of
Manchester

OXFORD
UNIVERSITY PRESS

OXFORD
UNIVERSITY PRESS

Great Clarendon Street, Oxford OX2 6DP

Oxford University Press is a department of the University of Oxford.
It furthers the University's objective of excellence in research, scholarship,
and education by publishing worldwide in

Oxford New York

Auckland Cape Town Dar es Salaam Hong Kong Karachi
Kuala Lumpur Madrid Melbourne Mexico City Nairobi
New Delhi Shanghai Taipei Toronto

With offices in

Argentina Austria Brazil Chile Czech Republic France Greece
Guatemala Hungary Italy Japan Poland Portugal Singapore
South Korea Switzerland Thailand Turkey Ukraine Vietnam

Oxford is a registered trade mark of Oxford University Press
in the UK and in certain other countries

Published in the United States
by Oxford University Press Inc., New York

© Oxford University Press 2011

The moral rights of the authors have been asserted
Database right Oxford University Press (maker)

First published 2011

British Library Cataloguing in Publication Data

Data available

Library of Congress Cataloging in Publication Data

Data available

Typeset by SPI Publisher Services, Pondicherry, India
Printed in Great Britain
on acid-free paper by
MPG Books Group, Bodmin and King's Lynn

ISBN 978–0–19–958908–1

3 5 7 9 10 8 6 4

Contents

Contents

Acknowledgements

The team of authors that produced this book has a continuous record of book and article output which goes back thirty years; and four of the authors have worked together continuously for some fifteen years. Our starting point remains the late John Williams' vision of a permanent research team, working outside disciplinary constraints to produce research that is conceptually minimalist, empirically resourceful, and politically resonant.

The Centre for Research on Socio-Cultural Change (CRESC) has since 2004 provided a broader context for our work and led to a new phase of funded research on financialization as well as new interdisciplinary collaborations with social science colleagues at the University of Manchester and beyond. We thank the Economic and Social Research Council (ESRC) for imaginatively funding this bold experiment and also Mike Savage and Josine Opmeer who made it work, creating the intellectual space in which we could have our conversations.

From the commissioning stage onwards, our book has been supported and encouraged by David Musson and Emma Lambert of Oxford University Press, who accepted frustrating delays and the late delivery of a lengthy manuscript. Some delay and hesitation was inevitable because this is an ambitious book about a changing object which led to sometimes heated internal debate amongst the team of authors as we made sense of the crisis and its implications.

In writing this book, we have drawn on a broader stock of ideas jointly developed with others who did not work on this project, especially two long-term collaborators, Peter Folkman and Sarah Green. The positions developed in this book owe much to CRESC's earlier *Alternative Banking Report* which was shaped by discussion with practitioners including Steve Francis of Vion Foods, Rob McGregor of Unite, and Alan McDougall of Pensions Investment Research Consultants (PIRC). More practically, Daniel Tischer helped us with the final assembly of the book in late 2010.

When a book has seven authors and ranges over technical and political issues, there will inevitably be differences of tone between chapters and unresolved issues, especially on matters of policy. This book is best thought of as an argument in a hybrid form because our eight chapters are neither a sole authored book held together by one controlling intelligence, nor a collection of essays where named individuals can properly take sole credit for developing particular chapters.

The authors' names appear in alphabetical order on the cover page because our imagination is collective and, after redrafting by many different hands, we are not always sure about who did what. If we had waited until all the individual authors agreed with every detail of the whole argument, this book would never have been finished. But we wrote this book because we were all convinced about the need to reframe the crisis as debacle and discuss the politics of reform as well as the technicalities of finance.

List of Figures

List of Figures

List of Tables

List of Abbreviations

ABS	Asset Backed Security
BIS	Bank for International Settlements
BVCA	British Private Equity and Venture Capital Association
CDO	Collateralized Debt Obligation
CDS	Credit Default Swap
CEO	Chief Executive Officer
CME	Co-ordinated Market Economy
ECB	European Central Bank
EVCA	European Venture Capital Association
FIRE	Finance, insurance, real estate
FSA	Financial Services Authority
FSF	Financial Stability Forum
GP	General Partner (in private equity)
IMF	International Monetary Fund
LBO	Leveraged Buy Out
LME	Liberalized Market Economy
LP	Limited Partner (in private equity)
LSE	London Stock Exchange
M&A	Merger and Acquisition
MEP	Member of the European Parliament
NED	Non-Executive Director
NGO	Non-Governmental Organization
NVCA	National Venture Capital Association
NWM	Nomadic War Machine
OECD	Organisation for Economic Co-operation and Development
OTC	Over the counter
PIK	Payment in kind
RBS	Royal Bank of Scotland

List of Abbreviations

ROA	Return on assets
ROE	Return on equity
S&P	Standard and Poors
S&PS	State and para-State
SEC	Securities and Exchange Commission
SIB	Securities and Investment Board
SIV	Structured investment vehicles
SPV	Special purpose vehicle
UKFI	UK Financial Investments

Introduction

Framing the Crisis: Accident, Fiasco, or Debacle?

There are only two stories: 'We name the guilty man' and 'Arrow points to defective part'. Everything else is PSJ—public service journalism. (Murray Sayle, quoted in an obituary in *The Times*, 21 September 2010)

Our intention was to write a book covering the financial crisis that began in 2007 in several high-income countries, concentrating on the United Kingdom but also covering the United States and the European Union. The aim was to answer two key questions in an accessible way which could influence social scientists and the political classes: how did finance come to cause the crisis, and why is it now so difficult to manage the consequences and to reform finance? As the chapters were drafted, we were increasingly troubled by a set of prior issues about how others were framing the crisis and how we should frame the crisis. Framing was relevant because it raised issues which, in academic terms, were about agency versus structure and, in popular terms, were about who or what to blame. Should we understand the crisis as an unfortunate accident caused by some kind of defect or mistake in a complex system; or did the crisis involve culpable irresponsibility or misjudgement by groups like investment bankers or regulators? Not least, framing matters because these issues are of broad interest and relevance for anyone interested in understanding present-day capitalism.

According to journalistic aphorism, there are only two stories: 'arrow indicates defective part' or 'we name the guilty men'. In a *Times* obituary, this was attributed to Murray Sayle, who also allegedly dismissed everything else as boring but worthy public service journalism. In other versions of the aphorism, Sayle, who was a great contrarian on issues like Bloody Sunday or the dropping of the first atom bomb, concedes there is a third kind of revisionist story because 'everything you thought you knew about this subject is wrong'. Our natural inclination was towards the third kind of story and we hoped to produce the academic equivalent of public service journalism with some revisionism. But, as we drafted chapters about financial innovation and the politics of reform, we were distracted by simultaneously reading the burgeoning academic and media literatures on crisis, which generally defaulted onto the two other stories by identifying the defective part or naming the guilty men.

Most notably, the elite British intelligentsia, including critical and independent key figures like the historian Donald MacKenzie, the regulator Andrew Haldane, and the *Financial Times* journalist Gillian Tett, was, by 2010, adopting variants on an accident account which associated financial crisis with disasters like the Challenger Space Shuttle or Deep Water Horizon. This framing had been adumbrated in the earlier emphasis on global imbalances in the work of figures like Adair Turner or Martin Wolf. But the critical intelligentsia added a new emphasis on mathematization and the performativity of formal knowledges. If the crisis was not an accident, our research also suggested that the crisis was not a fiasco in the classical sense familiar from the older social science literature by international authors like Bovens and 't Hart (1996) or Scott (1998); nor did we wish to endorse the attempts of those like Charles Perrow (2010) who blame the guilty bankers and politicians.

After some reflection, it seemed to us that the financial crisis could best be understood in a new and different frame as an elite debacle, which associated it with failed interventions like the American and British military ventures in Iraq and Afghanistan. This reframing was supported by research that indicated the importance of informal knowledges and of bricolage practices inside finance, which together open up new possibilities of attributing responsibility without scapegoating the guilty men; it echoes an original meaning of debacle as a confused rout. More broadly, the reframing of the financial crisis as debacle is also helpful because it situates the financial crisis in political terms as part of a much larger current problem about how and why the democratic system of political competition is not working to articulate alternatives and solutions.

The aim of this preface is then to present the book as an intervention in the ongoing debate about the crisis as accident. Through argument and evidence in the eight chapters we aim to persuade our readers to take our debacle framing seriously. Realistically, we do not aim to succeed by establishing a new mainstream orthodoxy but rather by provoking and persuading diverse readers to apply the debacle framing to their own work.

The *a priori* of accident

The definition and usage of the term 'systems accident' highlights the political and moral ambiguity of this kind of framing. Systems accident was originally used as a forensic category to describe an 'unanticipated interaction of multiple failures' in a complex system which is interactive and tightly coupled (Perrow 1984). The concept then provided the frame for classic accident case studies of engineering and process control disasters like the 1986 Challenger Space Shuttle disaster or the 1979 Three Mile Island nuclear accident. But, in current usage, systems accident has become the stock excuse of practitioners and corporate elites after things have gone disastrously wrong (Moran 2001). Thus, Tony Hayward, then chief executive of BP, when questioned in a Congressional hearing, described the oil spill from the Deepwater Horizon rig as 'a complex accident caused by an unprecedented combination of failures in a number of different, related processes, systems and equipment' (Plungis and Snyder 2010).

There is a large slippage between the original, austere forensic usage of the concept and the current, apologetic usage. For Perrow, the problem is about unanticipated or unforeseen, unknowable interactions between various components or events, under conditions of complexity and tight coupling. In his classic work, he was never a technocratic optimist who believed in fixing the defective part. Perrow argued more radically that complex systems which are tightly coupled should not be built because accident is inevitable (even though its precise form cannot be predicted *ex ante*). In the apologetic usage, the system has been built and failed disastrously and the corporate operator is trying to manage blame around the idea that accidents will happen. Thus, systems accident is not so much one explanation as an opening onto a field of accident explanation within systems.

But classic accident explanations typically share an a priori which is necessary to forms of explanation where 'arrow indicates defective part'. The system has one clear objective (such as oil from deep sea, electricity from nuclear power, or astronauts into space) so that success means safe and efficient performance of function. The accident involves a sequence of events and failures which go critical because of a decisive technical miscalculation or defective part (often organizationally embedded): at Three Mile Island, for example, the problem was the failure to recognize coolant loss consequent upon a stuck valve; with Challenger, the problem was poor design of the O ring component, compounded by low temperature after frost on the night before launch. There is an underlying fatalism about the past because accidents will happen in a complex world. Systems accidents are sometimes described as 'normal accidents' because under some combination of technological and social conditions we must expect catastrophic outcomes. But there is also technocratic optimism about the future because relevant interactions can be mapped and analysed; and on that basis future accidents can be prevented.

In earlier UK crises, like the Barings collapse of the mid-1990s or the secondary banking crisis of the mid-1970s, complacent practitioners had dared to try the 'accidents will happen' excuse (see Moran 1986, 2001). The 'disaster' metaphor has been much used in US media reporting of the crisis, which of course does suggest the crisis is, like a hurricane, an act of God for which no one is to blame. It is perhaps more surprising to see critical and independent elite members of the British academic, regulatory, and media intelligentsia all now presenting different accounts of the financial crisis as an accident within a system because the (rectifiable) problem is with systems, not actors. Thus, accident is invoked by Britain's most distinguished contemporary historian of finance, Donald MacKenzie. Following a classic pre-crisis study of the performativity (and counter-performativity) of mainstream finance, after the crisis, MacKenzie focuses on the role of default correlation assumptions.

Accident is also reinterpreted by the most intellectually radical of our current regulators, Andrew Haldane, financial stability director of the Bank of England. The Bank's house intellectual has lost faith in mainstream economics but favours a new, biological understanding of the financial crisis as ecological or epidemiological network accidents. In the media, the anthropologically trained business journalist Gillian Tett of the *Financial Times*, in her latest work on the crisis, produces another new account of the accident emphasizing the problem of fragmentation of understanding which is the consequence of technocratic elites acting in silos (Tett 2010).

In MacKenzie's (2010) account of the crisis, default correlation calculations within the ABS CDO (asset-backed securities collateralized debt obligation) class of credit derivatives has much the same significance as the mis-engineering of the O ring on the Challenger Space Shuttle. His working paper reports on a case study of 'evaluation practices' in complex instruments based on seventy-six interviews, focusing on the rise of a new derivative instrument ABS CDOs, or CDOs, whose assets were ABSs or residential mortgage-backed securities. The issued value of this class of derivative ballooned to $308 billion in 2006, mainly from pools of sub-prime debt. Different teams and valuation practices had previously been applied to estimate the risk of default on CDOs related to corporate bonds, and the risk of prepayment on ABSs related to mortgages. The problem of valuing ABS CDOs was solved by using existing corporate CDO models and borrowing their correlation values for the probability that different households within a diversified mortgage pool default simultaneously. The 0.3 value, lifted from experience of corporate bond cross default, both made ABS CDOs profitable and, within MacKenzie's performativity frame, resulted in the extension of mortgages to riskier households. In doing so, this brought into being a reality that did not conform with the underlying expectations of the model. Accident is explicitly invoked because the fatal miscalculation about default correlation resulted from 'two institutionally separate insights' (MacKenzie 2010: 79). The problem was not greed for fees but was instead 'reminiscent of the rigidities and barriers to information flow in the background of the Challenger disaster' (2010: 77).

Haldane is less socially constructionist about performativity but considerably more intellectually radical than MacKenzie about the uselessness of mainstream economics, the need to rethink the crisis as stress in a complex system, and to invent a new practice of macro-prudential regulation. Haldane's key paper on 'Rethinking the financial network' (2009*a*) proposes a move from physics-based concepts of economics to biology-based concepts with a new, epidemiological and ecological understanding. The financial crisis represents the behaviour under stress of 'a complex, adaptive system' on the model of the spread of SARS and HIV, or the collapse of fish stocks. There is an isomorphism about 'seizures in the electrical grid, degradation of eco-systems, the spread of epidemics and the disintegration of the financial system' (Haldane 2009*a*: 3). The explanation is that robust but fragile networks are 'accidents waiting to happen', so that modest events can precipitate a tipping point which will be made worse by homogeneous monoculture or hide-and-flight responses, which have their analogues in financial markets prone to illiquidity and dumping assets. Haldane is optimistic about the possibility of a technocratic fix for finance which would create a natural order with greater stability and resilience: this requires a new project to 'map the global financial system' and then 'vaccinate the super spreaders' (2009*a*: 24) or high risk, high infection individuals, and/or to institute 'central counterparties' (2009*a*: 29).

As an academically trained anthropologist, Gillian Tett has a rather different, more cultural take on accident, where actors play a larger role but systems limit information flow and understanding. Her popular book, *Fool's Gold*, told the story of the invention of derivatives by JP Morgan bankers and their subsequent diffusion, but did not turn the crisis itself into a coherent story. This task is now taken up in Tett's contribution (2010) to the *Banque de France Financial Stability Review*, which centres analysis on the problem of technocratic elites in their silos. There is an endemic twenty-first century problem about 'mental and structural fragmentation' in an increasingly interconnected world which helps to explain the disasters of complex credit or BP's oil spill in the Gulf. Insiders and outsiders alike could not 'join up the dots and see how systemic risks were building up in the (financial) system' (Tett 2010: 129). More precisely, there are two interrelated obstacles to understanding. First, there is a problem about technocratic elites operating in silos which are both structural, arising from the organization of banking and regulation, and cognitive, arising from how bankers and financiers conceive of finance. The second set of problems arises from Bourdieusian social 'silence': many topics, like derivatives before 2007, are not publicly discussed because they are thought boring, arcane, taboo, or unthinkable. Tett's culturally inflected fix is 'more holistic modes of thought' (2010: 129) via the employment of cultural intermediaries with an anthropological sensibility who can explain practices and mediate understandings of different worlds.

One of the peculiarities of all three accounts by MacKenzie, Haldane, and Tett is their weak visualization because there is no diagram of the accident. Classical systems accident analysis is usually supported by a process flow diagram: a sequence of malfunction, mis-steps, unanticipated and unregistered consequences produce a standard diagram of disaster in official reports and newspapers. But MacKenzie and Haldane provide no such diagram, and indeed their analyses in different ways all make the systems unnecessary or, as yet, unavailable. MacKenzie is preoccupied with transformation steps (not longer chains or circuits), as with his figures that show the ABS or cash CDO with pooled assets becoming tranched securities, or the transformation of 'mortgage backed securities into ABS CDOs' (2010: 107). Haldane (2009a) sidesteps process diagrams by identifying the need for (but not providing) a new macro map of the (whole) financial system. Tett sets up a related task because her problem of knowledge is actors but without a diagram that 'joins the dots'; like Haldane, her objective is greater legibility.

Yet, all three authors make strong assumptions about a world of expertise. This centres on the role of formal knowledge as a camera or engine, including of course the possibilities of the wrong lens or a misfire. MacKenzie's cumulative work on finance provides a history of mathematization which, in Tett's story, is what makes finance arcane; while Haldane proposes a re-mathematization of the world. There is no analysis of informal rhetorics, or how, for example, impossibilist ideas like shareholder value change the world. Neither is there reference to alternative (non-mainstream) economic paradigms: behavioural finance is not explored and the heterodox macroeconomics of the post-Keynesians and Minskians is ignored, even though the latter anticipated instability from finance. If we exclude Tett, whose mission is to persuade power to recognize its limits, there is little analysis of power and authority behind doxa: the heterodox have, in effect, over the past thirty years been purged from the academic communities which MacKenzie studies and Haldane inhabits.

Not a fiasco

Can the crisis be related to another set of policy literatures about fiascos? A fiasco was defined by Bovens and 't Hart (1996: 215) as '(i) [a] negative event that is (ii) perceived by a socially and politically significant group of people to be at least partially caused by (iii) avoidable and (iv) blamable failures of agents...'. These two authors put the primary emphasis on perceptions in constructionist studies (e.g. Bovens and 't Hart 1996; Bovens et al. 2001), where the task is not to explain fiasco but to explore the different meanings we give to fiasco. This is of limited relevance to our argument because we are fairly sure that the financial crisis will not turn out like the Sydney Opera House, which began as a fiasco and ended as a triumphant icon (Dunleavy 1995). But there is another literature on fiasco, represented by Scott (1998), which is much more relevant to our purposes and avoids crude scapegoating of villains like bankers. The problem, as we will argue below, is that Scott's account of crisis presents modernist governmentality as the central knowing subject of a unitary histori-cal process that always fails in the same way.

Scott's classic study (1998) presents an anti-modernist account of 'how certain schemes to improve the human condition have failed'. Fiascos are typically the result of what (after Foucault) we would now call governmentality, operating in a particular historical conjuncture. The focus is on a toxic combination of modern state power and the Enlightenment legacy of an obsession with legibility, simplification, and measurement. The result is high modernism as an ideology, which is shaping arenas as diverse as the modern city, economic planning, and the management of nature. 'Thin simplification' – knowledge derived from standardized measurement systems – overrides *métis*, the practical knowledge derived from everyday experience, with catastrophic results. This is interestingly anti-modernist because Scott's verdict echoes Oakeshott's argument (1962) against rationalism in politics and for the primacy of tacit knowledge based on elite experience over expertise and data in the practice of government.

There is much to be said for Scott's account, for it does help us to understand the Reagan and Thatcher projects that combined rhetoric with design for the reconstruction of political and economic institutions after 1979. What is crucial in Scott's view is the extent to which a project reflects the attempt to make something legible: standardization; the dominance of formal, official knowledge; and the performative use of state power together transform a multidimensional reality into something that closely resembles the maps, models, and images of the world used as norm by the elites pushing for greater legibility. As Moran (2007) has argued, in a paradoxical way, Thatcher and Reagan's attempt to transform society into a market place very much fits the template of high modernist socialist projects that Scott describes. In effect, the 'neo-liberal' project is the use of state power to remake a market society according to the image of the market propounded by mainstream economics. If the neo-liberal project has the same instruments, ethos, and epistemology, but different aims, this is a high modernist project even though what is being made is the opposite of Le Corbusier's 'machines for living'.

But this general position does not deal with the disconnects, anomalies, and contradictions so ubiquitous in present-day capitalism. We have serious doubts as to whether the neo-liberal agenda was operated or operable in every important area of policy. Our research has highlighted the many ways in which developments in the finance sector after the 1980s deregulation do not fit with Scott's assumptions. As we argue in Chapter 1 on the 'great complacence', the governmental approach pre-2007 in all major jurisdictions was the very opposite of an obsessive modern concern with control, monitoring, and surveillance at the expense of *métis*. Key regulators, like the Financial Services Authority (FSA) in the United Kingdom, did not pursue the legibility project, through a mixture of deference to market actors, passivity, and sheer incompetence. More generally, the evidence is that much of the failure can be laid at the door of policies that dismantled monitoring and control in the name of deregulation, placed excessive faith in market operators, and placed too heavy a reliance on the tacit, practical knowledge of those with expertise in markets. It was deference to *métis*, not its extinction, that helped create the crisis as policy elites bought into notions of market omniscience.

If Scott's notion of fiasco will not work for deregulated finance, we cannot then take an intellectual shortcut to explanation by naming the guilty men and scapegoating the legislators, regulators, and bankers who built and operated deregulated finance. This is the explanatory strategy of Perrow (2010) for whom, in effect, a kind of political financial complex has in the present day replaced the military industrial complex which Wright Mills (1956) analysed some fifty years ago. Perrow's denial (2010) that the financial crisis is a systems accident is useful and authoritative because Perrow originated that concept. But Perrow then immediately defaults onto naming the guilty men who turn out to be senior bankers and politicians who knew what they were doing. Elites of 'key agents who were aware of the great risks' and 'crafted the ideologies and changed institutions, fully aware that this could harm their firms, clients and the public' (2010: 309).

The problem is that Perrow's judgement is, in Scottish legal terminology, 'not proven'. Perrow observes a pattern of corporate donations by financial firms and of elite ties through the revolving door between finance and politics, but that indirect evidence does not prove that money or connections always or usually suborn the independent judgement of politicians and regulators. Furthermore, it is simply not proven to argue that senior bankers all shared the same cynical understanding of those like the former Goldman Sachs CDO trader 'Fabulous Fab' Fabrice Tourre (Jenkins and Guerrera 2010). Nor is it plausible to argue that they all or mostly knew what they did and understood the consequences of their actions if, as we argue in Chapter 2, the financial innovators were bricoleurs creating a changing latticework of circuits which neither practitioners nor regulators understood. As for warnings being ignored, in Chapter 1 we demonstrate that those in authority positions in central banking and regulation were all confidently supportive of financial innovation; while the warnings from the post-Keynesians and Minskians were general ones about the unsustainable housing bubble, not specific ones about how shadow banking would blow up the world.

So the question arising from our research (and our reservations about Scott and Perrow's explanations) is: can we have a non-accidental explanation which both recognizes the agency of bankers and regulators and assigns responsibility without supposing that they fully know what they do? If so, we would have new insights into the crisis.

Elite debacle and hubris

Our research has convinced us that investment bankers, regulators, and the political classes had different kinds of agency. Politicians and the media find it easier to make jibes about investment bankers both because they were managerially in charge and because failed senior bankers like Fred Goodwin or Dick Fuld behaved publicly in such a graceless way. But our research on financial innovation as bricolage in Chapter 2 suggests that no banking insider from one node had an overview of the changing latticework of circuits.

From this point of view, the crisis resulted from an accumulation of small, and in themselves relatively harmless, decisions made by individual traders or bankers and banks. It is hard to be so kind about the regulators and the political elite who made and implemented policy in finance. They typically bought into the high modernist macro project of 'perfecting the market' and at the sectoral level bought into a 'trust the bankers to deliver functioning markets' story. This promised everything and offered very little except the undermining of public regulation, while innovation delivered the exact opposite of the promises, as risk was concentrated not dispersed by a dysfunctional banking system. In our view, this complacence was an elite debacle.

When considering Anglo-American political and economic elites, we need to distinguish between the 1980s commitment to a project of social reconstruction in the image of a deregulated system of free market capitalism and the early 2000s complacency about financial innovation in the middle of a bubble which was misread as the Great Moderation or, in Chancellor Gordon Brown's words, the end of boom and bust. The 1980s position might have been naive, but the later 2000s position was certainly *hubris* in the more or less exact meaning of that word: an overbearing self-confidence that led to ruin. Among leaders of institutions it is, as Owen (2007) has explored, an occupational trait: the over-confident are attracted to leadership; and once in command, especially of well-resourced institutions like modern states, they are encouraged to concentrate on big picture 'strategy', leaving tedious evidence and detail to subordinate technicians. Their role is to exercise judgement in a world where uncertainty means that mundane evidence alone cannot guide choice.

If we are considering debacles and hubris, the point of comparison is not accidents like Challenger or Three Mile Island but foreign military adventures like Suez, Vietnam, Afghanistan, and Iraq, which start from hubris and end in debacle: that is, humiliating failure or collapse into defeat. The a priori of debacle is very different from that of accident in three ways. First, *informal knowledges are central to elite (mis)calculation*. This can take the form of over-estimating the enemy, as when Bush and Blair argued that intelligence showed Saddam Hussain had weapons of mass destruction. Or it can take the form of underestimation, as with the French commander who did not believe that the Vietcong could bring up artillery and bombard Dien Ben Phu.

Second, *intervention usually has multiple, fantastic, and contradictory objectives*, which are often disengaged from operating detail. The Iraq intervention was in this respect classic because it mixed high, and probably unattainable, aims of nation building and democratization with real politik about stabilizing the region, building a bulwark against Iran (and maybe controlling oil resources too).

Third, *matters are greatly complicated by the unforeseen improvisation of local players in response to events* and happenstance decisions by the major power. In the Iraq case, the key decision was that of Bremner and Rumsfeld when they disbanded the Iraqi army and thereby empowered every militant or gangster with a gun. In Afghanistan, the British deployment of lightly armoured vehicles used in Northern Ireland encouraged the use of roadside improvised explosive devices.

Thus, debacle is unlike an accident because the outcome is not reversible or fixable, nor even avoidable next time. A debacle which ends in defeat or withdrawal leads to shifts in the power balance; for the major power defeat is dangerous because it often (but not always) discredits the elites who embarked on the adventure.

The role of *hubris* in modern debacles is now being most closely documented in studies of the Iraq and Afghanistan conflicts – the former a subject also of Owen's (2007) study. Afghanistan and, especially, Iraq arose from a powerful tradition in British policymaking: the belief that Britain has a distinct providential mission to export values and institutions to foreign places, and to reshape civil society to accommodate those exported values and institutions. In the nineteenth and early twentieth centuries, this providentialism took the form of imperialism and of Christian missionary projects: two fine accounts are Colley (1992) and Cannadine (2002). The Iraq invasion is the greatest foreign policy fiasco for at least seventy years. It dwarfs even the Suez disaster of 1956, since its duration, damage, and magnitude have been much greater – especially in the suffering inflicted on the people of Iraq. Over 100,000 Iraqis have died as a direct result of the invasion, which ended with the humiliating withdrawal of US and UK forces as the dysfunctional democracy is on the point of being drawn in to the Iranian field of influence. It is only comparable to the succession of military disasters which led to the fall of the Chamberlain Government in 1940.

The public case for intervention in Iraq involved the manipulation of intelligence evidence assembled in secrecy; the decision processes which led to intervention, as detailed by Lord Butler's inquiry, show a pattern of casualness and informality so characteristic of the hubristic detachment from detail. Butler's verdict, though couched in the malicious understatement of a mandarinate taking its revenge on Blair, is nevertheless devastating. The charge is that the 'sofa government' reduced the scope for collective judgement.

> we are concerned that the informality and circumscribed character of the Government's procedures which we saw in the context of policy-making towards Iraq risks reducing the scope for informed collective political judgment. (Butler 2004: para 611)

What was going on here is graphically illustrated by Blair's own evidence to the (at the time of writing, ongoing) Iraq inquiry chaired by Lord Chilcott. His picture of the process that led to the decision to support an Iraq invasion is a perfect example of leadership hubris as he cites evidences and arguments that were available to every newspaper editorialist. Blair's defence is that a leader has the duty – and the capacity – to make an individual judgement in a risky world:

> As I sometimes say to people, this isn't about a lie or a conspiracy or a deceit or a deception, it is a decision, and the decision I had to take was, given Saddam's history, given his use of chemical weapons, given the over 1 million people whose deaths he had caused, given ten years of breaking UN Resolutions, could we take the risk of this man reconstituting his weapons programmes, or is that a risk it would be irresponsible to take? *I formed the judgment, and it is a judgment in the end.* It is a decision. I had to take the decision, and I believed, and in the end so did the Cabinet, so did Parliament incidentally, that we were right not to run that risk, but you are completely right, in the end, what this is all about are the risks. (Blair (2010) Oral evidence to the Iraq Inquiry, italics added)

In our view, reframing the crisis as debacle and focusing on hubris allows us to present much the most compelling account of the ongoing financial crisis. Finance is not only an economically unsafe and violently pro-cyclical sector but also part of a democracy that is not working.

11

1

After the Great Complacence

> *We should also always keep in view the enormous economic benefits that flow from a healthy and innovative financial sector. The increasing sophistication and depth of financial markets promote economic growth by allocating capital where it is most productive. And the dispersion of risk more broadly across the financial system has, thus far, increased the resilience of the system and the economy to shocks. When proposing or implementing regulation, we must seek to preserve the benefits of financial innovation even as we address the risks that may accompany that innovation.* (Ben Bernanke, Chair, US Federal Reserve, 2007a)

> *Yes, and in that story (The Thousand and One Nights) also the narrative is an object of exchange. Why do we tell stories? For amusement or distraction? For 'instruction', as they said in the seventeenth century? Does a story reflect or express an ideology, in the Marxist sense of the word? Today all these justifications seem out of date to me. Every narration thinks of itself as a kind of merchandise. In The Thousand and One Nights, a narrative is traded for one more day of life – in Sarrasine, for a night of love.* (Roland Barthes, *L'Express* interview, 31 May 1970)

How and why was the crisis an elite debacle? The chapter makes the case for this framing in two key sections about miscalculation by policy elites and catastrophic consequences for the public at large. It then explains how we need a new and different politico-cultural approach to present-day capitalism if we are to understand the origins of the debacle in the operations of unregulated finance and the subsequent frustration of reform, analysed separately in the front and back half of this book.

The opening section focuses on the informal pre-2007 story about the benefits of financial innovation, which was told in the period of what we call the *Great Complacence* when central bankers, regulators, and senior economists in international agencies repeated the same reassuring but ill-founded stories about the benefits of financial innovation and the 'Great Moderation'. These stories mattered because they framed the purpose, intent, and tone of policies towards finance and they legitimated a gross failure of public regulation around securitization and derivatives in the 2000s. This followed on from the more general undermining of public regulation of finance which began in the 1980s and reflected a collective belief that (financial) market forces, left to their own devices, would allocate capital efficiently, improve the robustness of financial markets, and deliver socially optimal outcomes. The judgement that financial innovation was a beneficial process (and part of a new golden age) was then made by technocrats in the 2000s with hubristic detachment on the basis of very little supporting evidence and argument.

This is followed up with a second key section which justifies the term debacle by briefly presenting some political arithmetic about the form and nature of the catastrophe after 2008. Although policy elites generally operate on Evelyn Waugh's principle of 'never apologise, never explain', what happened in and after the crisis was a doubly humiliating defeat. The finance sector which was supposed to bring benefits, instead imposed huge costs on the rest of the economy by requiring expensive bailouts and triggering recession, leading to substantial lost output. Worse still, the policy elites failed in their public service duty of preventing capitalist business from privatizing gains and socializing losses; this mechanism is illustrated by calculating the division of costs and benefits amongst the different stakeholder groups around the five largest British banks after 2000. Before (and after) the crisis, high rewards in the City of London and Wall Street meant that gains were heavily concentrated on the elite workforce, even as their PR assistants emphasized the benefits for ordinary shareholders and the exchequer. Afterwards the costs of crisis were borne by ordinary citizens: taxpayers, public employees, and service consumers in a new world of austerity and distributive conflict.

None of this is unusual in benighted dictatorships or oligarchies, where the privatization of gains and the socialization of losses usually indicate the presence of an uncontrolled and predatory elite. But this drama is different in several ways. First, technocrats like Ben Bernanke and Mervyn King are implicated in the making of a catastrophe: if these public servants cannot be accused of venality, it is perhaps more alarming to find them trading opinion on the basis of their authority and expertise. Second, the drama of reactionary consequences and cuts is now being played out in democracies like the United Kingdom and the United States which have mass franchises, electoral competition, and traditions of intervention for progressive redistribution. Yet, the post-crisis political drama (so far) does not have a 'never again' ending: the moneymaking financial elites are not clearly subordinated and the technocrats and politicians cannot agree on how to change their management of finance so as to prevent further disaster. All this despite the size and scale of a finance-led catastrophe which made the supposed earlier costs resulting from the promotion of sectional interests like agriculture or organized labour look very modest. The book therefore raises questions that are overtly political because we wish to interrogate the power of financial elites, the social value of finance, and the possibility of democratic control.

If the first aim of this chapter is to explain how and why the elite political debacle frame is relevant, the second aim is to explain the approach and apparatus used in later chapters of this book to explore the operations of finance – operations which create both the underlying problem and the difficulties of political reform. Our politico-cultural approach is conceptually minimalist and empirically resourceful because we do not start from a reified concept of capitalism which tells us what matters and how before we have done the research. For example, we do not work from any a priori knowledge of which institutions matter and how they fit together, as in the varieties of capitalism literature. Instead, we combine a cultural concern with stories and a political economy concern with politics so that we can develop a broad overview of the frustration of reform in several jurisdictions including the United Kingdom, the United States, and the European Union (EU). All this is reflected in the organization of this chapter. Thus, Section 1.1 on Bernanke's story and the Great Complacence is followed by Section 1.2 on story-driven capitalisms, which helps explain why this kind of elite story is so important. Contemporary elites have made the Barthesian discovery that stories are not necessarily frivolous distractions or cynical ideologies, but rather literary assets which acquire exchange value under certain conditions. Section 1.3 on the privatization of gains and socialization of losses is then followed by Section 1.4, which introduces some of the new concepts and apparatus which we bring to analysing and understanding the operations of the finance sector and the difficulties of political reform.

Bernanke's story, illustrated in the opening quote, about the benefits of financial innovation was comprehensively discredited by events after 2007 and that provides us with our point of departure in the succeeding chapters of the book. If most of what was interesting about the economic and social consequences of financial innovation was completely undisclosed in Bernanke's story, what exactly was going on in the area of the undisclosed? Chapters 2, 3, and 4 offer the reader, first, an alternative conceptualization of financial innovation, then evidence of finance as a kind of conjunctural bricolage, before exploring banking business models and conceptualizing hedge funds and private equity as financial war machines. Then again, if what has happened since 2007 is so catastrophic for ordinary workers, consumers, and voters, why is it now apparently so difficult to bring finance under democratic control in order to secure effective protection against further finance-led crisis? The short answer to this question is that elites who, before 2007, agreed on the benefits of finance and light-touch regulation now find it much harder to agree on the nature and form of effective re-regulation which is strongly resisted by the lobbyists from finance. That is addressed in the second part of the book.

1.1 The *Great Complacence*: Bernanke's story

If we use the framing of the debacle, informal pre-crisis stories told by policy elites are an obvious starting point. We therefore begin by analysing the pre-2007 stories about finance and the economy told in the United States and the United Kingdom by central bankers, senior regulators, and their economist colleagues in international agencies. Collectively, we denote this technocratic subgroup the 'econocracy', following the introduction of the term by Peter Self (1976), because they had both a major role in the governance of finance and mainstream academic backgrounds in economics.

But there are many other ways to begin a report or a book on the financial crisis and most of them can be illustrated through the various British responses to crisis that followed the collapse of Lehman Brothers in September 2008. The most serious official response was the *Turner Review*, produced in 2009 by the chair of the UK's soon to be defunct Financial Services Authority (FSA) at the request of Treasury. Turner starts boldly with structure and impersonal forces represented by the 'explosion of world macro imbalances' (2009*b*: 11) which produced more money than good assets in every market. By way of contrast, the best of the popular business books was Gillian Tett's *Fool's Gold* which, in line with the conventions of the genre, emphasized agency and begins with a vignette of the bankers from the JP Morgan derivatives team rough-housing around the pool in a Florida luxury hotel (Tett 2009: 3–7). And such beginnings matter because they are often difficult to escape. Thus, New Labour's July 2009 Treasury White Paper immediately undermined the case for radical reform of finance when its opening chapter stressed 'the importance of financial services and markets to the UK economy, and the pre-eminence of the UK as a global financial' (HM Treasury 2009*a*) rather than analysing the causes of crisis. The House of Commons Treasury Select Committee had more radical intent but failed to deliver a synthetic analysis which could sustain radical prescriptions because it never really recovered from an initial committee decision to produce several different reports on aspects of the crisis.

Beginnings matter, then; and in beginning with stories by the econocracy, we can open with a focus on one individual, Ben Bernanke, Chair of the Federal Reserve, who was one of the heroes of the hour after the banking system collapse was averted in autumn 2008. Like Gordon Brown, Bernanke was feted as the man who had saved capitalism (until the bills for saving capitalism had to be paid by taxpayers and public service consumers). *Time* magazine chose Bernanke as its 2009 Person of the Year because he 'led an effort to save the world economy' (Grunwald 2009) by injecting funds into financial markets, rescuing financial companies, and averting economic disaster. Just as in the case of Warren Buffet, the media has constructed a back story about

Bernanke as a brilliant and successful individual who lives modestly. A lower-middle class Jewish boy teaches himself calculus before collecting degrees and jobs from the Ivy League economics departments and then joining the Federal Board in 2002 and becoming chair in 2005. Yet Bernanke still wears cheap suits, takes out his own garbage, drives a Ford Focus, and his largest source of income and wealth remains textbook royalties (Grunwald 2009).

It is unkind but necessary to observe that there is another more interesting back story. Bernanke's mid-career move from head of the Princeton University economics department to the Federal Reserve is more than a personal history. It is emblematic of a historic change in the character of central banking and financial regulation. The elite of financial regulators and central bankers increasingly claim authority, as does Bernanke, from their academic credentials. Marcussen (2006, 2009) calls this the scientization of central banking and financial regulation: that is, those from mainstream economics backgrounds now monopolize senior positions in central banks, and the currency of argument within this group of econocrats is provided by economic data and the core concepts of the discipline. Our argument below focuses on one neglected consequence of this transition: those at the top of this econocracy, like Bernanke, used the authority conferred by their position and 'scientific' credentials to convert the assumptions of neoclassical economics into stories for laypeople about the benefits of financial innovation and deregulation. Such informal stories are not couched in the impenetrable language of economic 'science'. Instead, they offer broad-brush, 'commonsense' accounts in a vernacular, easily comprehensible to politicians and the lay public, and in a context where central bankers and finance regulators are managers engaged not only in making decisions but also in justifying actions.

One of the characteristics that distinguish elite econocrats like Bernanke is their commitment to this ambiguous kind of translation, whereby the technical language of economic 'science' becomes (or maybe authorizes) vernacular stories about markets in a language accessible to those without algebraic competence or an understanding of dynamic stochastic general equilibrium models of the economy. In this case, the important point is that leading members of this econocracy all told the same story about the benefits of financial innovation using the same arguments about the dispersion of risk and the increased resilience of financial markets as did Bernanke right up to the crisis. Bernanke's 2007 encomium for financial innovation is quoted at the beginning of this chapter but similar statements (with only minimal variation for local audiences) could have been cut from, or pasted into, any number of speeches by central bankers or authoritative reports from international agencies. Here, for example, are two quotations, one from Mervyn King, Governor of the Bank of England speaking in 2007, and the other from the semi-annual IMF Global Financial Stability Report of April 2006.

Securitisation is transforming banking from the traditional model in which banks originate and retain credit risk on their balance sheets into a new model in which credit risk is distributed around a much wider range of investors. As a result, risks are no longer so concentrated in a small number of regulated institutions but are spread across the financial system. That is a positive development because it has reduced the market failure associated with traditional banking – the mismatch between illiquid assets and liquid liabilities... (King 2007)

There is growing recognition that the dispersion of credit risk by banks to a broader and more diverse group of investors, rather than warehousing such risk on their balance sheets, has helped to make the banking and overall financial system, more resilient.... The improved resilience may be seen in fewer bank failures and more consistent credit provision. Consequently, the commercial banks, a core segment of the financial system, may be less vulnerable today to credit or economic shocks. (International Monetary Fund 2006a: 51)

Another common, collective theme was that financial innovation would 'democratize' finance because the efficient pricing and distribution of risk would result in an extension of credit to previously excluded firms and households. Bernanke took this line in a lecture in May 2007 when he argued that regulators should not overreact to emerging problems in sub-prime because 'credit market opportunities have expanded opportunities for many households' (2007b). On the same lines, a paper by Bank of England authors highlighted the way that, 'in recent years, there has been much greater scope to pool and transfer risks, potentially offering substantial welfare benefits for borrowers and lenders' (Hamilton et al. 2007: 226), including increasing 'the availability of credit to households and corporations' through a wider 'menu of financial products' (2007: 230). For Adrian Blundell-Wignall (2007: 2) of the Organisation for Economic Co-operation and Development (OECD), 'sub-prime lending is a new innovation... the big benefit is that people who previously could not dream of owning a home share in the benefits of financial innovation'.

These positive verdicts on financial innovation were complacent rather than foolish because position statements in the International Monetary Fund (IMF) report of April 2006, like the Bernanke lecture of May 2007, often registered qualifications and caveats about how financial innovation was not entirely or risklessly beneficial. But the force of these qualifications was neutered when they were always cast in the language of 'challenge' not 'threat' against the background of an enduring policy presumption that such challenges did not warrant changing the permissive pro-finance policy stance of regulators. Thus, the April 2006 IMF report talked of 'new vulnerabilities and challenges' (IMF 2006a: 1) and fretted in the subsequent September 2006 report about whether new instruments might 'amplify a market downturn' (IMF 2006b: 1). Bernanke's May 2007 lecture similarly adds a parenthetical qualification about the benefits of financial innovation, 'thus far' (2007a). But, in the same speech, he later adopts the standard language about 'risk-management challenges' associated with complex instruments and trading strategies based on leverage. In his conclusion he emphasizes 'the role that the market itself can play in controlling risks to public objectives'.

The story about the benefits of financial innovation seemed plausible because it was articulated in the middle of a period of prosperity, which was itself explained and rationalized with a broader narrative which emphasized a secular shift towards stability within the macro-economy. The phrase 'Great Moderation' was first used by the Harvard economist James Stock and the Princeton economist Mark Watson in a technical paper about how and why the business cycle had moderated and national income growth had become less volatile in the period 1984–2001 (Stock and Watson 2002). Bernanke (then head of the Princeton economics department) is thanked in the preliminary acknowledgements to the paper, and later the term was popularized across a number of his own speeches and papers. For the econocracy, their preferred policy mix of liberalized capital markets, light-touch regulation, and astute monetary policy had yielded a hugely benign low inflation, low volatility economy that was encapsulated in the phrase 'Great Moderation'. If such claims were validated by events for a period, the academic economists who originally coined the phrase were sceptical about the role played by central banks and had attributed most of the reduction in volatility to 'good luck in the form of smaller economic disturbances' (Stock and Watson 2002: 200). Against this, Bernanke argued that central bank policy was important in the moderation:

> I have argued today that improved monetary policy has likely made an important contribution not only to the reduced volatility of inflation (which is not particularly controversial) but to the reduced volatility of output as well. Moreover, because a change in the monetary policy regime has pervasive effects, I have suggested that some of the effects of improved monetary policies may have been misidentified as exogenous changes in economic structure or in the distribution of economic shocks. This conclusion on my part makes me optimistic for the future... (Bernanke 2004)

The story about benign moderation was taken up elsewhere in slightly different language (with or without an assumed or asserted connection between moderation and policy). In the United Kingdom, we can once again cite Mervyn King who in his first speech as newly appointed Governor of the Bank of England (2003: 3–4) announced that the 1990s in the United Kingdom had been a 'non-inflationary consistently expansionary – or "NICE" decade' of above-trend growth, falling unemployment, and improving terms of trade which allowed real take-home pay to increase without adding to inflationary pressures. As a result, Britain had achieved a 'new found position of macroeconomic stability'. While King saw the need for further supply-side improvements in productivity in the United Kingdom, others (especially in the United States) thought that macro policy alone could underwrite continuing steady prosperity. Bernanke had encouraged this belief in an earlier lecture in 2002, delivered after Alan Greenspan as Federal Reserve Chair had cut interest rates in response to the tech stock crash. Bernanke, then a newly appointed Federal Reserve Board member who had made his name academically with studies of the policy mistakes after 1929, promulgated what became known as 'the Bernanke Doctrine': that 'a central bank... retains considerable power to expand aggregate demand and economic activity even when its accustomed policy rate is at zero' (Bernanke 2002).

Against this background, many authoritative commentators in 2006–7 began to believe their own publicity and could not admit the possibility of recession, let alone finance-led crisis. The prognosis of J.P. Cotis, chief economist in the OECD in May 2007, asserted that:

> In its *Economic Outlook* last autumn, the OECD took the view that the US slowdown was not heralding a period of worldwide economic weakness, unlike, for instance in 2001.... Recent developments have broadly confirmed this prognosis. Indeed, the current economic situation is in many ways better than we have experienced in years. Against this background, we have stuck to the rebalancing scenario. Our central forecast remains indeed quite benign: a soft landing in the United States, a strong and sustained recovery in Europe, a solid trajectory in Japan and buoyant activity in China and India. In line with recent trends, sustained growth in OECD economies would be underpinned by strong job creation and falling unemployment. (Cotis 2007: 5)

There is much of interest here, not least the way in which the senior central bankers and public sector economists who repeated these stories were not sacked or disgraced after 2008, but confirmed in their jobs or promoted elsewhere. There is also the quite separate issue of the loose, informal nature of the stories told, and how their plausibility depended on economic context and repetition by all those in authority.

Bernanke was reconfirmed as Chair of the Federal Reserve by President Obama; Cotis, who signed off the OECD prognosis, was shortly afterwards recruited as Director General of the French National Institute of Statistics and Economic Studies. Of course, if Bernanke and Cotis had not been senior economists but junior social workers, one egregious misjudgement in a single case of probation or child welfare would result in an enforced resignation and the end of their career. There is no comparable punishment for central bankers, economists, or others in the upper managerial class, even though the welfare consequences of their misjudgements are hugely greater. Bernanke, King, and others show that obtaining an elite position is hard: to reach as high as governor of a central bank, it is nowadays necessary to acquire top 'scientific' credentials and to combine those with a mastery of vernacular storytelling about the virtues of deregulated markets. But once inside, standards of performance, competence, and accountability seem modest with few apparent consequences for mistakes.

We must also be queasy about the detached and imprecise character of the stories about financial innovation and great moderation. This is not just vernacular economics but also T.S. Eliot's 'mess of imprecision of feeling'.[1] Intellectual objects were never precisely defined: Bernanke and others were hubristically vague on financial innovation because they commended it as a good thing without ever engaging with the specifics of what was going on in the markets; meanwhile, the story about macro moderation grew to encompass much more than reduced volatility on quarterly measures. Neither of the two stories was empirically based. The benefits of (wholesale) financial innovation through derivatives and such like were confidently asserted but these benefits were not (and probably could not be) measured to the satisfaction of sceptics like Paul Volcker who believed it was retail developments like the ATM cash machine which had larger and more tangible benefits. As for the causal connection between reduced macro volatility and the newfound innovation of markets and wisdom of policymakers, even Bernanke had to admit that mainstream economists differed on this point. But the claims about innovation and moderation were plausible in the economic context before 2007 with its rising asset prices, low defaults, and sustained growth rates.

Any doubts about whether the future would be like the present were allayed by the repetition of a stock account in standardized language across a range of sources with no significant dissent. Some authors, like Taleb (2007), have focused on the technical choices and mistakes of those inside finance who modelled the future from a small number of past observations, assumed normal distributions, and underestimated the probability and power of extraordinary black swan events which can overwhelm firms and markets. But this needs to be set in context because such technical misjudgements are sanctioned in an environment where the policy elites regulating finance cannot see the possibility of harm, let alone catastrophe. And the power of policy elites is here less technical than *liturgical*. Their financial innovation is a liturgy in the vernacular which recites the many benefits of financial innovation, such as the extension of liquidity, the distribution of risk, improved pricing, and the democratization of finance. Its force, as in any liturgy, comes from repetition by expert authority figures and its effect is the

---

[1] From 'East Coker', No. 2 of Eliot's *Four Quartets*.

abasement of the political classes before financial innovation, rather like the Anglican congregation before the Lord in the 1662 prayer of humble access: 'We do not presume to come to this thy Table, O merciful Lord, trusting in our own righteousness, but in thy manifold and great mercies'.

In retelling the story about financial innovation and the great moderation, Bernanke donned the robes of a kind of clerisy led by experts – such as other leading central bank governors – who presented as technically founded analysis a story about the way markets and regulators had supposedly discovered a new economic alchemy that disposed of the problems that had historically afflicted market economies. The unexpected events which discredited the story after 2007 demonstrate conclusively that financial innovation was not as it seemed, nor as Bernanke represented it. This discrepancy between the reassuring disclosed and the dangerous undisclosed forms a main theme in our subsequent chapters. Still, this picture of a new clerisy ritualistically repeating stories itself raises a key question: why, in a world where debate between econocrats was conducted in an esoteric vocabulary of scientism, did a story like the narrative of the Great Moderation acquire such force? To understand that, we have to sketch some of the wider historical, structural, and cultural forces that have created story-driven capitalism. That is the purpose of the next section.

1.2 Story-driven capitalisms: elites and narrative exchange

This section attempts to provide a summary overview about how and why stories (especially informal and detached stories like Bernanke's) have become increasingly important in present-day capitalism. The argument here draws on and develops our earlier work, especially in books by Froud et al. (2006) on financialization and strategy in the United States and the United Kingdom and by Moran (2007) on the British regulatory state. The section brings together these accounts of business storytelling and political change and resets them in a Barthesian frame where the narrative is merchandise in a social transaction. What then appears is an account of the changing historical modes of narrative exchange in the twentieth century which shifted with democracy, the rise and fall of corporatism, and then the transition to financialized capitalism.

Stories matter in modern capitalist democracies: in market transactions, the voting booth, or in the kind of advocacy settings inhabited by econocrats, stories about actions, identities, histories, trajectories, and linkages are the springs of economic and political action which deliver a sale, an electoral majority, or a winning argument.

But this simple generic understanding needs to be set in a much more specific and changing historical context about various capitalisms over the twentieth century, especially if we are concerned with the raison d'être and context of elite storytelling. No doubt, elites have always told stories, sometimes to convince others, at other times because they were themselves convinced. But elite story-telling gains a new impetus in the early twentieth century, when mass democracy mobilizes new political and economic interests like organized labour, which potentially threatens unaccountable and self-serving elites. The question of whether and how elites will continue to escape democratic control is differently posed and answered in each new conjuncture. Hence, the insights of the past masters of elite studies, as in C. Wright Mills' analysis (1956) of executive elites in Cold War United States or in Bourdieu's analysis (1984) of haute bourgeois social capital in the French fifth republic, differ quite considerably. However, in both cases, they cannot easily be transposed or applied to different institutional and historical settings.

Storytelling became a more important device of elite power in the Anglo-American world following the era of Reagan and Thatcher. Deregulation, liberalization, and – especially in Britain – institutional reform destroyed many 'old boy' club elite networks and undermined the old ways in which elite power had been exercised. Capitalism has been increasingly enveloped in narratives so that storytelling is now a key weapon in the armoury of business and political elites. If Noel Coward celebrated the potency of 'cheap music' in *Private Lives*, our political and business elites have in the past thirty years exploited the potency of cheap stories in public life. This potency is considerable because their stories have a powerful constitutive effect: as we shall see, their new post-1980s stories about business and the economy, like the earlier post-1920s constitutional stories told in Britain, are important because they provide templates for the design and redesign of old and new institutions and regulatory regimes as well as a heuristic on policy stances.

But it would be wrong to represent this narrative turn as an epochal change which dates from Thatcher or Regan in the 1980s, because elite storytelling had been politically important all through the previous fifty years. Change is not about more or less storytelling, but about how the contours of narrative exchange have shifted so that the storytelling parties and beneficiaries change according to time and place. For instance, in the United Kingdom, from the early twentieth century, elite storytelling was designed to contain democracy and maintain political privilege through a *de haut en bas* narrative about how things are best left to existing, established arrangements whose delicate functioning would only be upset by the intrusion of majoritarian democratic forces. Hence, in the United Kingdom, there is a venerable tradition of constitutional mystification about 'arms length control' and such like, as discussed in Chapter 7, which has traditionally justified the unaccountability of elites in major institutions, from the House of Lords via the BBC to the City of London (Flinders 2008). All this was maintained in the face of successive 'modernization' attempts from the late 1960s onwards. The rhetorical tide for the past thirty years has increasingly favoured accountability and good governance which, under New Labour, required reform of the Lords, the BBC's Board of Governors, and re-regulation of finance. But this resulted mainly in the empowerment of other members of the upper managerial classes in non-executive roles. Just about the only consensus on the FSA-led regulatory regime, created for finance in 1997 in the name of greater accountability, is that it never seriously hampered bankers.

These narrative justifications for elite self-management in key institutions were also found in mainland Europe where they were intertwined with corporatist storytelling by the representatives of organized capital and labour who, on both sides, had to convince their own supporters of the social justice and economic sense of their claims and settlements on wages and prices. In countries like Germany or Holland, the negotiating rooms of corporatism were elite storytelling forums with employers and trade unionists in the Scheherazade role, as they spun stories designed to avoid the unpleasantness of being sacked or bypassed by their members or the political classes. Of course, the United Kingdom and the United States had not developed functioning corporatist modes of exchange; thus Reagan and Thatcher faced limited resistance when they planned an anti-democratic revolution which would diminish the area of story-driven political negotiation that had empowered organized labour in mainland Europe.

The Thatcher revolution, consolidated by New Labour, was anti-democratic because it diminished the area of formal political control over everything from council housing to utility industries by shifting them onto the market and/or into the hands of expert regulators as in the case of utility privatization. Rule of experts in many ways strengthened under the Labour government after 1997. In finance, the new settlement on financial regulation, with an independent Bank of England Monetary Policy Committee setting interest rates, boosted the role of expertise in economic management. Elsewhere, 'New Public Management' was applied to the National Health Service and to schools, which now relied on audit, targets, and league tables where, as in utility regulation, the 'consumer' cause was championed by proxy. But the rise of such techniques was itself an index of new issues about the end of 'the club' and the growing diversity of elite groups which were recruited into new roles such as that of utility regulator. This did not end the storytelling but shifted it into new arenas which were also being created by the rise of supranational regulation and jurisdiction from the EU to the committees of bankers organized around the Bank for International Settlements in Basel. This was all condensed into a deficit of democracy, a small circle of expertise, and a greatly enlarged sphere of industry lobbying through stories. Parallel developments in financialized capitalism occurred across much of mainland Europe and North America.

The process of financialization since the mid-1970s is often described as one which has given financial markets and motives greater influence over corporations and households. This process can be measured in terms of the rise of debt or financial assets and it can be conceptualized as epochal or as conjunctural (Ertürk et al. 2008). However, what happened after the 1970s brought a reinvented form of financialized capitalism that was differently organized and differently storied. In pre-1914 financialized capitalism of the German kind, as described by Lenin (1917) and Hilferding (1910), the dominant corporate players were banks and insurance companies which were individually connected at the board level with the industrial trusts that monopolized product markets, so that elite communication and negotiation went on informally in the boardroom and the club, and hence the 'interlocking directorates' of yesteryear which needed to include a banker and someone with political connections (Scott 1997). When the rise of pension funds and insurance companies gave intermediary fund managers a key role, much of this was rendered obsolete because fund managers had generalized, arms-length shareholder value objectives for all companies in their portfolio. There was then a new requirement for publicly listed company managers, in France or Germany as much as the United Kingdom, to make public promises about how they would deliver value and excuses about why they had not done so (Froud et al. 2009).

Other developments also increased the importance of business storytelling in a world where narrative increasingly holds open the space in which business operates. As Moran (2006) has emphasized, the end of British-style corporatism under Mrs Thatcher not only displaced organized labour but also threatened organized business and the traditional trade associations in the United Kingdom, which now had no negotiating partners. The Tory or New Labour default in favour of the market did not automatically deliver sector-friendly regulation and appropriate tax regimes which had to be defined case by case. Business in the United States and the United Kingdom has become increasingly detached from principled support for the party of the centre right and switched support to whoever it believed would win the next election (or placed an each way bet by offering financial support to both sides) in the hope of more favourable treatment afterwards. But stories were still necessary to motivate appropriate regulatory decisions by business-friendly politicians.

Furthermore, as Thomas Frank (2002, 2004) argued about the United States in the 1990s, the democratization of finance required the narrative co-option of the masses into elite-led financial processes (just as political democracy 100 years earlier had required the co-option of the masses into elite-led electoral processes). Again this was not about creating financialized capitalism but reinventing a different kind of financialized capitalism. When Tawney

(1921) and Bukharin (1927) criticized financialized capitalism in the interwar period, they focused on upper-middle class rentier claims to unearned income. Now finance has been democratized by the inclusion of the masses as consumers of savings and credit products: 70 per cent are homeowners in most capitalist countries except Germany, and everybody is credit-dependent in ways which provide feedstock for the wholesale financial markets. But wealth and income are increasingly unequally divided, partly because the major financial centres like London and New York have turned into machines for the mass production of millionaires from amongst the working rich in investment banking and fund management. Here, again, a story about effort and desserts is required.

Together, all these heterogeneous developments produced an explosion in business-led elite storytelling. That is an important part of the history of the explosive growth in lobbying and public relations, for the new lobbyists and PR professionals did not only – or even primarily – rely on suborning or manipulation, they specialized in providing stories that put their clients and their interests in the most favourable light, and preferably told stories that aligned clients' interests with some accepted notion of the public interest. Storytelling was no longer simply about these elites interpellating the masses to excuse and explain their entrenched power – as was the case in the first half of the twentieth century – because the new narratives were now just as importantly about different fractions of the elite signalling and trading with each other in a new kind of story-driven capitalism.

Developments were rapid for two reasons. First, since 1980, business and financial elites have made the Barthesian discovery that stories have exchange value at particular historical moments and that, after Thatcher and the increased pressure for shareholder value, this value can be cashed out as increased company profits, CEO bonuses, and such like. In this new order, stories were not so much merchandise but the new capital from which corporate reputations and individual careers could be constructed. Second, developments were rapid because the organizational preconditions for business storytelling were fairly minimal: any giant firm can buy in PR and corporate communications, while industry stories can be put together by loose distributive coalitions interested in regulation or tax regimes, without the expense of command and control organization. New business and financial elites do not need an executive committee of the plutocracy. Indeed, it is the absence of an executive or a club smoking room which necessitates much of their storytelling.

Behind the narrative explosion, the giant firm and industry response was complex as Froud et al. (2006) and Moran (2006) have argued. At the enterprise level, individual giant firms (especially in regulation-dependent sectors like finance and pharmaceuticals) increased their spending on 'do it yourself' lobbying and PR which bypassed trade associations, the traditional source of collective lobbying muscle. In pharmaceuticals, companies like GlaxoSmithK-line needed one story about the patient interest in shorter testing times and the social benefits of patent protection for Whitehall, Capitol Hill, and Brussels, and quite another for the stock market. Single-firm activity was backed up by collective industry efforts which involved loose coalitions of firms which did not so much negotiate outcomes as try to legitimate their sectional demands for business-friendly regulation with stories about their activity's social value. This was the model for sectional lobbying by finance in the United Kingdom, where organizations like the BVCA pressed the sectional interests of private equity while the City of London Corporation articulated the joint positions of private equity and others including hedge funds and banks on tax and regulation.

The shareholder value stories told to the stock market were inherently fragile, while the political stories about social benefits were always open to challenge. The single-firm's capital market story is about how value will be created by the firm going forward. As Froud et al. (2006) emphasize, the promises are often unrealizable and occasionally devalued by the fact that most giant firms have mixed financial performance, and all firms cannot produce supernormal profits all of the time. As for stories about the social value of the firm or industry, they share some general characteristics which make them vulnerable in different ways to charges of hypocrisy (Vilella Nilsson 2010). In social value stories, businesses (individual management and corporations) present themselves as the virtuous heroes at the heart of the processes of social change and progressive problem solving, which are often defined opportunistically to meet the current agenda of government. This kind of positioning leaves them exposed to NGO attacks on the hypocrisies of a sector like pharma whose 'for people not profits' narrative emphasizes research but whose cost composition suggests the primacy of marketing and predatory pricing, or it induces scepticism about integrated oil companies which are not beyond petroleum as much as one might suppose from their advertising campaigns.

The result is that business and politics become an endless pursuit of closure through mobilizing narratives which seldom obtain closure for long. This is different from the idea of 'capture' promoted in public choice economics which supposes that self-interested, rent-seeking special interests usually win at the expense of an indifferent public. With narrative 'closure', we have a more complex and cultural world with uncertain outcomes. Here business stories are used to motivate political action and inaction, but narratives compete, so that closure is a kind of temporary special case and not an inevitable permanent result. In story-driven capitalism, the normal activity of capitalist politics is interfering with another's narrative so as to secure action or inaction. Organizations, institutions, and positions provide location and partition which set limits on the authority, endorsement, or circulation of stories in a world where sectional agendas usually compete. For example, in turf wars between central bankers and non-bank regulators, where you stand usually depends on where you sit.

This point reminds us that we should recognize that there are many things in capitalism other than stories and, by implication, even a sophisticated Barthesian view of capitalism as narrative exchange is one-sided and partial unless it does justice to these heterogeneous other things. Hence, the analysis in our next section considers the redistributive impact of the finance sector before and after 2007, and our final section presents the fairly minimalist original conceptual apparatus about business models, political agendas, and such like which frames our argument.

1.3 Debacle: privatization of gains and socialization of losses

In later chapters of this book, we turn to the task of analysing what was going on inside the finance sector under the rubric of financial innovation. This section takes up the simpler task of replacing Bernanke's assertive pre-2007 story about the benefits of financial innovation with a very different post-2008 account of the costs of finance, which is more clearly evidenced and conceptualized. The term debacle is then justified for several reasons. First, and humiliatingly, while the leaders of central banking had asserted the benefits of finance before the crisis, their keen middle rankers were soon doing the political arithmetic on the huge costs of finance after the crisis. Second, and more fundamentally, the technocratic and policy elites had failed totally in their public service duty to prevent the exploitation of the state by capitalist business because banking privatized its gains before socializing huge losses. In consequence, ordinary taxpayers, public service employees, and public service consumers must now live in a new conjuncture defined by public austerity and distributive conflict within and between nations. Third, as we will argue in the second half of this book, this is a debacle because this defeat is not easily reversible, avoidable, nor fixable.

After the crisis, in all the major central banks and international financial institutions, liturgy about the benefits of financial innovation was replaced with technical calculations about the costs of finance. This was part of a shift towards questioning within these institutions because defeat or pyrrhic victory generally encourages unorthodox thinking amongst bright middle-ranking staffers. The unorthodoxy of Andrew Haldane at the Bank of England after the crisis parallels that of the military theorists of mobility like De Gaulle at the Staff College and Liddell Hart at the *Telegraph* after the First World War. We will consider Haldane's significance more broadly in Chapter 7, but here our focus is more narrowly on the political arithmetic about the post-crisis costs of finance. One of the more interesting aspects of this shift from liturgy to technical calculation is that the results of technical calculations are indeterminate and authors generally indicate ranges of costs depending on the assumptions and boundaries of the calculations. This makes little difference here because the numbers on costs vary only between the very large and the nearly unfathomable.

In an initial phase, after the major bank bailouts of autumn 2008, the technical calculations focused on how different national governments had paid large costs to bail out banks and markets after the failure of Lehman. By the middle of the following year in 2009, an authoritative estimate of bailout costs had been provided by the IMF in the July 2009 report by Horton et al. (2009) whose calculations are summarized in Table 1.1. In the case of the United Kingdom, the IMF calculates the 'direct up front financing' cost to the UK taxpayer as £289 billion, including here the cost of the Bank Recapitalization Fund, the Special Liquidity Scheme, and the cost of nationalizing Northern Rock and Bradford and Bingley. But if we add all the other Bank of England and HM Treasury loans and guarantees to the banking system, the IMF calculates the potential cost as £1,183 billion. On this basis, the cost of the 2008 bank bailout in the United Kingdom was somewhere between £289 and £1,183 billion, depending on whether and how the guarantees were drawn down. This cost would be ultimately offset by revenues from the sale of government stakes in nationalized or part-nationalized banks. Meanwhile, the direct costs were so large that public sector debt was set to double in relation to national income in several high-income countries (Reinhart and Rogoff 2009a, 2009b): in the United Kingdom, public debt rose from 36.5 per cent of GDP in 2007 to 63.6 per cent in 2010 and the public sector deficit rose from £634 billion to £890 billion. This is a huge unexpected cost arising from what Bernanke and King had a couple of years earlier represented as a beneficial process.

By 2010, most major high-income economies had moved into recession. It then became increasingly clear that finance (plus innovation) was effectively a violently pro-cyclical force determining the growth trajectory: the finance sector which had, through unrestricted credit growth, boosted output before 2007 would now, through deleveraging, damp output growth for the foreseeable future. Those who were making technical calculations of the costs of finance saw that the very large direct costs of bailout were dwarfed by the hugely larger indirect costs in loss of output induced by crisis. Haldane at the Bank of England now led the way in two key papers which presented the new arguments and some startling political arithmetic. One aspect of Haldane's argument was that the part of the increase in output before 2007 was itself illusory, insofar as the growth of financial output reflected increased risk

Table 1.1. The IMF's calculation of the UK treasury's subvention of the banking sector (as at April 2009)

	Announced cost of subvention (as at April 2009)				
	Total (£million)	Per head of UK population (£)	Per UK household (£)	% of GDP (2008)	% of public expenditure
Capital injection	56,398	919	2,230	3.9	9.7
Purchase of assets and lending by the treasury	199,564	3,251	7,891	13.8	34.2
Guarantees	718,718	11,709	28,419	49.7	123.3
Liquidity provision and other support by the central bank	208,240	3,392	8,234	14.4	35.7
Total	1,182,920	19,271	46,774	81.8	203.0
of which upfront costs of bank subvention	289,223	4,712	11,436	20.0	49.6

Note: Table does not include HM Treasury funds provided to support the Bank of England's operations. The sum provided was £185 billion and equal to 12.8% of GDP.

Source: Derived from 'The State of Public Finances: A Cross-Country Fiscal Monitor', IMF Staff Position Note, July 2009.

taking by the financial sector (Haldane 2010*b*, 2010*c*). But Haldane's truly spectacular result (2010*a*: 3–4) was the calculation that, in terms of foregone output (now and in the future), the net present value cost of the crisis was somewhere between one and five times annual world GDP in 2009. In money terms, this is an output loss equal to $60–200 trillion for the world economy and £1.8–7.4 trillion for the United Kingdom.

It is quite hard to comprehend the costs which banks have imposed on the larger economy when these lost output costs are, on Haldane's calculation in the UK case, anything up to fifteen times larger than the costs of the bailout which have wrecked our public finances. The numbers are so astronomically large and come in range form so it is worth emphasizing that the calculation is not an extreme one (Haldane 2010*a*: 3–4). The two key assumptions (of a trend output growth of 3 per cent and a discount rate of 5 per cent) are both arbitrary but moderate. The range of variation of between one and five times world GDP is obtained by assuming different fractions of the 2009 output loss are permanent: the worst case and highest loss is where 100 per cent of the output loss is permanent and the best case is where only 25 per cent of the output loss is permanent. Put simply, the implication is that on reasonably moderate assumptions and, if 75 per cent of the 2009 output loss is recovered, the costs of crisis are equal to world GDP. We can only agree with Haldane's own verdict that 'the scars from the current crisis seem likely to be felt for a generation' (Haldane 2010*c*: 87).

Worse still, the financial crisis is a debacle not simply because of its scale but because of its form. The technocrats and their political masters failed in their first duty as public servants, which was to protect citizens from the depredations of capitalist business which privatizes its gains to the benefit of employees and owners and socializes its losses at the expense of taxpayers and public service consumers. The idea that the banking crisis is about privatization of gains and socialization of losses has been in circulation since the bailouts of autumn 2008. But, interestingly, this is more the perception of independently minded outsiders rather than the staff officers at the Bank of England or IMF. The popularization of the phrase is probably most strongly associated with Nicholas Taleb, whose ten principles for a new order include 'no socialisation of losses and privatisation of gains' (2009), and it has recently been used by Mohamed El-Erian of Pimco when he returned to the IMF to warn about 'privatization of massive gains and socialization of enormous losses' (2010).

These assertions by contrarians and celebrities of the investment world have not been backed by calculations. So, Table 1.2 presents an illustrative calculation of stakeholder gains and losses in the five largest British banks from 2000 to 2009. This calculation illuminates the mechanisms and brings out the point that, in this case, the phrase about privatization of gains and socialization of losses is not hyperbole but sober description.

As the notes to Table 1.2 outline, the state receipts column excludes emergency loans, special liquidity schemes, state guarantees, and other financial support provided to these five banks. Nonetheless, the cumulative result after nine years from 2001 to 2009 (after allowing for all tax receipts) is that a huge (net) loss of more than £50 billion has been charged to the state by these five banks. Meanwhile, the cumulative private gains of employees are much larger at £242 billion, with shareholders seeing a positive cumulative return by 2009 of nearly £40 billion: in short, the private gains over nine years are more than five times as large as the huge loss charged to the state. The year-by-year totals are also interesting because they illuminate the mechanisms which underlie this result. The net receipts of the state are negative because of an offset cyclicality. The British banking sector's capacity to generate losses in a crisis of liquidity and solvency is significantly larger than its ability or willingness to pay taxes in the previous credit fuelled upswing: huge subsidies and a (net) loss of approximately £105 billion in just two years of 2008 and 2009 therefore outweighed the cumulative tax receipts of £54 billion in seven years on the upswing.

Shareholders and employees benefit because, first, their separate private gains are year by year much larger than tax receipts and, second, in the absence of any clawback mechanisms, they never lapse into offsetting losses. Shareholder receipts increase to a cyclical peak in 2006 and then are more or less suspended for one year only before being generously resumed. As for payments to employees, the growth of the wages fund is more damped than that of profits over the 2000s, but wages start from a higher level and the

Table 1.2. Cumulative stakeholder gains and losses of the five major UK banks, 2001–9

	Cumulative employee receipts (£million)	Cumulative shareholder receipts (£million)	Cumulative state receipts (£million)
2001	17,644	8,140	5,493
2001–2	35,282	−7,277	11,177
2001–3	55,223	66,850	18,027
2001–4	77,964	115,880	26,222
2001–5	104,937	112,202	35,830
2001–6	134,668	184,318	46,151
2001–7	166,874	142,031	54,089
2001–8	204,665	−37,761	14,051
2001–9	241,507	39,738	−50,140

Notes:
The banks included in the aggregate calculations are Barclays, HBOS, HSBC, Lloyds, and RBS.

Employee receipts is the summation of personnel expenses; shareholder receipts is the summation of dividends and increases in share price; the State's receipts is the summation of corporate tax receipts and the 2008 and 2009 bailout of Lloyds and RBS (2008: bank recapitalization plan; 8 October 2008: £20 billion RBS, £17 billion HBOS; 2009: bank recapitalization and guarantee; 26 February, RBS £25.5 billion; 3 November, Lloyds £6 billion and RBS £32 billion).

The calculation excludes all private sources of capital raised, for example, Barclays capital raised from China Development Bank (CDB), Qatar Investment Authority (QIA), and Temasek.

The bailout totals relate only to the five banks and therefore exclude bailouts of Northern Rock (£25 billion, 14 September 2007) and Bradford and Bingley (£42 billion 29 September 2008); emergency loans to HBOS and RBS, October 2008 (totaling £62 billion); special liquidity scheme/credit guarantee scheme (£500 billion in total); asset guarantee scheme, 24 February 2009 (£325 billion).

On 15 January 2009, HBOS raised £11.5 billion of capital (before costs and expenses) through an issue of £8.5 billion of new ordinary shares under a placing with HM Treasury subject to clawback by existing shareholders, and an issue to HM Treasury of £3 billion of new preference shares. Lloyds TSB raised £4.5 billion (before costs and expenses) through an issue of £3.5 billion of new ordinary shares under a placing with HM Treasury, subject to clawback by existing shareholders, and an issue to HM Treasury of £1 billion of new preference shares.

On 16 January 2009, the Lloyds TSB acquisition of HBOS was completed following final court approval and Lloyds TSB was renamed Lloyds Banking Group plc (LBG). The exchange of HBOS shares for LBG shares took place at an exchange ratio of 0.605 of a new LBG share for every one HBOS share held. As a result, the UK Government through HM Treasury owned approximately 43.4 per cent of the enlarged ordinary share capital of LBG. In addition, each class of preference share issued by HBOS, including the preference shares issued to HM Treasury, in the capital raising was replaced with an equal number of new LBG preference shares.

HBOS ordinary and preference shares were delisted from the Official List of UK Listing Authority, and admission to trading on the London Stock Exchange was cancelled on 19 January 2009 when trading in the new LBG shares commenced.

On 13 October 2008, the terms of the acquisition by Lloyds TSB were amended and, as part of the UK Government's coordinated package of measures, HBOS announced a Placing and Open Offer to raise £11.5 billion of new capital (consisting of £8.5 billion in ordinary shares and £3.0 billion in preference shares). The capital raising, underwritten by the UK Government, was made available to HBOS on condition that the acquisition by Lloyds TSB completed. On 16 January 2009, the acquisition of HBOS by Lloyds TSB was completed and the name of the combined group was changed to LBG.

RBS: At the Annual General meeting in April 2009, the authorized ordinary share capital of the company was increased by £7.5 billion through the creation of 30 billion new ordinary shares of 25p each. At a General meeting in April 2009, the authorized ordinary share capital of the company was increased by a further £4.2 billion through the creation of 16.9 billion new ordinary shares of 25p each. In April 2009, the company issued 16.9 billion ordinary shares at 31.75p each through a placing and open offer. The placing and open offer was fully underwritten by HM Treasury. The net proceeds were £5.4 billion.

Source: Annual report and accounts and Bankscope.

pattern is one of ratchet growth so that they increase continuously every year from 2001 to 2009. Quite remarkably, the huge crisis in 2008–9 is not reflected in a downward shift in the wages bill, which actually increases from £32 billion in 2007 to nearly £37 billion in 2009.

This is quite unprecedented. In a sector which is initiating crisis and requiring massive subsidy we would ordinarily expect downward pressure on both the wages bill and on numbers employed: in this case, the wages bill increases and the numbers employed decline only marginally from 1,046,000 in 2007 to 1,060,000 in 2008. It is also true that, from this stakeholder perspective, some £20 billion of losses are being socialized just to cover the (wholesale) workforce's expectation of increasing wages.

This account of socio-economic costs and benefits is important because it encourages a problem shift towards a much more explicitly political analysis. The issue is not simply about the huge costs which banking passed on to the rest of society after the crisis but also about the distribution of costs and benefits between stakeholders before and after the crisis. The phrase 'power without responsibility' was originally used by Stanley Baldwin at the beginning of the 1930s in attacking newspaper proprietors like Beaverbrook or Hearst, whose irresponsibility had political repercussions. After the 2007–8 crisis, such savagery has been turned against investment bankers like Lloyd Blankfein and firms like Goldman Sachs whose irresponsibility takes a purer financial form. Most famously, the *Rolling Stone* magazine described Goldman, 'the world's most powerful investment bank', as 'a great vampire squid wrapped around the face of humanity, relentlessly jamming its blood funnel into anything that smells like money' (Taibbi 2009).

If we avoid such rhetoric, and look back at the political arithmetic in this section, we nevertheless have a more sober problem definition about a pattern of costs imposed and losses socialized which would ordinarily be associated with the depredations of corrupt and uncontrolled elites in unfortunate third-world countries. How did this debacle happen in first-world democracies with honest technocrats in charge and why are we making such slow progress in dealing with the consequences and making sure it never happen again? This is surely the absolutely critical question of 2011. The central twentieth-century achievement of the high-income societies was, one way or another, to use democracy to secure mass social welfare in various post-1945 settlements. The twenty-first century issue we now face is whether we can use democracy to control and redirect the finance sector.

This question deserves a serious and extended answer which illuminates the undisclosed part of financial innovation and present-day democracy. The next section introduces the concepts which frame our argument in this book.

1.4 Apparatus: business models and agendas

Empirically resourceful and conceptually minimalist research can often produce interesting investigations that do not depend on a complicated apparatus. Such minimalism can be useful because concepts and a priori can easily become a procrustean device. But, in this case, the intellectual object in front of us is large, complex, and easily misunderstood. So, we need some apparatus for answering our questions about how financial innovation went wrong and why political reform of finance is apparently so difficult across a variety of political jurisdictions.

In answering our questions about financial innovation and the politics of reform, we prefer not to invoke concepts like 'Anglo-American capitalism' or 'neo-liberalism' which emphasize trans-Atlantic similarities of process or outcome, while suppressing or eliding differences between promise and outcome which are an important part of the explicandum. The conditions and changes around regulation of finance after the 1980s undermined three very different regulatory traditions of adversarialism in the United States, comitology and open methods of coordination in the EU, and regulation by consent in the United Kingdom. If we consider the slow pace of reform, different processes with various rhetorics, actors, and settings can produce apparently similar, reform-frustrating outcomes in the United States, the United Kingdom, and Europe. In the United States, the Obama administration had reforming intentions but the only policies which the administration can get through the legislature are full of compromises and loopholes which will be widened at the subsequent regulation writing stage. By way of contrast, the United Kingdom has a powerful executive, but the New Labour government did very little in 2009–10, and the Conservative/Liberal Democrat coalition has in effect postponed decision and sidestepped broader issues by setting up a banking commission, discussed in Chapter 6; the commission is most likely to do nothing except recommend breakup of the (state-owned) high-street banks. Both US and UK systems have so far failed, albeit in different ways, to deliver reform.

Something can be done by distinguishing between different kinds of stories which can be more or less memetic (Dawkins 1976) or instrumental. Bernanke's story about the benefits of financial innovation and the Great Moderation was mainly memetic: these narratives were simultaneously repeated in academia, by non-university economists, and within the finance sector so that they spread organically via repetition and were given credibility by contextual economic events and the broader backdrop of mainstream economics. Moreover, they were believed (in most cases genuinely) by practitioners, regulators, and others who often derived no direct benefit and hoped for nothing except understanding. In the second half of the book, we consider the finance sector's own 'social value of finance' narrative which centres on jobs created and taxes paid. This was, and is, more instrumental insofar as this story was formed and articulated by a small group or coalition with clear motives of furthering their interests. Their work on, and with, stories is rather like mass TV advertising with its endless repetition and simple updating of the same message in search of a suggestible but rather amnesiac target audience.

But distinctions between different kinds of stories will not do much unless they are connected with other concepts about how narrative elements can be variably integrated into political processes. Our key concept here is that of 'agenda' which can be either liturgical and consensual or political and divisive. In thinking about agenda, we do not have in mind the standard bureaucratic usage of agenda as the 'list of things to be done', a usage that dates from the late nineteenth century. If we consider the incantatory quality of Bernanke's story before the crisis, discussed earlier in this chapter, this links to an earlier liturgical usage and is distinct from later political usage of the term. In liturgical usage, agenda denotes matters of ritual or a prescribed set of forms for public worship (as in the Latin Mass). This was carried over from Catholic into Lutheran usage with the German concept of Agende or Kirchenagende (Schaff 1951). There is also a later political usage of agenda as 'a campaign, programme, or plan of action arising from underlying principles, motivations etc'. This usage is surprisingly recent and was included in the *Oxford English Dictionary* for the first time in the December 2007 additions, which give 1976 as the date of first usage.

On this basis, the book develops an argument about how the governance of finance was different before and after the financial crisis. It does so by playing between these two non-standard usages of the term and focusing on the changing role and balance of stories and interests. Immediately before the crisis, the governing agenda was narrowed by shared stories about the Great Moderation and the benefits of financial innovation. These reassuring liturgies operated in a frame of ideologies and interests that had for several decades increasingly undermined political questioning of, or resistance to, finance. After the crisis, the old familiar liturgies are replaced by competing stories from bankers, politicians, and regulators so that multiple political agendas conflict in a new conjuncture where the clash of interests, institutions, and ideologies becomes much more important.

Within this frame, the back half of the book offers a contemporary political history of the crisis as it has so far played across the United States and the United Kingdom, with some reference to the EU. It describes how overlapping elite groups – elected politicians, bankers, financial market intermediaries, agency technocrats, bureaucrats, and elite media commentators – responded to a crisis which suspended normal politics and, after Lehman went under, required extreme intervention whose outcomes are still uncertain but include the wrecking of public finances and a second phase of sovereign debt crisis and intra- and international distributive conflict. In Chapters 5 and 6, we also distinguish between overlapping moments of the crisis when different elite groups were in the ascendance, and where the efforts of the ascendant groups in one period become the basis for a different group project in the next. Thus, in the UK case, the extreme intervention of autumn 2008 empowered elected politicians who had forty-eight hours to prevent a global financial meltdown, but within the year it was business as usual for the banks who were making sizeable profits again by the summer of 2009, all with the tacit support of the Treasury even as they faced a new pushback from the Bank of England and FSA technocrats who tried to initiate reform.

The problem the technocrats faced was to understand the complex and multidimensional nature of what was going on in the area of the undisclosed under the rubric of financial innovation. Here, we develop four key concepts which allow us to think divergently in the front half of the book about the drivers and consequences of the antisocial structures and behaviours in finance. First, the concept of *business model* explains how and why financial innovation was so powerful in the stock market-quoted, corporate banking sector where profits were volume-based in a joint venture, profit-sharing arrangement between shareholders and senior investment bankers under the compensation (comp) ratio system (Augar 2005). Second, the Deleuzian concept of *war machine* helps us to understand the mobile opportunism of non-corporate finance organized into private equity and hedge funds which were, like most irregulars, less separate from constituted authority than they appeared to be. Third, the key concept of *bricolage*, in the strict Lévi-Straussian sense, highlights the inherent and unpredictable fragility of improvised latticeworks, which were smart at the links where bankers earned fees but dumb about the structural implications of changing values or behaviours. Fourth, we add the idea of a changeable *conjuncture* (i.e. a combination of asset prices, flows of funds, and legitimating stories) which makes some kinds of calculations and actions easy and profitable in one period but absolutely impossible in another. By putting these concepts to work, as we do in the first half of this book, we can present a differently conceptualized and better-evidenced account of the undisclosed of financial innovation.

The end result is a much clearer understanding in the front half of the book about the technical intractability of finance as an object of regulation. This intractability has not so far been intellectually registered or politically engaged because the integration of narrative into political processes so far deflects any attempt to cage finance. The complacency about ineffective regulation pre-2007 was rooted in the story about the benefits of financial innovation, and several other kinds of mystification, which all elites accepted and turned into an agenda. These other mystifications included constitutional mystification, which insulated the system of market regulation from democratic forces, and economic mystification, which presented narratives about the social value of finance so that sectional interests of finance could be presented as the national interest. The inability to impose effective re-regulation after 2008 was rooted in the general failure to construct any widely acceptable narrative which made sense of the crisis. A shift from pre-2007 liturgies to competing elite political agendas by 2009–10 was preceded by political default onto scapegoating and show trials of bad bankers like Dick Fuld and Fred Goodwin. This of course needs to be read in the context of the business model analysis in the first half of the book. The various elites were inevitably without an agreed agenda because they lacked the concepts to analyse financial innovation as fragile circuits embedded in shareholder value banking, which needs to be recognized as a transaction-generating machine.

Conceptual apparatus is not an end in itself and does nothing without supporting empirics and development; these are what the next six chapters provide. If we had been simply concerned with hanging the label of elite debacle on recent events, we could of course have been more economical with the development and written a shorter book. But we had a larger and more constructive aim of preparing the way for reform and in doing so by providing something other than a list of fixes because, if there will always be elite debacles, we do believe that we can collectively learn from events and prevent further debacle in finance. On the prospects for reform, after six chapters, we are able at least to indicate the two (surmountable) difficulties that stand in the way of effective reform. First, financial innovation, before 2007 or currently, is beyond any known technical mode of regulatory control because innovation takes the form of bricolage that creates complex lattice-works which are inherently fragile and fail in unpredictable ways with each new conjunctural change. Second, finance is presently beyond political control because criticism has not been turned into a relevant and politically actionable story to create a different kind of finance. We hope that these arguments and their implications will contribute to a future where rule of experts is less important than parliamentary democracy, which is absolutely crucial to the restraint of unaccountable finance.

In the first half of this book our question is about how crisis was generated. Chapters 2, 3, and 4 develop our answer, which is that innovation in and around the financial markets took the form of bricolage which did not consider the risks, uncertainty, and unintended consequences of volume-based business models and complex circuits. The direct implication is that finance needs to be simplified, rather than regulation made more sophisticated. In the second half of the book, our question is about why democratic political control both before and after the crisis has proved so difficult? Chapters 5, 6, and 7 develop our answer, which is that self-serving financial elites are not easily controlled by technocratic elites who are themselves recovering from knowledge failure, or by the rest of the governing classes concerned with political positioning for electoral advantage on issues which are technical, opaque, and illegible to the electorate at large.

2

Financial Innovation or Bricolage?

It's awful – Why did nobody see it coming? . . . If these things were so large, how come everyone missed them? (Queen Elizabeth II on the financial crisis, *Daily Mail*, 6 November 2008 [Greenhill 2008])

Capitalist civilization has not only been a successful civilization. It has above all been a seductive one. It has seduced even its victims and opponents. (Wallerstein 1995: 137)

So why did no one see it coming? In answering the question, this chapter develops a line of explanation which follows up Immanuel Wallerstein's insight about how capitalism works through promises, which mobilize supporters and seduce critics. Nobody (that mattered at the time) saw the crisis coming because everybody was seduced by a comforting story about the benefits of financial innovation. This chapter now presents a different and darker account of the framework and conjunctural conditions of innovation, and argues that securitization and the increasing complexity of derivative structures was a kind of bricolage which created a fragile latticework of counterparty obligations and exposures. Our argument focuses attention on the undisclosed or the gap between the promised benefits of innovation and the catastrophic outcomes of securitization. Here, we emphasize the role played by undisclosed circuits which concentrated risk at the financial core, and left governments with little option but to bail out those institutions once crisis occurred. This has now put huge obligations on governments who are passing on the burden of adjustment to taxpayers, public employees, and public service users.

Wallerstein invites us to consider the possibility that capitalism wins out because it has a more seductive story by virtue of more attractive promises. In the liberal collectivist world envisaged by William Beveridge and J.M. Keynes, as Wallerstein himself supposed, the relevant and credible promises were political ones about the possibility of reforming capitalism through democratic intervention to reduce polarized inequality. In the neo-liberal world envisaged by Ronald Reagan and Margaret Thatcher, as this book explores, the relevant promises instead are economic ones about the desirability and inevitability of perfecting capitalism through extending the market. We have in a sense lived through an extraordinary thirty-year experiment in the glamorization of capitalism. Discursively, through a kind of deindustrialization of the imagination, capitalism ceased to be a grimy system of repetitive industrial production and class conflict and has instead become a shiny system of financial innovation and well-groomed bankers. This chapter explains how these extravagant new promises were made and accepted prior to 2007, before turning to analyse how they were bound to disappoint because they did not engage with the actual processes and outcomes of financial innovation.

The first section of this chapter summarizes the mainstream story about the benefits of financial innovation, which originated from academics and was then generally repeated by journalists, regulators, and bankers. The coupling of finance and innovation established a normative bias in its favour with the growth of securitization interpreted as engineering which facilitated the efficient marketization of risk. These ideas were powerful because they spoke the lingua franca of mainstream economics, and its subsidiary financial economics, with self-reinforcing effects. Mainstream representations of financial innovation have therefore proved difficult to displace because they are underwritten by taken-for-granted assumptions and metaphors about utility-maximizing agents and efficient markets. Thus, key regulators, senior politicians, the elite 'commentariat', and many market 'insiders' failed to see it coming and failed to take avoiding action because the narrative of financial innovation is in a very precise sense a 'seduction', which doubly means 'to win by charm or attractiveness' but also 'to lead (a person) astray in conduct or belief; to tempt, entice, or beguile *to do* something wrong, foolish, or unintended'.

The promises about securitization were bound to disappoint because their idealizations were only loosely connected to financial market practices. Thus, much of what happened was not disclosed in the stories that circulated widely. The second section of this chapter presents our alternative account of financial innovation as bricolage in the classical Lévi Straussian sense, where bricolage represents a different, non-scientific improvisatory kind of rationality of making structures out of events and constructing latticework structures of interconnected circuits (not chains with a beginning and an end). Bricolage is a work of making structures under definite conditions which are not of the bricoleurs' choosing, and which involve both change and fixity, which we capture by invoking Braudelesque ideas about a present defined by the intertwining of different kinds of temporalities. Thus, the second section opens with an analysis of the conditions of innovation which distinguishes between a semi-permanent framework established after the breakdown of the Bretton Woods regime in the 1970s and the changing conjunctural opportunities of four- to seven-year periods. These periods are partly defined by a capital market configuration of asset prices, flows of funds, and specific kinds of coupons, all intertwined with a particular narrative of opportunity with supporting numbers. Put simply, the folly of financial innovation in the 2000s was to create a vast undisclosed latticework of counterparty obligations which turned into a crisis of liquidity and solvency when conjunctural circumstances changed.

Under these conditions, the behaviours of banks, hedge funds, private equity funds, and other financial actors could temporarily appear to conform to the expectations generated by the mainstream narrative, but only before generating unexpected and catastrophically different outcomes. The third section analyzes the undisclosed elements of the story of financial innovation, which was actually producing effects that were the opposite of what the story envisaged. Crucially, risk was not being distributed away from a few giant investment banks and financial conglomerates but was concentrated at the very hubs of the financial system. As the events around the collapse of Lehman and the rescue of AIG in September 2008 demonstrated, the unintended consequence of the concentration of risk through financial innovation was the obligation of governments to bail out banks and inject liquidity, regardless of the costs so as to avoid unacceptable consequences for corporate players (inside and outside the banking sector), markets, and citizens. The chapter ends with a brief concluding section about why mainstream economic accounts of the crisis that stress the reoccurrence of crisis in market economies, and hence downplay the uniqueness of this crisis, are limited.

From a broader perspective, the processes of innovation described in this chapter extended the boundaries of legitimate finance through bricolage and created new positions and transactional opportunities for enrichment for elite intermediaries and a handful of major banks. The second half of this book is about why it became politically difficult to remove or reconfigure such positions and opportunities.

2.1 Financial innovation and the promises of securitization

Financial innovation is a neologism which dates from the 1980s when finance and innovation were discursively coupled for the first time and used to describe the evermore complicated financial products that were, before the crisis, represented as financial engineering. The first half of this section does not aim to offer another brief history of financial innovation, as already well told by Bernstein (1992) or MacKenzie (2006). Instead, we here tell the story of how the term was used by financial economists and came to serve as the leading metaphor in the discourse on extending the market, before discussing the cluster of innovations which connected wholesale and retail on a hugely expanding scale in ways which delivered crisis after 2007. The second half of this section focuses on how none of this was anticipated because, within a mainstream frame, securitization promised great benefits including dispersion of risk, improved liquidity, superior capital allocation, and the democratization of finance.

It was US financial economists like Robert Merton and Merton Miller who first coupled the terms finance and innovation in the 1980s and thereby created a potent metaphor. Their linguistic coupling was foundational because it associated 1980s' developments in financial products and markets with widely shared ideas about innovation as a process with positive outcomes in the form of a higher level of economic welfare, either through enhancing static efficiency or dynamic efficiency. In effect, the metaphor was positively charged and imparted a bias in favour of financial innovation so that financial entrepreneurs naturally should be granted more leeway and constraining regulation should be removed.

The metaphor worked even without robust empirical proofs of its benefits. Miller defined financial innovation in a counterfactual way as something that produces economic growth in excess of what would otherwise have occurred (Miller 1986). But it was not easy to demonstrate this connection empirically and, as Philippon (2008) has demonstrated with a comparison of the 1960s and 1980s, there is certainly no simple connection between achieved growth rates and the quantum of intermediation or innovation in finance. Furthermore, as Tufano (2002) has noted, it is often easy to list but hard to measure the benefits of innovation. It is possible for instance to measure the (considerable) benefits of retail process innovations like ATMs or smart cards, but it is more challenging to measure the social welfare effects of new instruments in the wholesale markets – a point forcibly made by former Federal Reserve Board chair, Paul Volcker (2009). Where measurement has been attempted, the evidence suggests that effects are mixed and complex (see e.g. Allen and Gale 1994).

The definitional idea that financial innovation is everything that makes financial markets more efficient and/or extends their sphere of influence to deliver higher growth and welfare gains was an effective means of countering scepticism. While this was tautological it was also powerful because, in this frame, new products, techniques, and organizational forms would increase liquidity, allow risk to be managed, improve pricing, and address problems related to asymmetric information. By the 2000s, with the hockey stick growth of derivatives and other instruments, this definition had crystallized into the idea that the project of financial innovation was now about the marketization of risk. This definition was taken up by many, even by behavioural financial economists like Robert Shiller, who did not believe in efficient markets and rational actors. For Shiller, 'radical financial innovation' is 'the development of new institutions and methods that permit risk management to be extended far beyond its former realm, covering important new *classes* of risk' (2004: 2).

Within this narrative, the work of financial innovation is projected as a prosaic but heroic activity whose quality is captured in the notion of *financial engineering*. The representation of the activity as a form of engineering was crucial to confirming its status as a politically neutral, scientifically informed technical intervention which had exchange value among a wide array of different interests. The mathematically literate practitioner or finance professor was represented as analogous to an engineer using Newton's laws of force to test stress or compression in physical structures, or Brownian motion to understand the movement of suspended particles. The message of the analogy was that mathematical understanding could be applied to financial structures and processes to produce products and techniques that would increase the robustness and efficiency of the financial architecture. The metaphor of engineering encouraged the development of classificatory schemes about what different techniques or products were designed to fix or facilitate (see BIS 1986; White 1996; Litan 2010), as well as shortlists of the most important innovations of recent times. This was accompanied by a 'who's who' style popular history beginning with Bernstein's *Capital Ideas* (Bernstein 1992), which is a celebration of what is characterized as a 'revolution' in which the heroes are the talented finance academics and quants with their algebraic finance formulae. Technical formulae play much the same role in the business books about quants as did the launch chains of the Great Eastern in Howland's photograph of Isambard Kingdom Brunel.

The status of the great engineer is tied up with the global diffusion of a transformational technology like the steam ship, the automobile, or the personal computer. In the decade before 2007, securitization seemed to be just that kind of fundamental innovation. In technical terms, securitization is a two-step process of rendering assets liquid and fungible. First, illiquid assets such as the income streams from car loans or house mortgages are pooled. Second, financial engineering turns these pooled assets into a security (or tiers of securities) which can be sold on or traded at a secondary market. The security is a derivative because its value is derived from the underlying asset. However, despite the talk of financial innovation, the financial techniques and products were not new inventions of the 1980s. Securitization has a prehistory which dates back to the creation of proto-mutual funds in eighteenth-century Holland and trading took place before Black Scholes modelling developed in the early 1970s. But, whether measured by total value of contracts outstanding or by

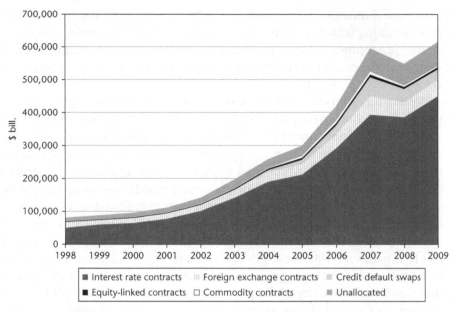

Figure 2.1. Total notional value of OTC derivative contracts outstanding at year end ($billion)

Source: BIS Quarterly Review, various years.

comparing that value to a standard comparator like GDP, there was dramatic growth and diffusion of securitization in the decade after the late 1990s.

As Figure 2.1 demonstrates, the notional value of contracts outstanding on over-the-counter (OTC) derivative markets increased 665 per cent from $80,309 billion in 1998 to $614,674 billion by 2009 with a peak in June 1998 of $683,814 billion. Measured comparatively, outstanding OTC contracts grew from around 2.4 times global GDP in 1998 to roughly 10 times by the end of 2009. Much of this growth came from interest rate contracts, particularly swaps, which reflect innovation in other markets, and in particular the rapid expansion of securitization in the 2000s which increased the financial sector's appetite for floating, mainly LIBOR-linked securities, though the growth of interest rate swaps can also be understood as a kind of virtual carry trade in its own right. Moreover, as Figure 2.2 indicates, beyond interest rate swaps, innovation led to the creation of new products like the credit default swap (CDS), which appeared out of nowhere in 2004 and grew into a $58,244 billion market by December 2007, virtually the equivalent of global GDP in that year.

Financial innovation also saw the spread of increasingly complex structured finance techniques into new markets such as residential real estate loans. This can be seen in Figure 2.3 which portrays the expansion of collateralized debt

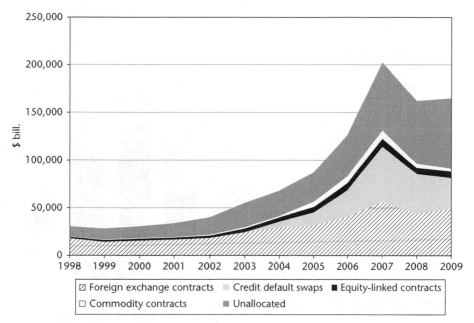

Figure 2.2. Total notional value of OTC derivative contracts excluding interest rate contracts outstanding at year end ($billion)

Source: BIS Quarterly Review, various years.

obligations (CDOs), which are tranched securities backed by mortgage-backed securities or other asset-backed securities, or, alternatively, CDSs which reference mortgage-backed securities in the case of synthetic CDOs. Between 2001 and 2007, issuance of cash and synthetic CDOs and collateralized loan obligations (CLOs) grew nearly 1,500 per cent to $1,078 billion, with much of that growth coming from novel and increasingly complex synthetic products.

The expansion of derivatives trading did not stimulate much discussion of what was going on in circles beyond those who had a professional interest in new developments; this was so, even though developments such as CDOs were effectively doing something new and radical by extending mortgage credit and creating a 'sub-prime market' for households which had previously been starved of credit due to their risky characteristics. Yet CDOs were rarely, if ever, mentioned explicitly in the majority of speeches and reports issued by institutions like the US Federal Reserve Board, the UK Treasury, the Bank of England, the IMF, and others. The *Financial Times* (*FT*) did have Gillian Tett providing specialist coverage but, more broadly, the *FT* like the rest of the press only focused seriously on securitization and derivatives after things went wrong in 2007.

As Figure 2.4 indicates, in 2006, when global CDO issuance reached $5.2 trillion (SIFMA 2007), this warranted just 116 articles in the *FT* throughout the

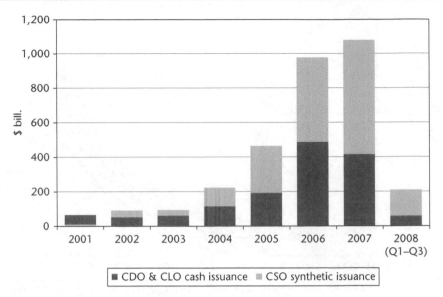

Figure 2.3. Total notional value of CDO, CLO, and CSO issuances

Notes: Collateralized debt obligation (CDO) is a type of asset-backed security. Collateralized loan obligation (CLO) is a type of CDO and underpinned mainly by leveraged bank loans. Collateralized synthetic obligation (CSO) is a derivative used primarily to speculate or manage risk.

Source: Creditflux Data+.

whole year, or just over two per week. Compare this with, for example, the activity of underwriting – an investment banking sideshow when measured in revenue terms – which generated 269 *FT* articles in 2006, while the automobile industry generated over 4,000 articles over the same period despite being just one quarter of the size of the CDO market in revenue terms.

Before 2007, securitization and derivatives were outside the field of the visible for most of those not directly involved and the banking industry could thus avoid difficult empirical questions about where the demand for these securities was coming from, and who would be left with the obligations if it all went wrong. Instead, financial economists and regulators who shared the paradigm of efficient markets developed a visionary exposition of the benefits of derivatives through four interconnecting promises. First, that financial innovation would de-risk core financial institutions; second, that it would free up capital in those institutions which would boost returns safely; third, that it would lead to a superior allocation of capital at a system level and produce liquidity in new markets and stimulate growth; and fourth, that it would 'democratize' finance – permitting the extension of loans to those households that had hitherto been excluded from the benefits of cheap credit.

The first claim was that financial innovation would encourage the efficient marketization of risk. New opportunities opened to individual institutions

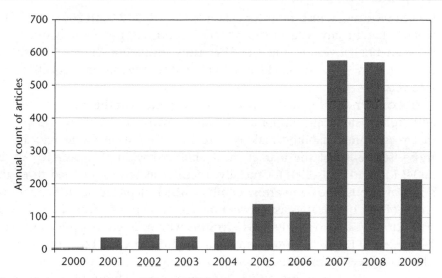

Figure 2.4. Annual count of *Financial Times* articles on CDOs

Note: The search excluded duplicates and used the terms 'collateralised debt obligation', 'collateralised debt obligations', 'CDO', 'CDOs', 'collateralised debt obligation', and 'collateralised debt obligations'.

Sources: Factiva database and *Financial Times*.

which could now hedge, market, or insure credit risk in a way that limited their exposure, leading to the efficient dispersal of risk at a system level. The vision of the transfer of risk was identified by the Federal Reserve as one of the driving motives of securitization for core financial institutions in the early 2000s (Gibson 2004). This view was reinforced by a plethora of structured finance textbooks, and public statements by the likes of Stephen Cecchetti, Head of the Monetary and Economic Department at the Bank for International Settlements (BIS), who argued mid-crisis that financial innovation had made growth more stable and business cycles less frequent and severe (Cecchetti 2009). This was only possible, he argued, because of the way in which structured finance allowed different kinds of risk to be isolated and commodified through new derivative constructs which could be tailored to the risk–return preferences of investors. Risk could be distributed to those actors outside of the core banking sector who were better positioned and more willing to assume the potential downside in exchange for a return on their investment.

Innovations in securitization required new organizational constructs, most notably off-balance sheet special purpose vehicles (SPVs), which were represented as a kind of firewall between banks and the new securities they were originating. Books on structured finance throughout the 2000s were replete with examples of how SPVs made it possible to issue 'nonrecourse' mortgage-backed securities transactions for example (Caselli and Gatti 2005: 2–3). SPVs meant that in any sale of asset-backed securities the legal contract was between final investors and the SPV, thus insulating the credit rating of the securities from any credit problems in the originating institution, and vice versa.

Risk could now be traded away from the core hubs of the financial system – and from systemically important banks in particular. This would provide macro-economic stability, making sure that risky assets were relocated to those 'segments' of the market most able and willing to bear it (e.g. BIS 2004; Kiff and Mills 2007). Crucially, these ideas were visualized through a series of familiar box-and-arrow exhibits which depicted securitization as a chain of risk dispersal as assets were moved sequentially from bank balance sheets to SPVs and to anonymous investors with different risk preferences (see Figure 2.5). If Lakoff is correct and the metaphor, whether literary or visual, is 'the main mechanism through which we comprehend abstract concepts and perform abstract reasoning' (1993: 245), then these exhibits played an important role in framing securitization as a rational process with a clear beginning and end which showed that risk could and would be traded away efficiently and safely.

A second, related argument claimed that securitization opened up opportunities to run banks more efficiently. This was related to regulatory changes around capital requirements which were forcefully lobbied for by organized financial interests at the Basel Committee on Banking Supervision. Banks argued that securitization limited their exposure to default risk and that they therefore should not be required to hold back as much capital as a buffer. This in turn would free up capital for further lending or investing, which would boost corporate returns and extend liqudity to new markets. In 2005, the Basel II agreement marked a turning point by allowing banks to reduce their capital reserves by securitizing assets and placing them off book. For example, before securitization, Dutch banks had to hold reserve capital equal to 4 per cent on mortgage loans under the risk-weighted capital adequacy ratios of Basel II. After securitization, these could be reduced to nil, freeing up bank capital for a new round of lending. Mainstream structured finance textbooks like Fabozzi and Kothari (2007) heralded Basel II as a great success and emphasized the new efficiency gains of securitization, which reduced funding costs and diversified funding sources, whilst simultaneously reducing credit risk.

If core financial institutions could now offload risk and free up capital, financial innovation would also improve liquidity and growth; this was the basis of the third supporting argument. Liquidity and growth could be created safely by using securitization to produce different, tranched credit-rated securities that could be matched to investors risk preferences. Most relevant in this regard was the transformation of risky mortgage loans into securities that were

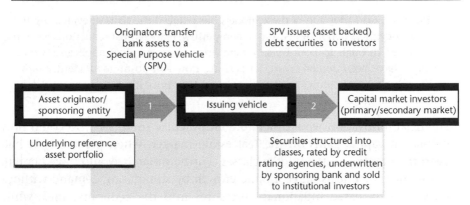

Figure 2.5. An example of a finance textbook representation of a basic (asset-backed) securitization structure
Source: Jobst (2007: 20).

rated from AAA to BBB or below. Before residential mortgages were securitized, it was argued, credit to many households was in short supply because pension funds and mutuals could not make consumer loans directly and did not wish to fund risky loans indirectly through their investment portfolios. Pension funds and mutuals instead invested in a combination of government bonds, equities, and blue chip corporate debt, where risk was limited and returns more certain. Securitization meant that pension and mutual funds could now fund risky loans by buying AAA-rated residential mortgage-backed securities, with no apparent downside when all of the default risk was in theory concentrated in the subordinated, lower rated tranches of the mortgage-backed securities. These lower tranches could be sold to hedge funds and other investors who were willing to take on more risk for higher returns by investing in higher yielding, lower rated tranches. The story was of win-win outcomes: households got mortgages from banks which could offload risk, as securitization lowered funding costs and boosted efficiency, whilst the creation of tranched securities meant new groups of investors could buy assets that matched their risk–return preferences.

This benign vision was supported with a fourth argument which focused on the democratizing benefits of financial innovation. The upside of liquidity creation was that households and corporations would have access to more credit for consumption or investment purposes. This credit could also be extended to a greater proportion of households, particularly those with lower incomes or chequered employment and/or repayment histories. This was in no small part due to new techniques for measuring default correlation. Banks and regulators were keen to assert that these techniques meant default risks were better known and caulculable, even with incomplete historical data. According to Alan Greenspan, then chairman of the Federal Reserve:

The widespread adoption of these models has reduced the costs of evaluating the creditworthiness of borrowers, and in competitive markets cost reductions tend to be passed through to borrowers. Where once more-marginal applicants would simply have been denied credit, lenders are now able to quite efficiently judge the risk posed by individual applicants and to price that risk appropriately. (Greenspan 2005)

Financial innovation would therefore enfranchise the poor who could now partake in capital gains on the real estate market, when previously it had been the preserve of the middle classes. Furthermore, it would have benign, self-reinforcing effects on economic growth by stimulating demand without pushing wage-based inflationary pressures into the economy; meanwhile competition and the efficiencies associated with securitization would reduce borrowing costs more generally, meaning we could all borrow more and more, with little regard to future obligations.

2.2 Framework, conjuncture, and bricolage

The previous section analysed the story of financial innovation whose exchange value was high when its many promises were apparently confirmed by events before 2007. This section aims to present a different account which engages with the specific conditions and character of financial innovation. This section not only attempts to explain the post-2007 crisis but also how it differs from earlier ones. In understanding conditions, we emphasize the difference between semi-permanent framework conditions and more conjuncturally variable circumstances which change within the decade. In understanding the character of financial innovation, we emphasize bricolage or the importance of a different, non-scientific form of rationality which involves the improvisation of structures from events.

Like many who write about financial innovation, we start with a descriptive list of general conditions which have enabled financial innovation. But we add an analytic distinction between semi-permanent framework conditions since the late 1970s and variable conditions which changed over shorter periods (the conjuncture). In drawing this distinction, we are influenced by Braudel's notion (1982) of multiple, intertwined temporalities moving at different speeds so that conjunctures or temporary configurations are embedded within a *longue durée*. If these ideas are transposed and used for economic analysis, we can first isolate a series of macro framework changes which established new conditions after the 1970s and released finance from the cage of national restrictions established in the aftermath of the 1929 crash and slump, and which continued under post-war national settlements.

The most obvious change after the 1970s was the breakdown of the compartmentalization within and between national financial sectors, driven first by the fiscal consequences of the Vietnam War and then by ideologies of deregulation. Forced by the growth of the stateless Eurodollar market, states increasingly lifted earlier restrictions on cross-border financial transactions, resulting in the gradual development of a transnational market in foreign exchange contracts. Over time, this transformed into an international inter-bank market, providing banks and other financial agents with an alternative liquidity supply outside national circuits of capital. This subsequently became the main source from which financial innovations were fabricated. During the next two decades, the transnationalization of bond, equity, and derivatives markets duly followed.

At the same time, financial pressures and the ideological force of neo-liberal arguments have, from the 1970s onwards, encouraged governments to retrench the post-1945 welfare arrangements they had set up to make amends for the great European wars and mass unemployment. As a result, households across the Western world have seen state-backed guarantees eroded, with households increasingly turning to financial markets to gain access to goods such as housing, higher education, and protection against unemployment, old age, or ill health. This 'Big Risk Shift' (Hacker 2006) has not only provided banks and other financial agents with an increased demand for retail debt instruments (credit cards, mortgages, life insurances, loans) but also ensured a steady supply of new and stable income streams, serving as feedstock for large-scale financial innovation in wholesale markets (Leyshon and Thrift 2007).

Pension reforms, international trade imbalances, and rising commodity prices, further led to a growing 'wall of money' chasing yield. Prior to the September 2008 meltdown, the volumes were staggering. McKinsey Global Institute (2008) estimated total pension savings under management by pension funds in 2007 to be around $28.5 trillion; mutual funds and insurers managed a further $27.3 trillion and $19.1 trillion, respectively; and private equity and hedge funds had assets under management totalling $0.8 trillion and $1.9 trillion, respectively. The fastest growth was booked by vehicles of state capitalism, sovereign wealth funds, which by late 2007 managed assets worth $6.1 trillion.

Digital technologies also mattered because the falling costs of information were transformative and opened up a new world of screen-based trading and decision-making. In wholesale and retail markets, the introduction of these technologies spawned new products and services, new modes of distribution, and new techniques of pricing and risk management, resulting in a rapid and radical transformation of global financial markets. In a broad sense, the virtualization of trade and the digitization of financial data were key preconditions for the broadening and deepening of financial markets depicted in the earlier exhibits. Only when the trade-in claims on (future) income streams was dematerialized, could the upscaling of derivative trading occur.

Finally, the algebraic development of financial economics facilitated the construction of a standardized set of techniques that allow anonymous traders, seated behind batteries of desktop screens, to recognize each other's expertise in the blink of an eye. The rise of finance as an economic sub-discipline, resulted in the mass production of quants with new pricing models like CAPM, Black Scholes, and Value At Risk, which can quickly be adopted, adapted, and deployed in the new digital environment described above.

Taken together, these developments, which mix some intended policies with many unintended consequences, resulted in a financial world in which funds were plentiful, capital was mobile, trading could easily be extended and upscaled, and in which there was a perpetual search for yield and the 'new, new thing'. These conditions are framework-setting and, at time of writing, appear nearly irreversible in that finance continues to feed off mass savings in a deregulated, virtualized, and border-crossing world even after the crisis. But these frame conditions are too general to explain the varying forms and directions of financial innovation in successive periods since the early 1980s. Or, put another way, within this general frame of facilitative conditions, the important questions are about what happens, where, and how in more precise terms. If financial market intermediaries respond to opportunities, then what structures an opportunity?

The Braudelesque idea of 'conjuncture' (between events and the *longue durée*) becomes important at this point in our argument. In our usage, 'conjuncture' refers to a distinctive but unstable set of circumstances within which events and episodes happen, to produce fragile periods of stability within a broader structural frame. A conjuncture typically is a four- to seven-year period partly defined by a capital market configuration of asset prices, flows of funds, and interacting intermediaries kept together by the exchange value of a shared narrative.

From this point of view, finance makes a particularly interesting object of analysis because conjunctural effects are prevalent for two reasons. First, a grand narrative can be constitutive with self-fulfilling prophesy results. Any story-driven conjuncture can have the effect of inflating asset prices if enough people invest, creating a virtuous circuit between market belief and returns on investment, validated by those who cash in their gains (before the *ex post* discovery that this is an asset price bubble where outsiders and newcomers play the role of greater fool). Second, innovation in finance has no property rights, so novelty and rapid upscaling are critical before inevitable commodification and shrinkage of margins occurs. Thus, what matters is scalable differentiation. In a world where profit arithmetically equals margins multiplied by volume, the intermediaries of the financial sector need a succession of blockbusters. The well-placed financial intermediary reaps profits by exploiting a conjunctural opportunity and contains losses by recognizing conjunctural change in real time. This kind of thinking is perhaps best captured by Citigroup's former CEO Chuck Prince in his now infamous comment about the need to carry on dancing as long as the music is playing (Nakamoto and Wighton 2007).

For these reasons, each new conjuncture crystallizes itself around different coupon instruments which carry investors' hopes of profit and generate intermediary fees for the well-positioned. The early 1980s saw the rise of the secondary debt markets, which were overtaken by the junk bond craze and leveraged buyout madness that ended badly with the conviction of Michael Milken of Drexel Burnham and the battle for RJR Nabisco between KKR and a number of other investment teams. The early 1990s saw the rise of telecommunications and media as a new site for financial speculation. This fad increasingly focused on equity, especially in new technology stock issues, which gradually morphed into the Internet bubble of the late 1990s. The early twenty-first century gave rise to a new conjuncture, this time dependent on leverage, derivatives, SPVs, and structured investment vehicles (SIVs) around securitized residential mortgage and other assets.

But under these conditions, what was the character of financial innovation in terms of the labour and its outcomes? Here, we break with mainstream finance accounts of financial engineering and with social studies of finance assumptions about performativity, which both imply some kind of rationalist application of, or formatting by, prior theoretization. We do so by introducing the idea of bricolage which, in the Lévi-Straussian sense, does not mean bodging improvisation and the absence of rationality but a different and non-scientific form of rationality. For Lévi-Strauss, bricolage is a 'parallel mode of acquiring knowledge' (1966: 13) and involves 'build[ing] up structures by fitting together events, or rather the remains of events, while science, "in operation" simply by virtue of coming into being, creates its means and results in the form of events, thanks to the structures which it is constantly elaborating and which are its hypotheses and theories' (Lévi-Strauss 1966: 22). Lévi-Strauss distinguishes between the scientist and the bricoleur 'by the inverse functions which they assign to events and structures as ends and means, the scientist creating events (changing the world) by means of structures and the "bricoleur" creating structures by means of events' (1966: 22).

The importance of this distinction is not only that it provides the idea of different rationalities but that it allows us to revisit and question representations of financial innovation as engineering or rationalist grand plan. Practices within financial markets were much more akin to bricolage, understood as the creative and resourceful use of materials at hand – regardless of their original purpose – to fashion new structures out of conjunctural events. Those events might include the repeal of the Glass–Steagall Act, the liberalization of derivatives markets, the introduction of Basel II, the growth of corporate law and accounting expertise, the taxation and corporate disclosure laws in havens like the Cayman Islands, and other conjunctural developments. This point emerges clearly in the semi-autobiographical accounts of ex-industry practitioners like Lewis (2009), Ishikawa (2009), and McDonald and Robinson (2009), who emphasize the quotidian way in which bankers identify profit-making opportunities and their artful adaptation to changing conditions. And also by academic anthropological accounts like that of Ho, who describes the trading strategies of individual traders as 'riding the waves as long as they come rolling in' (2009: 288); she also describes those of US investment banks as 'presentism' (301), 'a strategy of no strategy' (247), meant to 'milk the present' (295) or 'squeezing the most out of the present' (291).

If the financial world did not turn out the way it was envisaged in the textbooks, it did so because the practice of bricoleurs in banks, hedge funds, and other institutions escaped the disclosed representations of the activity. Bricolage, by definition, is changeable and opportunist; it is not rule-bound or confined by theory. For that reason the results of financial innovation were very different from those anticipated by the 'econocracy' who construct and inhabit a neoclassical economic world of impersonal and abstract market forces where the parameters for actor behaviour are understood within a narrow and rigid market frame.

To illustrate this point more forcefully, we aim now to show how the efforts of bricoleurs in financial markets produced private opportunities at the expense of economic stability. First, we show how bricolage facilitated the production of volume and complexity at a systemic level through innovations in the CDO market. Second, we show how the motive for this was the construction of fee-earning and/or transactional positions, which allowed bricoleurs to individually extract cash from the market. Finally, we show how the toxic combination of volume, complexity, and the search for fee-earning positions created fragile latticeworks of exposure and obligation or circuits that brought down major financial institutions and ushered in the worst crisis since the Great Depression.

During the 2000s, the changes in securitization, and mortgage-backed CDOs in particular, took the form of bricolage. None of the exotic structures that developed were part of a grand plan or engineering process which had, for example, synthetic CDOs as their end goal. The form and structure of those synthetic CDOs were the result of gradual improvisation by bricoleurs over time, who spotted the opportunities presented by events and, once created, those structures would then become the next event from which new structures could be fashioned. Figure 2.6 shows the outcome of this process: it is a fourth-generation CDO, developed from Deutsche Bank's Jazz CDO which

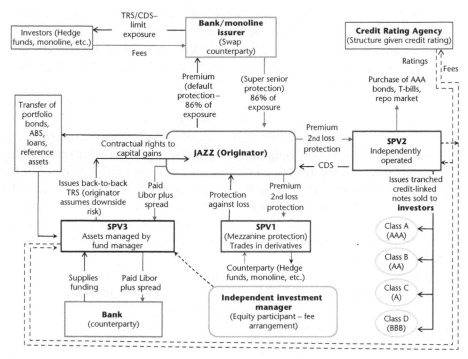

Figure 2.6. The Jazz structure (fourth generation)

was fairly typical of the kinds of structures developed from 2004 onwards. Its structure is the result of improvisation in CDOs over four phases. It is important, though, to note that this kind of structure did not mark the end of the innovation, as increasingly towards the mid-2000s single tranche, 'bespoke' built-to-order CDOs became the dominant form (Celent 2005; Lucas et al. 2007: 11).

In the first phase, during the 1990s, CDOs were 'true sale' deals used mainly to securitize commercial loans and corporate bonds (JP Morgan 2001: 4; Ng and Hudson 2007). In cash deals, loans were pooled by financial institutions and sold to off-balance sheet SPVs, which then issued tranched credit-linked securities that were bought by investors. This type of structure was a response to the Basel I accord of 1988 which made it a more efficient way of raising funding and obtaining regulatory capital relief. In the second phase, CDOs changed from true sale vehicles to synthetic and hybrid structures, which used CDSs rather than a true sale of assets to 'synthetically' transfer default exposure to counterparties. This kind of structure was an opportunistic response to US accounting rules which treated the purchase of protection via CDSs as a non-taxable event because no assets were transacted (Tavakoli 2008: 9). It was also attractive under Basel I as the AAA-rated super-senior tranches were awarded a 20 per cent BIS risk-weighting, which meant they were required to post 1.6 per cent rather than 8 per cent collateral on those securities held on their balance sheet. The changes to the market were sudden as synthetic deals moved from 14 per cent of the market in 2000 (JP Morgan 2001: 4) to 75 per cent of the market by 2003 (Tavakoli 2008).

With the explosion of synthetic CDOs came greater opportunity for bricoleurs, so that by 2002 and with a growing and increasingly liquid CDS market, it was possible to construct managed synthetic CDOs which employed fund managers to actively trade the underlying portfolio of credit derivatives to try to improve returns (or avoid losses). This marked a clear shift in the priorities of banks who built CDOs away from balance sheet management and risk transfer motivations towards the pursuit of arbitrage profits. With the principle of arbitrage established, a fourth phase saw bricoleurs develop increasingly complex structures, such as that in Figure 2.6 which used multiple SPVs to maximize arbitrage returns.

This particular CDO used at least three separate SPVs, which could be domiciled in any number of different havens such as the Cayman Islands, Delaware, or Dublin to take advantage of the particular taxation and/or accounting regimes to suit the particular function of the SPV. The CDO was also built on the growth of corporate law and accounting expertise and the intertwining of these professions with those of banking, as well as the introduction of the Basel II accord, which further encouraged the use of synthetics for capital relief reasons. Their foundations are also rooted in recently built structures, which become events in the next stage of construction, such as the growth of increasingly sophisticated derivatives, like total return swaps (TRS) and unfunded Credit CDSs; the expanding housing market which created an endless supply of feedstock in the form of mortgages; the increased willingness of companies like AIG and local government monolines to underwrite mortgage-backed securities and tranches of CDOs; and, as MacKenzie (2010) has persuasively argued, the default correlation assumptions that underpinned the pricing of such structures. In each of these cases, bricoleurs analysed events and built structures from them for private gain in an improvisatory manner that was not, and could not be, foreseen.

If that was how these structures were built, it is worth dwelling for a moment on Figure 2.6 to explain why CDOs were structured in this particular way. We appreciate that a complicated CDO structure such as this may be difficult for a lay reader to understand and for this reason we provide an explanation in Appendix 1. But the important point to consider is that this structure was built primarily to increase volume through greater complexity and leverage which would provide higher arbitrage returns. The volume comes from a number of sources. SPV3 as an off-balance sheet portfolio buyer and active fund manager bought a combination of bonds, asset-backed securities, mortgage-backed securities, loans, etc. as underlying collateral. This ultimately meant larger CDO deals which could be sold onto investors. Of course, scaling up the supply side is only possible if there is a market for the securities on the demand side. Volume therefore also comes from the use of multiple SPVs and different funding sources which open up the range of investors to whom securities could be marketed.

In this particular example, there are three sources of demand. First, the default risk on the super-senior tranches (which reference the lion's share of all the underlying collateral, usually in the region of 85 per cent) would be bought by a company like AIG or monolines via a CDS, and the securities would be held on the originator's balance sheet. Second, the mezzanine or '2nd loss' risk tranches would be sold to both SPV1 via a swap (who would in turn pass it on to another counterparty using another swap), and to SPV2 who would issue tranched credit-linked notes to investors like hedge funds, endowment funds, or even other banks. Third, the equity tranche would be retained by either the originator or the fund managers, or both.

Volume also came from the implied leverage involved in such deals, when the collateral posted by SPVs 1 and 2 was a small fraction of the underlying value of the asset pool held by SPV3, meaning institutions could gain exposure to the total return profile but needed to post only a small amount of capital. Volume and bricolaged complexity were therefore close relations, with originators gaining through the production of a large AAA super-senior tranche which was retained and funded by cheap short-term repo borrowing, creating large spread profits (Milne 2009; Gorton and Metrick 2010). Additional profits were also made on the arbitrage that accrued to the retained equity tranche when the fund management performance of SPV1 and SPV3 was good.

This understanding of a CDO as a volume-driven complex set of exposures and obligations takes us a very long way from the pictorial representation of CDOs as sequence of events along a relatively short chain, characterized in Figure 2.5. It suggests immediately that the robustness of the securities created depends primarily on technically correct assumptions about default correlation. This view is presented in a more considered way in MacKenzie's work (2010) on counter-performativity, which argues that the relatively low default correlation assumptions on mortgage-backed CDOs themselves encouraged the proliferation of sub-prime mortgages because they provided the impression that write-downs for investors would be limited. The subsequent extension of the sub-prime market, however, led to higher rates of default correlation which undermined the verisimilitude of the original models, so that the more the models were applied in a market setting, the poorer their explanatory power became (MacKenzie 2010).

The counter-performativity of the models is undoubtedly part of the story, but it is surely just part. Figure 2.6 suggests that the problem was equally one of moral hazard: the originator has little incentive to review the risk of default on poor quality loans or the derivatives which reference them when all the risk can be passed on to other counterparties, whilst maximizing positional fees and transactional profits. From the perspective of the bricoleur, the question of whether the models were correct or not did not matter, provided the risk could be spun off. The crisis was also borne out of uncertainty linked to the complexity of the structures: the lack of visibility about which institutions were exposed to what kind of risk when vehicles like SPV3 were bundling together fresh loans and tranches of mezzanine CDOs was a major factor in the ensuing liquidity squeeze because no bank was willing to lend money to or do business with an institution that was about to collapse. The result of bricolage was a credit crunch that resulted in a spiral of margin calls, sell-offs, mark-to-market losses, and further margin calls.

The exclusive focus on default correlation equations gives the impression that crisis might have been avoided with more robust datasets or different models that assumed higher correlation rates. But other models were available: interestingly, Fitch's rating system used a model which assumed higher default correlations which would therefore produce a smaller proportion of AAA-rated paper for securitization than if those same structures were rated by Moody's or Standard and Poor's. But bricoleurs understood the importance of AAA paper too well, so that Fitch's involvement in the rating of US residential mortgage-backed securities and mortgage-backed CDOs fell to almost zero by 2006 and 2007.

This raises the question of whether the problem was the assumptions of the models or the way in which bricoleurs chose to use some models and not others. The agency of the bricoleurs is an important issue, not least because towards the end of the boom it is alleged that certain banks sold securities priced in accordance with the credit rating agency models, whilst at the same time going short on those same structures. The implication is that they knew that the underlying quality of the portfolio assets was poor and would likely default. In this situation, the bank gets paid twice, once for arranging the deal and again for shorting their investors. Clearly, in a situation such as this, it would be too strong to suggest that the correlation assumptions format the economic world, even counter-performatively. This is a world of bricolage where correlation assumptions are just part of a broader battle of position and counter-position, where the objective is to create structures that enable the extraction of value or cash.

We consider the kind of 'war machine' strategies discussed briefly above in more detail in Chapter 3. But for this section we wish to retain our emphasis on the agency of the bricoleur and refocus the point made at the beginning of this chapter: financial innovation was important because it opened up space for financial elites to exploit new positional and transactional opportunities.

This is illustrated by Figure 2.7 which shows how one retail mortgage transaction generated at least seven fee-earning opportunities for a multiplicity of actors including mortgage brokers, retail bankers, and investment bankers in multiple roles as arrangers and fund managers, credit-rating agencies, and bond insurers. This is before we work in the various SPV managers, the likes of which we highlighted in Figure 2.6. Finance is now an industry where select groups can get seriously rich by finding one step in a 'volume-chain': for example, Salas and Hassler (2007) claimed that fund managers of an actively managed synthetic CDO would charge fees that ranged from 45 basis points to 75 basis points p.a. (i.e. 0.45–0.75 per cent) of the asset value of the CDO, so that a $500 million CDO on a 50 basis point fee deal would generate $2.5 million per year until maturity. Agents use justifications about marketizing risk, diversifying portfolios, maximizing returns, or optimizing rewards, but these rationalizations are (just like shareholder value in the giant corporation) not realizable programmes, only rhetorics with effects.

If we pursue the argument further, Figure 2.7 also shows that finance after securitization is an industry which has broken with the limits that constrain growth and profit that exist in other more mundane industries like car assembly, which epitomizes manufacturing. In any comparison between manufacturing and finance after securitization, two points stand out. First, there is an *internal* turnover constraint in manufacturing because it is only possible to book the turnover from an individual sale once. Additionally auditors have, since the early 1920s, enforced well-understood rules to prevent double counting when, for example, the assembler sells cars at end of line to its captive credit subsidiary. Second, there is also an *external* turnover constraint in manufacturing because the customers are households and firms outside the auto industry: all auto firms one way or another offer discounted product to workforce, suppliers, and dealers, but such auto sector sales could never sustain growth nor cover failure of external demand. Finance after securitization transcends these limits.

The finance sector actors involved in securitization deals are intermediaries in various roles, each taking a clip at one step in a chain of transactions, and anybody who creates a new step then charges a fee for service, which may open up opportunities for somebody else to book a profit too. The ability to increase the number of steps and charge fees is ultimately limited by the willingness of the end customer to buy the product, but as Figures 2.6 and 2.7 demonstrate, the end customers are often internal to the finance sector because it is banks, hedge funds, and pension funds which finance the final demand, either directly or indirectly by lending them the capital to do so. Furthermore, as Reuters blogger, Felix Salmon, has consistently argued,[1] the

---

[1] See http://blogs.reuters.com/felix-salmon/

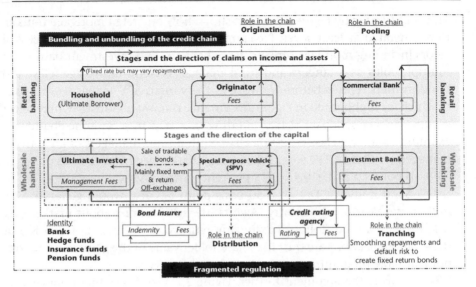

Figure 2.7. Business model of mortgage loan origination and securitization

use of CDSs allowed the mortgage-backed securities market to expand even when mortgage originations slowed down. This is because there is no limit to the number of CDSs that can be written on an underlying portfolio of assets, so that in theory the market is limitless. The sector therefore claims the exorbitant privilege of being able to create assets seemingly out of thin air and also to circulate them within the trade, selling to other institutions who are doing exactly the same thing.

Therefore, the illustration establishes the limitations of understanding securitization as a kind of chain because there is no natural beginning or end to this process. There are instead circuits between and behind the nodes. At its simplest, the hedge funds that are buying end-product securities may, for example, be borrowing from banks which are selling-on loans. In a more complicated way, if we return to Figure 2.6, it is entirely possible to conceive of a situation where SPV3 (which is actively managed) may at some point buy securities which are part of the CDO which references the portfolio, if, for example, the CDSs or credit-linked notes that come out of the other end are bought by another CDO that requires investors. The tiering of synthetics upon synthetics was a kind of financial parthogenesis as derivative products became the feedstock for new derivatives. From 2004 onwards, derivatives of one form or other became the principal form of collateral that went into CDOs sold to investors, so that institutions were, in effect, purchasing derivatives of derivatives or 'virtual' assets which reference real assets through swaps. In the antiques market, there is an old joke about how three antique dealers were stranded on a desert island with one Victorian chair and they all made a very good living out of it. If we imagine they were able to securitize the future income streams from the chair, trade those assets, and then place bets on the direction of the chair's price via the swaps market, at least two of them could very quickly double, treble, or quadruple their gains.

The picture or vision of circular movement and circuits within finance is a potent one; and one circuit in particular explains perhaps the most significant cause of the bank write-downs during the current financial crisis: the super-senior/repo circuit, as presented in the stylized diagram of Figure 2.6. The super-senior/repo circuit is relatively simple: banks securitized mortgages, which produced a significant amount of AAA-rated paper, particularly with the advent of synthetics. Roughly 85 per cent of all the paper produced would be AAA-rated and termed the 'super-senior' tranche. The default risk of this tranche was normally passed on via a CDS to a large insurance company like AIG or a monoline insurer. The AAA super-senior tranches were then retained by the originating banks and financed through repo market borrowing, which required the AAA securities as collateral. The bank would hold these securities either on the balance sheet, their trading book, or off-balance sheet by way of an SIV. The bank was then able to book the money on the spread between the short-term, low interest rate borrowing on the repo market and the long-term, higher interest return yield on the super senior, as if it was a simple carry trade.

The size of these repo deals was enormous: de La Dehasa (2008) and Mizen (2008) found that US bank conduits bought $600 billion and European banks $500 billion of CDO securities (in a market they were estimated to be worth approximately $2.2 trillion in 2006). This evidence is supported by Milne (2009: 175, 190), who found that the stock of bonds held by banks involved in yield trades (i.e. the practice of posting AAA-rated, mainly mortgage-backed, bonds as collateral for short-term repo financing) grew from virtually zero in 2002 to around $3 trillion, out of a total $4.8 trillion by the summer of 2007. This contributed some $100 billion per year to global banking sector profits and, incidentally, provided the bulk of the funding for the global credit boom. Evidence on individual banks seems to support this case. UBS, for example, stockpiled $50 billion of its own AAA-rated super-senior tranches by the time the first wave of the crisis hit, turning the Swiss behemoth into one of the biggest losers from the crisis, and earning it the derisive moniker of 'used to be smart'. Citigroup and Merrill Lynch had similar exposures. Meanwhile Lehman – which originally operated a 'moving, not storing' securitization business – from 2005 onwards succumbed to repo temptations; though it also suffered significant hits on stockpiled commercial and residential mortgages and subordinated CDO tranches (Valukas 2010: 540–1).

This is a circuit which ensured that risk was not dispersed, but rather concentrated around a small group of firms, leaving banks exposed to maturity mismatches and counterparty risks, and insurers heavily exposed to default risk. It is easy to see how circuits like this contain many points of fragility and vulnerability. For example, higher than anticipated default rates could lead to a credit-rating downgrade on portions of the super seniors, which might cause repo lenders to call for more or better quality collateral, sparking a fire sale of assets and a spiral of increased mark-to-market losses. Higher default rates might also distress insurers who could struggle to meet their obligations to the bank. Problems for the insurers might be exacerbated if they were thinly capitalized, when bankruptcy would render the insurance contracts worthless and undoubtedly cause further write-downs on the super-seniors. Repo lenders might get spooked and pull their money, leaving banks with no option but to dump illiquid, mortgaged-backed assets into a market with no demand, thus causing huge losses across the sector, and mass bank bankruptcy in many cases.

Of course all of this more or less actually happened. Mortgage defaults did rise and were more correlated than assumed; rating agencies did re-rate securities; AIG and many monolines did go bust under the weight of obligations which could not be met from their thin capital bases; banks did fire sell their assets, causing huge mark-to-market write-downs; and there was a run on the banks through the repo market, which practically made the entire global financial system insolvent. It is estimated that upwards of 20 per cent of the value of the $3 trillion posted collateral has been wiped out in mark-to-market losses, in addition to the value lost on the poor performance of the underlying loans (Milne 2009: 179).

The banks also had exposure to other non-bank institutions such as hedge funds, because in many cases they supplied, arranged, and/or syndicated the loans they required to make leveraged bets. Many hedge funds went bust after buying the riskier tranches of the same CDOs or after various other leveraged positions collapsed as all asset prices converged on a downward trajectory. Banks were also forced to bring off-balance sheet SIV exposure back onto their balance sheets once the first wave of the credit crisis hit in August 2007. A Fitch report found that of the twenty-nine SIVs they studied, five were restructured, thirteen were consolidated onto the sponsoring bank's balance sheets, seven defaulted on payments on their senior borrowings, and four unwound themselves (Hughes 2009). The SIVs that were consolidated or restructured accounted for two-thirds of total SIV assets while the defaulting SIVs represented 32 per cent. Financial innovation in this starkest of forms was a circuit, not a chain. The bubble inflated as a circuit and it went down like a circuit. All of this was hidden, undisclosed, and the implications remained unanticipated in Bernanke's story where rhetoric and visualizations of the activity pictured risk being moved to the peripheries of the financial sector and away from the large banks.

2.3 The concentration of risk

The argument so far has implications for how we understand the crisis of 2007 which was the outcome of the undisclosed consequences of financial innovation. Textbook definitions and chain visualizations emphasize the distribution of risk away from the originator as the defining characteristic and key benefit of securitization. Our analysis of bricolage and circuits instead explains the concentration of risk at the centre which, after 2007, brought down metropolitan banks like HBOS and RBS in the United Kingdom and Bear Stearns, Citigroup, and Lehman in the United States.

As we saw from Figures 2.6 and 2.7, the dominant industry representation of securitization is as a chain of transactions which move from retail loans made by banks on the left-hand side to generic 'end investors' pictured on the right-hand side of the diagram. The image was important because it powerfully framed the idea that risk was moving towards some 'safer' zone, to investors that were most able and willing to bear it. The implication was that finance was becoming safe, more robust, more stable, and more resilient than it was prior to securitization. But ultimately the representations simplified and obscured practice and made it difficult to observe how obligations had accumulated and where they travelled via pledges, collateral obligations, and short-term funding arrangements on and off the balance sheet.

Has much changed since 2007? As Figure 2.1 showed, the value of derivatives trading has not hugely declined. However, we are told that most of these classes of security gave no trouble in the last recession and are therefore no cause for concern in the future. The crash took out Lehman, Bear Stearns, and Merrill Lynch from US investment banking but the surviving investment banks and conglomerates now represent themselves as the survivors who can handle derivatives, as if they were recreational drugs that are safe enough for sensible users. However, this fails to engage with the consequences, which do not depend on the quality of the product or the individual firm's judgement but on the collective bricolage that concentrates risk.

If we were to consider the concentration risk and exposure to counterparty failure in a post-crisis frame, there are still serious questions that need to be asked. According to the Office of the Comptroller of the Currency's bank trading and derivatives 2010 first quarter report (Comptroller of the Currency Administrator of National Banks 2010), the notional value of derivatives held by commercial banks in the United States is $212.8 trillion. Of the 1,030 US commercial banks that submitted information on their derivatives exposure, the top five claimed 97 per cent of this notional value (Figure 2.8). Such concentration is quite staggering, and begs the question of what is actually hedged when so much value is held by so few institutions? And what would be

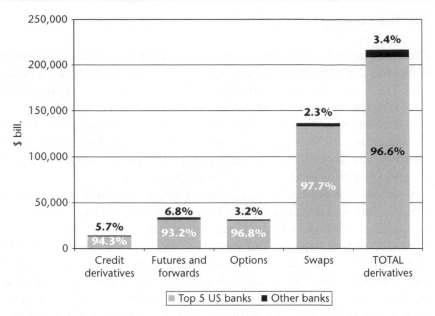

Figure 2.8. Analysis of US banks holdings of derivatives contracts (Quarter 1 2010)

Note: The top five banks are Bank of America N.A., JP Morgan Chase Bank N.A., Goldman Sachs Bank N.A., Citibank National Assn, and Wells Fargo N.A.

Sources: Comptroller of the Currency Administrator of National Banks, Washington, DC.

the implications for the value of all of these contracts if just one of them gets things fundamentally wrong? Clearly, netting does reduce some of the notional values – but netting is often difficult to implement in a bankruptcy situation, where complexity confuses simple measurements of exposure and who owes who what, as the experience of Lehman demonstrated. That JP Morgan has an asset base of $1,627,684 billion but derivatives exposure of $78,545,384 billion should be a cause of concern to us all, particularly when it is likely that their hedges are made with a smaller and smaller group of companies now that the likes of Lehman Brothers, AIG, Bear Stearns, and a raft of monolines went bankrupt or no longer exist.

The concentration of risk has continued even after the crisis, which is chilling news for the state and for society. The lesson of 2008, after letting Lehman go down and saving AIG, is simple: when risk is concentrated the state has to bail out players and markets, because the alternative is an unacceptable domino-style collapse. When banks take a major hit, the risk is offloaded onto government and ultimately onto taxpayers, public employees, and public service users. The government responds to these costs thus directly through recapitalization and cash loans, and 'synthetically' through guarantees, quantitative easing, asset/treasury swaps, etc; at the same time, households pay indirectly through public spending cuts, tax increases, job losses, and asset price falls on houses and pension rights. The role of government and households as risk-bearers of last resort – the socialization of risk – is the undisclosed 'other' of a hyperbolic financial sector which operates by way of bricolage. And if, as seems likely, reform imposes no onerous requirement for banks to hold more capital for their riskier activity, that reserve requirement too could be formally socialized, as states hold back public expenditure in the good years to build reserves for bank and market bailouts in the downturn.

This is all not adequately captured by the notions of 'too big' or 'too interconnected' to fail. For, if our arguments have force, the problem is not a matter of size or connections but of a continuing undisclosed concentration of risk which was denied by pre-2007 stories and visuals about chains that traded away risk. As we will argue in the closing chapter of this book, this problem definition suggests that the solution is not more sophisticated regulation but rather more simplification of finance which *inter alia* means limiting innovation by refashioning events in a way that frustrates the bricoleur.

2.4 Play it again

The problem with the recent crisis is to understand its similarity and difference from previous crises, which might allow some assessment of the implications for the future. The pertinent question is perhaps, why should this crisis be an invitation for radical reform if crises seem to be intrinsic to capitalism?

Radical and mainstream economists do not much help here for two reasons. First, economists tend to disparage financial innovation as a means through which new kinds of debt can be secured against assets so that new coupons, like junk bonds or derivatives, according to Galbraith (1994: 34), amount to no more than 'a small variation on an established design'. Second, economists tend to see cyclicality and recurrence in successive episodes so that Reinhart and Rogoff's book is oriented by its polemic against the foolish who in each cycle think 'this time it is different' and hence fail to see that it is just another boom ending in bust on the back of new products in a different conjuncture (2009*b*). The result is an expectations-led story about booms and busts.

On this account, the question is whether and how it is practical to promote a new sobriety and scepticism about tales like the new economy or the great moderation amongst traders, managers, and regulators. One academic response after the crash is to propose a reformed business curriculum by adding economic history courses to MBAs or finance masters, just as a decade previously ethics and social responsibility courses were being recommended after Enron. But, the recollection of an economic history elective taken ten years previously is unlikely to restrain exuberant animal spirits reinforced by this year's profit-taking. Equally, business curriculum reform does not begin to engage with the structural issues about bricolage and concentration of risk described in this chapter, or with the drivers and context of shareholder value and new business models which motivate the bricoleur as we argue in Chapter 4. If these issues are not addressed, then it is very likely that there will be a next time, which once again brings crisis to the metropolitan core with GDP loss and ongoing legacy burdens for households, even as the bankers return to bricolage as usual.

APPENDIX 2.1

Notes on Figure 2.6

The portfolio of bonds, asset-backed securities, loans, etc. is either sourced in the market or is from the originator's balance sheet. These are put in an off-balance sheet, separate legal entity (SPV3). The funds to acquire these assets are provided by a bank counterparty. The return profiles of those assets (interest payments plus capital gain) are then transferred to the originator in the diagram via a back-to-back TRS. The way that this works is that the originator pays SPV3 a 'LIBOR plus' spread based on the value of the underlying portfolio and assumes the downside risk. In return, it receives the interest payments on the underlying portfolio, including any capital gains that accrue. The funding bank counterparty receives a LIBOR plus spread. This structure now gives the originator the return profile of the underlying assets, but allows SPV3 to trade those assets and improve returns whilst domiciled in a tax haven, which means those transactions will not incur the costs they would have done had the originator performed this task-on-balance sheet.

The originator assumes the return profile and the downside risk on the underlying portfolio via the TRS. It will have to make good any deterioration in the value of the underlying portfolio, which would be payable to SPV3, who would then repay the bank counterparty. The originator then tranches this risk into three: an AAA-rated super-senior tranche where the default risk is 'sold' to a monoline or AIG, two mezzanine tranches where the risk is sold on synthetically to two additional SPVs (SPV1 and SPV2), and an equity segment. SPV1 passes on the risk in one or more of four ways.

1. Buy protection from a bank/monoline or some other counterparty via a CDS on the top centre of the diagram. This transfers the major part of the risk (roughly 86 per cent of the total exposure).
2. Buy protection from SPV2 (i.e. paying a monthly/annual premium to them) through a CDS. They in turn pass on the risk by issuing tranched credit-linked notes giving different degrees of exposure and return on the underlying portfolio.

The cash received is then invested in either AAA-rated bonds, T-Bills, or in the repo markets as collateral (because it costs SPV2 nothing to take on default risk exposure).

3. Mezzanine risk is also transferred through a TRS to SPV1.
4. First loss risk (i.e. the equity tranche) is borne by the fund manager(s). Returns are supposedly improved through active fund management: (*a*) of the underlying portfolio and (*b*) of credit exposure in SPV1, which purchases and sells CDS protection with other counterparties.

3

'Alternative Investment' or Nomadic War Machine?

> *[I]ndependent research and data demonstrate that private equity is a valuable asset class that is able to generate genuine alpha, making it particularly important for pension funds and insurance companies that want to boost returns in the face of ageing populations.* (British Private Equity and Venture Capital Association (BVCA) 2010)

> *Hedge funds engage in financial innovation by pursuing novel investment strategies that lower market risk (beta) and may increase returns attributable to manager skill. . . . Hedge funds' superior performance relative to other financial institutions and the market as a whole is in part attributable to financial innovation by the funds.* (Shadab 2009: 1, 51)

> *A record portion of the earnings that would go in their entirety to (Owners) . . . is now going to a swelling army of Helpers. . . . Helpers receive large portions of the winnings when they are smart or lucky, and leave (Owners) with all of the losses – and large fixed fees to boot –when the Helpers are dumb or unlucky (or occasionally crooked). Sir Isaac (Newton)'s talents didn't extend to investing (but if they did) Sir Isaac might well have gone on to discover the Fourth Law of Motion: For investors as a whole, returns decrease as motion increases.* (Warren Buffett, Letter to Shareholders of Berkshire Hathaway Inc., 2006)

In this chapter, we shift from analysing financial innovation with its emphasis on processes and products to exploring two groups of important financial actors: private equity and hedge funds. These groups are often represented as 'new' actors in that they operate in a field of 'alternative investments'. The quotations above illustrate the conventional differences of opinion about the benefits or costs of such alternative investments. As the first two quotations show, the large-scale growth of this new activity is built on its own promise that the skills of suitably incentivized new intermediaries will deliver 'alpha': above market returns and/or returns which are less exposed to market movements. These marketing claims, made by trade associations like the British

Private Equity and Venture Capital Association (BVCA), are endorsed by sympathetic academics like the lawyer Houman Shadab. But they are disputed by many others, including value investor Warren Buffet, who argues that new 'helper' intermediaries are simply making deductions through fees as assets are churned, so that net returns for retail investors are lower.

This disagreement about alternative investment intermediaries is, of course, part of a wider and established debate about virtue and vice in financial markets. But what is striking about the often very public debate on private equity and hedge funds is that they have been viewed either as better market operators or as worse rent seekers and speculators, operating in a market defined conventionally as a constellation of assets with differing risk–return characteristics. Within this essentialist, identity-centred frame, hedge funds and private equity are represented as a distinct part of the financial system, outside the mainstream. This chapter breaks with this assumption to reframe private equity and hedge funds as a mutable, integral part of the world of bricolage described in the previous chapter: hedge funds played a major role as service users, sellers of protection and buyers of asset-backed securities; meanwhile the debt used by private equity funds to fund their buyouts became feedstock for the markets as the debt was securitized and sold to investors like banks and hedge funds. These intermediaries were (like many others) bricoleurs operating within the conjunctural conditions of low interest rates and abundant liquidity in the 2000s.

But there was also something distinctive about their strategy which we can understand outside the market frame through the Deleuzian analogy of the 'nomadic war machine'. The concept of 'war machine' usefully invokes deception, power, threat, and tactical alliance, with the irregulars also operating symbiotically with regular forces, represented by the banks. Private equity and hedge funds then are not just traders but raiders who take positions and then try to 'make the positions work' using tactics like leverage, shorting, holding companies, and derivatives, often as weapons to secure advantage not just tools to facilitate trades. As was the case with the Vikings and other marauders, it is not fixed strategies that generate reward, but rewards which drive various tactics of value extraction and impose costs externally.

The chapter develops these arguments in three sections. The first, Section 3.1, presents data on the hockey stick growth of private equity and hedge funds and summarizes the narrative struggle over the representation of these activities, where there are sharp differences between the funds and their critics about their contribution to efficiency and their social responsibility. Section 3.2 tries to get beyond the essentialist arguments used by both defenders and critics of alternative investment by proposing a problem shift by analogy with Deleuze, drawing also on the argument of the previous chapter. This second section argues that private equity and hedge funds are like Deleuzian nomadic war machines, generating rewards for their managers by using devices like shorting as weapons not tools; it also shows how hedge funds and private equity are implicated in the latticework created by conjunctural bricolage so that they are intimately connected with the banks. The third and final section, Section 3.3, turns to consider the difficulties that private equity and hedge funds have had in negotiating conjunctural change since 2007. Their division of ownership rights and fee structure ensure high income and low risk for fund general partners regardless of performance, but they have struggled to deliver superior returns for investors in volatile markets under conditions of uncertainty.

3.1 Alternative investment funds (in a new conjuncture)

Alternative investment is part of the world of story-driven capitalism introduced in Chapter 1: doubly so, because this would-be 'new asset class' comprises a set of activities which divides opinion. Hedge funds and private equity are at the centre of an ongoing struggle to win or retain control over the representation of their activity, which is variably represented as economic function or dysfunction, but regardless of whether the narrative highlights good or bad, it is usually set within a market frame that is accepted by supporters and critics alike. Just as important, however, is the influence of the changing conjuncture, especially after 2000 when hedge funds and private equity could exploit leverage to generate returns for institutional investors disappointed after the end of the long bull market in equities. In this context, a defensive narrative of the benefits of the activity deflects intrusive regulation and sustains the inflow of new investment from which hedge fund managers and private equity general partners built new trading strategies and executed upscaled deals that generate jackpot rewards under their fee structures.

In alternative investment, as with financial innovation or banking considered elsewhere in this book, stories and representation matter. But alternative investment is different in some respects and generally more complicated because the players are a disunited and often quarrelsome coalition. For example, hedge fund manager Barton Biggs of Traxis Partners publicly queried private equity's ability to create sustained returns over time, and famously defined their success in the 2000s as little more than a leveraged bubble (Biggs 2008). Within the hedge fund industry there are divisions: some managers are wedded to fundamental analysis – the study of accounts, product market data, and so on – and are critical of other hedge funds that use technical analysis, which involves complex simulation software and trades on historic correlations between certain stocks and/or other assets. There have also been disagreements within the private equity industry: when there was panic about

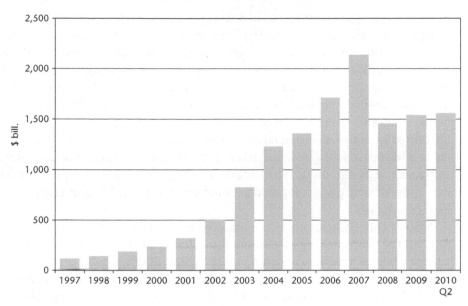

Figure 3.1. Hedge fund assets under management
Source: BarclayHedge Limited.

UK private equity in 2007, it was clear that maverick seniors, like Jon Moulton, did not stick to the official line like a CEO or front-bench politician when speaking to the press or giving public testimony. Strikingly, the most politically damaging quote of this panic came not from a politician or trade unionist but from Nicholas Ferguson, one of the founding fathers of British private equity. In an interview with the *Financial Times*, he broke the sector's taboo on talking about tax by criticizing rates that leave buy-out executives "paying less tax than a cleaning lady"' (Arnold 2007). After this, a BVCA spokesman rather stiffly told the *Daily Mail* that 'Mr Ferguson's views do not represent the industry as a whole' (Fleming 2007).

Academics have historically been more divided and uncertain about hedge funds and private equity than they were about financial innovations like securitization and derivatives, where financial economics anchored understandings without significant dissent and the economic models played a major role in rationalizing and instituting practice, as discussed in Chapter 2. The private equity industry of the 2000s is a partial successor to the leveraged buyout (LBO) movement in the US which gained notoriety in the 1980s when junk bonds were used to fund the purchase of ever larger companies, culminating in KKR's takeover of RJR Nabisco for $31.1 billion in 1989. At that point, Michael Jensen famously announced that the public corporation 'has outlived its usefulness in many sectors of the economy' because new organizations (like KKR) could control managers more effectively than dispersed shareholders (Jensen 1989: 61). But LBOs more or less vanished as the conjuncture changed and interest rates rose, which undermined Jensen's epochal claim and subsequently encouraged many to be cautious about endorsing private equity in quite the same way. As for hedge funds, many financial economists are sceptical of the claims made by the industry that they can generate superior returns consistently over time. This scepticism partly relates to the influence of the efficient market hypothesis, which was informed by an earlier generation's observation that most fund managers find it difficult to beat the market. Significantly, Shadab, the academic supporter of hedge funds cited in our opening quote, is not an economist but a libertarian lawyer opposed to state regulation and bureaucratic costs and constraints.

Against this background of internal division and academic disagreement, it is all the more striking to observe the rapid growth and increasing influence of hedge funds and private equity in the 2000s. Global funds under management by hedge funds increased from $20 billion of assets managed in 1997 towards $2 trillion in 2007, as Figure 3.1 shows. The number of funds also grew spectacularly from some 600 funds in 1990 to 9,000 in 2008. If the 1990s involved large percentage growth from a small base in funds managed, the remarkable point is that growth rates of 50 per cent per annum were sustained on a much larger base. Moreover, the throw weight of hedge funds is much greater because of the influence of active and sophisticated trading strategies. While hedge funds manage around 1 per cent of all assets in the financial sector, they account for between 25 and 50 per cent of all trading on major exchanges (Stalmann and Knipps 2007). Furthermore, their weapons of choice are sophisticated, and allow for both the element of surprise and control with the least commitment of resources. For example, in the mid-2000s it was estimated that up to 40 per cent of trading on the London Stock Exchange related to hedge funds' use of 'contracts for difference', which are derivatives that allow investors to bet on a change in stock price without owning the underlying shares (Ethical Corporation 2006).

The story of growth is similar in private equity, which was on a hockey stick curve of expansion at nearly 20 per cent per annum from small beginnings and modestly sized deals over the past fifteen years. The increased throw weight in the case of private equity case comes from the growing size of the companies bought. This is classically so in the United Kingdom where, for twenty years after the late 1980s, private equity bought between 1,200 and 1,600 companies a year but the individual purchases have become much larger. As Figure 3.2 shows, average equity investment per company

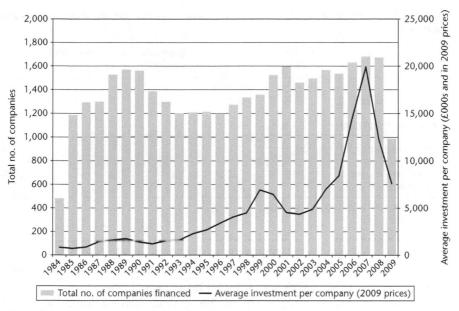

Figure 3.2. UK private equity worldwide investments

Note: Money values refers to direct investments from funds raised and therefore excludes financing used to acquire companies.

Source: British Venture Capital Association (BVCA).

(i.e. excluding debt) was around £1 million in the early 1990s, just £5.5 million in 2000 and no more than £13.5 million in 2006. As late as the year 2000, the average purchase was a £20 million privately held company or a division of a public company. That is all very different from the purchase of the high street chain Boots, in 2007, for £1 billion which represents private equity's first – and so far only – purchase of a giant FTSE 100 company and the high water mark of the private equity boom in the United Kingdom.

If we ask why these alternatives enjoyed periods of rapid growth, particularly since 2002, as argued in Chapter 2, the answer requires discussion of framework and conjuncture. The framework condition operated on the demand side as institutional investors were increasingly disappointed with modest returns from long-only, traditional investment in giant company shares and were prepared to allocate some of their funds to 'alternative investments' which promised to deliver more. The 1990s opened with the invention of proceduralized governance and value-based management, but as Froud et al. (2006) have argued, 'shareholder value' did not deliver a step like change in performance. More broadly, gilts may be less attractive but total returns on equity in the long run are modest. Table 3.1 presents evidence on the United Kingdom from the Barclays (2009) Equity Gilt Study and shows that, with all

71

Table 3.1. Returns from investing in equities, gilts, corporate bonds, index-linked funds, and cash

	Equities (%)	Gilts (%)	Corporate bonds (%)	Index-linked (%)	Cash (%)
2008	−30.5	11.7	−11.0	−2.1	4.2
Return over the past 10 years	−1.5	2.4	1.2	1.9	2.4
Return over the past 20 years	4.6	5.5		3.9	3.5
Return over the past 50 years	5.7	2.3			2.0
Return over the past 109 years	4.9	1.2			1.0

Source: 'Equity Gilt Study 2009', Barclays Capital.

dividends reinvested, the long-term real return on equities since 1900 is 4.9 per cent (the nominal annual return in 2008 was −30.5 per cent and in the year before crash, 2006, the nominal return was 11 per cent).

But, after the tech stock crash in 2000, conjunctural forces were even stronger on the supply side as they made it relatively easy for hedge funds and private equity to deliver on their promises of higher return in ways that encouraged greater commitment by retail funds. The crash of 2000 was widely taken to indicate the end of a bull market and the general policy response was to cut interest rates which made borrowing cheap. Moreover, funds were readily available: the recycling of trade surpluses from the Far East combined with securitization and derivatives which, from this point of view, represented unregulated private sector credit creation. All of this allowed leverage, magnifying returns for hedge funds and private equity, which was by then buying bigger companies with 70 per cent debt and 30 per cent equity in an environment where continuous holding gains on companies and all kinds of paper were underwritten by the sustained recovery of equity prices after 2002. On a monthly average basis the FTSE all-share index was at 3,500 in April 2007, more or less double the 1,735 level of March 2003 and well ahead of the previous 3,100 peak in March 2000.

At the same time the flow of funds into alternative investments needed narrative support, but this was complicated by the heterogeneity of the two activities and their rather different vulnerability to external criticism. Private equity's business model of dealing in companies was fairly intelligible, whereas hedge funds were dealing in coupons in ways that could not easily be turned into tabloid news stories. In the case of private equity, the activity was also increasingly newsworthy in broad sheet and tabloid media because expansion threatened the market position of more traditional fund managers, while its financialized operations which included closing production facilities and other forms of restructuring (Hall 2008) alienated trade unions. This was very publicly played out as a social panic about private equity which led to nearly six months of high profile media and political debate in 2007, including a Treasury Select Committee investigation (Montgomerie et al. 2008). The panic was the result of mounting concerns over private equity from a variety of sources but an important trigger was a sceptical letter to the *Financial Times* by a traditional fund manager, Michael Gordon (2007), who headed Fidelity in the United Kingdom. Before and afterwards, the most implacable and resourceful opponents of private equity were trade unions. One major union, the GMB, had been alienated by anti-union management at private equity companies like the AA which derecognized the union and instead sponsored a staff association; while the TUC was looking to develop its campaign on high pay which had previously focused on chief executive remuneration. All this can be tracked, as in Figure 3.3, by counting stories on private equity in the *Financial Times*, which rose to a peak of just under 6,000 articles in 2007 before falling away to under 3,000 in 2009 as private equity did fewer deals post-crunch and was crowded out by new concerns with bank failures, sub-prime, and collateralized debt obligations (CDOs).

Hedge funds were different because their opacity immunized them from severe or specific criticism as long as major funds did not fail in ways that

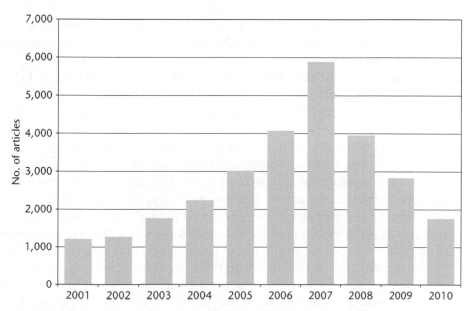

Figure 3.3. Annual count of *Financial Times* articles related to private equity
Note: 2010 data is the count between January and August.
Source: Factiva.

threatened the stability of the financial system, as had previously happened in the case of Long Term Capital Management, whose 1998 collapse resulted in a Federal Reserve coordinated bail out. The European Central Bank (ECB) did warn in 2006 that similar positioning and increasingly correlated hedge fund strategies represented a potential major risk (European Central Bank 2006: 44–5). But the benign conditions of the 2000s averted further threatening hedge fund failures and, when crisis hit after 2007, despite some high-profile failures and frauds, it was the big banks that spectacularly went under in ways which allowed hedge funds to parade their virtue. Indeed, independent hedge fund managers such as Greenlight Capital's David Einhorn got credit for warning of impending crisis and publicly going short on Lehman. When short selling of financial stocks in nervous markets became an issue in summer 2008, the practice was defended by middle-of-the-road financial journalists like the *Financial Times*'s John Gapper (2008), who argued that Einhorn's fees were rewards for enterprise. The industry took this line more aggressively in self-defence. Jim Chanos, chairman of a hedge fund industry group the Coalition of Private Investment Companies, argued that 'far from being the cause of the crisis, many short-sellers were warning months and years ago about problems in this area. Simply put, short selling is a vital investment strategy that responds to the market fundamentals and contributes to the integrity of stock prices' (Gangahar and Brewster 2008). When the ban on short selling finally did arrive in September 2008 the industry played the part of the injured party, because as one hedge fund manager put it, 'the banks screwed up and the hedge funds got blamed' (Magnus Nilsson, hedge fund manager quoted in Sherwood and Gemson 2008).

More generally, the narrative defence of private equity and hedge funds mixed two ingredients to produce a story that was both marketing pitch and a reactive defence against emerging criticisms of the industry. The first, positive ingredient was a free-market economic argument. This time it was not the syllogisms of economics, as in the circuitous inferences about financial innovation; in the case of private equity and hedge funds, it was the categories and a priori of economics which provided a shared language of justification. This was used by the industry as it pitched for low taxes and no regulation, and also by academics and regulators as they reasoned through what hedge funds did and how they should respond. Meanwhile there was a parallel, normative struggle that was related to the use of competing moral representations for popular as well as expert audiences. In this case, industry critics tried to hang the old trope of parasitic speculation on the alternative investment industry which responded in the modern narrative way by constructing an industry story about its contribution to market efficiency and social responsibility.

Apparent theoretical justification for private equity comes from agency theory developed by, amongst others, Jensen and Meckling (1976) and Fama (1980).

According to this approach, removing or moderating 'agency costs', typically informational asymmetries or misaligned incentives between shareholder principals and managerial agents, encourages managers to run corporations more efficiently for owners (Jensen and Meckling 1976: 310). These arguments are borrowed and used by the private equity industry in its narrative. For example, the UK's Walker report, which was an attempt to improve the image of the industry through enhanced transparency, contrasted the 'attenuation and impairment of the agency relation between owner and manager in the public company' with the 'direct alignment between (private equity) shareholder and (portfolio company) executive (which) minimises and may substantially eliminate agency tension in private equity' (Walker, D. 2007: 23). Similarly, the BVCA celebrated how 'private equity makes managers into owners, giving them the freedom, focus and finance to enable them to revitalise their companies and take them onto their next phase of growth' (BVCA 2007: 1).

In the case of hedge funds, we have already seen how market efficiency-based arguments about arbitrage underpinned the industry's 2008 defence of short selling. Even more striking was that those academics and regulators who did not buy into strong versions of the efficient market hypothesis also developed more general arguments about how arbitrage could improve the efficient functioning of markets. The Financial Stability Forum, based at the Bank for International Settlements (BIS), argued that the arbitrage function was further facilitated by the use of tools including derivatives (Financial Stability Forum 2007: 8); while Nyberg was highlighted the positive spin-offs from arbitrage in terms of improved pricing, efficient capital allocation, and risk management (2008: 1). Other commentators have argued that shorting would allow hedge funds to close price differentials across markets more swiftly (Duarte et al. 2005; Scholes and Blaustein 2005). Hedge funds' greater appetite for risk also led many, including the Financial Stability Forum, to claim that hedge funds are important suppliers of liquidity, particularly in risky markets such as emerging market bonds, credit derivatives, and distressed debt which reduces the need for core financial institutions to operate in these areas (Financial Stability Forum 2007: 8–9; Warsh 2007). Similarly, it is argued that hedge funds are vital suppliers of liquidity to markets at times of crisis when prices of certain assets drop precipitously.

But the more popular debate was, of course, about moral identities not efficiency. The critical tone of European reactions to private equity was set in 2005 when the leading German Social Democrat, Franz Müntefering, described private equity investors in Germany as 'locusts' who were stripping assets and destroying jobs (*Economist*, 5 May 2005). The imagery was equally strong in left and right newspapers in the United Kingdom during the private equity panic of 2007. The left-leaning *Guardian* wrote of 'wild west capitalism', where private equity 'corsairs' strip company assets, close company pension funds, and take advantage of tax loopholes for personal gain (Toynbee 2007). The right wing *Daily Mail* ran a series of articles, depicting private equity practitioners as 'City fat cats' and 'locusts' (Brummer 2007*a*), 'new robber barons' (Brummer 2007*b*), and 'pillagers' (Buckingham 2007). Others used emotive language about 'gamblers' and 'speculators' to understand hedge fund activity. In an *Observer* column, Will Hutton (2008) argued that the financial system 'consists of what are essentially gambling chips, such as credit derivatives, options, swaps, contracts for difference and stock lending for short selling. These are used by a vast global hedge fund industry to bet on movements of prices in the first financial system – shares, currencies, interest rates and commodity prices'.

Private equity hit back by developing its narrative of social responsibility. Organizations like the BVCA countered that private equity was not short-termist like the public company shareholder but rather a form of 'patient capital', which sought to build the firms they purchased with a time horizon of five to seven years. Further, the industry argued it was not in their interest to asset-strip a firm when the firm had to be sold for a profit after the holding period. According to Wol Kolade, BVCA chairman, 'we make money from building and growing the companies we own. We make money from creating value' (Kolade 2007). Moreover, this was done for the benefit of worthy stakeholders: the winners were: 'pensioners and people who benefit from pension funds that invest in private equity...it's ordinary working people who are the ultimate beneficiaries of private equity' (Walker, S. 2007).[1] Further empirical support was provided by adding up the jobs sustained and created by private equity (without of course considering how other styles of management or ownership would compare). Thus, the European Venture Capital Association (EVCA) highlighted the contribution to job creation by commissioning a survey that 'clearly demonstrates that European private equity and venture capital can make a difference to the European economy by providing sustainable, high quality jobs across Europe' (EVCA 2005). The EVCA claimed a million jobs were created by private equity between 2000 and 2004 and the activity would make a significant further contribution to the EU challenge of creating 20 million new jobs (2005). In the United Kingdom, the BVCA claimed that private equity not only created employment faster than other firms but it also generated faster growth, more exports, and investment so that the industry motif is 'investing in enterprise'; in similar vein the US National Venture Capital Association (NVCA) argued that private equity funds were always 'entrepreneurs first and financiers second' (2006).

Thus, mainstream discussion boils down to essentialist claim and counter-claim as private equity and hedge funds are set in a market context and then

---

[1] Simon Walker, BVCA Chief Executive.

credited with virtue or vice according to their economic function and/or moral identity, so that private equity funds are either 'patient investors' or 'asset strippers' and hedge funds are either 'arbitrageurs' or 'gamblers'. If we respond that maybe these funds are not always the same, then that raises the question of how we understand their variable character: as we argue in the next section of this chapter, this requires a different frame.

3.2 War machines: 'making the positions work'

In this section, we set private equity and hedge funds in a different frame by borrowing a Deleuzian analogy so that hedge funds and private equity are like 'nomadic war machines'. Their value-extracting activities then become visible and intelligible in ways that are important because they allow us to develop arguments about the character of bricolage and conjunctural opportunism introduced in Chapter 2. First, hedge funds and private equity are not separate from, but rather connected to, banks in complex latticeworks. Second, devices such as shorting and derivatives are not tools to facilitate work but weapons to exert pressure and force position. Third, within this frame, questions of morality, efficiency, and social contribution are irrelevant to the practice of finance because bricolage is about working the 'conflicts of interest' in finance.

The concept of nomadic war machine comes from the work of Deleuze and Guattari (1988). Nomadic war machines are a marauding, rootless army – a self-organizing structure without central control that exists for itself, and where the purpose of the march from battle to battle is the journey itself. They are countercultural by instinct, separate from mainstream values, and antagonistic to dominant apparatus and modes of intervention, but neverthe-less the irregulars will often be funded by the state or other dominant institu-tions in an attempt to harness the irregulars to do their bidding (in ways which can afterwards be denied). Our analogical use of their ideas is coherent with Deleuze and Guattari's original concept insofar as they argue that nomadic war machine is not a description of actually existing phenomena, but a representation of action that can be applied across a range of domains, includ-ing science as well as modern warfare (Deleuze and Guattari 1988).

This shift provides a parallax view, that is, one where a change in our observational position provides a new line of sight and thus interpretation of our object, adding perspective and depth perception. Within the analogical frame, if we suppose alternative investments act in financial not physical space, we can highlight new issues such as the connection between the alternative funds and more established institutions like banks. In the broader context of our book's developing argument, this allows us to locate alternative investment activity within the latticeworks of finance and develop the conjuncture–bricolage argument introduced in the previous chapter. Of course, financial actors operate in a changing economic landscape but they also have agency in creating that landscape by actively responding to conjunctural opportunities. Thus they help open up new positional and transactional opportunities through opportunistic bricolage which uses events to find or construct positions and then crucially makes the positions work.

Let us begin by showing how hedge funds and private equity were part of the latticework created by bricolage. To begin with, hedge funds and private equity were not separate from, but connected to, the banks. Most obviously, many banks and insurance companies had in-house hedge funds and private equity operations where the senior intermediaries were in effect franchisees dividing their profit with a supporting parent organization. Thus, Goldman Sachs, Lehman Brothers, and AIG had large-scale in-house private equity operations before the crisis; and, measured by assets under management, JP Morgan Chase was perhaps the largest hedge fund manager after the crisis. But the rest of the alternative investment industry was also connected by latticework which was vital to the rapid expansion of the financial sector during the boom and a major source of profit for the banks. This can be seen in their role as service users who operated symbiotically with banks, and also in their role in providing both the feedstock and final demand for CDOs.

Hedge funds and private equity both relied on banks for additional services such as prime brokering and the brokering of buyouts. For hedge funds, the closest and most important relation is with investment banks which act as prime brokers, supplying a range of essential services and profiting hugely from servicing hedge funds. For example, prime brokers lend hedge funds the securities they need to undertake short sales; they provide debt to allow hedge funds to leverage their investments; provide global custody services for the assets hedge funds acquire; and provide 'back office' accounting and portfolio information services. They can also aid hedge funds in accessing local shares abroad, provide cash management services, locate real estate and office space, provide headhunting services, and provide consulting on IT, compliance, and risk management. Small hedge funds usually have one prime broker while large funds have several. Morgan Stanley and Goldman Sachs each reported over $2 billion in revenues from prime broker services to hedge funds in 2006 (Annual Report and Accounts); and, in 2007, these two investment banks together had over 60 per cent of the prime broker market (Lipper 2007). However, in the fallout from the financial crisis, JP Morgan Chase, Credit Suisse, and Deutsche Bank increased their market share in 2008 at the expense of Goldman Sachs and Morgan Stanley. This led to consolidation in prime brokerage services and higher pricing for bank services and put pressure on hedge fund returns (Sender 2008b).

Within the latticework, alternative investment funds provided both the feedstock and the final demand for many debt-based securities. The expansion of alternative investments during the boom crucially depended on leverage supplied by the banks. The borrowed money allowed the financial sector to grow as it simultaneously created both feedstock and final demand: private equity debt in particular became feedstock for the securitization process, while hedge funds, and later private equity funds, became an important source of demand for the riskier debt securities produced in this process. As highly leveraged buyers and sellers of assets, alternative investment funds helped fuel an asset bubble from which fund managers profited handsomely.

As Figure 3.4 shows, UK bank-funded LBO debt grew by nearly 1,000 per cent between 2002 and 2006; this rapid growth was possible because securitization allowed sub-prime mortgages and other loans to be pooled, packaged, sold on, and then diced into structured financial securities. This debt provided feedstock – and in particular AAA-rated feedstock – for buyers who sought high-quality collateral. The other side of this debt was an interest-yielding asset for an investor, often banks but also hedge funds who were actively investing in the lower rated tranches.

If private equity and hedge fund debt, like subprime mortgages, became the feedstock for financial markets, hedge funds should also be recognized as

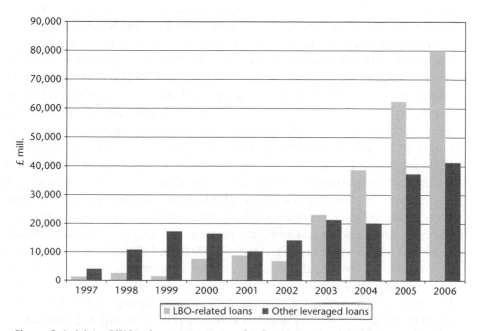

Figure 3.4. Major UK bank participation as lead arrangers in global leveraged lending
Source: Dealogic and Bank of England estimates.

'bottom-feeders' in the ABS/CLO/CDO chain, where they were an important source of demand for lower rated tranches. These crucially needed to be sold before banks could structure their securities, in the same way that a proportion of new houses had to be sold off-plan before construction could take place in the real estate market. Thus, CDOs could not have been constructed without hedge fund buyers taking up the riskier tranches, underlining hedge funds' role in the creation of complex latticeworks and circuits outlined in Chapter 2.

Hedge funds and private equity were undoubtedly an important part of the latticework, but how do we understand the nature of bricolage in this part of the financial sector? If we shift from the disclosed market frame to a more Deleuzian frame centred on nomadic war machines, the activity of hedge funds and private equity must also consider activity which seeks to 'make the positions work', that is, to extract value for intermediaries. Their activity needs to be understood in what nineteenth-century military theorist Claus von Clausewitz (1873) would have understood as a political space where position, power, force, threat, and deception are very much part of the business. Financial innovation was important here because 'making the positions work' required weapons, and these were provided by the legal structures of holding companies, tiered ownership rights, leverage, shorting, and derivatives.

This kind of activity can be illustrated by private equity's use of 'dividend recaps', which help recover the equity investment of the fund in a risk-free way. Dividend recaps are special one-off payments made by the portfolio operating company to the fund, often financed by extra debt, which is then loaded onto the acquired company's balance sheet. This practice was usually used to recover the private equity fund's original 30 per cent equity stake contributed when the portfolio company is purchased. After a dividend recap, the equity investors generally recovered their original investment stake and retained their claim on operating cash flows and resale returns, while the risks and costs of (a more indebted) portfolio company failing were passed on to bondholders and other stakeholders in the firm. This kind of strategy was widespread: it is estimated that roughly one-fifth of all private equity debt stems from the use of dividend recapitalizations. The British and US trade press in the 2000s was certainly full of brief reports of dividend recaps. For example, they were used at artificial sweetener manufacturer Merisant Worldwide Inc., which was re-leveraged twice in 2003 for $270 million in dividends. This more than covered the original fund equity investment of $160 million. Or, we can consider Thomas H. Lee Partners LP (THL) which followed a leveraged buyout in 2004 with more debt to fund dividends of $187 million in 2005 and $174.9 million in 2006, allowing THL to recoup its entire $361.8 million equity (Tenorio 2010). Such weapons made it possible for private equity investors to recover their equity stake, realize a large profit, and maintain the rights to capital gains in the event of a further recap or sale, whilst limiting their exposure to a corporate vehicle that may subsequently collapse.

An example will show how, in the worst case of company failure, private equity partners can walk away with decent returns before a portfolio company goes into bankruptcy. The outcome and role played by dividend recap in Focus DIY can be seen in Table 3.2 which illustrates how cash extraction realized large returns on investment by creating a debt-burdened retail company which subsequently failed, leaving other stakeholders bearing the costs.

In 1996, Duke Street Capital bought 45 per cent of Focus DIY: subsequent acquisitions of Do It All, Wickes, and Great Mills made Focus DIY by 2002 the second largest DIY group in the United Kingdom with 430 stores and a debt burden of £650 million (Davey 2002). The sale of 28.9 per cent of the business for £340 million to another private equity group, Apax Partners, and the issue of more debt in November 2002 allowed Duke Street Capital to recover all of its original equity input through a special dividend (Smith 2002). The sale of Wickes in 2003 for £950 million then netted the equity providers a large dealing profit of £369 million, so that the limited partners (typically outsiders like pension funds) more or less doubled their initial investment, while the general partners (the insiders, or private equity fund partners) realized a 950 per cent gain. However, as a consequence, when Wickes was sold the remaining Focus business was left burdened with so much debt that it could not survive a minor downturn in DIY retail sales. After successive credit downgrades (Anon 2005; Anon 2007b), Focus breached its loan covenants in June 2007, and was sold to US hedge fund, Cerberus, for just £1 (Anon 2007a). The final loss of equity was of no great significance for the investors because the equity loss of 2007 was much smaller than the gains already captured from refinancing and restructuring during 2003–4. Other stakeholders were less fortunate. Senior debt holders were repaid in full but those holding mezzanine

Table 3.2. Duke Street Partners extractions from Focus DIY (Duke Street Partners acquired Focus DIY in 1998 and Cerberus acquired it in 2007 for £1)

		Limited partners (97.5% investment) (£million)	General partners (2.5% investment) (£million)
Outlay	Equity investment	331.5	8.5
Income	Refinance (2003)	331.5	8.5
Net extraction		288.4	80.8
Multiple gain on outlay		1.9	9.5

Notes: While under Duke Street ownership, Focus DIY acquired other DIY companies: Do It All in 1998 for £68 million, Wickes in 2000 for £290 million, and Great Mills in 2000–1 for £285 million. In 2002, Apax Partners acquired a 28.9% holding in Focus DIY and during 2003 Duke Street Partners refinanced the enlarged company. In 2004, Wickes was sold to Travis Perkins for £950 million. In 2007, Focus was sold to Cerberus for £1.

Source: Report and accounts and IPO document.

notes received only 40p in the pound for their debt. Duke Street also left the Focus pension funds with a deficit which they were forced to top up with £8 million after intervention by the Pensions Regulator (Cohen and Arnold 2008).

This represents a kind of positional bricolage which exploited the long-standing different rights of debt and equity. It was elaborated in the mid-2000s through new innovations like payment in kind (PIK) and 'cov-lite' loans which gave creditors fewer rights in a bankruptcy or default situation. The significant characteristic of PIK loans is that the borrower can pay with 'paper' (i.e. shares or other securities in the company) rather than cash, while 'cov-lite' loans are those where breach of covenant would only be tested in specific circumstances, such as when the company proposes to issue more debt. These features were very useful when things did go wrong after 2007: out of forty-three bond deals done with a PIK feature, at least eight borrowers had already suspended cash payments and were paying in bonds by summer 2008 (Sender 2008a). These developments directly empowered private equity and weakened many banks which were left with less recourse protection than public company debtors who have the ability to take over the company when covenants are breached. In a period of competition between banks to expand and securitize their loan portfolios, the issuance of mezzanine debt with fewer covenant protections expanded at the expense of senior debt with traditional protections. By the mid-2000s, Europe was moving closer to the American model where senior debt accounted for only a few per cent of total capital (FSA 2006: 33).

In their different way, hedge funds were equally resourceful in using new innovations as weapons not tools. Taking one example, the development of measures, including codes of practice to improve corporate governance in public companies, created a host of profitable opportunities for bricolage by activist hedge fund managers. Guidelines designed to encourage shareholders to take a more active interest in the companies they invest in had the unin-tended effect of empowering hedge funds through a particular kind of *activism* with the ability to influence corporate payout policies or major strategic moves in public companies in unanticipated ways. In the United Kingdom, a series of reports by Cadbury (1992), Greenbury (1995), and Hampel (1998) together created a structure of proceduralized corporate governance intended to operate in the shareholder's interest. This was to be promoted by non-executive directors inside firms and by more engaged (long-term) institutional investors outside.

The collapse of Enron and WorldCom further encouraged this tendency towards proceduralization in the United States with the Sarbanes–Oxley Act the eventual response. All this created opportunities for old and new 'raiders' inside and outside the firm to take actions that would have an effect on the share price of the target company and allow profit-taking, before the raider moved on to the next target. This was the game played by Carl Icahn, William Ackman, Nelson Peltz, Chris Hohn, Eric Knight, and others in companies like Time Warner, McDonald's, Cadbury Schweppes, Deutsche Börse, and Shell. They variably used a variety of mechanisms to effect change, including proxy fights which allow shareholders to vote on key issues at AGMs; hostile 13-D letters which publicly criticize management; levered positions through 'contracts for difference' which allow buyers to enjoy the underlying rights of a share without owning them, while covering positions with swaps; and anticipating events by short selling of stocks. Thus, in 2005 it was (in European terms) aggressive and novel when a London-based hedge fund, the Children's Investment Fund, used shareholder activism to stop the Deutsche Börse bid for the London Stock Exchange (LSE) to allow Deutsche Börse to use its spare cash to pay higher dividends instead; many hedge funds also made money out of the fall in the LSE stock price after the deal fell through.

Fears about hedge funds using these devices as weapons were raised by the European Parliament in 2007 when it was alleged that hedge funds were buying voting rights in companies where they held an overall short position, thus raising serious conflicts of interest (Naik 2007). Acharya and Johnson (2005) also claim that, 'hedge funds often purchase small syndicate stakes in firms precisely to acquire non-public information to aid them in arbitrage trading' (20–1). Not surprisingly, it is alleged that hedge funds are involved in insider trading: between a quarter and a half of all merger announcements are preceded by abnormal share price moves, driven largely through the options market where hedge funds are most active (Scheer 2007). These misgivings were reinforced in late 2008 when many believed that hedge funds in the United States and Europe were spreading rumours to undermine banks stocks in which they held short positions. Thus, UK regulators banned the use of short selling in 2008 in the belief that rumour spreading and shorting were being used as a weapon to realize profits in a climate of fear, not as a tool to create market efficiency (Mackintosh 2008).

If many of these allegations about use of weapons are difficult to prove, it is clear that war removes old restraints as the irregulars increasingly break established conventions, or use whatever is not forbidden. But the logic of this particular process is that it encourages mimesis and the ever wider use of new weapons, so that war machine-like activity changes the general norms and customs of market behaviour. For example, in 2008, Porsche, a relatively small company, attempted to take over Volkswagen (VW), a much larger industrial giant, through the use of cash-settled derivatives. The fact that the derivatives were cash-settled meant that Porsche's stake did not have to be disclosed. When Porsche finally revealed that it held 31.5 per cent in derivatives in VW, it meant that there was an equity free float of only 5.8 per cent, creating panic among hedge funds which then had to cover their short positions.

Hedge funds bid up VW's price by 348 per cent in two days and in doing so made an estimated collective loss of around €10–15 billion (Milne 2008). The weapons of hedge funds are adopted by other actors, like Porsche, and can even be used against hedge funds. In consequence, it becomes increasingly difficult to define who or what a hedge fund is.

If private equity and hedge funds were using financial innovation not just as tools to facilitate trades but as weapons in a kind of guerrilla war against the corporation, the discussion of morality can be displaced. The preoccupation with morality is encouraged by the self-serving public narratives of the alternative investment industry and also by media and regulatory criticism of 'conflicts of interest' in finance. However, this particular framing of the problem can be unhelpful. The notion of 'conflict of interests' presupposes that an individual or organization is involved in multiple activities where one interest corrupts the conduct or reporting of the work carried out in another activity. This in turn assumes an ideal of impartial and independent action, which may be relevant to conduct in a Weberian bureaucracy or the restraint of political corruption, but is irrelevant to the practice of finance where the work of the bricoleur is to manage multiple activities so that the interest in one activity generates profitable opportunities in another.

The aftermath of the crisis has exposed much bricolage of this kind. The best-known case is that of the Abacus CDO structured by Goldman Sachs to meet the risk and return preferences of a hedge fund client, Paulson & Co. It is alleged that the hedge fund asked for high returns, and this implied the construction of a portfolio with riskier securities, which Goldman sourced from the market. Goldman then marketed the remaining tranches to investors in 2007, whereupon Paulson & Co decided to take short positions through CDSs on those tranches, gambling that they would default and fall in value. Goldman's marketing literature to other investors did not disclose that Paulson & Co had been involved in the structuring of the portfolio and had indeed bet against the CDO. Goldman Sachs was subsequently fined a record $550 million in damages for its part in the affair (Guerrera et al. 2010).

The Abacus scandal is one of many egregious examples that have surfaced as the role of hedge funds and banks in sustaining the housing bubble becomes much clearer. The backdrop to the Abacus case was the growth of 'build-to-order' CDOs in the mid-2000s, which meant banks would construct single tranches with particular risk–return profiles to suit client tastes and the banks would then subsequently retain, sell on, or re-securitize the remaining tranches. Hence the opportunity for those such as the Magnetar hedge fund which facilitated the creation of a few of the worst-performing CDOs by helping to structure CDOs and then betting against the structures they helped create. Many hedge funds realized that the loans and securities that went into CDOs were extremely toxic and they designed structures to exploit this situation (Ng and Mollenkamp

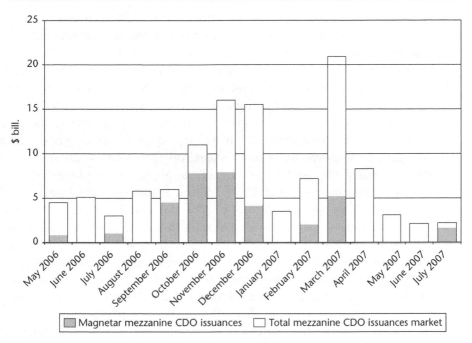

Figure 3.5. Magnetar's share of the mezzanine CDO issuance market
Source: Dealogic.

2008). Because banks had to sell the lower tranches before they could structure the CDOs, hedge funds used their power and influence as the default buyers of these tranches to insist on 'more risk' for higher returns; that is, they demanded that riskier loans (such as sub-prime loans, cov-lite private equity loans, or lower rated tranches from other ABSs or even other CDOs) be put into the structure. Magnetar then bought the lower rated tranches of these CDOs which yielded something in the region of 20 per cent annual returns (Ng and Mollenkamp 2008) and used them to fund short positions on the whole structure, knowing that if the BBB securities defaulted, it was very likely that the whole structure would default (Gapper 2010). In many ways this was the perfect hedge – if the boom continued they would receive modest returns from the 20 per cent interest on their lower rated tranches minus the cost of the short positions; if the whole structure went bust they would receive a jackpot win from the credit default swaps. As Figure 3.5 demonstrates, Magnetar was instrumental in driving Mezzanine CDO issuance at the peak of the boom, acting as arranger in over $34 billion worth of CDOs between mid-2006 and mid-2007 alone.

These examples demonstrate that hedge funds do not simply and passively take positions in a universe that consists of a given constellation of assets; instead, their actions shape markets and their attempts to 'make the positions work' do not necessarily result in the correction of prices. In this instance, their actions helped sustain the sub-prime boom and undoubtedly created significant private gains. Roughly, 96 per cent of all Magnetar's deals were in default by 2008, whilst Magnetar's founder, Alec Litowitz, drew $280 million in 2007 alone and the banks who managed the CDOs earned somewhere in the region of $3–4 million per annum (AR – Absolute Return + Alpha).[2]

This kind of bricolage has continued unhindered after the crisis. One example of this is the way in which Barclays drew on ex-employees in a hedge fund to improve its balance sheet, on terms unfavourable to the institution, but which were hugely beneficial for the ex-employees. On 16 September 2009, Barclays sold $12.1 billion of mainly monoline insured toxic assets to a hedge fund, 'Protium'. The purported aim of the exercise was to limit Barclays' balance sheet exposure to monoline collapse. Protium was managed mainly by ex-Barclays employees and received an annual management fee of $40 million. Protium funded the purchase of the toxic debt using a private equity-type structure: 30 per cent of the purchase was funded by equity raised from limited partners and 70 per cent funded by a loan supplied by Barclays itself. Crucially, the interest payment on the loan taken out by Protium from Barclays was subordinated to the management fee which meant that the general partners in Protium were paid before the interest on the loan. This still left Barclays exposed to the risk on the assets because, if they were to default, there would be little left after Protium's management had been paid.

Protium's fees can therefore be thought of as a kind of guaranteed bonus for the cleaning-up of Barclays' balance sheet that is necessary in the new conjuncture. This is a perfect example of how the problems that we now confront should not just be seen as a problem of institutional malfeasance but rather bricolage by individuals working in the shadows of their institutions, who are building structures from events for private gain. To understand how this is possible we need, in the next section, to understand some of the characteristics of alternative investment activities, in particular how different ownership claims structure rewards.

3.3 The division of ownership (and conjunctural change)

It is important to understand the processes and character of bricolage because they helped create the fragile latticeworks which were – and still are – the

---

[2] According to data compiled by specialist hedge fund magazine *AR* (Absolute return and Alpha), which produces an annual rich list of hedge fund partners used by amongst others the *Sunday Times* in its annual rich list.

medium of crisis. But while the actions of bricoleurs may influence the shape of events which constitute each new conjuncture, they do not control them completely. For this reason, alternative investment strategies and business models change to engage with new profit opportunities which present under different conjunctural circumstances. This section illustrates the point by describing the highly leveraged pre-2007 business model of private equity and hedge funds. It then considers how all this was challenged by conjunctural change after 2007, since when private equity and hedge funds have struggled to adapt and deliver returns.

Before discussing strategies, we need to briefly describe the basic characteristics and business model of alternative investments. Both private equity and hedge funds are mainly structured as limited liability partnerships with two classes of partner: the managing financiers are general partners (GPs) who contribute around 2 per cent of the equity fund in private equity, but often much more in hedge funds, with the remaining funds provided by a range of outside investors, the limited partners (LPs). These outside investors are typically high net worth individuals, pension and endowment funds, or even hedge funds that invest in alternative investments. The GP of these funds is remunerated in two ways: an annual management fee of 1–2 per cent on funds invested and a performance fee of 20 per cent of profit, which is generally paid after achieving a hurdle rate of return.

The fund's purchasing power is enhanced through leverage to cover most of the cost of either buying companies in the case of private equity or taking positions on various assets in hedge funds. In private equity, the standard purchase formula was typically 70 per cent debt and 30 per cent equity (Ertürk et al. 2010), whereas hedge funds could be anything up to ten times levered when taking positions, although the average ratio throughout the boom was around 200–250 per cent, depending on which source we read. The '2 and 20' remuneration structure of private equity and hedge funds are widely reported, but the question of who sets (and benefits from) the ratios is seldom analysed. Similarly, the relevance of the partnership form is often ignored. Yet these arrangements define the business model, which is political in the sense that it ensures a division of returns by constructing a hierarchy of ownership rights and claims that guarantee a return to the GP. It also positions the GP as an indispensible intermediary between the LPs and their investments.

The '2 and 20' fee structures of both private equity and hedge funds set a very high threshold of returns to GPs during the 2000s boom and encouraged the pursuit of larger funds and riskier borrowing. The 2 per cent management fee incentivized GPs to increase their funds under management because a small percentage of a greater number means a bigger fee, regardless of performance. This is easier to demonstrate in the case of private equity than hedge funds, where information is notoriously difficult to access. In the case of private equity, Metrick and Yasuda's study (2007) found that US buyout fund GPs can make twice as much from flat 2 per cent management fees as they can form the 20 per cent performance-related carry (driven by the profit from the sale of the business). This is supported by our analysis of private equity management accounts (Folkman et al. 2007). As Table 3.3 shows, a 2 per cent fee on a large fund alone brings in £16–32 million per partner over five years, compared with £4–5 million per partner in the smaller fund. Similarly, if we look at the 20 per cent carry alone, a successful mid-market fund earns £5–£15 million per partner over five years, whereas the same 20 per cent on a large fund generates £25–£50 million per partner. The incentives to scale up are obvious: first, the flat 2 per cent fee delivers more according to size and regardless of success; second, the logic of 20 per cent of profits regardless of fund size is that, in an asset price-led boom, a GP's carry in a moderately profitable large fund can be more lucrative than both the management fee and the carry in a highly profitable smaller fund.

Leverage was also important in a routine way in boosting returns to private equity and hedge funds. This is most easily demonstrated again in the case of private equity, which typically bought portfolio companies with 30 per cent equity from its own funds and 70 per cent debt from outside sources. This had many effects as it both increased private equity purchasing power and pushed up the price of buyout targets to a peak of ten or even twelve times cash flow in 2006 and 2007 (Chassany and Alesci 2010). But, most important, with low interest rates after 2001, debt capped the returns to the majority of capital providers at a modest rate and thereby concentrated returns for those holding a smaller equity tranche. The simple act of leveraging up with cheap debt as a substitute for expensive equity is a very basic form of financial engineering which provides a counter to the industry's claims about rewards based on

Table 3.3. Fees earned over five years on successful mid-market and large private equity funds

	Mid-market fund	Large fund
Funds under management	£250–£500 million	£4–£8 billion
Management fees: 2% of committed capital over five years	£25–£50 million (£4–£5 million per partner)	£400–£800 million (£16–£32 million per partner)
Number of full general partners and their share of the carried interest ('Carry')	6–10 partners share 100% of the carry	20–30 partners share 75% of the carry
Carry over five years available to general partners	£40–£120 million	£625–£1,250 million
Based on carry as 20% of fund profits	(£5–£15 million per partner)	(£25–£50 million per partner)

Notes: Returns over five years on funds which are still operating; figures converted into ranges so that source cannot be identified; representativeness was confirmed by an experienced observer.

Source: Anonymized management accounts.

management ability, alpha creation, and solutions for agency problems. If the public company was displaced, the majority of investors in corporations would become bond holders excluded from the upside gains from dividends and share price appreciation which were previously spread widely through ordinary shares. With '2 and 20' structures this would have the effect of diverting a disproportionate stream of cash flows and profits from the sale of corporate assets to a very small number of private equity GPs who have positioned themselves at the apex of a hierarchy of ownership claims.

This can be demonstrated by a thought experiment on the FTSE 100 in the stock market golden years of the 1980s and 1990s (Figure 3.6). If we consider the FTSE index survivor companies who were in the index continuously between 1983 and 2002, their equity was worth £47 billion in 1983 but share prices appreciated so that, twenty years later by 2002, the shareholders had a capital gain of £391 billion on their equity holdings. During the same period, some £167 billion had been paid out in dividends so that the cumulative gain (without reinvestment of dividends) was £558 billion. If the £47 billion of equity had been converted into bonds which paid 3.75 per cent above LIBOR, there would have been no capital gain on the bonds and interest payments of just £108 billion for bondholders.

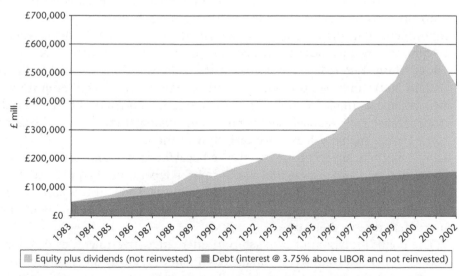

Figure 3.6. FTSE 100 survivors: cumulative gain on £46.98 bill invested in 1983 and cashing out in 2002

Notes: FTSE 100 survivors are a group of companies with continuous membership of the FTSE 100 since December 1983. The initial 1983 investment is the actual value of shareholder equity in those companies in 1983. All equity changes are based on market values. Interest and dividends not reinvested. Nominal values.

Source: Datastream.

From this point of view, the use of debt by private equity represents a kind of banal privatization of the old liberal collectivist social imagination. The private equity practice of substituting cheaper debt for equity is a reprise of Keynes' *General Theory* proposals (1936: 374–7) for the euthanasia of the rentier under which low-interest coupons (like bonds) would be substituted for shares. Of course, Keynes made his proposals with two broad social aims: to stabilize the macro economy and reduce unemployment created indirectly by fluctuating shareholder expectations; and to encourage more investment to defeat 'the dark forces of ignorance' and increase society's production possibilities (1936: 155–7). In comparison, private equity's use of cheap debt is for the private advantage of the minority of equity providers amongst whom some partners are more equal than others under '2 and 20' payment structures. In this sense the private equity GP, like Marglin's putter-out (1974) in the industrial revolution, constructs a hierarchical division of labour and of income claims which is not technically necessary but is personally advantageous. Moreover, through refinements like dividend recaps, the private equity GP can also recover costs and pass on risks in ways which were not available to earlier intermediaries.

The argument so far is about equity versus debt. If we consider an individual case example, we can show that the political division of ownership also works within the two classes of equity to secure disproportionate gains for the GP who, in a rising market, will always get a much higher return on initial investment than the LP. Table 3.4 presents the results for Yell, the classified telephone directory business which was acquired from British Telecom by Hicks, Muse, Tate & Furst, and Apax Partners in May 2001 for £2.14 billion (Bream 2001) and then floated at a handsome profit of £1.4 billion just over two years later (Budden 2004). This was a classic mid-2000s 'buy and hold' deal, because Yell's management team was not changed and most of the gains came from a higher valuation of cash flow at the sale date. In Table 3.4, we have hypothetically reconstructed the Yell deal for equity holders on standard industry terms, and assume that the GPs put in 2 per cent of equity and drew 20 per cent of profit when the public offering was made; in this simulation, the GPs would have earned 15.6 times their initial stake while the LPs did no more than double their stake.

The political division of ownership in alternative investment, as described above, works to advantage the financier GP under virtually all circumstances, insofar as some fees are drawn regardless of performance. But the political division of ownership works best under three key conjunctural conditions: strong inflow of investable funds from would-be LPs; liquid markets in corporate assets; and the ready availability of cheap credit. These conditions became problematic when Lehman Brothers collapsed and since then private equity and hedge funds have struggled to put together new tactics and strategies which

Table 3.4. General partner and limited partner returns on Yell investment 2001–3

		Limited partners (98% investment) (£million)	General partners (2% investment) (£million)
Outlay	Equity investment (2001)	592.7	12.1
Income	IPO share (2003)	1,269.5	200.4
Net extraction		676.8	188.3
Multiple gain on outlay		2.1	15.6

Notes: Yell acquired on 22 June 2001 and IPO on 3 July 2003 (25 months). Gains exclude post-IPO shares held by the partners and debt still invested in Yell. While Yell remained under private equity ownership, the company made pre-tax losses.
Source: Report and accounts and IPO document.

can plausibly *ex ante* and reliably *ex post* deliver the returns which are necessary to keep things going. Hedge funds, particularly those that specialized in fixed income arbitrage and other non-equity-based trading strategies, were left with illiquid securities in their prime broker's margin account which could not be financed when LIBOR rates rose and banks stopped lending to each other in mid-September 2008. Hedge funds with fewer liquid assets received margin/collateral calls which in turn led them to distress sales of portions of their portfolio into already depressed markets. The lack of credit also pushed hedge funds into forced deleveraging at a time when investor redemptions also rose.

Such growing problems were both compounded and poignantly underlined in December 2008 when a hedge fund run by Bernard Madoff was found to be operating a ponzi scheme which had lost its clients an estimated $64.8 billion. Investors *en masse* pulled their money out of hedge funds and piled into cash: investor funds under management with hedge funds fell by 9 per cent in Q4 of 2008 and a further 7 per cent in Q1 of 2009, with redemptions totalling $254.9 billion, whilst money market funds saw their investor funds increase 12 per cent over the same period (Citigroup 2010: 22). The combination of collateral calls, the evaporation of credit, and investor redemptions wiped out the positions of many hedge funds, causing significant bankruptcy in the sector and encouraging others to wind up their activity. By March 2009, hedge funds had lost nearly $600 billion – just under one-third of their assets under management – from their peak in June 2008, with just under half of that coming from investor redemptions and the remainder from performance write-downs. If their own marketing claims were to be believed, 2008–9 was a time when management skill, flexible investment strategies, and incentivized remuneration structures should have allowed hedge funds to differentiate themselves from broader market indices. Instead, their performance in a period of conjunctural change correlated strongly with beta (or average market) returns, suggesting the bold alternative investment promises about alpha creation and the possibility of 'absolute returns' under all market conditions were deeply exaggerated.

The crisis affected private equity differently because the drying up of liquidity immediately removed levered buyout possibilities, suspending a business model of hold-and-sell based on rising corporate asset prices. By mid-2010, the industry was struggling to raise new outside funds (Lex 2010*b*); although, after record inflows in 2006 and 2007, some firms remained flush with funds raised pre-crisis but not yet spent on buying portfolio companies. If attracting new investors has proved increasingly difficult, this is because returns on current portfolios have been poor, with multiple write-downs of portfolio values and some fund dissolutions in the absence of any solid investment prospects. For example, in 2009, Candover closed down its £2.7 billion mega fund (Arnold 2009), following the folding of Carlyle Capital Corp in 2008; meanwhile, other private equity houses wrote down the value of their investments – Blackstone, Permira, and Terra Firma wrote down 30, 36, and 45 per cent of the value of their total investments, respectively. In the midst of the crisis, estimates suggested that between 20 and 40 per cent of private equity partnerships would dissolve between 2009 and 2011, while 50 per cent of all companies backed by private-equity funds might default on their debt by 2011 (Meerkatt and Liechtenstein 2008). Others estimated that write-downs in the leveraged buyout sector may eventually be in the region of $1 trillion, prompting the conclusion that there could be a second wave of financial crisis, equal in magnitude to the preceding sub-prime crisis (Kosman 2009). Of course, not all such predictions have so far been realized but they are significant in that they underline both the scale and the interconnectedness of the alternative investment funds.

At this point we can broaden the discussion to consider the returns achieved by private equity and hedge funds and engage critically with the debate about the contribution of these new financial actors. The ability to generate higher returns is central to the narrative of alternative investments: the issue is of such importance that the BVCA has developed a rapid response capability so that it can produce an instant rebuttal of independent reports which examine the discouraging evidence on high fees, mediocre returns, and windfall gains (see BVCA 2010; Morris 2010). It would be unrealistic to expect all alternative investment funds to consistently outperform conventional funds; moreover, differences in trading strategies are likely to lead to significantly different performance within the sector. Hedge funds in the aggregate represent a bundle of all the possible trading strategies in financial markets which include trading on macro events, on stock market direction, on events such as merger or distress, and on arbitrage opportunities. Each strategy is likely to deliver variable returns given diverse tactics and changing conjunctural circumstances, but these different outcomes will not be easy to identify on an *ex ante* basis, nor will the previous winning strategy necessarily be appropriate in the next year or quarter.

Private equity is in some ways more straightforward because here there is an identifiable activity of trading in companies. But total returns from the activity depend on the addition of gains from three sources whose contributions will all vary cyclically in an unpredictable way: financial engineering gains from leverage, sale and lease back of assets, and such like; trading gains from buying low and selling high; and operating gains from increased revenue or better cost ratios. Success in one conjuncture does not imply success in another by any absolute measure or relative standard against stock market investment.

These general problems are nicely illustrated by the variable returns from hedge funds since 2000. As Figure 3.7 demonstrates, hedge funds did not manage to consistently beat the S&P 1200 stock index even in the good years from 2003 to 2006, when returns from equities or hedge funds or funds of funds were strikingly similar. If there is little outperformance in the good years, superior long run returns from hedge funds depend on avoiding underperformance in the bad years. On the evidence so far this is most easily done when there is a clear directional story upon which to trade. In 2001–2 this involved carry trade profits and shorting the dollar, while in 2008 it was

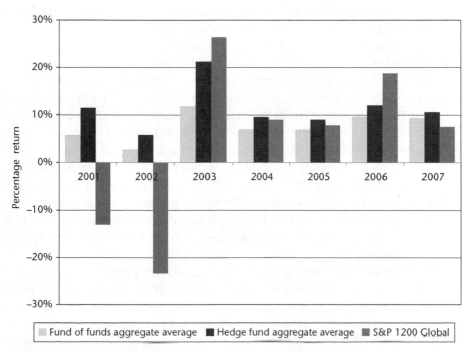

Figure 3.7. Comparison of aggregate returns for fund of funds, hedge funds, and the S&P 1200

Source: Dealogic.

shorting bank and financial sector stocks (until that practice was banned). But, on aggregate, hedge funds find it very difficult to make money out of perplexing uncertainty which leads to volatility. According to Hedge Fund Research, the average global macro fund, which specialized in trading on fluctuations in the global economy, lost 1.2 per cent in the first half of 2010 after small gains in 2009 (Chapman 2010). The macro funds had not anticipated sudden deterioration in the euro zone in May and June, followed by temporary stabilization in July, leading to British hedge fund manager, Hugh Hendry's, eloquent complaint that global macro funds were 'lost in a wilderness of mirrors' (Jones 2010).

Private equity faced a different problem which was not uncertainty but effective lock out from the markets on which they had depended before 2007 to sustain deal flow. Acquisitions were problematic because leverage was constrained by limited availability of credit and selling on was impossible until the stock market recovered. According to trade researcher Preqin, the additional problem was that global private equity needed to make acquisitions because it had a cash pile of some $1 trillion of committed but uncalled capital that was raised during the boom years of 2005–7. Some $400 billion of that capital had to be spent or returned to investors and, if these investors did not recycle returned capital into new private equity funds, the industry was going to lose a huge fee earning opportunity as well as a net outflow of funds.

The industry has tackled this problem in two ways: by doing deals on smaller companies with less aggressive leverage; and through secondary buyouts, whereby private equity firms sell portfolio companies to one another. According to Dealogic, in the United States and Europe in the first half of 2010, secondary buyouts had a record share of private equity deals, as their $15.8 billion worth of transactions represented 47 per cent of all European buyouts by value (Bollen 2010). This is valuable for the industry because it locks investors of uncalled capital into a five-to-seven-year cycle of paying fees to the private equity fund that makes the acquisition, while also helping the private equity fund that makes the portfolio sale to book a profit. Incidentally, any investor who had committed capital to both vending and acquiring funds would pay two sets of transaction fees for the same company.

Both private equity and hedge funds by 2010 had problems about finding sustainable and credible strategies. But they had at least beaten-off the threat of re-regulation. The British panic on private equity ended in a fudged compromise which raised taxes modestly on the general partner's carried interest which had been taxed as capital gain not income; and it led to the industry-friendly Walker Report which recommended improved transparency and disclosure by more reporting in the sector. The requirements of the ensuing 2007 code of conduct were not onerous, though by January 2009 only half of private equity firms had met the disclosure requirements 'without exception' (Robbins 2009). The EU initiative to regulate hedge funds and private equity firms was immediately more threatening because, unlike the British political classes, some members of the socialist group in the European Parliament did have stomach for a fight. But after national governments had intervened, the *Financial Times* could report that what remained of the EU proposals is 'essentially a box ticking exercise that requires funds to disclose more about their investment objectives and strategies . . . [but] will not fundamentally change the way the industry operates' (Editorial, *Financial Times* 2010) When details were agreed in October 2010, the *Financial Times* reported that the leading UK industry body, the Alternative Investment Management Association, gave a 'cautious thumbs up', commenting that the deal was much less far-reaching than the original proposals (Tait 2010). This outcome reflects the general difficulty of enacting significant financial reform, as discussed in the second part of this book.

In conclusion, private equity and hedge funds were not dead by 2010 but rather finding things to do while awaiting a more favourable conjuncture. They have, however, already changed the world in two respects. First, they have changed the world by mimesis, as it is increasingly difficult to tell one actor from another when banks and industrial companies can use weapons just like private equity and hedge funds. Second, they have increasingly moved valuation into Hendry's 'hall of mirrors' (Jones 2010). In this respect, Holmes (2009) makes a convincing argument that the alpha returns for hedge funds in the upturn (and their investment losses in the downturn) should not be understood as an act of the so-called discovery in the marketplace, with market and fundamental prices converging through a process of arbitrage. Rather, the prices achieved, and thus the returns generated by hedge funds and other actors, reflect the relative success of the war machine under changing conjunctural circumstances; thus it is difficult to assert the presence of a real 'fundamental' market value of the assets traded when prices are *created* through the investment and divestment act, and are not *discovered*.

This point is perhaps most striking as we write in autumn 2010 when alternative investment funds are struggling. The combination of fragility in financial markets, unpredictable corporate revenues and returns, fluctuating economic data on unemployment and house prices, and ballooning national government debt has led to bouts of general fear between periods of modest optimism about some kind of 'new normal'. The toxic result is both significant correlation and volatility across all assets which, for example, make it impossible for hedge funds to get a directional read on the markets or to find a steady earner like the yen dollar carry trade in the early 2000s. Of course, no one group of bricoleurs is responsible for the underlying change in conjuncture but the volatility that defeats artful strategies is partially the logical consequence of war machine-like activity over a prolonged period where the proliferation of cash extraction strategies has produced a market of multiple weaknesses where no one understands the value of things or their relative risks.

4

Banks Misunderstood

There's no reason to apologise for the actual profits (in British banks). A third of the money goes in tax, which means huge sums are going into schools and hospitals....Another third goes to shareholders – and I'm not talking about fat cats driving Ferraris; I mean pension funds looking after the interests of all of us. (Angela Knight, incoming chief executive of the British Bankers' Association, in an interview with the *Independent*, Prosser 2007)

Banks have an ethical obligation to strive for sustainable value creation and stability, similar to the obligations we have for the environment. This entails the need, both in credit provision to customers and in internal affairs, to assess everything in terms of sustainability. That [implies]...for instance, that never again would a CEO of a German bank present a short term profit rate of 25 per cent as a realizable corporate goal, thereby raising expectations to insiders and outsiders which can never be fulfilled...[This is] an instance of idolatry. It reminds me of the dance around the golden calf. Luther said: 'to that which your heart goes out, is your God'. In our society money has become our God. (Bishop Wolfgang Huber, *Berliner Zeitung*, 24 December 2008, our translation)

These two quotations come from different moral worlds. Angela Knight represents the smooth processes of elite circulation and expedient public defences of the indefensible. Knight was a talented junior Conservative Treasury minister whose rise was blocked by electoral defeat in 1997 and afterwards built her second career as lobbyist and spokesperson for finance in Britain. In early 2007, as incoming chief executive of the British Bankers' Association, she was defending bank profits on the grounds that they boosted tax revenues and returns for pensioners. This trope about the poor and otherwise indigent rentier dates back to the mid-nineteenth century when (before the democratization of finance and increased life expectancy) the shareholders of railway companies were always widows and orphans. Bishop Huber, in late 2008, represents the awkward principle of individual Protestant conscience. In the Bishop's moral universe, banking represents not greed but idolatry or the worship of false gods, which is of course the first prohibition in all Protestant or reformed versions of the Ten Commandments. Just as in the case of Queen Elizabeth, the Bishop as an outsider has perhaps a much sharper perception of the issues around finance and crisis than most insiders.

If Queen Elizabeth's question was, why did nobody see it coming?, Bishop Huber's question is how did banking CEOs, like Josef Ackerman of Deutsche Bank, set an unsustainable 25 per cent return on equity targets as 'a realizable corporate goal'? It is a great pity that, under current norms of elite circulation, a dissident like Bishop Huber will not be recruited into a non-executive board role where he could directly put his question to a bank CEO.

The aim of this chapter is to answer a more elaborate version of Bishop Huber's question. Specifically, we are concerned with two related questions about the pre-2007 period: why were high profit targets set in banking; and how could returns of 15–25 per cent on equity be (unsustainably) delivered before the crisis? The high returns before the crisis are immediately puzzling because investment banking had always been a small-scale activity focused around new issues of securities and merger advice, which could not sustain giant companies. At the same time, retail banking had traditionally been a low return utility activity which, after 1980s deregulation, was increasingly exposed to increased competition. Sections 4.2 and 4.3 of this chapter answer our questions and explain the apparent paradox. Section 4.2 analyses the pressures on all public companies from the early 1990s under a stock market regime of shareholder value where sectoral and company excuses for low returns were not acceptable to fund managers or analysts. Section 4.3 analyses how banking business models changed with the rise of mass marketing in retail and proprietary trading in investment banking, so that, when leverage was added, these volume-driven business models could (unsustainably) produce high returns for shareholders.

But this chapter also tackles a series of equally interesting questions about the irrelevance of academics and regulators, who either failed to register the transformational changes in banking business models, or did not understand that the profits of change were unstable and unsustainable. Thus, the first section of the chapter begins by analysing the academic conceptualization of the role of banks in contemporary economies. In doing so, it considers the mainstream economics that dominates research-based departments and institutes, with commitment to markets and rationality assumptions, elaborated through algebraic formalization and published in a small number of highly ranked journals. We then turn to consider the voluminous, institutionalist varieties of capitalism literature. This filiates from Michel Albert and from Peter Hall and David Soskice, and represents an important part of the post-disciplinary world created by the splintering of previously unitary disciplinary formations like political science and sociology. The fourth and final section of this chapter considers the post-Keynesians and Minskians who can, with some justification, claim to have foreseen a crisis, because they had more generally understood the instability of finance-led capitalism. While we should be grateful for such prescience, it is also important to register the limits of Minsky's kind of technical analysis, which does not engage the political domain that is the theme of the second half of this book. Put simply, getting it (partly) right before the crisis is not the same as having a solution after the crisis.

4.1 Academic understanding: banks as intermediaries?

This section introduces and discusses academic understanding of banks in the mainstream economics literature, where banks are credited with functions like intermediation and risk transfer. This is a good example of how an over-developed interest in identifying the reasons for what exists has distracted mainstream economists from the more interesting task of evaluating stories about what exists. We then show that much heterodox social science, like the varieties of capitalism literature, does little better because the heterodox buy into mainstream accounts so that intermediation between firms and households becomes taken for granted.

In mainstream economics and finance, banks have always posed a theoretical problem because, in informationally efficient markets, intermediaries like banks should not exist. The early literature on banking tried to explain this anomaly: from Gurley and Shaw (1955) onwards, the standard answer has been that banks exist as intermediaries because financial markets are informationally imperfect, with the consequent existence of transaction costs (Klein 1971; Benston and Smith 1976) and informational asymmetries (Leland and Pyle 1977). On this account, banks pool retail household deposits which are transformed into wholesale diversified claims on productive firms. Evaluation of credit risk, which individual households are not capable of performing themselves due to the existence of informational asymmetries, then becomes a very specific banking function in the economy that justifies the existence of banks. Banks achieve their profit objectives by intermediating between the economic units that have surplus funds (households) and those that require funds for investments (firms). This view of banks in mainstream economics continued for quite some time. As late as 1993, Bhattacharya and Thakor wrote that: 'to summarize, intermediation is a response to the inability of market-mediated mechanisms to efficiently resolve informational problems' (1993: 14).

From the early 1980s onwards, the changing framework conditions described in Chapter 2 have led an increasing number of mainstream economists to question the relevance of transaction costs and informational asymmetry and therefore of financial intermediation theory. This led to confused debate about whether disintermediation threatened credit-creating banks in a new historical period and how banks could still exist if their theoretical justification had more or less disappeared (Boyd and Gertler 1995; Miller 1998). In effect, as banks were not withering away, a new theory of banks was needed that would (like the old one) try to specify a new universal logic to explain the role of banks in the economy. In this context, Merton and Bodie (1995) shifted the debate to a functional approach to financial systems as opposed to an institutional approach, by emphasizing in their modelling what banks do rather than why they exist. Allen and Santomero (1997) then announced their new theory of financial intermediation as risk transfer within wholesale markets: instead of traditional theory, 'we offer in its place a view of intermediaries that centers on two different roles that these firms currently play. They are facilitators of risk transfer and deal with the increasingly complex maze of financial instruments and markets' (Allen and Santomero 1997: 1462).

The new emphasis on risk management displaced the old question in the financial intermediation literature about 'why banks exist?' but still retained the question 'would banks survive?' in a world of disintermediation and reintermediation. Disintermediation has since become an important research topic in mainstream economics: for example, Schmidt et al. (1999) and Allen and Santomero (2001) investigated whether bank-based economies of continental Europe would converge to market-based economies. Schmidt et al. (1999) concluded that in the United Kingdom, Germany, and France, disintermediation had not been significant enough to change the role of banks but noted a relatively increasing role of markets in France. However, Allen and Santomero (2001) announced the decline of traditional banking business due to competition in intermediation and the associated rise of fee-producing activities by banks in the United States and the United Kingdom which, as we shall see, is a very significant development:

> The world financial system has changed significantly in recent decades. In the US, banks and many other types of intermediaries have moved away from their traditional role of taking deposits and making loans. Although their share of intermediated funds has fallen they have not shrunk relative to GDP, and they remain an important part of the financial system. They have achieved this by moving away from simple balance sheet intermediation toward fee-producing activities. (Allen and Santomero 2001: 290)

The corporate form of banks also became an issue with a wave of banking mergers, in the 1990s, initially in the United States after deregulation, and then in the EU and Japan. *Inter alia*, these increased bank size and created large financial conglomerates which were actively encouraged by many national authorities. The EU Second Banking Directive of 1989 encouraged universal banking in the EU, as did the Treasury Report of 1991 and the Financial Services Modernization Act of 1999 in the United States. Meanwhile, in Japan, the Financial Services Agency's Financial Reform Programme had similar aims.

Explaining and analysing the existence of these new kinds of banking giants became another important research topic in mainstream literature before the crisis. Mainstream economics, of course, has struggled to find a rationale for corporate mergers when the empirics show that they do not generally create shareholder value for the acquiring firm. Mainstream finance has also struggled to find a rationale within the finance sector because studies of bank and financial services mergers report mixed results and do not consistently find scope or size economies. For example, econometric studies of the effects of bank mergers in different jurisdictions and different periods provide no convincing case for the existence of economies of scale and scope due to size and diversity (Rhoades 1993; Benston 1994; Milbourn et al. 1999; Vennet 2002; Casu and Girardone 2004; Campa and Hernando 2006; Stiroh and Rumble 2006).

So, after two decades of strenuous effort, mainstream economics updated its story on the rationale for banks by shifting towards risk transfer theories but, in doing so, it failed to explain why banks have become larger multi-activity conglomerates, because size increases without any obvious economic rationale. Thus, as the crisis was breaking, mainstream economists were agnostic about many developments, arguing that more research was required. In 2007, after the crisis had started, Feldman and Lueck of the Federal Reserve Bank of Minneapolis returned to issues raised by Boyd and Gertler (1995) at the annual conference of the Federal Reserve Bank of Chicago in 1994. Nearly fifteen years later, Feldman and Lueck still could not decide the question of whether banks as intermediaries were in decline:

> The new technology of banking continues to transform how banks operate. It also makes it possible for competitors, both new and old, to take on banks. . . . We simply do not have the data needed to adjust the balance sheets of all financial firms to properly determine their relative market share. (Feldman and Lueck 2007: 48)

This observation of mainstream indecision raises the question about whether heterodox approaches have done better in understanding developments in banking. There are many kinds of heterodox economics which derive their identity partly from being unlike mainstream economics. Below, we look at the varieties of capitalism literature which, in the decade after the mid-1990s, made strong inroads in the wider social sciences as a frame for looking at contemporary capitalism. This makes an interesting case because the varieties of capitalism preoccupation with cross-sectional national differences, understood in stereotyped bank versus market terms, blocked any recognition of the changes in banking which Allen and Santomero registered as risk transfer. The heterodox concept of banking was in many ways more conservative than the mainstream.

The master problem for the varieties of capitalism literature was not why do banks exist or survive but how does the financial system influence national economic performance. The varieties of capitalism literature is methodologically nationalist, and uses banking as an important variable in classifying economies according to the relative importance of banks and stock markets for productive firms. Finance is then analysed as a system embedded in an overall institutional structure of national complementarities. In Hall and Soskice's version (2001) of varieties of capitalism, the banks are 'patient' capital in a coordinated market economy (CME) and the stock market is footloose capital pursuing higher returns in a liberal market economy (LME).

> We would argue that British firms must sustain their profitability because the structure of financial markets in a liberal market economy links the firm's access to capital and ability to resist takeover to its current profitability; and they can sustain the loss of market share because fluid labor markets allow them to lay off workers readily. By contrast, German firms can sustain a decline in returns because the financial system of a coordinated market economy provides firms with access to capital independent of current profitability; and they attempt to retain market share because the labor institutions in such an economy militate in favor of long-term employment strategies and render layoffs difficult. (Hall and Soskice 2001: 16)

Thus, the logic of financial intermediation is held to be variable by nationality in cross section and, on this basis, the literature turns to taxonomic issues. The problems of classification are then about identifying the metrics and criteria which measure the relative importance of stock market and bank, and also about resolving contradictory evidence in ambiguous national cases so that these can be related to ideal-type constructs such as CMEs.

Thus, Hall and Soskice and others have introduced empirics on the ratio of stock market capitalization to GDP, household portfolios, bank loans as source of corporate finance, and the role of banks in the governance system. Using these metrics to score different cases resulted in endless debates on how various measures give divergent results, while many measures are contestable even in seemingly clear-cut cases such as Germany. For example, Hackethal and Schmidt (2003) and Schmidt and Tyrell (2003) emphasize the importance of gross lending by banks, which accounted for 80 per cent of non-financial firms' finance between 1970 and 1996, but earlier studies by Edwards and Fisher (1994), Corbett and Jenkinson (1996), and Mayer (1998) used net lending as the measure and on this basis concluded that banks in Germany were not major providers of finance. There is then the further complication that change is measurable on such empirical criteria, but the nature and implications of any such change are often ambiguous. By the mid-2000s, everyone appeared to agree that 'the large for-profit banks in Germany have been systematically exiting their close relationships with industrial companies' (Vitols 2005: 364).

However, researchers differ about what this change means: Vitols (2005: 12) anticipates an outcome which stops 'far short of convergence to the Anglo Saxon system', whereas Schmidt and Tyrell anticipate a long-run German 'transition to a capital market-based system' (2003: 50).

Finally, there is the problem of how to classify ambiguous and intermediate national cases. Thus, Schmidt and Tyrell credit Germany with a bank-based financial system and Britain with a capital market-based system before concluding that the French system 'has not been stable' (2003: 47). Amable (2003) provides the most sophisticated attempt to classify empirical cases. Using cluster analysis and multiple criteria, he finds that Germany belongs to a group of countries where an ideal bank-based system exists. This group includes Japan, France, Austria, Italy, Portugal, and Spain, and it is characterized by a high credit to GDP ratio, an important share of insurance companies among institutional investors, little M&A activity, weak development of accounting standards, and a lagging venture capital sector. But we would also note that, as the empirics become more complicated, Amable finds five distinct variant types of capitalism where Hall and Soskice hypothesized just two.

Despite (or because of) this increasing sophistication, the varieties of capitalism literature has lost itself in typological discussions and failed to register the changing activities of banks in both bank and capital market-based economies. Because they were exploring their theory built around the bank versus market opposition, these authors failed to register the adjustment of reality whereby Landesbanks in Germany could divert from their national productive role of supporting SMEs to an international financial role of the greater fool, as they became depositories for toxic assets created by the US banks. In our view, this development was partly driven by an attempt to compete with shareholder value-driven banks and their highly profitable volume-driven business models. These more general developments are considered in the next two sections. Section 4.2 explains how the rise of shareholder value as the metric of corporate performance played out in banking, where it was possible to generate high profits before the crisis. Section 4.3 then turns to analyse the new business models in retail and wholesale banking, which generated profits and remained undisclosed in the narratives about intermediation constructed in mainstream economics and varieties of capitalism literatures.

4.2 Shareholder value-driven banking

Shareholder value was the new corporate objective for quoted giant firms in the 1990s. The financial results of shareholder value by the 2000s were generally disappointing but not in the case of banks. This section examines the exceptional sector and explains how leverage was used to produce shareholder value in banks and other financial companies. It also observes that (unsustainable) profits sedated the critical faculties of non-executive directors, analysts, and fund managers who might otherwise have seen a crisis coming.

Froud et al. (2006) provides an overview of the impact of institutional investor demands for shareholder value on giant US and UK firms. The argument presented on outcomes has two elements: first, financial disappointment was inevitable because capital market pressures cannot shift product market limits in mature, competitive industries like car assembly where the delivery of value is almost impossible except through brief rallies which are cyclical and understood as such by everybody; and, second, the unintended consequence was a narrative turn as underperforming corporate CEOs rehearsed their excuses and claimed ever higher pay. Froud et al. (2006) did not focus on banks because of the difficulties of using the financial accounts of banks in making sense of their business models and hence the sectoral differences in value production were not highlighted.

While the bubble lasted, banking delivered a spectacular (albeit unsustainable) growth of profits in the 2000s which consolidated a long-run rise in the proportion of giant firm profits generated from finance in the United States, the United Kingdom, and other jurisdictions. Figure 4.1 presents data for the period since 1979 on the share of S&P 500 profits (income) generated by the finance, insurance, and real estate (FIRE) sector as a whole. The share of FIRE sector giant firms in total S&P 500 profits increased from 6.2 per cent in 1979 to 13.6 per cent in 1991 and then reached 39.1 per cent in 2002. Figure 4.2 shows the profits from deposit-taking (retail) banks over the decade from 1997 to 2007: retail banks (including commercial banks with investment banking activities) accounted for an average 11.3 per cent of total profit (income). At their peak in 2002 and 2003, retail banks accounted for more than 20 per cent of total S&P profits. Interestingly, the share of banks in S&P profits did not increase every year because oil and mining profits were high during the commodity boom that ran in parallel to the finance bubble.

As Figure 4.1 shows, FIRE's share in giant firm profits is substantially larger than the FIRE sector's share of US employment, which was more or less flat: in 2002, FIRE firms accounted for 39.1 per cent of S&P profit, and the FIRE sector employed 10.4 per cent of the workforce. This was hardly a miracle of efficiency because the profit was achieved by tying up a huge share of giant firm assets in finance. As Figure 4.1 suggests, the FIRE sector's share of giant firm assets was usually twice as high as its share of profits; moreover, its share of giant firm assets increased steadily in the 2000s from 58.3 per cent in 2000 to 69.4 per cent in 2007.

If the United States invented a new kind of unproductive (but hardly weightless) economy, so had the other high-income countries with the exception of Germany and Japan. The importance of finance plus commodities in

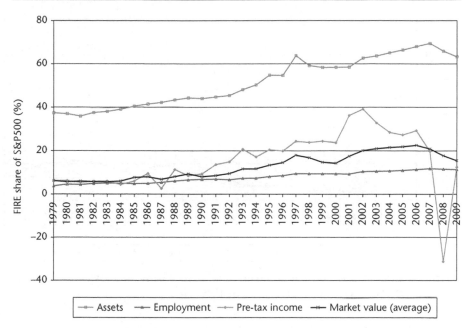

Figure 4.1. S&P 500-listed FIRE companies' share of assets, employment, profit (pre-tax income), and market value

Note: FIRE refers to finance, insurance, and real estate.

Source: Compustat.

generating giant firm profit in the bubble years emerges very clearly from Figure 4.3, which presents the trends in the FTSE 100 or the British giant firm sector. As Figure 4.3 shows, in the five years before 2007, the performance of the FTSE 100 was completely dominated by the commodities boom and the finance bubble. In those years, companies from oil and mining and from FIRE together accounted for more than 70 per cent of total FTSE 100 profits. The FIRE category is dominated by finance, which on average accounts for more than 30 per cent of all FTSE 100 profits over the bubble years when finance's share of UK employment was flat and its share of output was no more than 8 per cent. The miracle of the City of London and Wall Street was that such a small sector by traditional output and employment standards could generate such large profits, and in rigorous value terms this was more a trick than a miracle if two-thirds or more of giant firm assets were tied up in producing finance sector profits.

But stock market analysts were not very analytic about such issues. Instead, they praised profits at banks like Northern Rock (without inquiring how they were made) and endorsed moves like RBS' serial takeovers, including the overpriced acquisition of ABN Amro (without suspecting it would end in tears). Thus, according to ING in September 2006, 'Northern Rock has

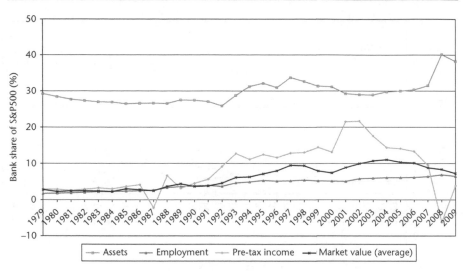

Figure 4.2. S&P 500-listed deposit taking, commercial bank, and saving institutions share of assets, employment, profit, and market value
Source: Compustat.

managed to transform itself into one of the UK's top residential secured lending powerhouses.... We expect asset and profit growth to continue to outpace the market, and Northern Rock is the envy of its peers...' (Sarangi 2006: 2). Analysts were apparently relaxed about RBS' valuation of ABN Amro in the bidding war with Barclays: analysts at Dresdner Kleinwort described the consortium approach by RBS, Santander of Spain, and Fortis of Belgium as 'close to perfect.... We believe they could offer up to €38 per share' (Treanor 2007). As Treanor (2007) also reports, Keefe Bruyette & Woods analysts estimated that the consortium could offer €39.5 per share, well above the €34 that had been suggested as the price being considered by Barclays. As long as shareholder value-driven banks were delivering profits, analysts sanctioned whatever they wanted to do.

Corporate governance was no more of a control via outside pressure from institutional investors or internal criticism by board directors. Proceduralized corporate governance, as invented by the Cadbury Report in the United Kingdom, has been greatly strengthened after successive crises (Ertürk et al. 2008). But this kind of corporate governance is more of an accelerator of initiatives in the absence of profit than a brake on irresponsibility when profit is being made. In general, a dearth of profits strengthens the scepticism of non-executive directors (NEDs) and the activism of outside shareholders, while an abundance of profits sedates the critical faculties of outsiders and becomes a matter of boardroom celebration as managers ride high on the tide of rising stock markets (Ertürk et al. 2008). Hence, there are few records of

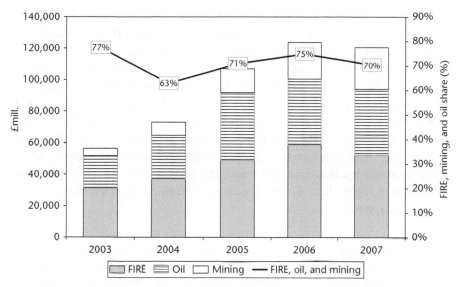

Figure 4.3. FIRE, oil, and mining share of FTSE 100 pre-tax profit (nominal values)
Source: Datastream and report and accounts.

institutional shareholders in banks who asked awkward questions before 2007 about management rewards, risk management, and sustainability of growth in profits. Under the proceduralized corporate governance regime, these issues were directly the responsibility of NEDs. But, just as in the earlier case of Enron, the NEDs on the boards of US investment banks like Lehman or converted former UK building societies like Northern Rock did not question business models which appeared to be working. For example, the Lehman examiner Valukas' findings were:

> Lehman's Board fully embraced Lehman's growth strategy. In a January 2007 Board meeting, the directors were informed of the large increase in the risk appetite limit for fiscal 2007, and of the firm's intention to expand its footprint in principal investments, and they agreed with Lehman's senior officers that Lehman needed to take more risk in order to compete. All of the directors told the Examiner that they agreed with Lehman's growth strategy at the time it was undertaken. (Valukas 2010: 76)

The simplest question was how so many banks of all kinds (in retail and wholesale across many jurisdictions) were able to turn in returns on equity of 15 per cent or more and thus become the sweethearts of the stock market. The short answer is through leverage or borrowing to expand capital employed in a favourable conjuncture: that is, the banks borrowed cheaply to expand their asset base from which they could make profits for shareholders whose equity base was much smaller. Hence, the banking sector's insatiable appetite for assets which we observed in the case of the US S&P 500. The arithmetic of leverage was such that a bank that had a meagre and declining return on assets (ROA) (or capital employed) could earn a handsome return on equity (ROE). Figures 4.4a and 4.4b present the relevant data for a group of British banks: these graphs show that the pattern was one of sustained, high ROE, combined with wafer-thin ROA ratios which declined in three of the four cases after 1998 and in all four cases after 2006. As Haldane (2009b) has noted, this in turn implies that banks' impressive performances for shareholders before the crisis were not the result of strong economies of scale or scope or high value-added innovation; instead, the driver was financial engineering in the form of higher leverage, new sources of funding, and an increasing velocity of transactions.

> During the golden era, competition simultaneously drove down returns on assets and drove up target returns on equity. Caught in this cross-fire, higher leverage became banks' only means of keeping up with the Jones's. Management resorted to the roulette wheel... leverage increased across the financial system as a whole. Having bet the bank on black, many financial firms ended up in the red. (Haldane 2009b: 3)

A broader, sectoral view of banking in the United States, United Kingdom, and Mainland Europe after the mid-1990s directly shows the importance of leverage in all three areas and indirectly suggests that laggard national sectors and

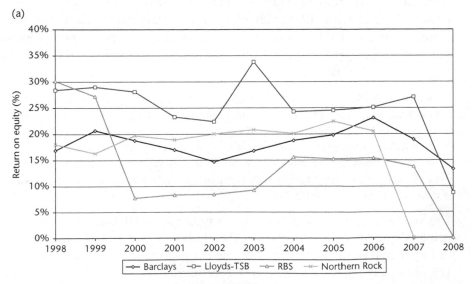

(a)

Figure 4.4a. Return on equity for selected UK banks

Note: Negative return set to zero.

Source: Thomson One Banker.

(b)

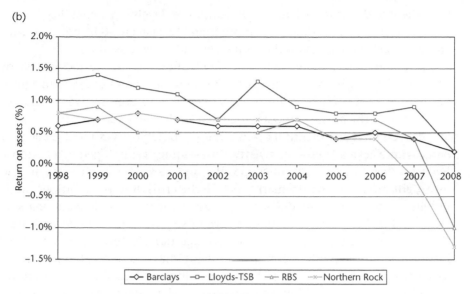

Figure 4.4b. Return on assets for selected UK banks
Source: Thomson One Banker.

firms were under pressure to deliver at least 15 per cent ROE. Such stock market competition amongst the shareholder value-oriented banks in effect set performance targets for mutuals like building societies in the United Kingdom and Landesbanks in Germany. Haldane (2009*b*) analysed seventy global banks in 2007 and confirmed such ROE-driven behaviour amongst global banks:

> First, the downward slope is consistent with global banks targeting a ROE, perhaps benchmarked by peers' performance. The Bank [of England]'s market intelligence in the run-up to crisis suggested that such 'keeping up with the Jones's' was an important cultural influence on banks' decision-making. Second, . . . banks kept up in this competitive race by gearing-up. Banks unable to deliver sufficiently high returns on assets to meet their ROE targets resorted instead to leveraging their balance sheets. (Haldane 2009*b*: 3)

Figures 4.5a and 4.5b present data on the profitability of large banks with assets of more than $50 billion in the United Kingdom and more than $100 billion in the United States and the Eurozone in 2010. The contrast between slim returns on assets and handsome returns on equity is very clear: the United States, the United Kingdom, and Eurozone banks all had ROA of less than 1.5 per cent but all three had converged on 15 per cent plus ROE by the mid-2000s. These graphs are also suggestive of pressure to conform to the norms of shareholder value. ROE is consistently higher in the United States, where the banking sector's rate of return never falls below 15 per cent, while UK banks have a different pattern of cyclicality but are never far behind. On the other hand, Eurozone banks start from lower levels of profitability, which in the mid-1990s is running at no more than 7–8 per cent ROE, but then rises and after 2003 converges on the 15 per cent achieved elsewhere.

The differences between ROA and ROE underline the attractiveness of leverage, allowing banks to enhance performance for shareholders with equity holdings (and for senior investment bankers whose bonuses were turnover related under the business model discussed in the next section). In an era of low interest rates and plentiful capital, every profitable investment made by a bank with a leverage ratio of twenty times equity capital, generates simply twenty times as much revenues, profits, and fees, as was the case in the overnight interbank money market before the crisis. But, the multiplicand is not guaranteed and it can all go wrong if asset prices start falling and markets close, and if the central bank does not then step in to provide cheap funds. Without such central bank support, leverage quickly turns into a crisis of insolvency and illiquidity because asset values have to be written down and losses recognized, as assets cannot easily be sold and cheap short-term funding is no longer available. Whatever happens in high street retail banking, the inevitable result in the wholesale markets is distressed parties, extreme risk

(a)

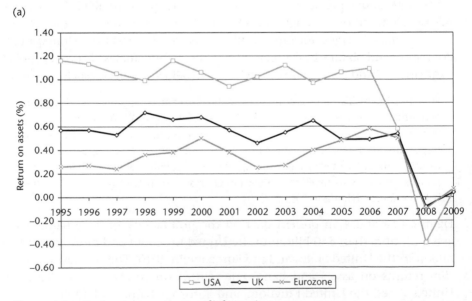

Figure 4.5a. Bank return on assets split by region

Note: Selection criteria is US large banks with assets larger than $100 billion in 2009; UK banks and building societies with assets larger than $50 billion in 2010; Eurozone commercial banks, savings banks, cooperative banks, real estate and mortgage banks, investment banks with assets larger than $100 billion in 2009.

Source: Bankscope.

(b)

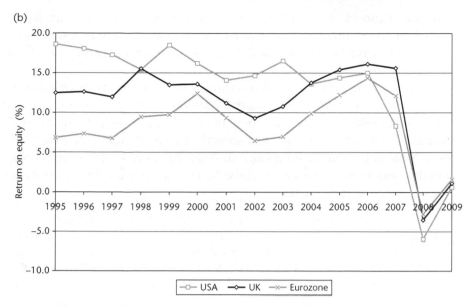

Figure 4.5b. Bank return on equity split by region

Note: Selection criteria is US large banks with assets larger than $100 billion in 2009; UK banks and building societies with assets larger than $50 billion in 2010; Eurozone commercial banks, savings banks, cooperative banks, real estate and mortgage banks, investment banks with assets larger than $100 billion in 2009.

Source: Bankscope.

aversion by sound counterparties, and a run on any vulnerable players within the leverage-dependent 'shadow banking system' (Gorton and Metrick 2010).

Before 2007, such dysfunction was all in the future and the main symptom of the mid-2000s was a spectacular ballooning of bank balance sheets as the asset-hungry banks defended or increased their profits for shareholders. As Figure 4.6 shows, bank balance sheets ballooned in all major jurisdictions, including those like France which did not include a major financial centre like London or New York. All this should have been a public cause for concern because the assets of the banking system were public liabilities if things went wrong. National governments had one way or another guaranteed retail deposits in most jurisdictions and, in any case, national governments would not easily allow large or interconnected banks to fail. A highly leveraged bank system could and did then have a frightening size in terms of total assets, which could be many times that of national GDP as illustrated in Figure 4.7: in the Dutch and the UK cases, the banking system was by this measure five times as large as GDP by 2008. And, as Turner has noted, this ballooning of bank assets in relation to GDP '... was dominated not by the banks' relationship with UK households and companies, but by a complex mesh of intra-financial system claims and obligations', fuelled by wholesale funds not by

111

customer deposits (Turner 2010*b*: 17). Leverage was, therefore, the driving force behind the privatization of gains and the socialization of losses, multiplying profits and bonuses in good times and multiplying losses and bailouts in bad times.

Of course, hindsight is a wonderful thing and as soon as this crisis got under way, irresponsible individuals and risky corporate behaviour were identified and scapegoated. Northern Rock had relied on volatile short-term wholesale markets to finance the phenomenal growth of its mortgage book, rather than on reliable long-term retail deposits: in 2006, 76 per cent of Northern Rock's funding was from wholesale markets. In announcing its 2006 preliminary results, the bank stated that:

> Northern Rock has four distinct funding arms enabling it to attract funds from a wide range of customers and counterparties on a global basis. In recognition of our broad and innovative access to a cost effective and diverse capital markets investor base, Northern Rock was awarded the prestigious International Financing Review's 2006 Financial Institution Group Borrower of the Year award. (Northern Rock Plc 2006: 9)

In another case, that of RBS, it was clear *ex post* that Fred Goodwin's strategic mistake was to overpay for ABN Amro, which was not a profit source but a burdensome set of liabilities given that ABN Amro had invested in toxic assets and contributed £20 billion to the £28 billion loss at RBS in 2008 – the biggest

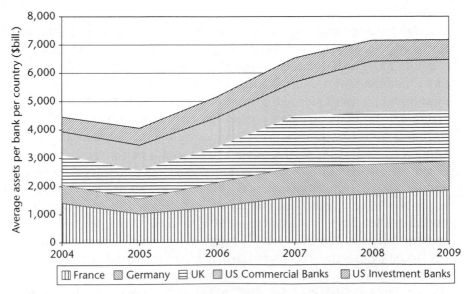

Figure 4.6. Average assets per bank split by domicile (US$ billion)

Note: The average asset per bank is the average of six banks in France, Germany, UK, and US commercial banks, and five banks for US investment banks.

Source: Bankscope.

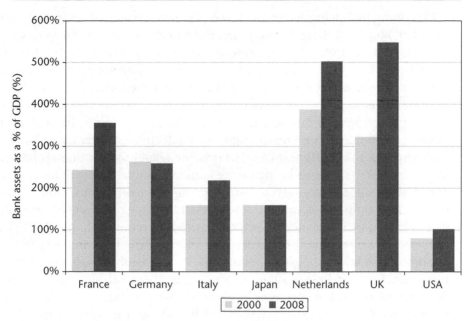

Figure 4.7. Total bank assets as a percentage of GDP
Sources: IMF World Economic Outlook Database, OECD Banking Statistics, and Bank of England.

ever loss in British corporate history. British Prime Minister Gordon Brown was 'angry' at the 'irresponsible' actions of Fred Goodwin, who was knighted on Brown's advice in 2004 for services to banking (Bawden and Waller 2009). The representatives of proceduralized governance were more penitent and confessional, as they had been after previous crises. The International Corporate Governance Network (ICGN) represents institutional shareholders (private and public pension funds) responsible for managing global assets worth $15 trillion, accepted that poor governance was to blame:

> It is true that shareholders sometimes encouraged companies, including investment banks, to ramp up short-term returns through leverage.... Corporate governance failings were not the only cause but they were significant, above all because boards failed to understand and manage risk and tolerated perverse incentives. (ICGN 2008: 1)

It is not surprising that bankers' bonuses quickly became an issue because they were an intelligible symbol of excess for a mass audience that did not understand leverage and such like. The G-20 demanded the implementation of new standards on bonuses acting on Financial Services Board's (an international coordinating body of central banks and financial authorities) advice. The Institute of International Finance, a global association of financial institutions, nodded in agreement (IIF 2009).

Everything had changed and much was now being criticized and called into question. But, in all these debates, shareholder value-driven business models of banks were not questioned. Quite the opposite: governments that have been forced into bank nationalization, plan exit strategies of trade sale or flotation which will realize gains for the taxpayer because the banks have been turned around and are, once again, generating shareholder value. Generally, and for publicly quoted banks within the private sector, the aim is to ensure shareholder discipline through more effective governance of banks, which relates risk and reward but retains the shareholder value objective, while new entry strategies of increasing banking competition will inevitably attract shareholder value-driven firms, like supermarket chains, from other sectors. The continued dominance of shareholder value principles is above all demonstrated by the mandate for UK Financial Investments Limited (UKFI), the state holding company for nationalized banks. After the enforced nationalization of UK banks, the government could not think of what to do except to run them for shareholder value before selling them off, and nationalization was reinvented as a private equity style turn around (as discussed in Chapter 6). The chief executive of RBS will earn an incentive payment of £6.9 million if he doubles the share price (Jenkins 2009): that is acceptable to UKFI because the 'overarching objective [is] protecting and creating value for the taxpayer as shareholder' (UKFI 2009a: 74). However, it is not clear whether the banks have been nationalized or the Treasury has been privatized as a new kind of investment fund.

Moreover, media reports of negotiations so far on the modification of the banking accord, Basel III, indicate that shareholder value considerations, and the protection of profits on equity, has been a major objective of regulators. Reports suggest regulators are concerned not to undo the gains of leverage by raising capital reserve requirements so that profitability is spoilt. The capital reserve requirements that were published in August 2010 were much less stringent than the initial proposals that dated from December 2009. The size and definition of tier one capital in Basel III has been recalibrated in such a way that, according to Nomura, European banks will only need €200 billion in extra capital, a third less than under the December proposals, and US banks only $115 billion, half of what was in the December proposals. The commentariat has criticized this as caving in to industry lobbying, but insiders claim a higher rationale because 'regulators worldwide became alarmed that the combined effect of the (original Basel III) December proposals would hobble banks' ability to lend and shrink their profitability to potentially unsustainable levels' (Masters and Murphy 2010: 5). This claim is interesting, both because regulators accept the banks' threat to withdraw lending without inquiring into what they are now lending on and because regulators do not question the appropriateness of shareholder value in banking, although this was model was responsible for the 2007 crisis. The next section focuses on changes in the business models of retail and investment banks to explore how a shareholder value orientation encouraged the activities that undermined the banking sector.

4.3 Business model changes

If the crisis was about what happens when leverage is added to banks under pressure for shareholder value, the crisis is also tied up with changes in bank business models, or the ways in which they recover costs and generated profits. The crisis confusingly brought down banks with many different kinds of business models, including Wall Street investment banks like Bear Stearns and Lehman Brothers (which were leveraged wholesale traders), aggressive new-style UK retailers (like Northern Rock and Bradford and Bingley) which funded risky mortgage lending by wholesale borrowing, and the old-style reckless (like some Irish banks or HBOS) which lent unwisely on commercial property. The aim of this section is to set all this detail into perspective by presenting an overview of changes in wholesale and retail bank business models. In many advanced capitalist countries, the deregulation of finance was associated with a shift from old business models of intermediation to new business models of retail mass marketing and wholesale trading which made banks into transaction-generating machines.

Insofar as banks are intermediaries, their major source of income will be interest earned on the spread between interest paid to depositors and interest charged to borrowers, and a shift from intermediation can be crudely measured by a decline in interest income (or a rise in non-interest income) as a proportion of bank profits. Table 4.1 presents the relevant empirics for banks in six countries between 1984 and 2007. While banking systems still betray historically rooted institutional differences, in each of these countries, interest income as a source of overall banking revenue have declined vis-a-vis non-interest income. This last category combines retail fees and commissions earned by selling financial products like mortgages or pension plans, and from wholesale earnings either from various kinds of trading or from charges for services rendered at the nodes of the wholesale latticework.

As Table 4.1 illustrates, the simple average for six countries rises from 25.5 to 47.3 per cent in twenty-three years, with non-interest income significantly above this level in France as well as in the United Kingdom. The outlier is Germany where non-interest income hovers between 20 and 30 per cent, due to the federalist structure of the banking system in those two countries (Verdier 2000). Non-interest income after 2003 primarily came from trading income in wholesale markets, even in countries like France. The staggering ratio of 75.2 per cent in France in 2007 in Table 4.1 probably tells us what the

Table 4.1. Non-interest income as percentage of net interest income plus net non-interest income

	1984 (%)	1990 (%)	1995 (%)	2000 (%)	2003 (%)	2005 (%)	2007 (%)
France	n.a.	22.6	45.5	60.9	56.7	62.2	75.2
Germany	18.0	26.8	21.0	35.8	27.1	29.7	24.9
Italy	24.6	22.0	19.8	36.1	30.2	32.1	36.1
The Netherlands	24.7	28.4	33.3	47.0	39.2	45.9	54.2
The United Kingdom	35.6	38.7	42.7	43.2	46.4	54.1	53.9
The United States	24.7	33.0	35.3	42.8	44.6	40.7	39.3
Simple average	25.5	28.6	32.9	44.3	40.7	44.1	47.3

Source: OECD Bank Profitability Statistics and Bankscope.

likes of Jeróme Kerviel of Société Générale were engaged in before it blew up in 2008. However, the US banks had already started to suffer the impact of the dot-com crash on fee income after 2001, and the trading losses in CDO markets in 2007. The decline in interest income is driven by several distinct developments. These include the secular decline in nominal interest rates in the 1990s after the 'conquest of inflation', which had the unintended consequence of reducing spread between deposit and lending. Figure 4.8 shows that the pressure continued through the bubble because in the United States, the United Kingdom, and in the Eurozone, net interest margin declined in the decade before 2007 from 3.0 to 2.0 per cent in the US case and from 1.5 to 1.0 per cent in the two other cases.

But this is only part of the story because, if traditional intermediation was inexorably less attractive, it encouraged retail and wholesale banks (and the new conglomerates combining both retail and wholesale) to get further into retail mass marketing and wholesale trading, which are of course connected through the markets because products like mortgages provide the feedstock for the wholesale markets. We first discuss the transformation in retail business models and then move to wholesale. In each case, we will emphasize the connection with leverage, complexity, and velocity which in wholesale is tied in to the 'comp ratio' business model which incentivizes senior bankers. Most critical analyses of the banking after the crisis focus on the hyperbolic growth of bank assets in relation to the productive sectors of the economy and the role complex securitization played in making such bloated banks unstable. Turner (2010*b*), for example, insightfully analyses these secular trends in banking. But these studies tend to overlook the bank business models that drove these quantities and qualitative changes. Bank business models that are both shaped and justified by the shareholder value principle,

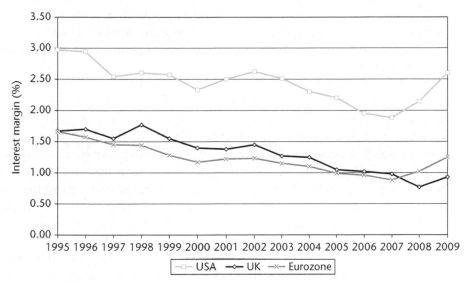

Figure 4.8. Bank net interest margin split by region

Note: Selection criteria is US large banks with assets larger than $100 billion in 2009; UK banks and building societies with assets larger than $50 billion in 2010; Eurozone commercial banks, savings banks, cooperative banks, real estate and mortgage banks, investment banks with assets larger than $100 billion in 2009.

Source: Bankscope.

but ultimately favoured the banking elites at the expense of shareholders, require a closer intellectual scrutiny.

The customer-facing changes in the retail business model are less radical than those envisaged in the new economy literature of the 1990s (see e.g. Evans and Wurster 1997; Llewellyn 1999), where retail bank branches and bookstores figured as examples of obsolescence because their activity would surely move onto the Web in ways that put incumbents with bricks and mortar investments at a serious disadvantage. Instead, incumbents in retail have moved the routine transaction, standing order, and account statement part of retail onto the Web but retained their branches because customers want them, and market share of mainstream retail business therefore requires a branch network. Consider the evidence from the United Kingdom: 80 per cent of consumers say that their preferred channel of arrangement for current accounts is a branch, and company shares of the current account market are closely correlated with the extent of a particular provider's branch network (Datamonitor 2008). Branches are also the material support of customer inertia which is such a striking feature of retail banking. Only 7 per cent of British current account customers switch in any twelve-month period and 65 per cent of consumers have held their current accounts for more than ten years (Ipsos MORI 2008). Before or after the crisis, retail consumers mistrust banking in

117

general but have more trust in their primary bank. In a 2009 survey, the average consumer rating of trust in the banking sector was 2.1 out of 5 but the average trust rating in their (current account) primary bank was 3.4 out of 5 (Datamonitor 2009).

But this put retail banks under pressure. If market share requires retail branches which incur high rents and staff costs, how could banks recover these costs (especially when spreads on intermediation were declining)? One expedient was cross-subsidy from other retail activities like credit cards, with higher margins than account-based business where margins were also boosted by fee charges for overdrawn account holders and such like. But the major development was to use the bank branches for retail mass marketing of products like insurance policies, mortgages, and pension plans on which the retailer earned an upfront fee which was typically calculated either as a percentage of the value of the product or as a fixed amount. For example, most mortgages require typically a 2 per cent fee to cover arrangement and booking. This major shift is reflected in the visible changes of layout in retail bank branches. Intermediary retail banking operated out of branches that were dominated by the long counter across which money was paid in and out by bank clerks, while the manager in a side office made decisions about lending to households and businesses. By the 2000s, bank branches are dominated by cubicles and workstations where advisers sell financial service products like mortgages and pension plans, and decisions about personal loans are made over the phone in minutes by junior call-centre staff using FICO scores[1] and other assessment techniques.

There were other equally important but much less visible changes because the new retail business models were increasingly volume-based and connected via mortgage securitization with the wholesale markets. In an old-style intermediation operation, the volume of lending depends on the availability of deposits, where limits are set by the balance sheet of the firm. The relation applies in the case of a national retail chain but is most obvious and constraining in the case of a community bank which operates a closed circuit between local savers and borrowers. Thus, James Stewart in Frank Capra's 1946 *It's a Wonderful Life* stopped a bank run by warning panicking savers about the effects their withdrawals would have on local borrowers. But, after deregulation and securitization, banks can obtain funds to lend and/or ramp up fee-earning transactions by reaching beyond their balance sheets. Banks can, for example, obtain new funds to lend by borrowing short-term on the overnight money market. Similarly banks do not have to hold loans on their balance sheet because they can be securitized and sold on, so that the bank can lend and

---

[1] FICO scores are risk scores produced from models developed by Fair Isaac Corporation. Various proprietary versions are used by different credit risk assessors.

lend again. The new volume-based business model is the end result because, as in any retail operation, banks will try to cover high fixed costs by ramping volume.

The results are transformational. While some banks remained retail only (in that they do not have trading divisions), most banks were increasingly connected to the wholesale markets, especially through the securitization machine described in Chapter 2. Figure 4.9 presents data on the size of the deposit base of UK commercial banks relative to total assets in 2007. Leading up to 2007, the sharp decline of the importance of saving accounts as a source of funding for banks is a direct reflection of the increasing amount of short-term borrowing on money markets as well as the securitization of assets to provide alternative sources of funding. This was inevitably a source of new risks in retail banking, which has always had to manage a mismatch between short-term liabilities and long-term assets. Turner (2010b) underlines the systemic risk that arises out of this, what is usually termed, a customer funding gap: 'this funding gap and reliance on wholesale funding created significant vulnerabilities for the UK banking system which crystallised in 2007 and 2008' (Turner 2010b: 17). The wholesale markets themselves then become the equivalent of James Stewart's panicky savers because retail banks are increasingly vulnerable to mood swings on the overnight money market and other debt markets, and to crisis-led closure of securitization processes which depend on willing counterparties and liquidity (Gorton and Metrick 2010).

The consequences of this retail revolution for the consumer are also very mixed. The volume requirement encourages aggressive selling of investment, insurance, pension, and mortgage products in the retail branches, while high fixed costs mean the stripping out of back-office functions and customer support which has no direct revenue stream. All this is covered by a large marketing spend on advertisements which feature friendly, helpful retail staff. Thus, in the United Kingdom, RBS has been promoting its NatWest brand under the slogan 'helpful finance'. A series of TV commercials by Yipp Films uses real staff and customers to illustrate how NatWest has 'money sense advisers' in more than one thousand branches. The voice-over sententiously claims 'they are not there to sell but to give you free impartial advice'. When the consumer body *Which* sent researchers to NatWest branches, it found that only four out of twenty sessions offered impartial advice while sixteen of twenty sessions ended in attempts to interest the consumer in NatWest products, which were the only products mentioned in six sessions (Bachelor 2009). The branch network is then the place where the implied promise of good advice is betrayed as an adviser on incentive pay 'sells to' the retail household.

The developments in the business model of wholesale finance have been rather different. Investment banks have always lived off fee income and the revolution here was about the changing sources of income with the relative

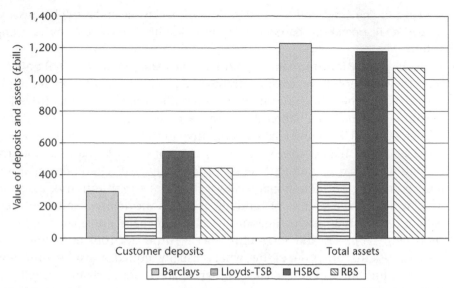

Figure 4.9. Customer deposits compared against total assets in four UK banks, 2007
Note: HSBC data is converted from US$ to £.
Source: Report and accounts.

decline of fee income earned from advice and issues, as 'proprietary trading' became the main source of profit for investment banks. In the late 1980s, investment banking earned fees by providing corporate advice to productive firms, especially on M&A, and by issuing bonds and shares for corporate customers. From the early 1990s, investment banks increasingly moved towards becoming principals in the financial markets and shifted into own-account trading by setting up trading desks for derivatives and such like – just as, more recently, investment banks have set up hedge funds and private equity funds in their own right (as well as advising others on such deals). The connection with volume and leverage is of course very strong because, as we have noted in Chapters 2 and 3, leverage increases the returns on profitable trades and deals by allowing traders to take larger positions.

The shift to proprietary trading should be straightforwardly measurable but it is difficult to track empirically, even for stand-alone investment banks that are public companies and obliged to report results by segment. The measurement problems are caused by limited accounting disclosure in the first half of the 1990s and the continuing absence of a standard set of segment categories for identifying and classifying investment bank activities. In 2005, when Goldman Sachs reported earnings 50 per cent higher than the analysts' forecast because of better than expected results in proprietary trading, Lex of the *Financial Times* commented that Goldman Sachs was a 'black box . . . albeit one that continues to deliver pleasant surprises' (Lex 2006). However, Bank of England economist Andrew Haldane, who has become famous for his unorthodox analysis of the crisis and banking as discussed in Chapter 1, is critical of this kind of commentary:

> Many practitioners and policymakers were seduced by the excess returns to finance during that twenty-year golden era. Banks appeared to have discovered a money machine, albeit one whose workings were sometimes impossible to understand. One of the South Sea stocks was memorably 'a company for carrying out an undertaking of great advantage, but nobody to know what it is'. Banking became the 21st century equivalent. (Haldane 2009b: 2)

Figures 4.10a and 4.10b look inside the black box by presenting data on Goldman Sachs, a leading investment bank that has no retail activities. Goldman Sachs distinguishes between three categories: first, investment banking advice and services; second, proprietary trading and principal investments; and, third, investment management for clients. Already in 2003, revenues from proprietary trading were larger than those from traditional investment banking and their importance has since increased (albeit unsteadily because investment banking advice was and is a cyclical business). By 2007, proprietary trading accounted for almost two-thirds of Goldman Sachs' revenues and assets, and the bank was, in its own right, the largest hedge fund manager in the world. For European investment banks, Goldman Sachs and its American peers were the new pattern and exemplar. A McKinsey report in 2006 discussed how European investment and corporate banks played a lead role in developing credit and equity derivative markets, and makes the point that the late 1990s and early 2000s were a time of significant product innovation by these institutions as they sought to develop competitive positions against the US banks by emulating their prop trading successes (Roxburgh 2006).

The question of what has happened to proprietary trading since the crisis is illuminating. And the short answer is that it has become very much less visible because of the threat of re-regulation, but it has not gone away because it remains lucrative. Its continuing importance is indicated by the effort invested in new ways of finding funds for levered trades. There can be no doubt that, after the crisis, proprietary trading has to negotiate a new climate of disapproval which is encouraging all kinds of relabelling and circumvention. The British regulatory response has been more emollient as the regulator, the Financial Services Authority (FSA), accepts the banks' claim that proprietary trading played only a marginal role in the crisis (Hughes 2010), but the Obama administration has pressed ahead with curbs on proprietary trading by banks, and the legislature has passed the so-called Volcker rule that forces banks to unwind own account trading. The US banks have responded by reclassifying their activities and drawing a distinction between 'flow trading' that should not be counted as proprietary trading and 'pure prop trading'; the latter turns out to be of only marginal importance to the revenue and profit of banks, ranging from 10 per cent in the case of Goldman Sachs to 1–2 per cent in the case of European banks such as Barclays, UBS, and Credit Suisse. If this does not satisfy the Securities and Exchange Commission (SEC), the banks can no doubt in the next stage construct arms-length (but profitable) arrangements whereby their star traders set up independent prop trading firms and, following the analysis in Chapter 3, the nomadic war machine can take a different form, with a new group of irregulars armed and provisioned by the banks.

The maintenance of volume is critical because of the 'compensation (comp) ratio' practice embedded in the business model of wholesale banking in Wall Street, London, and other major centres. In investment banks like Goldman Sachs, or in the wholesale divisions of conglomerates banks like Barclays, the understanding is that the senior investment bankers will (through base pay and bonus) receive a definite percentage of net revenues, usually somewhere between 40 and 50 per cent. While there has been criticism of how bankers are paid in bonuses since the crisis, nobody has questioned the basic comp ratio principle that senior bankers should receive a semi-fixed proportion of the turnover. This makes the investment bank a kind of profit share arrangement

(a)

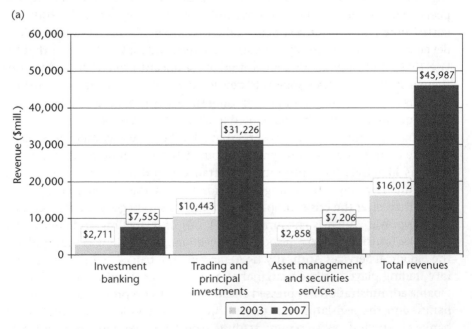

Figure 4.10a. Goldman Sachs revenues in 2003 and 2007
Source: Report and accounts.

(b)

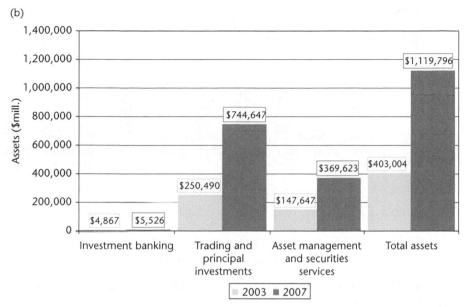

Figure 4.10b. Goldman Sachs assets in 2003 and 2007
Source: Report and accounts.

between shareholders and senior investment bankers who, at firm and trading desk level, have a direct and simple incentive to increase turnover. Figure 4.11 shows the total compensation cost for all employees for the major US investment banks, Goldman Sachs, Merrill Lynch, and Lehman, up to the crisis, as well as the amount that went to shareholders in the form of dividend and/or cash (share buy-backs).

The comp ratio system combines the worst features of the soccer star system and of CEO pay, but under finance sector-specific conditions which encourage explosive results. In a major soccer club, the players will get a substantial chunk of around half of revenue and, as in investment banking, it is difficult to cut pay when revenue falls through relegation or non-qualification because of easy exit for star players. And just as in a football club, the owners' returns get squeezed when times are bad. Looked at another way, an investment banker's pay is like that of UK and US senior executives, who are effectively paid according to company size (Froud et al. 2008). However, while CEOs in non-financial firms generally have limited opportunities to increase turnover organically if acquisition is blocked, senior investment bankers operate under different sectoral conditions where bricolage can be used to increase turnover by adding extra steps to transactions circuits, and leverage can increase the value of trades. From this point of view, the financial crisis was simply what happened when the comp ratio provided the incentive for

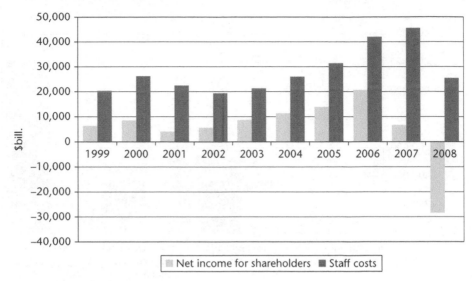

Figure 4.11. Combined employee costs vs. net income in Goldman Sachs, Merrill Lynch, and Lehman
Note: 2008 data excludes Lehman.
Source: Thomson One Banker.

bricolage, which was facilitated by the availability of new instruments and easy leverage. Turner (2010*b*) argues that proprietary trading that drives bonuses in investment banking enriches position-taking bankers rather than creating liquidity-related efficiency in financial markets:

> ... an emerging body of analysis which suggests that the multiple and complex principal/agent relationships which exist throughout the financial system, mean that active trading which both requires and creates liquid markets, can be used not to deliver additional value to end investors or users of markets, but to extract economic rent. (Turner 2010*b*: 40)

If we put together our analysis of retail and wholesale banking business models, this is not intermediation but banking for itself and banking has become a giant transaction-generating machine. As we have seen, the ongoing daily socio-economic cost of this in retail banking is mis-selling which undermines the bank's claim to help the customer; in wholesale banking the ongoing daily socio-economic cost is conflicts of interest which undermine the bank's claim to advise clients. As with retail mis-selling, this problem of wholesale conflict of interests is repeatedly discovered and punished, but not so fiercely as to prevent further misbehaviour. In investment banking, the pattern has been set by the ritualized interaction of US regulators with investment banks and conglomerates over conflicts of interest and mis-advice: a case is prepared and charges are filed before an out-of-court settlement is struck whereby the bank pays a fine without admitting guilt. The size of the occasional fine is such that this is an acceptable cost of doing business.

This pattern was very clear after the dot-com boom when the top ten investment banks in the United States (including Citigroup, Goldman Sachs, Merrill Lynch, Lehman Brothers, and JP Morgan) reached a general settlement with the authorities and paid a record total of $1,387.5 million in fines (SEC 2003). In the case of Citigroup, the fine settled issues arising from its multiple, conflicted relations with WorldCom: Citigroup provided analysis and advice on WorldCom shares for its institutional and retail clients, while it was also advising WorldCom management on strategy, and lending to and underwriting securities for WorldCom. In addition, Citigroup served as the exclusive pension fund adviser to WorldCom and executed significant stock option trades for WorldCom executives, while at the same time conducting its own proprietary trading in WorldCom shares.

After the financial crisis, the same thing happened all over again. In Chapter 3, we have already noted Goldman Sach's involvement in the sale of a complex synthetic CDO, Abacus 2007-AC1, which caused a loss of $1 billion for investor customers of Goldman Sachs, but produced a profit for the hedge fund Paulson & Co., another client. Here, we can focus on the legal outcome: the 2009 SEC case against the bank ended when Goldman Sachs reached a settlement neither denying nor admitting guilt and paying a fine of $550 million. This was the largest such fine ever levied, but no more than a week's trading revenue for Goldman (Treanor 2010). In 2010, the Director of the SEC's Division of Enforcement, Robert Khuzami, claimed 'This [Goldman] settlement is a stark lesson to Wall Street firms that no product is too complex, and no investor too sophisticated, to avoid a heavy price if a firm violates the fundamental principles of honest treatment and fair dealing' (SEC 2010*b*). Our analysis has rather differently suggested that violation of those principles is part of the business model.

4.4 Banking after a Minskian moment?

In this section, we pay our respects to those who got it right. The post-Keynesians and Minskians did see a crisis coming, though we argue that they missed out on the reinvention of banking and banking business models so that their diagnosis fails to capture what is at stake in the financial sector. The chapter then ends with a brief overview of what is at stake if we follow this analysis, and the arguments of Chapters 2 and 3. This serves as a counterpoint to the discussion of the limited and hesitant politics of reform in the second part of this book before the issues are taken up again in Chapter 8, where we indicate the limits of technocratic reform.

Of course, not everyone fell for the story of beneficial financial innovation and the line about banks as credit and risk intermediaries. In an important article, Dirk Bezemer (2009) has reviewed the pre-2007 work of post-Keynesians and Minskians, like Wynne Godley and Steve Keen, and demonstrated that this group did see the unsustainability of the credit bubble in housing and warned that this could produce some kind of crisis. On the law of large numbers in mainstream economics, we would of course expect some (outlier) individuals to anticipate this crisis; the obvious example is the maverick Nouriel Roubini, who identified the housing bubble in the first half of the 2000s and predicted that it would lead to crisis. But Bezemer's argument is that the heterodox as a group had a collective, theoretical basis for their prescience because 'accounting or (flow of fund) macro-economic models helped anticipate the credit crisis and economic recession' (2009: 1) when mainstream equilibrium models did not. Understandably, the heterodox critics were also unclear about the timing of crisis and about the importance of the shadow banking system which would make crisis much worse.

Even so, Bezemer's conclusion is uncomfortable for all who believe in academic league tables and credentialized knowledge. The heterodox economists who did see it coming were a marginal internal group within the profession who had lost out in thirty years of movement to and strengthening of the mainstream in prestige economics departments. Thus, one of the most relevant and accessible applied economists currently is Steve Keen, who is an associate professor at the University of Western Sydney (which is of course not the same as being a full professor at the University of Sydney). Mainstream economists have, since the crisis, continued to treat such living dissidents in the time-honoured academic way by not citing them at all. But the media and internal critics of the mainstream, like Paul Krugman and Joseph Stiglitz, did show a new interest in the founding fathers of the dissident schools who were all safely dead. As the *Wall Street Journal* rightly noted shortly after the outbreak of crisis: 'In time of tumult, obscure economists gain currency' (Lahart 2007).

The rediscovered founding fathers were John Maynard Keynes and Hyman P. Minsky but, as we shall see, the endorsement of Keynes was short-lived and the interest in Minsky was not particularly discriminating. Some, like Skidelsky (2010) in the United Kingdom, insisted that the giant state interventions to save banks and shore up aggregate demand proved Keynes had the answers, but that looks much less plausible three years after the crisis began in view of huge fiscal deficits and sovereign debt problems in high-income countries. Minsky gained more enduring recognition because his work provided a much more detailed analysis of the role of banks in the economy, and indeed he had predicted the recurrence of financial instability induced by bank lending and credit. The media took this up, so that the *New Yorker* and others enlisted Hyman Minsky as a prophet and labelled the crisis as a

'Minskian moment' (see e.g. O'Connell 2007; Thomas 2007; Wilson 2007; Cassidy 2008; Mason 2008), as the following quotation illustrates:

> Twenty-five years ago, when most economists were extolling the virtues of financial deregulation and innovation, a maverick named Hyman P. Minsky maintained a more negative view of Wall Street; in fact, he noted that bankers, traders, and other financiers periodically played the role of arsonists, setting the entire economy ablaze. (Cassidy 2008)

So what exactly did Minsky argue? Like other post-Keynesians, he rejected the neoclassical notion of automatically equilibrating markets and insisted on the need for a theory of instability and an associated control practice: 'identifying a phenomenon is not enough; we need a theory that makes instability a normal result in our economy and gives us handles to control it' (Minsky 1986: 10). Minsky's distinctive contribution comes from his focus on financial markets, banks, and credit as causes of instability. Keynes had related instability to disequilibria in labour and product markets, initiated by speculation in liquid (stock) markets, but Minsky put the primary emphasis on instabilities arising in capital markets initiated by bank lending and debt. When the monetarists opened up a debate on free markets, full employment, and inflation with the Keynesians in the early 1980s, Minsky was one of the first to point out the growing importance of credit money issued by banks in influencing investment decisions:

> One proposition that emerges from Keynes's theory is that, from time to time, a capitalist economy will be characterized by persistent unemployment. The neoclassical synthesis accepts this result, even though a deeper consequence of the theory, which is that a capitalist economy with sophisticated financial practices (i.e. the type of economy we live in) is inherently unstable, is ignored. (Minsky 1986: 100)

Interestingly, Minsky supposes that banks exist to create credit for productive investment activities, just as in mainstream economics. But, in contrast to neoclassical economists who see money as neutral, Minsky holds that the intermediary activity of banks can become speculative and disruptive.

> In an economy in which the debt financing of positions in capital and financial assets is possible, there is an irreducible speculative element, for the extent of debt-financing of positions and the instruments used in such financing reflect the willingness of businessmen and bankers to speculate on future cash flows and financial market conditions. Whenever full employment is achieved and sustained, businessmen and bankers, heartened by success, tend to accept larger doses of debt-financing. (Minsky 1986: 177)

To be able to distinguish conceptually between productive and speculative credit creation, and identify imminent bubbles, Minsky distinguishes between different types of 'financial structure'. When the present value of cash flows from capital or financial investments is sufficient to pay off debt, companies are what Minsky calls 'hedge financed'. When cash flows pay is sufficient to pay off interest only (and not the principal) then financing is 'speculative', according to Minsky; this happens when bankers tend to get innovative and help the economy grow. Under 'Ponzi financing', the third fragile 'financial structure' distinguished by Minsky, debt and financial innovation is used to pay off interest. This is the moment when the system becomes crisis-prone and is arguably what we witnessed in 2007.

> The way in which a speculative boom emerges and how an unstable crisis-prone financial and economic system develops are of particular importance in any description of the economic process that is relevant for this economy. Instability emerges as a period of relative tranquil growth is transformed into a speculative boom. This occurs because the acceptable and the desired liability structures of business firms (corporation) and the organizations acting as middlemen in finance change in response to the success of the economy. (Minsky 1986: 173)

The eponymous 'Minsky-moment' refers to a bank-induced economic depression, when overvalued assets drop to their true value and most of the credit pumped into the economy suddenly leaves it again.

> During periods of tranquil expansion, profit-seeking financial institutions invent and reinvent 'new' forms of money, substitutes for money in portfolios, and financing techniques for various types of activity: financial innovation is a characteristic of our economy in good times.... Therefore, in a capitalist economy that is hospitable to financial innovations, full employment with stable prices cannot be sustained, for within any full-employment situation there are endogenous disequilibrating forces at work that assure the disruption of tranquillity. (Minsky 1986: 178)

And at the end of the day it is the 'Minskian moment' that resets the expectations of future prices and values to a more 'healthy level'. This suggests that breakdown in financial markets, such as in the aftermath of the failure of Lehman Brothers, is nothing but unwillingness to trade resulting in lack of liquidity. The solution that follows from this is the injection of liquidity by central banks after the crisis, even if they earlier failed to 'take away the punch bowl'. Although banks are the endogenous source of bubbles and financial excess, their balance sheets after the crisis can be repaired by liquidity injection from the central bank so they regain their economic health to finance the next cycles of investments. This is Minsky's favoured technical fix which follows from his analysis, just like Keynes' preference for low interest rates flows from his argument about volatile expectations and the marginal efficiency of capital.

This Minskian apparatus of thought opens up a number of debates and issues, not least as to whether 2007 was truly a Minsky moment (Davidson

2008; Kregel 2008; Dymski 2009; Keen 2009). But, that debate should not distract from a more fundamental point about Minsky's *a priori*. Minsky was, like Keynes before him, what might be called a technical optimist about economic fixes for the problems generated by capitalism as a progressive system for generating welfare. Minsky believed in technical progress and explicitly endorsed the necessity of financial innovation: he also believed in the possibility of steering a capitalist economy through new kinds of theoretically guided economic practices.

For Minsky, financial innovation was a special kind of creative destruction. It was intrinsic to banking because 'a banker is always trying to find new ways to lend, new customers, and new ways of acquiring funds, that is to borrow; in other words, he is under pressure to innovate' (Minsky 1986: 237). And thus financial innovation should not be suppressed: ' . . . capitalism without financial practices that lead to instability may be less innovative and expansionary; lessening the possibility of disaster might very well take part of the spark of creativity out of the capitalist system' (Minsky 1986: 328). This did not of course imply positive approval of any and all forms of financial innovation; in the 1990s after shareholder value, Minsky was pessimistic about the predatory nature of what he called 'money manager capitalism'.

> The pension fund and mutual funds have made business management especially sensitive to the current stock market valuation of the firm. They are an essential ingredient in accentuation of the predatory nature of current American capitalism. . . . Money manager capitalism has led to a heightening of uncertainty at the firm and plant level; in particular, it has made the lot of middle management in firms unsure. (Minsky 1996: 363)

But more fundamentally, as we saw above, Minsky never renounced his optimism about technical fixes for banking and credit-led instabilities. Government and central banks can, as Greenspan would put it, 'mop up after the bubble bursts' and are together capable of sorting out the Ponzi-like balance sheets of banks and private companies before the economy launches itself to the next cycle of full employment and bust. Minsky thus provides us with a useful and unique vocabulary to discuss endogenous instability in present-day capitalism but simultaneously sees central banks as neutral, apolitical institutions with tools adequate for the job of stabilization. Framing capitalist instability in Minskian terms therefore directs us to a technocratic debate in both policy and academic circles about which policy interventions and which forms of bank regulation will restore order in credit and risk markets before they embark on another finance-led economic cycle.

Thus, Minsky shares the *a priori* of other heterodox economists who have never broken with the post-1945 pioneers who formulated 'hydraulic Keynesianism' and first conceived of the macro economy as a mechanism of stocks, flows, and ratios which generated employment, inflation, and all the rest. Before algebraic expression was standardized, this conception was materialized in the early plumbers' models of the macro economy as fluid moving in pipes between reservoirs. This basic concept has survived even though heterodox and mainstream economists have (after monetarism, Minsky, and all the rest) several times rethought which fluids and flows really matter; the corollary of the hydraulic concept is the idea of a technically informed policy practice (fiscal or monetary) which would steer the economy or damp fluctuations. But what if the problem is not knowing what to do as an expert policy adviser on the basis of a tight technical calculation of the best intervention in a world where economics contributes to perfectible rationality? What if the problem is understanding and changing other policymakers (including central bankers) whose loose, informal calculations of expedient intervention operate in a world of limited knowledge and ongoing mess? The post-Keynesians may have seen the crisis coming but are they prepared to provide advice? This is a serious question when the history of post-1945 economic management demonstrates the difficulty of constructing a credible technical management practice (Keynesian or monetarist) from limited knowledge, and under conditions of socio-political intrusion.

At this point it should be noted that our argument raises questions about Minsky's technical optimism which has been explicitly renounced by the current generation of Minskians and post-Keynesians who share our pessimism. Post-Keynesian economists tend to disagree with the mainstream media that this is a 'truly' Minskian moment (Davidson 2008; Kregel 2008; Dymski 2009; Keen 2009). For example, Davidson (2008) claims that the banking sector is not faced with a Minskian liquidity problem that can be resolved by a lender-of-last-resort central bank, but instead is suffering an insolvency problem that requires a different set of policy tools than Minsky proposed. Kregel (2008) argues that the current crisis is not an outcome of an endogenous Minsky process because the new banking of 'originate and distribute' led to the loss of banks' ability to evaluate credit as they no longer derive profits from credit intermediation. Dymski (2009) too emphasizes the transformation of banking from an interest income-driven machine of Minsky to a fee income-driven business, showing how this transformation invalidates a Minsky-inspired rescue of banking. Against this background, Keen argues that current problems of liquidity and solvency around wrecked balance sheets are beyond technical remedy and policy interventions so far have made things worse:

> However, though I am proudly Minskian in my economics, I expect the bailouts to fail. Minsky, I fear, was an optimist. The basis for this opinion is the feeling that, even though Minsky gave Ponzi finance a key role in his 'Financial Instability

Hypothesis', he did not foresee the extent to which misguided government action would rescue Ponzi financing from itself, and therefore renew it, in the name of systemic stabilisation. (Keen 2009: 9)

There is a large discrepancy between the pre-2007 romance of financial innovation and our own much darker story about finance and banking, as discussed in Chapters 2, 3, and 4 about conjunctural bricolage, the nomadic war machine, and the reinvention of banking through new volume-driven business models. Taken together, the message of these chapters is that finance and banking were not so much out of control as beyond control, so that some form of finance-led crisis was nearly inevitable and its consequences would be dire. And, though our analysis is more elaborate and multidimensional, we agree with the current generation of Minskians about the difficulty of expert management and mitigation by technical means. This is not an engineering problem and, on this basis, it is time to turn to a more explicitly political analysis in the second half of the book which examines whether what is beyond technical control can be brought under political control.

5

Prelude: Regulation Undermined Before 2007

In the second half of this book, we turn from an analysis of financial innovation, its processes, and actors to examine the regulation of these activities, both before and after the crisis. The arguments developed in the first half of the book raise issues about the difficulties in controlling bricolage, whether by banks, hedge funds, or private equity. Therefore, the next three chapters take up these issues using a more explicitly political analysis, starting from a discussion of how effective regulation of finance was undermined before 2007. Some of the key conceptual ideas introduced in the first four chapters, including the role of elites, storytelling, and the difficulties of democratic control, are developed through analysis that ranges across different jurisdictions.

The chapter begins by considering the general conditions which weakened quite different traditions of regulation in the United Kingdom and the United States. It then turns to consider and deconstruct the mystifications about the social value of finance which had peculiar power in the United Kingdom, partly because the constitution of the United Kingdom is built on mystifications and also because its continuing economic decline makes it peculiarly susceptible to narratives of success and transformation – narratives which claim that contemporary policymakers have bucked the historical trend of dismal failure and relative decline. It finally considers the failure of supranational regulation. The different arguments interconnect because this chapter describes a closed world of pre-2007 elite shared understandings about the importance of non-intrusive regulation of finance, based on a story about finance and financial innovation as self-evidently a socially valuable activity. In the British case, we present counter evidence which shows that finance actually made a very limited social contribution.

In this chapter, we focus first on national political and financial elites whose mystifying stories about the nature and contribution of finance were mutually reinforcing, though, as we argue, open to challenge. Through the chapter we develop the argument that the regulatory failure to control financial innovation was rooted in two kinds of mystification originating in the modus operandi of political and financial elites: constitutional mystification about regulation, and a mystifying narrative about the social value of finance. Mystification here is not a conspiratorial process because elites have to convince not only others – they have to convince themselves. Thus, it is as much a process of self-mystification as of mystification for the purposes of elite management of wider social forces, and one of the crucial problems is that elites often have no other knowledge, not even the cynics' advantage of knowing their statements are not true. This problem has particular currency in the United Kingdom because of the relative weakness of the economy since the 1980s: the perceived strengths of the finance sector appeared to make it a new national champion capable of giving the United Kingdom a comparative advantage and a dynamic, post-industrial future.

The chapter explores a closed world of shared understandings of the groups of political and financial elites who believe in the value of finance. The first section, Section 5.1, uses the notions of framework and conjuncture introduced in the first part of this book to analyse the regulatory origins of the crisis in both the United Kingdom and the United States. Here, we develop an argument that the crisis was not so much about regulatory failures in specific jurisdictions but about the way that ideologies and interests supported the official liturgies of the benefits of innovation and the great moderation, thereby effectively drowning out any counterstory about finance in the United Kingdom and the United States. The second section, Section 5.2, turns to the specifics of the UK case and argues that the pre-2007 regulatory regime was the product of a constitutional mystification about the advantages of self- or light-touch regulation, combined with a widely circulating mystifying narrative about the national economic benefits that would ensue. However, though politically unchallenged, our argument developed in Section 5.3 suggests that this narrative is empirically problematic. When we consider evidence on tax paid or employment created as examples of the contribution of the finance sector, we find that the benefits are less significant than suggested by elite narratives. In the fourth and final section of the chapter, Section 5.4, we turn from the national to the supranational level to consider why alternative stories did not emerge from those regulatory organizations that might have been expected to have understandings and narratives quite different from those prevailing at the UK or US national level. Here, we develop an argument that the crisis has revealed an absence of democratic institutions that could, from a different political basis, challenge the mystifying narratives that fog the national scene.

5.1 Regulatory origins of the crisis: framing and liturgies

The crisis that developed from the 2007 credit crunch was not a straightforward matter of regulatory failure in one jurisdiction leading to collapse of nationally embedded financial organizations. Indeed, during what we have called the 'Great Complacence', many countries actively encouraged the development of a domestic and international financial services industry; they were in thrall to this growing sector and its apparent contribution to the economy. In this section of the chapter, we consider why what had appeared to be reasonably robust national regulatory systems in the United Kingdom and the United States failed to prevent the crisis in the banking sector.

The argument is developed in three stages, and in doing so we echo the framework and conjuncture set-up that was employed in the earlier chapters of this book. First, we establish the problem: our explicandum is massive regulatory failure across several different national jurisdictions with historically different traditions of regulation. Second, we introduce a partial explanation for regulatory failure: our analysis explains how multiple conditions of interests, institutions, and ideologies in the United Kingdom and the United States after the 1980s combined to undermine resistance to finance. Third, this section goes beyond the methodological nationalism which is implicit in much discussion of interests and institutions: our emphasis here is on the liturgies about the great moderation and the benefits of financial innovation which were equally important on both sides of the Atlantic. In the conjuncture between 2000 and 2007, these stories were shared by regulators, academics, bankers, media, and politicians, and served as the keystone in the arch of complacency. Here, we pick up on arguments outlined in Chapter 1.

The scale and longevity of the crisis is generating an explanatory literature of comparable magnitude, and this literature draws inspiration from many points of the theoretical and ideological compass. But whether the crisis is viewed as a vindication of theories of efficient markets (Minford 2010) or as a further episode in the prolonged structural crisis of the capitalist order (Burnham 2010), there can surely be one point of agreement: it was at root a massive failure of regulatory practice. It could be argued that the failure of a single institution, like Northern Rock in the United Kingdom, was compatible with a robustly functioning regulatory system, for after all it is hardly reasonable to expect regulatory institutions to abolish all risk of enterprise failure. But the prevention of precisely such a systemic meltdown as almost happened in October 2008, and the hugely damaging consequences for the wider economy which followed, is exactly what we should expect of a regulatory regime. And indeed, while Northern Rock was a single failure, that case exhibited wider features of the dominant UK regulatory style – complacency, incompetence, and subjection to market actors (Treasury Select Committee 2008).

Making sense of this comprehensive regulatory failure is plainly difficult, for what we are looking at here is a multinational and international problem about the failure of many different regulatory regimes (configured in many different institutional ways, in many different political environments, and exhibiting many different regulatory cultures). It is hard to correlate the incidence of crisis with particular institutional arrangements, or with regulatory styles: for instance, the two systems at the heart of the crisis – the United States and the United Kingdom – exhibited quite different regulatory cultures, different historical trajectories, and different political settings. The British system was indeed marked by a historically engrained regulatory culture which marginalized the role of law and stressed the priority of regulation practised in a cooperative fashion with market actors. Some of the more catastrophic failings in the supervision of Northern Rock can indeed be traced to this style of 'light-touch' regulation (House of Commons Treasury Committee 2008*b*). In its defence, it could be argued that the British style had proved quite robust: the failure of Northern Rock in 2007 was, after all, the first public run by depositors on a bank since Overend Gurney in 1866.

But that is quite a blinkered test. The British system also gave us the fiasco of the Barings collapse in the mid-1990s, and this fiasco was in part traceable to an earlier instance of light-touch regulation where supervisors placed excessive trust in the regulated (Moran 2001). Some of the most influential postmortems on the British case, notably the Turner Review, draw the lesson that a transformation is needed to a more intrusive, adversarial culture (Turner 2009*a*: 88–9; 2009*b*: 88–9). However, the more aggressive, legally based, and adversarial system in the United States also has a mixed record, having in the fairly recent past given us the savings and loan fiasco, and the Enron and WorldCom swindles. The British system certainly privileged market institutions and actors and helped marginalize the institutions of democratic accountability, but the striking point here is that the historical experience hardly points to its unique vulnerability to the kind of systemic meltdown experienced in 2007–8.

Even if we could trace the origins of the British failure to informality, market friendliness, and light-touch regulation, we would then still face the problem of explaining the much more significant American failure – more significant because it was the American meltdown that precipitated the crisis of October–November 2008, and because it was in the United States that the sheer scale of collapse was greatest. For the United States had a very different set of regulatory arrangements, and moreover arrangements which seemed to guard against the potential deficiencies of the British system: not only did it possess a system with a well-established history of adversarial regulation of business but there were long-established and technically proficient regulatory bodies and a tradition of powerful democratic oversight both of the regulatory process and of the markets. These arrangements had been laid down after the crisis of the Great Depression, and had proved robust, at least in averting systemic collapse, for almost seventy years.

The critical question, therefore, is: why was this robustness undermined so drastically? In part, there are clues in the regulatory history of the decades before the great crash when multiple conditions encouraged complacency about regulatory dangers. After the Great Depression there was a long period of prudential stability in financial markets. This prudential stability decayed from about the middle of the 1970s, with the onset of the era of financial deregulation. Notable instances in the Anglo-American systems included: the secondary banking crisis in the United Kingdom in the 1970s; the savings and loan crisis in the United States in the 1980s; the collapse of the House of Barings which led to the reconfiguration of the UK regulatory system in the late 1990s; and the dot-com bubble right at the end the millennium. These failures might have been expected to alert regulators to the growing fragility of the prudential foundations of financial institutions. The market practices which led directly to the systemic crisis have now been well documented, mainly by journalists and other commentators including former insiders (see e.g. Tett 2009; Turner 2009b). As we argued in Chapters 2 and 4 of this book, complex derivative instruments, that were supposed to manage and minimize risk, became embedded in volume-driven banking business models with the rise of proprietary trading. The central conclusion of Chapter 2 is that the outcome was a fragile latticework of interdependence and counterparty obligations which was highly vulnerable to changing market values or behaviours (see also Engelen et al. 2010). After the crash, unfolding revelations about accounting and trading practices at giants like Lehman and Goldman Sachs show these markets were built on conflicts of interest and tolerated a culture of opportunism that blurred the line between sharp practice and criminality (Dorn 2010; Valukas 2010).

The development of this fragile system, and of blindness to its regulatory dangers, depended on ideologies, institutions, and interests which framed the whole period after the 1970s as one when the power and authority of regulators was increasingly diminished and constrained. These conditions are important because they have also helped shape the post-crisis landscape and we consider each one briefly below, using the United Kingdom as the illustrative case.

At the intellectual root of blindness lay the rise within the economics profession of theories of efficient markets that ascribed to market processes and institutions a superior capacity (superior to regulators) to monitor, measure, and anticipate risk. These theories conquered large parts of the profession and were central to the account of the workings of finance which was taught in the leading business schools (Buiter 2009; Ormerod 2010). Equally significant, the connection between academic economics, market practices, and regulatory styles in the period leading up the crisis has a concretely structural form. In the generation before the great crash, financial economics – especially through business school education and in the role of professional economists in consultancies and in research departments of financial institutions – became an important component of corporate life. This corporatization of a discipline which had hitherto been organized in relatively autonomous academic hierarchies was important in reinventing the media-visible and publicly engaged economist, who was no longer a professor against the background of a book case but the 'chief economist' of a giant investment bank captured against the background of a dealing room.

The account of how markets (supposedly) managed risk in an efficient manner was closely allied to the institutional reconfiguration of market regulation which occurred in this period. Institutionally, the period is marked by contradictory tendencies. Most obviously, especially in the United Kingdom, it was a period of significant institutional innovation designed to strengthen public supervisory arrangements: the original deregulation of markets in the 1980s was accompanied by the creation of a public regulatory regime around a Securities and Investments Board (SIB), which was charged with responsibility to supervise an array of Self Regulatory Organizations that covered the major markets. In that reconfiguration in the mid-1980s, the Bank of England was still powerful and prestigious enough to retain control over banking supervision (Moran 1991). The Barings collapse, coupled with the return of New Labour in 1997, led to three critical developments: the Bank was stripped of its lead responsibility for banking supervision; a newly created Financial Services Authority (FSA) was endowed with comprehensive responsibility for regulation of the financial system; and a Standing Committee chaired by the Treasury was created to coordinate the roles of the three key institutional actors – the FSA, the Bank of England, and the Treasury. This looked like a considerable increase in public control over the markets: for instance, the reforms centralized in the FSA responsibilities which, in the US system, were divided between several agencies at the Federal level and numerous agencies at the level of individual states.

But we now know that at the same time as these institutional innovations were happening, the new theories of market efficiency were also encouraging a considerable 'naturalization' of markets – that, after all, was the critical feature of the intellectual superstructure erected by the corporatized disciplines of financial economics, accounting, and financial law (Bernstein 1992; MacKenzie 2006). That naturalization was accompanied by three related developments.

First, this was a period when democratic governments became increasingly attached to doctrines of signalling credible commitments about sound money policies to financial markets, the most important sign of which was the spread of arrangements for independent setting of short-term interest rates by technocratically governed central banks (described in Roberts 2010: especially 23–46). Second, in both the United States and the United Kingdom, the emphasis on naturalizing markets had impacts on both the resources and the style of regulatory institutions. The SIB in the United Kingdom, despite being a very tentative step in the direction of public regulation, was subject to constant attacks for its interventionism; the Barings fiasco showed that, despite the history of bank failures, from the 1970s the Bank of England practised a high-trust, non-interventionist style for elite institutions. The history of the FSA in the first ten years of its life was also one of accommodation to the markets, and of self-consciously light-touch regulation. In the United States, from the Reagan era, there was persistent pressure on regulatory agencies to soften adversarialism, and a constant pressure on their resources. At the root of this was a conviction that the very innovativeness of markets was itself a powerful protection against prudential failure: that the complexity of the instruments devised and traded in markets were themselves powerful mechanisms of systemic risk management. As Alan Greenspan put it, as late as 2002:

> These increasingly complex financial instruments have been especial contributors, particularly over the past couple of stressful years, to the development of a far more flexible, efficient, and resilient financial system than existed just a quarter-century ago. (Greenspan 2002, 2004)

But there were also more brutal forces at work. If historically engrained ideologies of market-friendly regulation shaped British behaviour, sheer lobbying muscle defanged American adversarialism. In particular, the defenders of deregulated markets were able to use their financial muscle to produce compliant behaviour from members of Congress hungry for campaign funds. For instance, well before the crash the Bush Administration was worried about the market practices of the two giant mortgage corporations, Fannie Mae and Freddie Mac, which eventually had to be taken into public ownership in the midst of the crisis. But its efforts to impose regulation were successfully obstructed by the two institutions, which used their lobbying muscle to mobilize congressional allies (ironically, typically Democratic party allies) to block the Administration's banking reform proposals (Thompson 2009).

This process of hemming in the power and authority of public regulators was connected to a third development: the effect of both the intellectual naturalization of markets, and of the pressures on public regulators, was to empower interests in the markets. The intellectual and institutional developments are inseparable from some of the wider structural features of financial markets in this period: the rise to dominance of the doctrine of shareholder value, which legitimized the supremacy of one group – holders of property rights – in decisions over the fate of enterprises; the rise of trading in those property rights as a source of profit; and the rise of a plutocratic elite which extracted historically unprecedented rewards from prop trading and from managing processes of financial intermediation in activities like private equity (Froud et al. 2006; Erturk and Solari 2007; Engelen et al. 2010). Under the so-called 'comp ratio' system, described in Chapter 4, senior investment bankers had established a kind of joint-venture arrangement with shareholders which entitled them to a half share of turnover which they could increase at will (see also Augar 2005). More so than in any other period since the US Robber Barons profited from the national market, the UK and US investment bankers who profited from financial innovation were standing next to a huge, open till and, predictably, wanted everybody else to get out of their way.

Making sense of the roots of regulatory failure in the great banking crisis bears directly on our understanding of the post-crisis governing agenda. The crisis was not straightforwardly an intellectual failure (e.g. as argued by Turner 2009a: 39), nor can it be assimilated to the kind of fatalism about human nature which lies behind those accounts that picture it as the latest in a long line of instances of human credulity (Reinhart and Rogoff 2009b). Rather, it had its origins in a combination of theoretical understandings, institutional arrangements, and economic interests which have often carried over into the world of crisis management and post-crisis reconstruction. But the emphasis on continuity and the general analysis of frame conditions is incomplete because the favourable environment for banking and finance had to be established and maintained in each new conjuncture. And there is then an interesting and important question about how things were allowed to get completely out of hand in the upswing of the 2000s which followed the tech stock crash in spring 2000.

As we noted in Chapter 2, when opening the London School of Economics' new building, Queen Elizabeth asked the social scientists: why did nobody see it coming? In Chapter 4, we added our own qualification and observed that parts of the problem (including asset price bubbles and the rise of consumer debt) had been spotted by a range of authors. Theoretically, the new literature on financialization in the 2000s had identified the probability that a more financialized capitalism would be troubled by asset price bubbles and wealth effects rather than commodity price inflation and trade union pay demands (Boyer 2000). Practically, as Chapter 4 notes, a dissident minority of academics, from behavioural finance as well as Keynesian and Minskian macro economic schools, did see it coming. More precisely, the dissidents had focused on the rise of house prices (especially in the United States), correctly identified this as an asset price bubble, and predicted it would end in financial market panic and economic recession. None of them, of course, predicted the gravity of the present ongoing crisis because the shadow banking system could not be analysed from the publicly available accounts of the leading investment banks, which disclosed only an alarming ballooning of assets and liabilities. However, in our view, the publicly available evidence was alarming enough to justify major macro policy correction and some kind of investigation into the black box of investment banking which was producing such remarkable increases in profits. Likewise, and from the opposite end of the financial system, the growth in consumer credit was helping to fuel a consumption boom that was viewed as unsustainable and destabilizing by some commentators (Schor 1998; Manning 2000).

How and why were the macro economic Cassandras ignored? As outlined in the opening chapter of this book and developed in our subsequent discussions of academic theory of finance and banking, the prescient warnings were ignored by regulators, politicians, and the majority of the commentariat because policymakers, regulators, and much of academia had bought into, and thus through their silence contributed to, the great complacency. Understanding was powerless because Western regulators, academics, bankers, and politicians accepted the overlapping stories about the end of boom and bust and the benefits of financial innovation. Right up to the summer of 2007, the endless repetition of these liturgies by all authority figures everywhere deflected attention from the bubble.

There was, then, a set of stories that served to create a new mystification: one that represented the new worlds of deregulated, 'efficient' financial markets as having solved 'old' problems of boom and bust, financial instability, and risk management. But in the United Kingdom, there was also an older kind of mystification that continued to have huge power and which contributed greatly to the crash. This was a mystifying narrative about the superiority of distinctive UK modes of self-regulation – a narrative that had its roots in the historical connections between City and political elites – and that served powerfully to enhance the control over regulation exercised by financial interests in London.

5.2 London fog: constitutional and regulatory mystifications

The previous section tells a story about the broad framework and specific conjunctural conditions for regulatory failure, based on general arguments about the United States and the United Kingdom. In this section, we develop this analysis, using the specifics of the UK case, to argue that the regulatory regime in place prior to 2007 was not simply an outcome of New Labour obsession with the City (though that is part of the story), nor can it be explained only as the product of deregulation post Big Bang. Taking a longer view, its roots lie deep in the culture of business, especially financial, regulation in the United Kingdom. The regulatory system that was created in 1997, and that failed so disastrously, was the product of two conflicting forces (which helps explain its many gaps, silences, and inconsistencies). First, the historically dominant mode of constitutional mystification – one that removed the regulation of markets to a protected sphere of self-regulation – had been eroded over a period of more than thirty years, despite the development of a post-1979 narrative that argued for the insulation of markets and decision-makers from 'politics'. Second, the need to create regulatory arrangements that proceduralized control in a light-touch form had the effect of minimizing the kind of detailed, intrusive intervention associated with the law and public regulatory agencies. This then was consistent with the mystifying narrative about the social value of innovative markets in the City of London. In short, the regulatory settlement post-1997 was full of contradictions but made 'consistent' by massive doses of mystification – hence 'London fog'.

In the United Kingdom, after the late 1980s, finance became a domain of high politics where agendas were set by industry leaders, sympathetic technocrats, and supportive elite political sponsors. If political participation narrowed, so did intellectual debate as two mystifications supplied what Wright Mills once called the 'vocabulary of motivation' for elite economic and political practices in finance. The first mystification was a variation on the venerable laissez-faire narrative about self-regulation that helped legitimize a particular regulatory order by conferring on financial markets the right to run their own affairs. The second mystification was a more contemporary narrative about the social and economic value of finance in the wider economy. That narrative helped to politically empower finance as a sector by emphasizing the importance of an economic regime and a 'light-touch' regulatory regime tailored to the needs of financial markets.

The first of these mystifications about 'light-touch regulation' was a kind of ghostly return, framed by the peculiarities of British historical development. The City is the oldest, and the most distinctive, part of the business community in the United Kingdom. Key markets and institutions – the Bank of England, the London Stock Exchange, and Lloyds in insurance – can be dated back to the creation of what Cain and Hopkins (1986) call the 'military fiscal state' at the end of the seventeenth century. Britain's early entry into industrialism preceded the development of any democratic political forces, and created a politically privileged and broader business elite which promoted regulation beyond the law or public controls. The expression of this was in doctrines of self-regulation and cooperative regulation (Moran 2006, 2007). These doctrines were peculiarly well embedded in financial markets, dominated as they were by the oldest, most entrenched of business elites. The doctrine of self-regulation in financial markets was structurally reinforced after World War I by the reorganization of the Bank of England so that it functioned as the voice of the City in government, and by the reorganization of City markets – mostly into cartels – so that, under the eye of the Bank of England, markets could regulate participants. Before and after the rise of the labour movement, the appearance of formal democracy after World War I, and the rise of an interventionist state, the City represented regulation as a matter of flexible control by market actors with practical experience: in other words it privileged market actors and institutions over the actors and institutions of the democratic state.

The decline of the industrial spirit in metropolitan England in the later nineteenth century led to a fusion of metropolitan political, administrative, and financial elites which was memorably described at the start of the twentieth century by Hobson (2006) in *Imperialism*. In this process, those in financial occupations experienced collective upward mobility. For much of the nineteenth century, the stock jobbers' trade, for example, occupied the same twilight world as that of the bookie; by the end, stock jobbing became a respectable occupation for public schoolboys – the first old Etonian jobber dates from 1891 (Kynaston 1995: 318–25). Marital and business alliances connected financial, aristocratic, and political elites (Lisle-Williams 1984). The growth of financial markets through the twentieth century (producing finally the City of London's 'Big Bang' in the 1980s and the growth of proprietary trading in the 1990s) led to the emergence of new and more numerous financial elites who claimed meritocratic provenance and whose world was European or global as much as national. But the political representatives of the new elites were incorporated into a national reworking of the old style British alliance of the post-industrial elites. This reworking was personified by David Cameron, as Tory opposition leader in the first phase of crisis and coalition prime minister from May 2010. An old Etonian with an aristocratic wife, family wealth of more than £30 million, and a CV including a stint in corporate PR, David Cameron described his father – erstwhile senior partner in Panmure Gordon – as 'a fourth or fifth generation stockbroker'. As leader of the opposition in a 2007 interview, Cameron endorsed utterly conventional views about 'innovative financial services . . . (as) important industries of the future' (Jones 2008).

The mystification of self-regulation proved hard to sustain in the age of globalized markets, financial innovation, and the new business models that developed from the 1980s onwards (Erturk and Solari 2007). Big Bang was accompanied – in the Financial Services Act 1986 – by the reconstruction of regulation around the SIB. This reconstruction was designed simultaneously to provide a more robust system of controls while preserving the autonomy of markets from the 'usual suspects', such as lawyers and democratically elected politicians. That is why the SIB was a complex half public, half private body presiding over the institutionally convoluted system of 'Self Regulatory Organizations' (SROs) that were supposed to supervise separate markets – and, incidentally, why the Bank of England continued to control banking supervision. It was these arrangements that were discredited by successive regulatory failures, and above all by the massive failure of light-touch regulation to foresee and forestall the crash of the House of Baring in 1995 (Moran 2001). The subsequent creation in 1997 of a new regulatory body, the FSA, with considerable formal power did represent an inching towards a more formal, publicly controlled system. But the strength of the historically entrenched regulatory ideology, and the strength of the interests in the markets, ensured that the new FSA was rapidly colonized by that old ideology. Until 2007, the FSA practised market friendly, light-touch regulation in the belief that this regulatory style promoted innovation and guaranteed London's place as a leading global financial market place (House of Commons Treasury Committee 2008b).

Why was so much invested in the reinvention of an old regulatory style for a new order? If it was explicitly designed to enhance London's competitive advantage, why was it so important to have a globally leading financial centre? And why were the conventional views of narrowly based metropolitan elites so widely accepted? One answer lies in the bureaucratic politics of international financial diplomacy. By the 1980s, the United Kingdom was a declining military and diplomatic power with a palsied manufacturing sector. But its financial regulators punched above their weight in the networks of international financial regulators: the Bank of England, for instance, regularly provided the chairs (including the founding chair) of the key Basel committees concerned with banking regulation. And they punched above their weight because London was a financial centre of an importance well beyond the scale of the wider UK economy. Possessing a leading global financial centre was thus the equivalent, in international financial regulatory politics, of a permanent seat on the UN Security Council or possession of an independent nuclear deterrent.

But there was also a new supporting economic narrative about the social value of finance, which, from the 1980s onwards, legitimized the objective of strengthening London's comparative advantage. In this narrative, finance became the goose that laid the golden egg, so that what was good for the global financial centre in London was also good for the UK economy. These narratives were a deliberate creation of organizations like the City of London Corporation with its annual reports extolling the contribution of finance to London and the wider economy (see e.g. CEBR 2005), as well as sector-specific reports like those from the British Private Equity and Venture Capital Association

(BVCA) that represent a specific set of interests.[1] Much of this was assimilated into standard Treasury discussion of the contribution of finance in the modern UK economy (HM Treasury 2005).

The old constitutional mystifications that legitimized market-friendly regulation did have some (contestable) evidential foundations because it could be argued that regulatory systems based more on the law and adversarial regulation, like that in the United States, were also prone to regulatory failure. But the new narrative about the social value of finance to the wider economy was more or less pure fantasy. As we demonstrate in the next section of this chapter, employment in the finance sector did not increase after the early 1990s, and the profits of finance were disproportionately captured by foreign-owned investment banks and financial services conglomerates which had, by the mid-1990s, taken over British-owned firms, treated the City as one arena of their trading system and recruited a cosmopolitan workforce into a sector built on tax avoidance whose tax contribution of the City was always limited.

Yet, the fantastic new mystification about the social value of finance exerted a powerful hold over the minds of participants in financial markets, financial regulators, and economic policymakers by the 1990s. It was powerful because it was promoted by the heft of a new lobbying and PR machine and because it remotivated an old political pattern of alliance amongst metropolitan elites which was part of their historic lineage. The narrative about the social value of finance was so potent because it served to align the calculations of different elites (in markets, the core executive, and the regulatory agencies) about the benefits of financial innovation, and because it was congruent with the historically engrained culture of consensus amongst (old and new) metropolitan elites who were once again in the saddle during the years of Thatcherite triumphalism. Thatcher's control of the state, of course, rested on the way the electoral system gave power to a party supported by only a minority of votes concentrated in the metropolitan south-east – in the very England sketched so memorably by Hobson almost a century earlier.

However, the mystification involved here was more fundamentally potent because it was consonant with the new economic rhetoric about enterprise and rewards which was part of the post Thatcher settlement. The regulatory narrative in the decade after the return of Labour to government in 1997 was couched in new language about 'light-touch' regulation: see, for example, Gordon Brown's annual keynote speeches at Mansion House as Chancellor of the Exchequer when, in 2006, he reflects on the creation of a light-touch regime and its successes in the form of the growth of derivatives markets

---

[1] The BVCA has published a number of annual reports that cover the contribution of the private equity sector to the UK economy. See for example the series: *The Economic Impact of Private Equity in the UK* (2005, 2006, and other years).

(Brown 2006), or, in 2004, when he stated that he wanted to encourage 'risk takers' (Brown 2004). The City was viewed by the new Labour government as both a tax cash cow and as an engine of growth, job creation, and innovation in the UK economy. But the City was also pictured – and pictured itself – as operating in an international climate of ferocious competitiveness in which comparative advantage accrued to the financial centre which most effectively pursued market-friendly regulation (City of London Corporation 2000; Centre for the Study of Financial Innovation 2003).[2]

Why was New Labour after 1997 overpowered by this ghostly return where a new kind of neoliberal rhetoric about competitiveness hybridized with the self-serving historical excuses for regulation of the City by the City? An answer turns on both the long-term regulatory history of the City of London, and the tactical contingencies that faced Labour in the years of Conservative ascendancy. The decline of class-based political parties with mass membership opened the way for the hijacking of the Labour Party by a small clique who saw that centrist swing voters were the key to electoral success and delivered three election victories in a row. The New Labour project was based on enthusiastic acceptance of Conservative doctrine about economic transformation and private sector enterprise that follows from flexibilized labour markets and lower income and corporation taxes. Politically, New Labour distanced their party from the trade unions and thereby made Labour financially dependent on, and sympathetic to, City donors and other high-wealth individuals. A new style of politics had also emerged whereby business supports not the centre right but whatever side is winning, in the hope of sympathy after the election. The comprehensive listing of large (in excess of £5,000) donations by *Power Base* documents this shift: in 1999, at the height of New Labour triumphalism, for example, 60 per cent of Labour's income came from individual donors (20 per cent from donors over £5,000). The trade unions, which once generated 90 per cent of the Party's income, by then provided only 30 per cent (and only three high-value donations in 1998–9) (Power Base 2010). The virtually bankrupt state of the Party by 2010 reflected the fact that wealthy donors had now deserted in favour of placing their high-value bets on the winning Conservatives (and to a lesser extent on their Liberal Democrat partners) (White and Saner 2010).

The change in political mindset signalled by the new flows of party funding was also reflected in the economic mindset of New Labour in office. The party accepted the 'success' of the experiment in economic management which

---

[2] Note, for example, concern about the City's position in the Global Financial Centres Index (published since 2006), where the major international cities are compared with each other in terms of their success in capturing the growth of the sector, as well as their attractiveness vis-à-vis each other.

originated in the Thatcher response to the economic crisis of the 1970s, even though, as we show elsewhere (Buchanan et al. 2009), the experiment begun in 1979 did not fundamentally change the feeble capacity of the British private sector to create jobs. Instead, New Labour made policy framework changes like independence for the Bank of England and, in a confused way, tried to claim the credit for a fifteen-year boom sustained by equity withdrawal from appreciating house prices, and by increasing public expenditure – an increase that in one way or another accounted for more than half the job creation from 1997 to 2007 (Buchanan et al. 2009). The continuing decline of the manufacturing base was tolerated on the assumption that compensation would come from paradigm change to knowledge or creative industries and from building the City's strength in the global financial services industry.

The financial crisis left that strategy in ruins; in the contest for Labour's leadership after the May 2010 defeat, all the leading Labour leadership contenders were left looking helplessly at the large hole in the table. But the hole in the table was not only due to the financial crisis; it was also due to something more fundamentally damaging still. The whole presupposition of New Labour's economic policy – that financial services, and particularly the City, could power a new service-based economy – turns out to be a costly fantasy. Even at the height of the Brown boom the contribution of finance to public revenues and jobs was nothing like that suggested by the rhetoric of the City and its political cheerleaders. The notion of a City-led revival of the British economy turned out to be yet another species of mystification – as we now demonstrate in the next section of this chapter.

5.3 Deconstructing the social value of finance

So far in the chapter we have argued that mystification has been at the heart of the exercise of power by business elites. In the case of finance, it takes two forms: a mystifying constitutional ideology that pictures 'self-regulation' as the most natural and effective mode of regulation, thus delivering control into the hands of the industry; and a mystifying narrative about the social and economic value of finance, which seeks to elevate financial markets to a position where they are perceived as critical to the nation's economic health. In this section, we focus on the latter. The social value narrative works by: first, representing the sectional interest of the trade as a national, social interest as in the case of British 'big pharma' (Froud et al. 2006); and, second, putting business at the centre of a story about delivering social and economic benefits. But mystifying narratives are not immune to empirical interrogation and challenge. They can be deconstructed by scrutinizing their claims about, for instance, the employment or tax benefits that their activities are supposed to produce. And we show in this section that this narrative – which did convince politicians, civil servants, regulators, and leaders of financial institutions themselves – does not pass the test of evidence.

Before and after 2007, finance repeated endlessly a story about the benefits it brought to the wider economy and society. The narrative was built round two particular sets of claims which we scrutinize here: claims about the contributions to taxation from the sector and claims that the finance sector was a major creator of new employment.

Taxes paid by finance have to be estimated because no official source directly gives a total for taxes paid by the sector. The Wigley Report published by the Mayor of London (2008) imputed the tax contribution of the finance sector using methods derived from a PWC study for the Corporation of London. Wigley used this method to estimate taxes paid in one year, and we have used the same method to estimate taxes paid by the financial sector over five years. It is widely assumed that tax revenues from finance were a key source of funding for New Labour's social programmes. But, as a pro-cyclical sector built on tax avoidance, the finance sector actually delivered remarkably little revenue in the boom years before it was bailed out at huge cost to the taxpayer in the crisis. Table 5.1 shows that, over the six years from 2002 to 2008, tax receipts from finance totalled £193 billion and averaged just 6.8 per cent of total government receipts. The manufacturing sector employed many more workers under strict PAYE rules, which make tax avoidance and evasion difficult. As a result, over this period, manufacturing delivered double the tax revenue as financial services.

We return to this question of benefits and costs in a moment, but an alternative way of measuring the finance sector's tax contribution – one that was widely used to reinforce the 'golden egg' theory – is to focus on the absolute size of the finance sector's contribution to the Exchequer. Table 5.2 shows this as the total of taxes paid by finance over five years from 2002 to 2007. The five-year total is £203 billion which includes £101 billion of taxes borne plus £102 billion of taxes collected (principally income tax and national insurance). This is a large total partly because there is a strong bubble effect: government tax revenues from the finance sector rose by almost 50 per cent after 2002 as the finance bubble inflated. But this kind of calculation has an inherent bias because it accentuates the positive and eliminates the negative: taxes paid have to be balanced against the subventions required by finance. We here attempt exactly this kind of balanced calculation. On the one hand, the finance sector pays taxes, especially in good times; and on the other hand, the sector also imposes costs on other taxpayers insofar as the sector requires market subvention, system guarantee, and corporate bailout when things go wrong.

Table 5.1. UK finance and manufacturing sector's share of UK tax paid as a share of total government receipts

	Finance sector			Manufacturing sector		
	Total taxes paid by employers and employees (£ million)	Employers share of sector's taxes (%)	Sector's taxes as a share of government receipts (%)	Total taxes paid by employers and employees (£ million)	Employers share of sector's taxes (%)	Sector's taxes as a share of government receipts (%)
2002/3	25,333	48.8	6.4	63,167	32.7	16.0
2003/4	25,184	50.0	6.0	62,273	32.8	14.7
2004/5	29,661	49.4	6.6	62,516	33.4	13.8
2005/6	34,366	52.4	7.1	62,993	33.8	12.9
2006/7	38,488	51.9	7.4	63,503	34.5	12.2
2007/8	39,679	52.9	7.2	63,375	35.2	11.6
Total for six years	192,711	51.1	6.8	377,827	33.8	13.4

Notes: Employer taxes category summate corporate tax plus employer's national insurance; employee tax category summates income tax and national insurance.

Sources: Nomis, HMRC, ONS, and PriceWaterhouseCoopers.

It is obvious that the biggest imposition from finance on the public purse came as a result of the bursting of the bubble in 2007–8. After the bubble burst, the UK government had to pay staggering sums for the bailout. The most authoritative estimate of bailout costs is provided by the International Monetary Fund (IMF) in the July 2009 report by Horton et al. (2009). The IMF calculates the 'direct up front financing' cost to the UK taxpayer as £289 billion; this includes the cost of the Bank Recapitalization Fund, the Special Liquidity Scheme, and the cost of nationalizing Northern Rock and Bradford and Bingley. But if we add all Bank of England/HM Treasury loans and guarantees, the IMF calculates the potential cost as £1,183 billion. As all the guarantees have not been used, the actual cost is between £289 and £1,183 billion and certainly well above the base figure of £289 billion. These upper figures of £1,000 billion or more are so surreally large that they are difficult to comprehend. If we guesstimate the final actual cost as £550 billion, that is nearly £10,000 for every person resident in the United Kingdom or just under £35,000 per family. In terms of public expenditure, £550 billion is roughly the size of the total public expenditure budget for 2009, ten times the schools budget and six times the total spend on health.

The fiscal consequences of the great crash are thus immensely important given the agonizing cuts in public spending which the British economy will undergo in the coming years. But they are also important in considering the well-established narrative about the finance sector as the goose that laid the golden egg for New Labour. Our analysis shows that in the years leading up to

Table 5.2. The financial services sector's share of total UK tax borne and paid as a share of total government receipts

	Taxes borne by the UK finance sector					
	Taxes borne as a share of total government receipts					Taxes borne by the finance sector (£ million)
	Corporation tax (%)	Employer's national insurance (%)	Business rates (%)	Non-recoverable VAT (%)	Share of total government receipts (%)	
2002/3	1.9	1.3	0.3	0.7	4.1	16,344
2003/4	1.8	1.2	0.3	0.7	4.0	16,981
2004/5	1.9	1.3	0.3	0.8	4.3	19,423
2005/6	2.4	1.4	0.3	0.7	4.7	23,006
2006/7	2.4	1.5	0.3	0.8	4.9	25,531
Total for five years	2.1	1.3	0.3	0.8	4.4	101,285

	Taxes paid by the UK finance sector					
	Taxes collected as a share of total government receipts				Taxes collected by the finance sector (£ million)	Total taxes borne and collected by the finance sector (£ million)
	Employee taxes and NI (%)	Stamp duty (%)	Insurance taxes (%)	Share of total government receipts (%)		
2002/3	3.3	0.7	0.5	4.5	17,693	34,037
2003/4	3.0	0.6	0.5	4.1	17,452	34,433
2004/5	3.3	0.6	0.5	4.4	20,074	39,497
2005/6	3.4	0.7	0.5	4.6	22,183	45,189
2006/7	3.6	0.7	0.4	4.7	24,594	50,126
Total for five years	3.3	0.7	0.5	4.5	101,996	203,282

Note: NI refers to national insurance which is paid by employers and employees.

Sources: Derived from Nomis, HMRC, ONS, and PriceWaterhouseCoopers.

the crash, the 'golden egg' was actually quite small; and it shows that in the years of the great crash, the 'goose' of the financial sector gobbled a hugely disproportionate share of the communal corn – far more than was consumed by education, health, or other big-spending public services. The cost of post-crisis subvention so far is manifestly larger than the finance sector's tax payment in recent years; after this experience, a prudent accountant would then probably recommend setting aside all the finance sector's future tax receipts as provisions to cover the cost of subvention when things went wrong. The cost of subvention will of course be reduced by subsequent sales of stakes in part and wholly owned banks. But that is itself cause for concern because it encourages civil servants to extract the highest price by selling off assets without confronting the underlying problem, namely that the sequence of tax payments, bailouts, and asset sales suggests that the state is only manoeuvring around uncontrolled subsidy for a pro-cyclical sector. From this point of view, the issue is not the size of the finance sector in itself but inflated and unsustainable wholesale finance which carries with it huge social risks – risks that were realized in a devastating manner in 2007–8. The surreal logic of this problem is that only the state has the balance sheet to stabilize finance and the state should increase its capital reserves (at the expense of current expenditure on services and jobs) so that it can better manage the cyclicality of finance.

Given the hugely unfavourable figures on tax revenue and bailout cost, it is doubly disconcerting to find that the United Kingdom gets relatively little in return by way of job creation. On the issue of employment, the City arithmetic is not so much illogical as frustratingly incomplete partly because the employment contribution of finance is peculiarly difficult to understand and measure from the available figures. The UK finance sector includes wholesale finance in the City, and retail utility banking and insurance across the country. The sectoral employment totals for finance thus conflate two quite different classes of bankers: the masters of the universe in the City and the disposable white collars on the high street. Furthermore, the boundaries of the sector are increasingly blurred. The finance sector like others is vertically disintegrating and therefore we must consider not only finance employment inside the finance sector but also para-finance employment in other sectors sustained by demand originating in finance. The main issue here concerns the amount of general business service employment which is sustained by demand from the financial sector. After considering these complications, we have reviewed the direct evidence on finance sector employment, and added estimates for para-finance employment. Three key points immediately become clear.

1. *Despite rapid expansion of finance output and profits from the mid-1990s, the total numbers employed in the finance sector were more or less flat.*

Figure 5.1 sets this modest total and flat trend in context. The total of 1 million directly employed in the finance sector is less than half the total of those employed by British manufacturing even in its current emaciated condition, and no more than a quarter of those employed in manufacturing ten years ago. The trend of financial services employment is flat, but there has been a huge expansion in business services employment where employment has nearly doubled from a base of 2 million in the early 1990s towards 4 million at present.

Why are there so few jobs in financial services? The explanation is rooted in business models and activity characteristics; these explain why the finance sector, which accounts for 8 per cent of output, accounts for a share of the

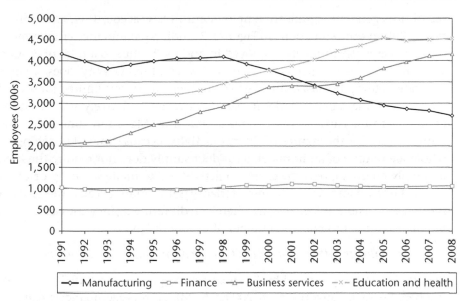

Figure 5.1. Comparison of UK employment in selected sectors
Note: Data refers to employees and excludes self-employed.
Source: Annual Business Inquiry, ONS.

workforce that is declining towards 4 per cent. On the one hand, there is constant downward pressure, in the name of efficiency, on numbers of retail banking employees on the high street: they are a cost to be reduced by banks pursuing shareholder value. In wholesale banking in the City, by contrast, one employee can lift a lot of money; huge output is generated by small numbers, who are enriched through bonuses and fees. The activity characteristics in wholesale are reinforced by a business model in investment banking which, as in law and accounting partnerships, is designed to generate high incomes for a small number. The practice of the investment banks is to increase the numerator by ramping up 'prop trading' activity (as discussed in Chapter 4) while limiting the denominator by operating a form of labour market closure so that relatively few new recruits are hired and those in post are promoted under an 'up or out' system of culling, whereby those who are not promoted will leave.

2. *Numbers employed are not hugely increased by adding para-finance and out of sector employment sustained by demand from finance.*

UK call centres or data processing centres providing services for retail finance are counted inside the finance sector; we do not think there is a large para-finance component in general business services (e.g. though it does include call centres working both for finance and other companies). The wholesale

sector does generate significant employment in law, accounting, and consultancy. But on our estimations in Figure 5.2, adding para-finance employment
only increases the numbers employed in and by finance to a total of around
1.5 million or 6–6.5 per cent of total UK employees. Why does finance
generate so few jobs *outside* finance? The numerical effect is limited for several
reasons. The main beneficiaries in para-finance are a relatively small number
of high-earning partners in law and accounting. More fundamentally, the
limits are set by the nature of finance activity because the retail selling or
wholesale trading of an immaterial product simply does not require the kind
of supply chain support necessary to activities like manufacturing or other
kinds of retail. More generally, immateriality is important because the product
is often expansible at low cost, as when a credit rating agency uses a standard
template contract to rate any number of new derivatives.

3. *Regionally, the effect of finance is to concentrate rather than diffuse prosperity.*

Reports like those produced by Bischoff, which present the 'official' story of
the benefits of finance (Bischoff 2009: 15–28), emphasize finance's regional
contribution. It is indeed true that retail employment is geographically
distributed, and there are also significant concentrations of wholesale activity
in the North-West and Scotland: these two regions together employ just over
one quarter of the finance sector workforce. But that is less than half the story.
From 1998 to 2007, finance sector employment actually decreased in the

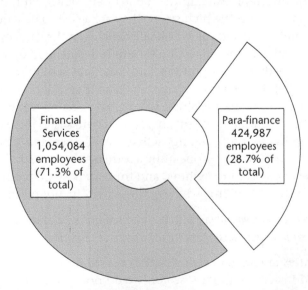

Figure 5.2. UK financial services and para-finance employment in 2007
Note: Total employees in both sectors is 1,479,071.
Source: Nomis, ONS.

Table 5.3. Analysis of London and its surrounding regions' intra- and inter-regional employment change in the finance sector between 1998 and 2007

London and the surrounding regions	Employees	London boroughs	Employees
East	−14,074	All London boroughs except	−32,909
South East	−17,372	Tower Hamlets	
South West	−1,560	Tower Hamlets	45,095
London	12,186		
Net change in finance sector employment	−20,820	Net change in finance sector employment	12,186

Source: Nomis (from the Annual Business Inquiry), ONS.

South-East, South-West, and Eastern English regions, and finance sector employment also decreased in all the London boroughs except Tower Hamlets. Table 5.3 presents our calculations and shows that, for example, the direct increase in finance employment of 45,000 in Tower Hamlets (which includes Canary Wharf) was balanced by an employment loss of 33,000 in all other London boroughs. Wholesale finance is thus an island of wealth surrounded by much deprivation in the capital. The expenditure of the wealthy few has a strong but narrowly focused impact on house prices in select London suburbs and on luxury goods and services whose production and distribution has high import content and does little for deprived Londoners.

All the argument and evidence above is about the finance sector as whole. If we consider banking more narrowly defined, then the totals are simply much smaller. The time series evidence on banking employment is not particularly informative because it shows an increase in employment in the mid-1990s, which is caused entirely by reclassification of an existing workforce when the building societies converted into banks. According to the British Bankers Association (2006), the 'UK banking industry' provided employment for 432,000 at the end of 2006 or just under half of those directly employed in financial services in the first-half of the 2000s (British Bankers Association 2006). Nearly 80 per cent of the employment in 'major British banking groups' was actually in retail activity and most of that would exist even if Canary Wharf was derelict.

This chapter has mainly focused on the Anglo-American systems, but the stories of silences, tensions, and failures detailed in the preceding sections are replicated elsewhere. In particular, it is important to get a sense of the single-most important regulatory system outside the Anglo-American arena: that of the European Union (EU). Its importance lies partly in the financial weight of the institutions which it covers, and also in the very special characteristics of the politics which surround those financial institutions – notably that developed in the EU.

5.4 Silences, tensions, and failures in other systems

The worlds of the supranational financial elites present a very different environment from those described above. This section considers what happens, in particular, when the influence of democratic politics is removed, as in the case of the Bank for International Settlements, or relaxed, as in the case of the EU.

Mystification, we have argued, has been a driving force shaping the kinds of stories told by elites about both the social purpose of finance and about its regulation at the national level. The fundamental reason for this has been the need to reconcile the continuance of elite financial power with the existence of formally democratic politics. Stories are needed about the social value of finance to provide it with public interest justification, and stories are needed about regulation to create systems that reconcile the exercise of regulatory power with independence from the institutions of the democratic state. And since these stories are – in open, liberal societies – subject to constant challenge and scrutiny, they always have an unstable, contingent quality. But the demands for public interest justifications, and for a reconciliation with democratic politics, are eased (or in some instances entirely relaxed) when we move beyond the sphere of national politics. For beyond the national sphere, there are no well-developed democratic institutions.

The point is most obvious in the world of global banking regulation. The focal point of this lies in the committee system of the Bank for International Settlements (BIS), an institution that originated as a fairly informal club of leading central bankers during the Great Depression. A key institution is the Basel Committee for Banking Supervision, which had its origins in the international banking crisis of the 1970s, when the BIS became the centre of global efforts at the coordination of prudential banking rules, and following the 2007–8 crisis, became the centre once again of attempts to formulate a renewed set of globally applicable rules.[3]

This world of global banking supervision centred on Basel is marked by three highly distinctive features. First, it is the very epitome of a world marked by highly scientized policy discourse whose 'stories' are about the adequacy of technical rules governing prudential banking. Second, in part, because this is a world marked by a high level of scientization, it is also a world dominated by networks of banking – mainly central banking – technocrats. The barriers to entry to this world are formidably high because of the technical complexity of the issues that are dealt with, and the language in which those issues are debated. This is not a world penetrated by democratic politics, and it is not one which needs a story to effect a reconciliation with democratic politics: it

---

[3] Basel II is the summary name given to the attempt to develop coordinated rules of prudential supervision. As discussed in Chapter 4, the latest set of rules is referred to as Basel III.

has been self-defined as a technical arena where democratic political debate plays no part. But third, this is a world where the agreements thrashed out have big implications for important economic interests, notably because prudential rules impinge in very direct ways on the profits and competitiveness of individual banks and national banking systems – a feature we examined in some detail in Chapter 4. It is thus also one which is entangled in the very highest politics of international financial diplomacy (Quaglia 2007, 2010).

As an example of the technically closed character of this world consider the following characteristic text, introducing a boxed feature detailing risks to financial stability.

> From a financial stability perspective, it is useful to decompose the risks faced by the financial sector into systematic, sector-specific and idiosyncratic components. The aim of this Box is to apply a latent factor model framework to achieve such a decomposition for both the banking and insurance sectors. Principal component analysis is a dimension reduction technique that makes it possible to approximate large multivariate datasets with a limited number of factors which account for the largest share of the changes in the original data. The variance of the data can be explained by a model of unobserved factors that are common to all or most of the variables, and an idiosyncratic component which corresponds to variable-specific factors. In this way, each variable can be represented as a linear combination of common factors plus idiosyncratic ones. (European Central Bank 2007: 115)

The text comes from a European Central Bank (ECB) Report and shows, incidentally, the extent to which this 'scientized' discourse has also penetrated the regulatory system in the EU. This is also true of the wider network of banking supervisors that surrounds the Bank. For example, the Committee of European Banking Supervisors (CEBS) comprised forty-six active members from respective national regulatory agencies. (The past tense is used because it has been subsumed into a successor institution, for details see below.) Of this number, three were professors at the universities of Amsterdam, Portugal, and Vienna (Arnold Schilder, Pedro Duarte Neves, and Andreas Ittner), whilst a further three were university lecturers (Rumen Simeonov, Jukka Vesala, and Mihaly Erdos). At least eight of the members held PhDs, whilst a further three had postgraduate qualifications in economics. Of the remaining members, the majority were trained research economists (Macartney and Moran 2008; Macartney 2010). But the kind of story which elites have had to tell in the EU is rather different from the stories told by the scientific 'clerisy' in supranational regulatory organizations. In particular, after the 'central bankers' coup (Wyplosz 2001) which created an ECB largely independent of democratic control, it was necessary to fashion a narrative which reconciled the existence of very different systems: the scientized system that characterized the technocratic aspirations of the ECB; the 'comitology' system through which the

European Commission organized its decision-making, and which made Brussels one of the most densely populated lobbying systems of any leading policy-making centre (a feature explored in more detail in Chapter 6); the system of intergovernmental bargaining represented by the institutions of the Councils of Ministers; and an embryonic system of formal democracy represented by the European Parliament, whose powers had been steadily augmented in each successive treaty since the introduction of direct elections to the Parliament in 1979.

The balance struck between these systems has varied between policy arenas, and over time. But the striking feature of regulatory policymaking in finance was the dominance of corporate interests and the independence won by the key institution, the ECB, from external control, democratic or otherwise (Dyson and Marcussen 2009). The dominant story about the substance of policy has been traced by Macartney (2010) as one involving 'variegated liberalism': a process by which elites coming from different national traditions nevertheless – especially through the processes of reform associated with the Lamfalussy Committee – struggled after the publication of the Lamfalussy Report to move to the creation of a single market in financial services in the EU.

It was this set of arrangements which were weighed in the balance and found so spectacularly wanting in the financial crisis. Key policymakers like the governor of the ECB were forced into issuing 'don't panic' appeals: in August 2007, as the crisis in German banks made it abundantly clear that this was more than an Anglo-American problem, Trichet could only say 'I call on all parties concerned to continue to keep their composure'. And the responsible Commissioner was reduced to flapping his hands in the face of the immobility of the Brussels system in the crisis: 'We are making progress, but I would not want to put it any stronger than that.... We are moving to the next stage. You can only move as fast as you are allowed' (Barber 2007). The management of the crisis in the two critical EU national systems that felt first the full force of the collapse – Germany and the United Kingdom – was largely done by *national* rather than supranational EU actors (Macartney and Moran 2008). Subsequent attempts to strengthen the EU regulatory system have, in Pauly's massive understatement, been 'inelegant' (Pauly 2009). They amount to an attempt to strengthen existing modes of coordination and communication via the creation of a European System Risk Council and the consolidation of three existing sets of financial supervisors into a single European System of Financial Supervisors (Quaglia 2010).

There are two important reasons for that limitation. First, the debates over the substance of regulatory change have reanimated – for instance, in the British case – a narrative that pictures national governments as the defenders of the competitiveness of 'their' national systems in the face of EU regulation threats; that has been a theme uniting the behaviour of both the Brown

Government and of its coalition successor. Second, despite the failure of the EU to cope with the crisis in 2007, it has quickly reverted to its pre-crisis pattern. The most striking instance of this is the production of the de Larosière report in 2009. The diagnosis in the report bears a striking resemblance to that offered for the United Kingdom by the Turner Report – unsurprising, perhaps, because de Larosière's high-level group was composed of national financial regulators, including Turner's predecessor as head of the FSA. But what is most striking about the report is the extraordinarily narrow range of interests and actors to whom it listened. Beginning in November 2008, at the moment of greatest fragility in the financial system, it held eleven-day-long meetings. Those who gave evidence included neither a single elected politician nor any of the numerous groups in civil society with views about the organization of finance. The witnesses consisted of two sets: the members of the regulatory elite, such as Trichet, EU Commissioners, and Baron Lamfalussy; and representatives of the trade associations (mostly EU-wide but including some national voices) for the main corporate interests from insurance, banking, and securities (de Larosière 2009: 70).

This summary overview of the most important supranational regulatory systems reveals several distinctive features that return us to some of the themes of Chapter 1. These worlds are densely inhabited by what we there identified as a kind of clerisy: a caste that has emerged to dominate financial regulation in the last generation, which has its own specialized vocabulary, its modes of communication and debate, and its own distinctive way of telling stories about the financial world. As the de Larosière high-level working group's notion of witness calling and consultation shows, this clerisy is both structurally and culturally closely attuned to the world of corporate finance. And in these supranational settings the need to create mystifying narratives that can help elites cope with the threat of democratic politics is either much relaxed (the EU) or virtually absent (the networks surrounding the BIS in Basel). What this has done to the process of crisis management and reconstruction is something we return to in Chapter 6.

6

Open and Shut? Democratic Opening *vs* Regulatory Closure After 2008

> *Around us we must build a new Bretton Woods. A new financial architecture for the years ahead. Sometimes it does take a crisis for people to agree that what is obvious and should have been done years ago can no longer be postponed. But we must now create the right new financial architecture for the global age.* (Speech by Gordon Brown, 13 October 2008)
>
> *Most banks world-wide appear poised to comply easily with the tougher capital requirements regulators and central bankers unveiled Sunday. Bank shares jumped Monday . . . (as) investors expressed relief that the landmark regulatory agreement . . . didn't include tougher provisions and that banks will have the better part of a decade to comply with the so-called Basel III rules.* (Lead story in the *Wall Street Journal*, 14 September 2010)

The two quotations above illustrate the gap between great expectations of necessary reform in autumn 2008 and the modest outcomes by way of achieved reform some two years later. After Lehman went down in September 2008, the severity of the crisis in terms of bank collapse and market seizure plus the need for extreme policy response encouraged (and indeed seemed to reward) promises of fundamental and thorough reform. President Barack Obama's Chief of Staff, Rahm Emmanuel, chose to retread the classic line about not letting the crisis go to 'waste'. British Prime Minister Gordon Brown grandiloquently insisted on the need for a 'new financial architecture' and invoked the Bretton Woods conference of 1944, just as authors like Eichengreen (2009) were envisaging an enhanced role for the IMF and global regulatory oversight by a new 'World Financial Organisation'.

Fast forward some two years to September 2010 and none of this had happened. The first significant piece of international re-regulation came in September 2010 with new capital adequacy rules for banks under the so-called Basel III rules. After bank lobbying and special pleading by national governments on behalf of their banking sectors, the new rules required a modest increase in tier one capital from 2 to 3.5 per cent by 2013 and then to 7 per cent by 2019. Such increases did not spoil the bankers' game, given that most banks already meet the new requirements. Moreover, these new requirements might incidentally open opportunities for gains from regulatory arbitrage as hedge funds, and energy companies (which compete with investment banks) are not subject to such cost increasing requirements. The stalling of reform was equally evident in domestic politics by autumn 2010, when the US legislature had both passed and watered down the Geithner/Obama reform proposals and the UK executive had appointed an 'independent' commission to look at banking reform while it got on with the more urgent business of austerity via public expenditure cuts.

This chapter and the next tackle the question of how the impetus to reform failed. In summary, democratic reform of finance (by the executive and legislature under established systems of electoral competition) failed because competing technocratic and political elite groups could not agree on what was to be done technically or how reform was to be turned into a politically actionable story for the public at large. At the same time, financial elites remained remarkably resilient and politically effective in defending the status quo and frustrating reform. But this summary verdict on outcomes so far is uninformative unless we also recognize that the political process that delivered non-reform was deeply unsettling, and consequently that the outcome (so far) is thoroughly unstable. The crisis was a moment of danger (and opportunity) for all elite groups because it unsettled their established assumptions. But UK financial elites had the easier defensive task insofar as their main objective was to preserve the old order rather than envision a new one.

This chapter begins an analysis – developed further in Chapter 7 – of crisis and post-crisis management in the United Kingdom, United States, and the European Union (EU) focusing on elite responses in a sequential analytic narrative. We focus on different elite groups rather than examine each jurisdiction in turn because, from early in the crisis, the jurisdictions shared some common political dynamics despite very different institutional structures and processes. The distinct dynamics at work across the different jurisdictions are illustrated from both the United Kingdom and the United States with some cross reference to the EU. The first shared dynamic is one of repoliticization as first the crisis and then the unprecedented political intervention of autumn 2008 turned finance into high politics. Democracy intruded because the expertise of the financial sector and its regulators was called into question by the near collapse of major institutions. This opens onto a second shared dynamic of narrative struggle, because action or inaction about reform has to be justified by a story. Amidst a multiplicity of competing stories from elite groups, financial elites in the United Kingdom held an advantage because they could immediately reuse an old story about the social value of finance for defensive purposes to try and close down discussion of radical options on reorganization. But the outcome was not so much closure as disorderly un-ravelling. This has left finance uncontrolled, but those who press for reform still have much to play for – as we note in the next chapter.

The chapter has four sections. Section 6.1 explores political responses in the United States and the United Kingdom immediately after the crisis and argues that the overall effect was a repoliticization of finance but with no clear overall outcome for particular groups of elites. Given the struggles between elites that emerged during this process of repoliticization, Section 6.2 turns to lobbying as an important response by financial elites in three jurisdictions (the United States, EU, and the United Kingdom) to limit the extent of reform. In Section 6.3, we draw on Olson's concept of the distributional coalition to understand how small groups can obstruct change and impose costs on society more widely; this section also highlights the importance of stories that support the sectional interests of the financial elites, drawing on Wright Mills' concept of vocabularies of motive. The fourth and final section, Section 6.4, illustrates these two ideas with a case study of inquiries and reports into finance, includ-ing comparisons between those published in the post-crisis period and those from earlier decades.

6.1 The crisis as repoliticization

Crises, famously, are turning points: a critical moment occurs when the patient is irrevocably transformed, for better or worse. But crisis also often raises questions about the limits of technical knowledge and practice: in many crises the medical expert either does not know what will work reliably or maybe even what to do next. So it was with the crisis after 2008, which in a short space of time completely upset the governing agenda of market actors and of the econocracy and threatened the insulation of financial markets from democratic control; a passive approach to financial regulation was no longer sustainable and intervention had to be improvised as events challenged estab-lished understandings and expectations. The cumulative impact was to threaten the technocratic experts and finance interests who had dominated in the era of 'light-touch' regulation outlined in the previous chapter. In both the United Kingdom and the United States, there then followed a dynamic of repoliticization. The crisis, and its management, had six major, immediate political effects, as outlined in this section. All of this was strikingly contradic-tory because some effects weaken and others strengthen specific elite groups who are, partly in consequence, increasingly caught in processes of elite competition and conflict.

160

- *Effect 1. The politics of financial market regulation on both sides of the Atlantic was reconfigured*

For about three decades before the crisis, the notion that financial markets should be kept free from political control dominated the minds of market actors and policymakers. That was the reasoning behind light-touch regulation, the naturalization of market processes that pictured risk management as the domain of market innovation, and the removal of politicians' control over short-term interest rates in favour of committees dominated by econocrats. Econocrats, as we saw in preceding chapters, are a subspecies of technocrats produced by the economics profession which has come to dominate, in particular, central banking in the last couple of decades. In short, in the story that shaped financial regulation before the crisis, democratically elected politicians were largely written out of the script. The events of 2007–8 are a moment when a thirty-year-long experiment to insulate financial markets from democratic control came to an end; what succeeded it, we shall see, was a brief 'democratic' moment followed by a continuing struggle between a range of elite groups for control of regulation.

The narratives of the crisis of autumn 2008 are concerned with the assertion of control by some democratic actors, typified by the rejection of the first version of the Troubled Assets Recovery Program by the US House of Representatives (Swagel 2009; Paulson 2010). More generally, they are a narrative of events in which the details of banking had been turned into the material of high politics on both sides of the Atlantic. Debates about regulation shifted arenas: they were no longer confined to the domain of low politics, populated by technocrats, but were the subject of investigation by elected politicians, and the stuff of front pages rather than financial pages. Perhaps the culmination of this transformation was the series of 'show trials' of prominent bankers by committees of the legislature in both the United States and the United Kingdom in 2008–9. These were occasions when legislators used public hearings to skewer bankers unused to the cut and thrust of (public) hearings before committees of the legislature. After a House of Commons Treasury Committee hearing in the United Kingdom, for instance, Sir Fred Goodwin and some other former leading bankers appeared on the front page of the tabloid the *Sun* under the heading 'Scumbag Millionaires' (Hawkes and Pascoe-Watson 2009): this was precisely the kind of setting that the politics of banking had been designed for three decades to protect them from. At first glance, the shifting of arenas looks a comparatively unimportant procedural change. It was nevertheless fundamental, precisely because it involved an implicit rejection of an assumption that had dominated the government of financial regulation for several decades: that it belonged appropriately to a domain of low politics dominated by market actors and econocrats.

• *Effect 2. Adversarial regulation was strengthened*

Adversarial regulation – the notion that the regulator should not trust the regulated and should use the weight of the law against them – is a well-embedded tradition in American regulatory culture (Kagan 2001). It derives from a mix of a populist legacy and a pervasive culture of adversarial legalism. It is perhaps the best-established, and the most distinctive feature, of the culture of regulating American business, viewed comparatively, and it has certainly been a striking point of contrast between financial regulation in the United Kingdom and the United States. But adversarialism had been at its weakest in the regulation of financial markets. The system created in the 1930s around the US Securities and Exchange Commission (SEC), for instance, relied heavily on 'franchising' the business of daily regulation to private bodies, like stock exchanges, and to professional bodies in accounting, and, since the appointment of the notorious speculator Joseph Kennedy as the first chairman of the SEC, the Commission had been close to the markets. The era of deregulation, in addition, was not kind to the adversarial tradition in financial markets. Although crises like Enron and WorldCom led to some reconfiguration of accounting and auditing regulation, the regulatory agencies were under severe resource pressure; the intellectual climate favoured light-touch cooperative regulation, and attempts to extend regulation over practices and institutions that subsequently proved troublesome were successfully rebuffed by the lobbying muscle of the financial services industry (see the history of the Bush Administration's attempts to regulate Fannie Mae and Freddie Mac in Chapter 5).

But we also know that all this took place in a culture where there still existed a general, background murmur of hostility to Wall Street and to big business, and where the drift of public opinion over the preceding three decades had been hostile to big business, in particular to Wall Street (evidence summarized in Moran 2009). This background hostility meant that it was not difficult to set off the wave of American popular hostility against Wall Street in the autumn of 2008. Secretary Paulson's first plan publicly to underwrite the banking system's untradeable debts reawakened that hostility. By 2010, both Congress and the SEC were on the job, including pursuing Goldman Sachs on fraud charges (SEC 2010 *a* and *b*). What was described in various media accounts as the 'show trial' of senior Goldman Sachs executives by the Senate Permanent Subcommittee on Investigations (Kerpen 2010; Newmark 2010), harrowing though it may have been for the executives, was only a sampler: the subcommittee has only been using Goldman Sachs as a case study in its longer running investigation of Wall Street (Senate Permanent Investigation Subcommittee 2010). The SEC had also been reinvigorated under new leadership and was presenting itself to Congress in a much tougher language of adversarialism (see Chair Schapiro's testimony: Schapiro 2010).

In the United Kingdom, after almost a generation when leading politicians of all main parties had celebrated the City of London as an emblem of British economic success that should be left to get on with its own affairs, both government and opposition now pledged to tighten legal controls. More important still, technocrats like Lord Turner, the new chair of the Financial Services Authority (FSA), and econocrats like the Governor of the Bank of England, and his executive director for financial stability began to use explicitly adversarial language in their account both of what had gone wrong in the past and what needed to be put right in the future (Haldane 2009*b*; King 2009*b*). Turner's review for the FSA, and his subsequent intervention dismissing much financial innovation as 'socially useless', was an attempt to create a conscious turning point in the regulatory culture: it disavowed the 'light-touch' approach that had shaped the Authority's behaviour from its foundation; used dismissive language about the supposed benefits of much innovation in markets; and embraced a more adversarial and 'intrusive' regulatory style (Turner 2009*b*, 2010*a*).

That attempt to stake out a distinctive position in the regulatory landscape was in part a manoeuvre in something we describe below: the turf struggles between regulatory agencies set off by the crisis and its aftermath. But it is significant that in these struggles to defend agency turf (and, in the case of the FSA, even the very existence of the Authority), it was felt necessary to resort to the language of adversarialism in a system that had hitherto made a virtue of cooperative regulation. The new spirit of adversarialism also spilled over into the challenging public confrontations between legislators, regulators, and, most important, executives from failed institutions, as politicians began to sense that electoral advantage could be gained from publicly confronting the leaders of the financial services industry.

- *Effect 3. Large parts of the financial system were taken into public ownership*

The age of deregulation was also an age of privatization, in which politicians, especially in the United Kingdom, competed with each other to privatize key industries. The Conservative hegemony in the 1980s had turned the United Kingdom into world champions in the scale of privatization. For the New Labour governments from 1997, the perceived electorally suicidal and economically anachronistic practices of 'old' Labour were symbolized by the party's commitment, in its ill-fated 1983 general election manifesto, to take parts of the banking system into public ownership. Unsurprisingly, therefore, New Labour in 2007 was at first driven only slowly and reluctantly in the direction of accepting any new forms of public ownership. The first great event of the crisis occurred in September 2007 when the Treasury was obliged to replace the limited guarantees for depositors by a state guarantee that soon amounted to an assurance that public money would guarantee all deposits in

163

the failing bank, Northern Rock. But the initial response of policymakers was to dither and resist public ownership: in the months immediately after the collapse of Northern Rock, millions were spent on consultants in a failed attempt to offload the stricken bank.

The scale of the systemic collapse in October–November 2008 concentrated minds wonderfully. The authorities were obliged to establish the United Kingdom Financial Investments (UKFI) as a vehicle for managing public ownership of a huge tranche of the banking system. By July 2009, UKFI owned 70 per cent of the voting share capital of Royal Bank of Scotland (RBS), and 43 per cent of the Lloyds Banking Group. Or as John Kingman, then UKFI Chief Executive, put it in more homely terms in introducing UKFI's first Annual Report: 'Every UK household will have more than £3,000 invested in shares in RBS and Lloyds' (UKFI 2009a: 2). In the United States, apart from the 'nationalizing' of a huge volume of bank debt, two leading suppliers of housing mortgages were also taken into public ownership: the Federal National Mortgage Association and the Federal Home Mortgage Corporation. These events dramatized how far the wheel of policy had turned. Fannie Mae was created under President Roosevelt's New Deal as part of the attempt to cope with the last great global financial crash. It was privatized in 1968 near the start of the modern era of free-market triumphalism, and two years later Freddie Mac was created as a private sector competitor.

The huge extension of formal public ownership, combined with the even more extensive state underwriting of the banking system in the crisis, is the single-most important structural consequence of the crisis: it is the key to the ensuing fiscal crises of states and the interrelated sovereign debt crisis which together have been so central to post-crisis economic management. But it is also the key to much of the subsequent politics of the financial system, for this dramatic reversal of long-established policy raised an obvious question: on what terms would the new state presence in the financial system be established? Since the state had socialized banking losses, what price (if any) would be exacted in return for socialization? The problem of how to answer that question has shaped the way interests and institutions have manoeuvred in the post-crisis world, but it also deeply affected the role of politicians in the management of the crisis itself.

- *Effect 4. Politicians became managers of the financial system*

The wave of nationalization was itself the sign of a wider shift: a great increase in the importance of politicians in financial management. On both sides of the Atlantic, the ferocity of the crisis sucked governing politicians into the detail of managing markets: brokering mergers and takeovers to rescue failing institutions; extending the guarantees of protection to depositors in retail banks against the threat of collapse, to the point where the state was guaranteeing virtually all deposits in the system; and using treasury and central bank resources to supply the financial markets with liquidity to try to keep trading going.

Some of the most important effects were felt in the high politics of the EU. Before the crisis, financial regulation in the Union had been a classic zone of low politics: a domain dominated by dense networks inhabited by corporate elites and econocrats. After the crisis, competing visions of a reconstructed regulatory order and 'grandstanding' in defence of the interests of national markets became central to the high politics of the Union. A possibly even more profound consequence was to raise, to the highest level of political sensitivity, issues hitherto buried in the Growth and Stability Pact that underlay the system of economic government in the European Union. The trigger for this was the attempt by Greece to manage the fiscal fallout of the crisis.

The Euro had protected weak Eurozone economies like Greece and Ireland from the fate succumbed to by Iceland (a catastrophic devaluation of the national currency). But this had come at the price of putting huge strain on the Growth and Stability Pact, and pushing to the head of politicians' agendas in the Eurozone the problem of how to manage fiscal imbalances in member states. The first response in May 2010 was a bailout package designed to buy some time in the markets and to take market pressure off the Greek Government, which was effectively locked out of the bond markets, as well as to prevent the contagion spreading via Portugal to Spain. By autumn 2010, it was clear that this had not worked: the Greek Government had to offer 11 per cent interest on its ten-year borrowings because the markets were anticipating default and a hair cut of 30 or 40 per cent. But the (unresolved) European dimension of the crisis was made more salient still by the fifth effect identified below.

- *Effect 5. The 'Anglo-American model' of capitalism was challenged*

The notion that the United Kingdom and the United States are part of a single model of capitalism is an intellectual oversimplification which matters because it has exercised a powerful hold over the minds of business people and politicians in these two countries, leading to a belief that it represented the model of the future for the rest of the capitalist world. In other words, in the period before the crisis, the liturgies about the Great Moderation and innovative financial markets were bound up with a kind of meta-preference for a particular – perhaps imagined but still influential – model of market-based, flexible, and innovative capitalism. The 'other' on this construction was commonly a model – equally possibly largely constructed from the imagination – identified with the leading nations of the EU, a mainland model that was pictured as restricting labour market flexibility and financial innovation.

While the claimed benefits of labour market flexibility remain largely unchallenged, the events of 2007–8 unsettled the idea that the future rested with lightly regulated financial markets where virtually all assets were turned into tradable securities. Indeed, it is not too extreme to say that it reconfigured the mind world of important parts of the technocratic elite. The crisis in the United States set off a long period of public soul-searching, especially when considered alongside instances of collateral damage, like the failure to spot and stop the fraudster Bernard Madoff. The results even included some recantations from some of the high priests of the previous era, of the kind quoted earlier from Alan Greenspan. In the American case, this soon became entangled with an extended, and not yet concluded, series of turf battles between regulatory agencies, as discussed later in this section. Meanwhile, in the United Kingdom, the immediate effect of the crisis was an even more comprehensive destruction of the intellectual capital of the regulatory technicians who had in the mid-1990s constructed a new regulatory system which was built much more completely than in the United States on the intellectual presuppositions of market-friendly, light-touch control. As we shall see, some parts of the regulatory elite in the months after the crisis tried to preserve as much as possible of 'business as usual'; in other parts – notably in the new leadership of the FSA and in parts of the Bank of England – very different regulatory philosophies began to exercise influence.

- *Effect 6. An extended series of turf wars began*

In the very heat of the crisis in October–November 2008, the participants had to act so quickly that they had little time for reflection, still less for deliberation on the future shape of the regulatory system. But as policymakers have begun to survey the ruins left by the crisis, three interlinked factors, already discussed above, came together to convert the process of regulatory reconstruction into an extended series of turf struggles between regulatory agencies: the attempt to recast a regulatory philosophy to replace that discredited by the crash; the rising salience of issues of regulatory construction and reform in high politics, especially among elected politicians; and the debates about how to shape the post-crisis financial system. In the case of the United States, even in the middle of the crisis, for instance, it was obvious that the stage of institutional reform would soon be reached. It was also apparent that this stage would create great opportunities and dangers for the agencies and that the realization of these opportunities and dangers would depend critically on cultivating key Congressional allies. The new Administration's first attempt at substantial regulatory reform – flagged in the Treasury's *Financial Regulatory Reform* (2009) – represented a considerable widening of the Fed's jurisdictions. The process of trying to manage reforms through Congress set off a prolonged bout of inter-agency struggles for turf, including competitive briefing of journalists and advocacy of competing positions in Congressional hearings – processes that even pressure from Treasury Secretary Geithner could not shut down (Paletta 2009; Paletta and Solomon 2009).

These intra-elite struggles took a more publicly dramatic form in January 2010 with President Obama's announcement of proposals presented as an attempt to revive the spirit of Glass-Steagall: proposals, notably, to prohibit any bank holding deposits under public guarantee from operating hedge funds, private equity funds, or trading on its own book – 'proprietary trading'. Briefings to journalists suggested that the turn by the President to these measures, and to populist rhetoric ('If these folks want a fight it's a fight I'm ready to have'), was the result of a struggle for the President's ear in the preceding months between competing sections of the technocratic elite offering more or less radical visions of reform. The prominence of Paul Volcker at the President's public announcement, and the fact that the proposed prohibitions would be known as the Volcker Rule, confirm this.

The new proposals had a tortuous progress through Congress (see Paletta 2010) but were finally enacted in July 2010 as the Wall Street Reform and Consumer Protection Act. They are the most sweeping reforms of the regulatory structure since the New Deal reforms, and like those reforms, their full impact will only be seen in the process of implementation. But their appearance reinforces the way the process of regulatory reform is now entangled with turf battles in the US system. It also shows that these battles spillover between the US and the UK systems: the Obama proposals in principle strengthened the hands of those in the British technocratic elite, notably in the Bank of England, advocating more radical structural reforms.

That intellectual struggle in the United Kingdom is in turn also now bound up with turf struggles. The system of financial regulation created in 1997, and now discredited, amounted to a considerable loss of jurisdiction by the Bank of England, principally as a punishment for its incompetence in supervising Barings, the elite City house that crashed so spectacularly in 1995. The debate about the reconstruction of the system after 2007–8 allowed the Bank to reopen this division of regulatory labour. The Governor made crystal clear in his June 2009 Mansion House speech that the Bank supported a more radical structural reconfiguration of the banking system than was envisaged in, for instance, the Treasury. Moreover, he also made a clear bid for an increase in the Bank's regulatory authority.

To achieve financial stability the powers of the Bank are limited to those of voice and the new resolution powers. The Bank finds itself in a position rather like that of a church whose congregation attends weddings and burials but ignores the sermons in between. Like the church, we cannot promise that bad things won't happen to our flock – the prevention of all financial crises is in neither our nor anyone else's power, as a study of history or human nature would reveal. And experience suggests that attempts to encourage a better life through the power of voice is not enough. Warnings are unlikely to be effective when people are being asked to change behaviour which seems to them highly profitable. So it is not entirely clear how the Bank will be able to discharge its new statutory responsibility if we can do no more than issue sermons or organise burials. (King 2009*a*)

By 2010, this turf war had become enmeshed with adversarial party politics. The adversarial party system in the United Kingdom demands that opposing teams of party politicians adopt policy that distinguishes them from their opponents. Adversarialism demands that oppositions create a reverse image of governing policies, almost regardless of ideological consistency. Thus, it was that the Bank found an unlikely ally in the form of the Conservatives who, attempting to distinguish themselves from the Brown Administration, advocated a recentralization of regulatory jurisdiction in the Bank, and flirted with some of the more radical proposals for a reconstruction of the banking system.

There is a recurrent theme in the account given above: the impact of the financial crisis was profoundly to disturb established, consensual patterns of elite relations in the financial system. Before the crisis, there was a liturgical consensus about the benefits of financial innovation and the appropriateness of light-touch regulation; after the crisis, the political developments described above broke the consensus and opened new divisions. So crisis changed the relations *within and between* elite groups, just as it changed relations between elites and democratic electorates after three decades in which democracy had been written out of the script. But it did not democratize financial politics or disempower financial elites. Individuals like Fuld and Godwin may have been scapegoated, but the broader group of senior bankers and other financiers was not excluded from the process of reform. Because of the highly specialist (and seemingly impenetrable) world of financial instruments and markets, some industry insiders were co-opted into the process of sorting out the mess and the rest could insert themselves into the process by lobbying. Thus, the paradoxical outcome of the crisis has been bickering competition between different elite groups with different reform agendas overshadowed by the successful regrouping by financial elites who lobbied to water down reform measures, and organized into distributional coalitions which told stories that encouraged a process of regulatory closure. We describe the lobbying in the next section of this chapter before turning to analysis by exploring the notion of distributional coalition and regulatory closure.

6.2 Three worlds of lobbying

If the impetus for fundamental reform of the banking and related financial system was lost by 2010, the slow and limited pace of reform of the financial sector in both national and supranational contexts raises questions about how, and by whom, is regulation shaped. It also opens up for examination the continuing influence of different elite groups in and around finance who are themselves challenged by other elites such as technocrats with a responsibility for (or a stake in) the regulation of finance. How have financial elites been able to operate so as to ensure their continuing significant role in shaping the regulatory framework around finance, and in doing so, minimize the extent of reform? The answer developed in the next three sections of this chapter is that financial elites have organized into distributional coalitions and committed massive resources to political lobbying whose effectiveness is increased by storytelling about the social benefits of finance. If we are concerned descriptively with what happened and how, this section provides the short answer to these questions, which is that reform of the financial sector stalled because finance sector lobbying succeeded.

This section examines lobbying by finance in the United States, the EU, and the United Kingdom in turn. The paradox is that the political forms and conditions of lobbying were very different in the three jurisdictions which were nevertheless equally susceptible to the influence of finance. This was more than enough for finance to win, because if finance succeeded in blocking significant reform in investment banking in either London or New York, it would nullify reform efforts elsewhere. It is easier to make these arguments than to provide simple measures of the influence of finance in different jurisdictions. Lobbying can most easily be tracked in the distinctive political setting of the United States which combines large-scale lobbying with effective disclosure of lobbying activities by individual corporations and trade associations. The finance sector, health care, pharmaceuticals, and defence contracting have long been amongst the major political lobbyists in the United States using the conventional measures of lobbying such as expenditure or exchange of personnel through revolving door appointments. In other jurisdictions with different institutional structures, lobbying activity is less transparent but also very important because financial elites have not been excluded from the reform of financial regulation, particularly in relation to the mapping of options. In the EU, the continuing deficit of democracy and the small size of the central bureaucracy make Brussels a congenial arena for lobbyists with any claim to expertise. What we observe in the specific UK case is a typically fudged British compromise with new-style disclosure of financial contributions to political parties but in a hard-to-understand form combined with old-style influence for City insiders who are close to the political classes.

In the United States, there is no shortage of evidence about how the interests of finance are intertwined with political and regulatory institutions. This glorious transparency in the United States allows all kinds of NGOs, bloggers, journalists, and others to provide measures of lobbying muscle and interest, and to speculate about the attrition of the original objectives of reform laid out by the incoming Obama administration into a set of relatively circumspect new rules. For example, the NGO Public Citizen reported in 2010 that, since early 2009, nearly 1,000 lobbyists have worked on at least one of the nine bills that together 'rewrite the rules governing derivatives'. Using House of Representatives disclosures, they estimate that lobbyists representing opponents of reform outnumber pro-reform lobbyists by more than eleven to one (Public Citizen 2010).

Of course, this is neither new nor a practice unique to the finance industry. In terms of continuity, Kevin Connor (2010) documents the lobbying process that surrounded the earlier deregulatory process, including legislation such as the Financial Services Modernisation Act 1999 (Gramm-Leach-Biley) and the Commodity Futures Modernisation Act 2000, which kick-started the growth of derivatives trading in the 2000s and facilitated the ensuing growth of the investment banks. Connor also details the longstanding practice of the movement of personnel between government and banks, noting that the six biggest banks have each hired more than forty 'revolving door lobbyists' since the 2008 bailout of Bear Stearns.[1] While the revolving door is certainly not an invention of the current crisis, what is new according to Connor is that banks are using more covert forms of lobbying, with banks funding both established organizations, like the US Chambers of Commerce and the Business Roundtable, as well as shadow organizations which can promote the interests of the derivatives industry more easily than banks that have benefitted from bailouts and other support. In short, faced with the threat of reform, banks have cleverly adopted some of the most sophisticated, latest tactics of the corporate lobbying industry.

The wider nature of corporate lobbying also shapes an additional important feature of finance industry activity: contributions to election campaigns. The US system creates an almost insatiable demand from politicians for campaign money, while the ability of Congressmen to shape regulation creates a huge supply of that money from affected interests. Hence, donations to election campaigns have been a traditional and important link between politicians and the finance sector. Ralph Nader, amongst others, estimates that over ten years to 2009, $1.7 billion was given as campaign contributions by the finance sector. The Centre for Responsive Politics calculates that political contributions from the FIRE (finance, insurance, and real estate) sector dwarf all others (including health and defence), with a total of $2.3 billion given to individual

---

[1] Connor provides profiles of some of most significant lobbyists. Overall, all of the 243 lobbyists working for the six big banks had worked in federal government (Congress or the White House): for example, thirty-two have been staffers to the Senate Banking Committee, while twenty-six staffed the House Financial Services Committee.

candidates and party committees between 1989 and 2009 (Renick Mayer et al. 2009). According to other commentators, the influence of the finance sector is not to be counted simply in campaign billions nor in numbers of mid-level lobbyists passing between government and industry, but in the much smaller numbers of key positions held by those whose background in finance might affect their ability to govern in the public interest. Seniors who passed through the revolving door include two Treasury Secretaries: Hank Paulson served as chief executive of Goldman before he became Treasury Secretary in 2006, while Robert Rubin, who was Treasury Secretary from 1995, had previously worked twenty-six years for Goldman and retired from government office to a senior position in Citigroup. For Simon Johnson, ex-IMF economist and prominent critic of what he terms the 'Wall Street takeover', it is the connections at senior level between banks and government which have been most decisive. Johnson and Kwak (2010: 6–7 and Chapter 7) describe the major US banks as an oligarchy, whose political power comes not simply from campaign contributions but from the economic power of Wall Street firms who are the present-day equivalent of the giant industrial trusts of the early twentieth century.

If the immense political weight of the finance sector in the United States cannot be denied, the European context is very different and, on the face of it, less favourable to political influence by finance. The members of the EU are distinguished by different political systems and party politics, and the collective outcome is one where the interests of finance have never been explicitly dominant because of established counterweights in the form of organized labour, the role of non-financial business, and opposition to predatory finance from social democrats and (traditionally minded) centre-right politicians. Franz Müntefering's jibe about private equity as 'locusts' represents the hostility of many European politicians who have been openly suspicious of the finance sector, especially new intermediary financier groups such as hedge funds and private equity. It might therefore be expected that the European regulatory system would be more resistant to the lobbying of finance. On the contrary, although there is limited direct evidence of finance sector influence, there is considerable indirect evidence that finance is structurally well placed to frustrate the European reform process. This follows from the features sketched near the end of Chapter 5: notably, the way much policymaking in Brussels is done in Commission-sponsored expert groups dominated by econocrats and industry representatives.

Some commentators, like the *Brussels Sunshine* blog, argue that Members of the European Parliament (MEPs) are too close to the finance sector and that there is a need for 'a change in political culture and vision, away from the pre-crisis thinking that what is good for mega-banks is good for society' (2010). In 2010, the French Green MEP, Pascal Canfin, started a campaign to counter financial lobbying that seeks to influence EU policymaking (McCann 2010). According to

Canfin, unlike other industries such as environment or health, NGOs and other pressure groups that are concerned with finance issues are limited in number and influence, and therefore do not function as a countervailing force to large international banks and other financial institutions. This is corroborated in a very detailed report by the Alter-EU NGO which presents a breakdown of the nineteen finance sector-related active expert groups. Eight of the expert groups are classified as industry dominated because, as Alter-EU argues (Alter-EU 2009: 5–6), the Commission often breaks its own rules about the composition of expert groups designed to prevent any one group becoming dominant. Within the nineteen groups as a whole, the 229 industry experts outnumber the 150 civil servant members while the finance industry provides more than four times the combined number of experts from academia, consumer groups, and trade unions (Alter-EU 2009). The finance industry justifies this as the provision of specialist information and advice about technical issues such as derivatives or capital adequacy. In practice, MEPs and civil servants often have no alternative sources of (independent) expert advice on finance so that, by default, the industry's views and positions go unchallenged. These particular observations about finance sector lobbying are consistent with Coen's wider picture (2007) of the explosion of business lobbying in Brussels from the early 1990s.

The specific national context of the United Kingdom is different from that of the European Commission which has to reconcile diverse national positions and demands while defining some kind of supranational European project which adds value politically and legitimates Brussels. In the United Kingdom, the context is very different because here the government whole-heartedly sponsors the financial sector and only half-heartedly buys into transparency and account-ability. The finance sector became the national champion for successive Conser-vative and Labour governments largely by a process of elimination because other sectors like manufacturing were always manifestly unsuccessful or, like pharma-ceuticals, subject to reputational damage. UK national interests have long been perceived to be directly linked to the finance sector and, particularly after the 1980s deregulation, successive governments of the right and left have acknowl-edged the significance (economic and political) of the sector through words and actions, as outlined in Chapter 5. Yet, if the City of London has been in direct competition with New York for a share of burgeoning activities, there is no competition for transparency in the UK's disclosure of the political influence on the sector. Thus, lobbying in the United Kingdom is a much less tightly regulated activity and financial contributions to political parties are disclosed in a way which makes it easy to identify individuals but more difficult to identify groups and sectors. Successive Conservative and Labour governments have had difficulties about party funding which have produced scandals about sources of donations and allegations about bought peerages (the so-called 'cash for hon-ours') and other favours in return for donations and loans from those with business fortunes often made in the City, sometimes without paying their taxes in the United Kingdom (see for instance Moran 2011). Probably more significant was the easy access which City elites had to the New Labour Treasury under Gordon Brown, so that they were able, for example, able to get tax concessions such as the treatment of private equity partners rewards not as income but as capital gains taxed at a low rate. The obsequious relation of the Treasury to the City was then performed in several ways: before the crisis, New Labour recruited reforming but mainstream City figures, like Paul Myners, as junior Treasury ministers; and, after the crisis, New Labour allowed finance to draft and disseminate its defensive story in an official report with a foreword by Alastair Darling. Overall, the UK government's susceptibility to City influence undoubtedly increased under New Labour.

This sketch of the activities of financial lobbies in three key institutional settings is useful in helping us begin to understand the limits on reform in the wake of the 2007–8 crisis. But by itself it does not take us much beyond the description of three different jurisdictions and suspicion about the United States as, in Greg Palast's phrase (2002), 'the best democracy that money can buy'. The descriptions do not offer us a way of making analytical sense of what is going on because such analysis requires some explanation of why finance lobbying is (unusually) effective. These explanatory issues are approached in Simon Johnson's account of the role of Wall Street banking elites, before and after the crisis. Johnson uses the idea of a 'coup' to explain the paradox of limited regulatory reform and address the central issue of why finance lobbyists have an easier life than tobacco or pharma lobbyists. A coup is not only about the composition of committees but about the ability of the finance sector to 'amass a kind of cultural capital – a belief system' (Johnson 2009). As Johnson notes, the finance sector is just like tobacco, pharma, and defence in that it spends large amounts on lobbying and campaign finance, but the finance sector is different because it has much less need to 'buy favours' when 'Washington insiders already believed that large financial institutions and free-flowing capital markets were crucial to America's position in the world' (2009). In other words, Johnson is arguing that the return on lobbying expenditure is high for cultural and ideational reasons. In the next two sections of this chapter, we take this argument about cultural capital a couple of steps further and argue that effective lobbying depends on elite organization and storytelling.

6.3 Distributional coalitions: organizing financial elites

In this and the next section, we are concerned with the organization of financial elites and their narrative inventiveness. The argument is that distributional coalitions plus defensive stories initially allowed financial elites to escape the punishment and constraint which often befalls discredited elites who are responsible for costly debacles. This outcome was all the more remarkable given the asymmetry in the distribution of losses and gains across society in a financial debacle which involved the privatization of gains and the socialization of losses. The next and final section of this chapter considers how this was justified for outsiders by a finance sector story of self-importance and social contribution. Before turning to finance's story, this section takes up the immediate task of introducing the classical interest group and elite theorists who have reflected on the organizational conditions under which minority groups can articulate sectional projects and defend sectional autonomy against the economic interests of the majority within democratic systems of political competition.

For this specific purpose, Bourdieu's ideas about social capital, as invoked by Johnson and others, are less relevant than those of Mancur Olson on distributional coalitions and C. Wright Mills on (elite) vocabularies of motivation. If Olson's work from the 1970s or Wright Mills' from the 1950s is relevant, their work must be treated with caution because they presume or imagine a form of capitalism which is very different from present-day financialized capitalism. Writing at the end of the long post-war boom, Olson's economic idea of a distributional coalition highlights how small groups can gain by obstructing change and thereby imposing costs on a wider society, while Wright Mills' socio-political ideas about the power elite highlight how executive power can frustrate democracy at the same time as he draws on his earlier work about motive as a social category. Wright Mills in the 1950s and 1960s provides a left political analysis of managerial capitalism in the long boom after the Second World War when the Cold War was a political and economic project, as well as a military mission. Olson in the 1970s and 1980s provides a centre-right economic analysis of how, at the end of the long boom, sustained prosperity and stability entrenched interest groups who became obstacles to further economic growth. Neither Wright Mills nor Olson wrote about financial elites as a distinctive group such as the one that is so striking in and after the Great Complacence of the 2000s, when political and regulatory elites were particularly receptive to a narrative about the benefits of finance.

Olson was concerned with how rent seeking through distributional coalitions plays an important role in economic development where the distribution of income and wealth can become as important an issue as wealth creation and growth (Olson 1982: 44). Distributional coalitions comprise organized groups of special interests, their advisors, and lobbyists whose attempts at rent-seeking redistribution have the effect of reducing economic wealth. When powerful sectional groups are threatened with losses from reforms, they choose blocking tactics. The gains (or avoidance of loss) to that discrete group are far outweighed by social losses as sectionalism diverts effort from wealth creation to distribution of income and wealth. Olson provides several centre-right, pro-free market examples of this kind of diversion into distributive struggle, as with small groups of producers who resist free trade and obtain protection, or organized labour which resists technological change.

Writing after the oil crises at the end of the long boom, in the shadow of the Reagan and Thatcher experiments, Olson (1982) argues that political stability can foster distributional coalitions which effectively obstruct economic development, while opportunity created by crisis is one way in which powerful coalitions can be broken or marginalized. Subsequent supporters have developed Olson's (contestable) insight into a philosophy of history. Thus, Mokyr and Nye (2007: 2) argue that where governments act to create institutions that are effective counters to distributional coalitions, as in the case of the British industrial revolution, the conditions of economic growth can be established. Critics such as Cameron (1988) have riposted by questioning many of Olson's assumptions.

We do not have to take sides in this dispute because we are intrigued by the differences, not the similarities, between Olson's then and our now. A first key difference is that Olson's assumptions about a conservative sectional coalition standing in the way of market forces does not apply to the pro-market financial elites of the deregulatory and post-crisis era. In Olson's vision, producer and worker groups like farmers or labour unions would typically lobby to restrain free-market forces by promoting intervention, for example, through protectionist policies or prohibitions on technological change which might undermine their interests (see Lane 1995; Jones 1999 for examples). In the finance sector, the coalition is differently oriented towards maintaining market freedoms by broadly preventing anything (especially new interventions and regulatory change) that would constrain financial innovation, free movement of capital, and the ability to take risk to earn private profits, before dumping losses onto the state's balance sheet (which did not figure in Olson's economic universe).

The second key difference is that Olson supposed that the distributional coalition was an organizational form that was initially sustained by stable prosperity and then found its mission in blocking change. In the finance sector, loose coalitions seek to maintain the conditions for profitable bricolage which are the result of rapid changes that would otherwise stress the representative capacity of trade associations with corporate members or trade unions with individual members, who in the United Kingdom and the United States are in any case denied a corporatist negotiating role. Thus, in any of the high-income countries, banks and hedge funds will be divided on specific regulatory reform proposals, such as breaking up large banks or requiring higher capital ratios, according to sectional calculations about opportunities for bricolage around their business models. If multiple lines of division around sectionalism would make trade organizations ungovernable or dysfunctional, loose coalitions are well adapted to frustrating reform through narrative re-framing of the socio-economic issues with stories about the social value and contribution of the finance sector.

This takes us into a world of new financial elites who operate very differently from the US cotton farmers or the auto workers union. And the scale of their depredations is much larger because present-day finance is both the basis for extracting huge gains and for causing more extensive collateral social and economic damage because the distributional coalition around finance can undermine the macro economy by creating costly recession rather than slow down beneficial growth. However, Olson's distributional coalition insight remains relevant in several ways. It focuses attention on the asymmetrical distribution of concentrated benefits and widely distributed losses because the benefits of the growth in the finance sector were largely concentrated within the sector, while the costs of the bailout of the banking and other sectors have been spread very broadly across the population, including the substantial secondary effects that result from dealing with public expenditure deficits. We can also put to one side trade unions and other mass demons of the 1970s neo-liberal imaginary: finance is the new sector of the 2000s, whose elites have unprecedented opportunities both to enjoy large rents and cause exten-sive collateral social and economic damage and these intertwined develop-ments might be considered the major financial innovation of our times. The idea of coalition emphasizes the loose organization of disparate groups more committed to storytelling than negotiation with social partners, partly because the various fractions of finance can often agree on very little except a collective story about their self-importance and social contribution which justifies their collective activity and thereby prevents punishment and main-tains influence.

If we then turn to consider C. Wright Mills (1956), his theorization of the power elite is both much more subtle than anything in Olson but also appar-ently less relevant insofar as Wright Mills analyses how managerial capitalism undermines democracy . The focus is on a small number of individuals, 'the higher members' at the apex of the major political, military, and economic bureaucracies (1956: 271) who occupy 'the command posts' and 'give the orders' (1956: 272). In Mills' view, such elites were able to use their positions to pursue their own discretionary projects which, in the 1950s, included committing America to a Cold War sustained by the 'coincidence of eco-nomic, military and political power' (1956: 278). This exercise of managerial prerogative subverted democracy and undermined accountability. Or, more exactly, formal political democracy survived but there was in Cold War Amer-ica 'the decline of politics as genuine and public debate of alternative decisions' (1956: 162). All this is explicitly represented as a historically specific form of exercise of power because Mills explicitly identifies four previous 'epochs' when the power elites operated differently and, from this point of view, would presumably now recognize current financialized capitalism as a sixth and different epoch.

If so, it would have to be admitted that the exercise of power is different. As Chapters 3 and 4 demonstrate, the financial sector is not generally organized into a few major hierarchies or giant bureaucracies with a handful of executive seniors at the apex. The major investment banks and conglomerates employ thousands or tens of thousands but they interact with a multiplicity of smaller players like hedge funds and private equity partnerships which employ tens or hundreds and broadly depend on a favourable conjuncture for their profitable growth. The prevailing forms of fee-based remuneration and bonuses in the banks ensure that key individuals are incentivized to pursue personal gain through a variety of only semi-visible intermediary or financier activities (Folkman et al. 2007). If successful, the result is collective high performance by some giant firms, but this is not the same as the top-down giving of orders in pursuit of particular projects of corporate and wider significance. The finance sector also does not really have any super-ordinate project analogous to the Cold War that C. Wright Mills emphasizes. Moneymaking through bricolage, as outlined in Chapter 2, generally requires the establishment or maintenance of a largely deregulated, lightly taxed sector; yet subgroups would generally disagree on any specific framework proposal because it opened or closed various arbitrage possibilities for different intermediaries.

But these points are hardly decisive objections, if we remember that C. Wright Mills' view of power was structural but never reductionist when he argued that 'we cannot infer the direction of policy merely from the social origins and careers of the policy makers'. His famous 1956 book backs this position up with some discussion of 'social similarities and psychological affinities' amongst the groups with shared backgrounds who pursued the Cold War project. But there is an altogether more interesting discussion of related issues in Mills' brilliant 1940 *American Sociological Review* article which aims to establish that 'motive' is properly a sociological category linked to action not a psychological propensity. Here, motive is an 'answer to questions of social or lingual conduct' (Mills 1940: 904) which provides the basis not only for what an elite group might do but also the 'vocabularies' it uses to articulate and justify its interests. Motives are socially defined; they are not so much about individual needs and calculations as about social justifications of practice or ideology. By implication, an elite effectively exists only as and when it has produced a 'vocabulary' which under conditions of elite pluralism and mass democracy would need to be socially intelligible and acceptable to outsiders. Put another way, elites with shared (social) background and rotating positions need a motive which supplies an 'unquestioned' answer (Mills 1940: 907). All this is highly relevant to our financial elites (and also the political and policy elites that have been public promoters of the industry) because C. Wright Mills' idea about the vocabulary of motive adds a behavioural context to the story told by the industry.

What do we gain if we bring together Olson and C. Wright Mills with our earlier arguments in an attempt to understand this chapter's question about how present-day financial elites successfully prevented the introduction of any new financial order? To begin with, we can understand that the economic and social power of financial elites is primarily a domestic form of what Nye (2004) in international political economy has called soft power. Financial elites work mainly not by giving orders or coercing others but by co-opting others. Their position is of course greatly strengthened by their near monopoly of expertise on complex finance, illustrated by the way that the finance industry fills the places in the so-called expert groups of the European Commission because politicians have to address problems and regulatory reform can often be represented as a technical not a political problem. However, financial elites have seldom been represented as attractive role models. The deregulation of finance opened up the denigration of the greedy financier in a range of genres from popular movies like *Wall Street* in the 1980s through to sober business best sellers like Philip Augar's *The Greed Merchants* in the 2000s.

To counteract these stereotypes about individuals and groups, financial elites need a narrative about the economic importance and social contribution of the financial sector. If this is accepted by senior politicians, as we saw in Chapter 5, the interests of the financial sector become those of the nation and the role of political elites is to promote the competitiveness of their national sector and prevent clumsy re-regulation which will kill the goose that lays the golden eggs of tax revenues and other benefits. Elite politicians in many countries make speeches that rhetorically underscore their commitment to reforming finance and caging its private interests, but all this is effectively undermined if they accept the story of the contribution of finance whose political corollary is that any reform must be acceptable to finance.

Another implication is that we need to move beyond the long-established mainstream economic ideas about regulatory capture (Stigler 1971; Levine and Forrence 1990), which generally fuse simple utilitarian concepts of group interest with asymmetry arguments about how the political process of regulation is easily subverted or misdirected when small groups capture concentrated benefits and large groups pay thinly spread costs. The billions of campaign finance in the United States or the domination of key expert groups in the EU are certainly indicators of the significance (economic and political) of the finance sector, but they do not necessarily imply a cause–effect relation between US contributions and committee scrutiny or individual votes by elected politicians. Nor do they demonstrate any direct cause–effect relation between participation by expert finance and the collapse of regulation. This is not to argue that the key ministries and regulatory bodies have not been captured by those industries that are supposed to be the object of regulation in the public interest (indeed much evidence suggests that this is likely to be so, both in general as well as in the specific case of finance). However, regulation develops within broader frameworks of understanding, where narratives frame what is possible or necessary. On this basis, in any world that is not simply venal, the possibility of regulatory capture depends on a prior stage of regulatory closure through narrative means.

The next section of this chapter uses the UK case to show how financial elites went about the job of (re)telling their story about the contribution of finance in and after the crisis. Of course, this does not mean that there were no challenges to the narrative. Some of the most interesting developments post-crisis have been the way that several elite policy figures have questioned finance and made the stories more complex, as we explore in Chapter 7. However, the often controversial (and sometimes rather academic) pronouncements of figures like Adair Turner of the, now marginalized, FSA or Andrew Haldane of the Bank of England are seemingly of more interest to the commentariat than to political elites. Moreover, the potency of these unsettling, questioning stories has been diluted by a new political vocabulary of deficit reduction which indicts previous governments that have been too profligate and built up public debt to an excessive level, and now require large-scale expenditure cuts to placate the bond markets. Through some strange shift, the finance sector ceases to be the villain and the markets become the judge of government action with coercive power in reserve.

6.4 Going for closure: the Bischoff, Wigley, and Walker reports

This section explores case material on narrative closure from the United Kingdom. If the United States is the jurisdiction where lobbying activity is most extravagantly funded, the United Kingdom is the jurisdiction where narratives about the social contribution of finance are most highly developed as the means through which finance has acquired an extraordinary hegemony over public policy discourse as it closes down alternatives. The crisis of 2007–8 was immediately disorienting for most critics and would-be reformers of finance because they needed a new story about what had gone wrong, and therefore what should now be done, and all this would take a couple of years or more. In the meanwhile, in 2008–9, the defenders of finance had one great advantage as they could try to head off reform by repeating and updating their pre-crisis story about the social contribution of finance which had been used previously to open the space of light-touch regulation. As we shall see also, this attempt at closure was not successful.

After 2007, the finance sector used the old story for new defensive purposes through the Bischoff and Wigley reports, which brought together city elites and co-opted two key political figures. The first report was co-chaired by Win Bischoff, former chairman of Citigroup, and Alastair Darling, as Chancellor of the Exchequer. The second report was commissioned by Boris Johnson as Mayor of London from a group headed by Bob Wigley, European chair of Merrill Lynch. The two reports had been commissioned before the crisis and were ostensibly neither about the causes of crisis nor about the solution of re-regulation. Bischoff's remit was 'to examine medium to long term challenges to London's continued competitiveness in international financial markets' (HM Treasury 2009b), while the Wigley Report was a 'review of the competitiveness of London's financial centre'. This provided the financial establishment with the very timely opportunity for a two-step analysis. In a first step, the reports updated the old story by recounting the contribution of financial services to the national economy; then, in a second step, the City identified the conditions necessary to maintain this valuable activity which incidentally included some-thing like the regulatory status quo.

This syllogism was powerful because the political classes on both front benches had a bad case of Stockholm syndrome – the syndrome by which those captured identify emotionally with their captors. After the crisis of 2007–8, the Bischoff and Wigley reports encouraged their continuing identi-fication with their captors. This was manifest in the processes of *buy-in* and *copy-out*. First, leading politicians explicitly bought into the syllogism about the social value of finance and made a commitment to nurture the sector. In his foreword to the Bischoff Report, the Chancellor of the Exchequer writes that 'financial services are critical to the UK's future' (Bischoff 2009). In a press release accompanying the Wigley Report, the Mayor of London says 'Bob's team have identified what needs to be done and I will pull out all the stops to protect London's position as the world's premier financial centre' (Mayor of London 2008). Second, the social value claims from the Bischoff Report are copied out and used as a framing device in other official reports, especially the July 2009 White Paper on *Reforming Financial Markets* (HM Treasury 2009a). In its first chapter, the White Paper begins by reviewing not the causes of crisis but 'the importance of financial services and markets to the UK Economy and the pre-eminence of the UK as a global financial centre' (Bischoff 2009: 17). Claims and evidence from Bischoff are simply copied out and dropped into the text of the White Paper, which reproduces the story and, unsurprisingly, ends by proposing nothing radical.

The White Paper was an example of what we call closure: that is, it operates by framing, and narrowing, the political world of possible interventions. The White

Paper is important because its slipshod copying out of Bischoff's claims indicates that senior civil servants have been co-opted, just like elected politicians, through the narrative of the City as the goose that lays the golden eggs. We showed in Chapter 5 that the claims in Bischoff and Wigley about the social benefits of finance were highly contestable. But what is extraordinarily revealing about both these reports is that, despite the mounting evidence from the crisis that the financial sector was hugely dysfunctional for the economy, there was no internal dissent (e.g. in the form of a minority report). This, as we show below, was because the distributional coalition monopolized the speaking and writing parts which together produced the two reports as a kind of performance. Many groups in the wider society – from consumers to producers – have an interest in the operations of wholesale finance both in itself and because it connects with the availability of retail finance. But none of these other interested non-City groups were consulted in the information-gathering, problem-defining phase before Bischoff and Wigley told their story about (the benefits of) finance and drew their policy implications. The membership of these inquiries contained no non-financial businesses and their trade associations; no trade unions (despite the unionization of retail finance workers); no NGOs to represent consumers or press social justice agendas; no mainstream economists or heterodox intellectuals; and very few politicians or civil servants.

The exclusion of other voices and the privileging of finance can be empirically demonstrated in several ways if we consider the membership of groups, the composition of secretariats, and the witnesses called. The most accurate statement in the Bischoff Report was its subtitle: 'a report from UK based financial services leaders to the Government'. The working group that produced the Report had twenty-one members whose biographies we have analysed. Altogether, the group had 662 years of work experience which are classified in the pie chart in Figure 6.1. Taken together, finance and parafinance support services accounted for 75 per cent of all the years of work experience, with banking and fund management alone accounting for 38 per cent of those years of work experience. This calculation understates the influence of finance if we remember, for example, that the CBI (Confederation of British Industry) is represented by Richard Lambert, an ex-journalist with a thirty-year career in 'media' which was actually at the *Financial Times*, the UK's national business and finance newspaper.

The secretariat and research arrangements are even more striking, because of course it is at this level that the concerns and content of any report will be shaped. The details of Bischoff (2009) are especially illuminating. This was, after all, an officially published report, crown copyrighted, and available on the Treasury web site. That might lead readers to expect a report that was drafted by civil servants. In fact the 'secretariat' and the 'sherpas' (to use Bischoff's language) were overwhelmingly drawn from the distributional coalition. The

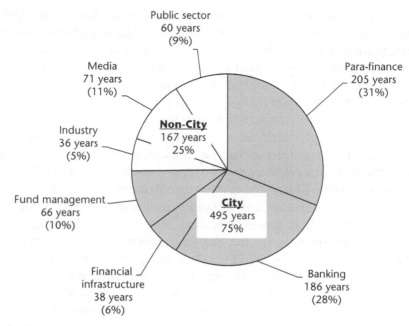

Figure 6.1. An analysis of the Bischoff Report

Note: Number of panelists: 21; total number of years' experience: 662; average number of years' experience: 32.

Source: Publicly available information on the members of the Bischoff Working Group.

eight-strong secretariat contained just one civil servant and four employees from Citi plus three from the City of London Corporation, the City's 'local authority' which has traditionally acted a booster for finance. The Citi contingent was led by Alan Houmann, Director of European Governmental Affairs, and the City of London by Paul Sizeland, Director of Economic Development. So, the Bischoff Report was researched and written by the functionaries of finance PR and lobbying who have made careers out of telling stories about the beneficial effects of the activities of firms in the financial sector.

Unlike Bischoff, the Wigley inquiry did call witnesses, but the range of witnesses only testifies again to the deficit of democracy. Wigley's witnesses were overwhelmingly drawn from the same distributive coalition that provided the working-group members and secretariats. These question and answer sessions were a matter of finance speaking to finance. Altogether, Wigley called seventy-one witnesses whose expertise we have classified. Figure 6.2 illustrates the quite striking results: of the seventy-one witnesses, some forty-nine came directly from finance and a further fifteen came from consultancy activities which generally have revenue connections to finance. Quite remarkably, the public sector provided just one witness: presumably the knowledge and expertise of HM Treasury or Department of Business Enterprise Regulatory Reform (as it was then known) were irrelevant to the story that Wigley told about the importance of defending this valuable activity.

The United Kingdom has become a very peculiar place where the main employers' organization, the CBI (supposedly a Confederation of British *Industry*), is headed by a retired financial journalist and where finance company lobbyists can include authorship of Treasury reports on their CVs. However, our democracy once worked very differently in scrutinizing the City. We can see this if we compare Bischoff and Wigley with earlier major reports into the operations of the City, the choice of financial policies and the role of finance in sustaining business and economic progress. Bischoff and Wigley are the latest in a long line of such exercises: they stretch back to the Wilson Committee into the Functioning of Financial Institutions (1980), the Radcliffe Committee on the Working of the Monetary System (1959), and the Macmillan Committee on Finance and Industry (1931). Several key points of difference stand out if we benchmark Bischoff and Wigley against the more inclusive practice of representation and the pluralist notion of the report in these earlier classic inquiries. In terms of representation, committee members in pre-1979 inquiries were a diverse group with academics, elected politicians, trade unionists, and industrial employers substantially represented. The standard practice was then to initiate and sustain debate by inviting written submissions and hearing evidence from witnesses who represented a broad range of interested groups.

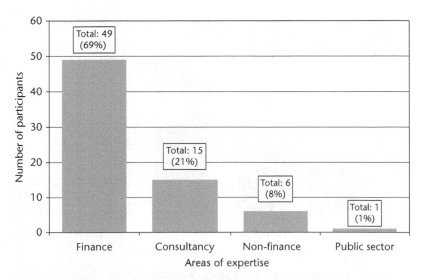

Figure 6.2. The Wigley Report – an analysis of the expertise of the witnesses

Note: Total number of witnesses: 71.

Source: London: Winning in a changing world – interviewees and workshop participants list.

If we consider the Wilson Committee, for example, it received 352 written submissions which are analysed in Figure 6.3. Some 173 submissions, almost exactly half, came from individuals who were not directly speaking for organizations; as for the written submissions from organizations, the eighty-one written submissions from non-financial organizations actually outnumbered the sixty-nine submissions from financial institutions. The Wilson Committee's membership, like its written submissions or oral hearings, represented a particular practice of politics. Harold Wilson's committee on the City, just like his Labour Party, included and balanced different points of view which were performed at every stage in the inquiry; by way of contrast, Bischoff and Wigley develop and push one view point to the exclusion of all others.

If we consider final reports, practice again changes quite fundamentally because the pre-1979 reports are often messy, inconclusive, and pluralist. Public inquiry before Thatcherism was legitimately a forum for intellectual debate and political differences, not a Bischoff-style attempt to impose a narrative wrap and pitch one story intended to compel belief and justify (pre-existing) policy choices. This is most clear in the case of the Macmillan Committee which discovered the 'Macmillan gap' in funding for medium-sized companies through a vigorous contest of views. The Macmillan Committee members included heavyweights such as the eminent economist John Maynard Keynes and Ernest Bevin, the outstanding trade union leader of his generation. Moreover, the views expressed in written submissions and oral

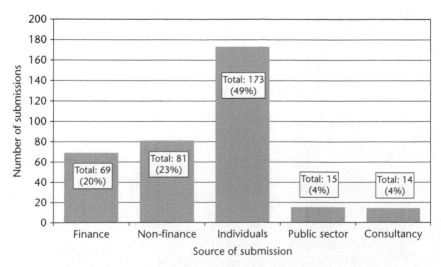

Figure 6.3. The Wilson Committee – analysis of submissions

Note: Total number of submissions: 352.

Source: Committee to Review the Functioning of Financial Institutions (Report – Appendix 1: Organizations and individuals who submitted evidence).

testimony ranged all the way from Governor Norman's inarticulate Bank of England orthodoxy to Major Douglas' cranky Social Credit. And, all this was reflected in the final 276-page report whose structure is analysed in Figure 6.4. This exhibit shows that dissent, reservation, and addenda to the majority report accounted for one-third of the pages in the full report. Thatcher and Blair would no doubt have regarded this is a hopeless failure but the Macmillan Report represents a healthier pluralist outcome than the Bischoff and Wigley reports.

If we return to the current period, then perhaps the most reassuring part of the attempt at closure after the immediate crisis response in 2008 was that it did not succeed: in a few months from summer 2009 it was apparent that it was unravelling. One key event here was the commissioning of a career banker Sir David Walker to produce an official report on how improvements in corporate governance and remuneration within the finance sector could miti-gate risk taking by banks and bankers. Walker's interim report published in July 2009 and his final report published in November of the same year represented more of the same kind of closure, extended now to an attempt to capture the reform agenda. The Walker Report is vague on its working methods, merely listing two categories of contributors: those contributing analyses to the Review and those who 'participated' either 'by submitting formal reports or in informal discussions' (Walker 2009: 108). The list of the first is much shorter than the second; it is plain that these contributions were

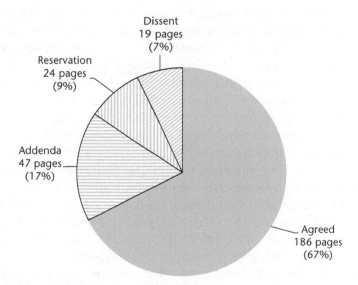

Figure 6.4. An analysis of the Macmillan Report
Note: Length of the Report: 276 pages.
Source: Committee on Finance and Industry (Report).

the most weighty, and the list is entirely dominated by corporate contributors, mostly from the financial services sector.

Unsurprisingly, given the range of witnesses, and the fact that the author of the report is steeped in the City's traditional view of the world, the Walker Report made only the most anodyne proposals for reform, either of governing structures or remuneration policies at the top. Thus the failure of governance to prevent risk taking was met by demands for more governance with stronger non-executives and risk committees. On pay, there were half-hearted proposals to identify the number of high earners in each bank with Walker refusing to contemplate a more open regime of pay disclosure on the grounds that transparency would drive talent abroad.

However, letting a career banker define the agenda of banking (governance) reform was a provocative step too far, especially when that same banker had previously produced an anodyne report on private equity at a time when the sector was under intense public scrutiny (D. Walker 2007). Thus, the timidity of Walker's proposals were noted by many commentators on publication of his interim report which was, as the *Financial Times* observed, 'widely seen as tamer than some had feared' (Jenkins and Parker 2009). By the time the final report was published in autumn 2009, the *Guardian* was able to make a story out of the considered and dismissive comments of various trade unions, civil society groups, and opposition politicians whose position on Walker's proposed reforms was summed up in (Liberal Democrat) politician Vince Cable's comment about 'nothing like enough' (Allen 2009). The interim report appeared in summer 2009 at a moment when parts of the City narrative had, as we have seen earlier in this book, began to unravel under three related sets of pressures: first, the impact of critiques of the role of a large financial sector from econocrats, like Haldane and King at the Bank of England; second, the impact, as we saw earlier in this chapter, of turf struggles between regulatory agencies; and, third the impact of electoral competition in the general election campaign of 2010, as banking became (briefly) the object of attention once more.

This third impact may yet prove critical. The unprecedented and unexpected outcome of the UK General Election of May 2010 was that competing views of how banking should be reformed were now embedded within the Conservative/Liberal Democratic coalition for control over policy. The creation of the 'Independent Commission on Banking' was the coalition's solution to the problem of how to cope with profound differences about how far reform should include major structural change in the banking industry itself, and the shaping of the terms of reference and the membership was plainly the result of some hard bargaining, notably between the (Conservative) Chancellor, George Osborne, and the (Liberal Democrat) Business Secretary, Vince Cable (HM Treasury 2010). The initial signs are that the struggle so far has been won by those committed to a mainstream economics agenda of breaking up some of the, mostly publicly owned, banks to create more competition on the High Street. The Banking Commission is headed by Sir John Vickers and includes Clare Spottiswoode; both made their public careers implementing Thatcherite privatization with added market competition. The Commission does also contain some independent voices, including *Financial Times* columnist Martin Wolf. Regardless of outcome, the existence of the Banking Commission shows that closure of agenda and restriction of speaking parts has not fully succeeded. If it has failed, that is, at least partly, because other elite sections would not go along with closure and attempts at alternative narratives have emerged. By summer 2009, some econocrats had begun to think heretical thoughts about the role of banks in the UK economic system, and in the next chapter we will consider how these econocrats tried to assemble some intellectually defensible account of banking regulation from the ruins of the crisis of 2007–8.

7

The Limits of Expertise: The United Kingdom as an Unhappy Family

> *A family with the wrong members in control – that, perhaps, is as near as one can come to describing England in a phrase.* (George Orwell, *The Lion and the Unicorn*, 1941)
>
> *What happened was that I volunteered to serve as UKFI non-exec, for obvious reasons, because I think this is the worst financial crisis we will ever face and, if we blow it, we are going to lose a generation of prosperity, and I have had a lot of experience of prior banking crises and downturns. What happened was Philip Hampton went to RBS, and I was with my wife on a brief holiday in Malta and I got a phone call, saying, 'Will you do this?' and of course I said yes.* (Glenn Moreno on becoming chair of UKFI in 2009)

If democratic politicians were central to crisis management in 2008, they were marginalized once again after the crisis by various kinds of technocrats. The failure to sustain financial reform in the succeeding couple of years is therefore about the limits of expertise and technocracy and that, in turn, requires a chapter which engages with the specifics of a major national case because post-crisis reform will be won or lost at the national level. International reform of finance will certainly be ineffective when the G7 and G20 or Basel Committee are fora for national governments to pursue divergent national agendas, while the EU's deficit of democracy opens Brussels to the industry lobbyists. At the national level, the most interesting cases are the United Kingdom and the United States because they contain the two major international financial centres which would (both) have to be curbed if reform is to be effective. And, if we are interested in the role of technocratic policy elites in sponsoring financial reform, the United Kingdom is the more interesting case for historical reasons.

In an earlier period, self-confident elite figures, like Beveridge and Keynes, played a major role in British twentieth-century social and economic reform.

More than a generation ago, Fred Hirsch (1976) was apprehensive about whether such altruistic policy elites would survive in a marketized world. It is therefore immediately reassuring to find that in 2010 the United Kingdom still has elite reformers like Mervyn King, Andrew Haldane, or Adair Turner in positions of responsibility at the Bank of England and the Financial Services Authority (FSA). But this chapter argues that the reform outcomes are so far disappointing because the technocratic legatees of John Maynard Keynes and William Beveridge have severed their predecessors' connection with social democratic values and popular politics which gave them traction. We do not expect Haldane to write Liberal or Labour party manifestos as Keynes or Tawney did, nor would we expect Turner to write a report that sells more than 600,000 copies as the Beveridge report of 1942 did. But the current complete disconnect between the technocrats and politics disempowers reform.

Of course, national cases of failed reform raise issues about specifics and the differences between cases. In statistics or popular science writing (Diamond 2005), such differences are covered by the so-called Anna Karenina principle that all instances of failure are unique because, as Tolstoy observed, every unhappy family is unhappy in its own way. But the family metaphor reminds us of that other famous quote by George Orwell: how England is a family with the wrong members in control. From this point of view, the limited scope of financial reform (so far) in the United Kingdom is symptomatic of the limited and diminished power of altruistic technocratic policy elites to drive substantial reforms here and, we guess, in other high-income capitalist countries. The problem is not that the supply of altruism is limited but that the reforming altruists are not in control.

The first two sections of this chapter illustrate aspects of this disappointment. Part of the problem is that elites are divided by crisis. Conservative policy elites inside the bureaucracies are often well placed to frustrate post-crisis reform by mobilizing established elite network contacts and reusing familiar organizational devices and tropes. Section 7.1 illustrates this problem by considering how the UK Treasury neutralized bank nationalization after it could not be avoided; the opening quote from Glenn Moreno shows how the Treasury did so by drawing on a tight network of safe City figures to run the key management agency at arms length. Another part of the problem is that reforming policy elites are themselves often divided, inevitably slowed by the obligation to think through complex problems and increasingly by a kind of self-denying ordinance: they operate in a technical frame without the political allies who could lead a popular coalition for reform to challenge the distributional coalition. Section 7.2 illustrates these dilemmas by considering the limited consequences of pro-reform interventions by radicalized elite technocrats like King, Haldane, and Turner.

But there is also a more fundamental and interconnected problem about the limits of the technocratic imaginary which helps explain the disconnect from politics. Why do these would-be financial reformers make no connection with politics in the broad sense of the democratic competition to formulate policy alternatives? Our argument is that this is because they accept a definition of their role as experts who have little to say to anybody outside the metropolitan bubble (and its media and intellectual followers). And that is not a matter of social distance but of political and economic values. The current generation of policy elites are no more remote from the masses than Beveridge and Keynes, who both came from a lost Edwardian world and always carried with them what Keynes' biographer, Roy Harrod, called 'the presuppositions of Harvey Road' (1951: 192–3) after the upper middle class household with servants in Cambridge where Keynes was brought up. King and Haldane could not be further from Harvey Road: the former the product of Wolverhampton Grammar School, the latter the meritocratic product of the universities of Sheffield and Warwick.

However, the current generation of elite reformers have lost sight of the old Beveridgean and Keynesian vision which connected apparently technical problems like social insurance with capitalism's failure to provide economic security for the politically enfranchised majority (Cutler et al. 1986; Williams and Williams 1987). The separation of financial reform as an expert sphere for technocrats in the present-day imaginary takes us into an engineering world where an arrow indicates a defective part within systems that can be mapped and redesigned for greater safety. The third and fourth sections of this chapter expose the limits of the technocratic imaginary by presenting our own alternative and more radical analysis of finance and the problems of the British economy. Section 7.3 makes the argument about how the United Kingdom has the wrong kind of finance because the circuits from finance encourage asset price inflation not productive transformation; it also observes that this much is admitted by radical policy elite critics of British banking like Turner. This is complemented by Section 7.4's analysis of the unsustainable British national business model which under successive Conservative and Labour governments relied on public sector job creation, especially for women and in the ex-industrial regions. The problem of jobless growth does not figure in current expert discussion of financial reform because it implies deep-seated, structural problems which require us to make a connection between radical reform of finance and fixing a broken national business model.

This argument about the irrelevance of experts will seem paradoxical to present-day social scientists who are interested in 'knowledge', preoccupied by the relation between knowledge and power and infatuated with experts. Moreover, the political patter of the EU and others about a knowledge-based society fits with the emphasis on reflexivity in authors like Giddens (1991, 1993).

Late Foucauldian analysis of capillary power leads to Miller and Rose's argument about 'liberal governmentality' and technologies which produce docile subjects (Miller and Rose 1990; Lemke 2001; Rose and Miller 2008). Actor Network Theory, influenced by science and technology studies, envisages a world largely made of expertise, while analysts of performativity celebrate the capacity of formal knowledge to format the world. The more free-form work of authors like Timothy Mitchell on the 'rule of experts' (2002) opened up new and related perspectives on the British imperial project. While we recognize the contribution of these approaches, one of the lessons of the recent events is that there are limits on knowledge and expertise both beforehand in foreseeing crisis and afterwards in managing crisis and reform. Hence, our argument for a different framing of the problem as an elite debacle, as well as much more radical thought about solutions which connect unsafe finance with larger capitalist failures.

7.1 Neutralizing bank nationalization: bureaucrats and City networks

The first problem of radical policy elites is that many bureaucracies nurture a different kind of conservative expertise which is often very effective at blocking reform. This is historically the case with the British Treasury mandarins who played a major role in frustrating the left's radical proposals for public works in the 1920s and 1930s or again in blocking policies of devaluation plus planning in the 1960s. The Treasury was much more tolerant of Mrs Thatcher's right-wing radicalism after 1979 because it destroyed primitive forms of British collectivism and simplified the tasks of economic management. Thus, in the period of the great complacence, the Treasury under Gordon Brown could act as a kind of right-wing, neo-liberal think tank within a complacent set of assumptions about how capitalism had solved its big problems. But, after the crisis of autumn 2008, the Treasury had to revert to its historic mission of blocking radicalism, and more especially blocking policies which might open the way for new democratic priorities in finance and/or increased scrutiny of elite privileges. The blocking challenge of 2008 was nevertheless new and different: in autumn 2008, the Treasury and the Bank of England had no alternative but to sanction bank nationalization, something that would have been unthinkable before the crisis. Therefore, after 2008, the challenge was to neutralize a policy that had already been adopted but which had possibly radical implications. This section explains how the Treasury ensured that nationalization would make no difference.

The Treasury rose to this new challenge as arguably the most successful young civil servant of his generation, John Kingman, acted in the spirit of earlier Treasury mandarins and the establishment caste from which he came. (His father, Sir John Kingman, was a distinguished Oxbridge mathematician turned University of Bristol Vice Chancellor; his mother, Valerie Cromwell, was Director of the History of Parliament.) Under John Kingman's direction, the old constitutional mystifications and the shareholder value trope were together deployed to ensure it was to be business as usual in newly nationalized banks. All this was especially important in wasting the crucial year of opportunity between the downfall of Lehman Brothers in September 2008 and the summer of 2009, when popular hostility to bankers was strong. Kingman's initiative deflected and dissipated the impetus for banking reform which could have been pressed by instructing the nationalized banks to do things differently. Under Treasury auspices, the interim result was a timid British government White Paper on financial reform published in July 2009 which promised to change very little, and a Banking Act which, in April 2010, enacted more or less exactly the timid original proposals (Froud et al. 2010*b*).

Extreme intervention to prop up the banking system resulted in *faute de mieux* nationalization of banks like Northern Rock and Royal Bank of Scotland, which passed into public ownership, just as the state also acquired a substantial minority stake in Lloyds TSB. Public ownership is not of course democratic control, but it did represent a democratic threat to elite power. A major part of the banking system was now state owned and controlled so that elected politicians could, in principle, always ask what state-owned banks were doing about lending to business or executive pay and instruct them to do something different. At this point the fusion and interpenetration of elites became important. The challenge of democracy was headed off by a few key figures at the Treasury: in addition to Kingman (who later left to work for Rothschild), Paul Myners the ex-fund manager who had been brought in by Labour as a junior Treasury minister played a key role.

Their key institutional creation was United Kingdom Financial Investments (UKFI), a new holding company for government majority and minority stakes in banks, where City grandees in the chairman role worked alongside Kingman as founding chief executive. The creation of UKFI was a critical institutional move in sheltering the operations of the publicly owned institutions from democratic control. But this kind of social defence by closing elite ranks requires a narrative justification to motivate anti-democratic practice. In the case of UKFI, this was provided by combining an old constitutional mystification – about the importance of preserving operational autonomy by 'arm's-length' control – with newer tropes about shareholder value. The Treasury's mobilization of both old tropes and elite City personnel has ensured that bank nationalization was a policy reversal that delivered more of the same.

The paroxysm of crisis required an improvised policy response which, as we have noted, worked through high democratic politics and involved Chancellor and Prime Minister in nationalizing Northern Rock and managing the systemic crisis of 2008. Afterwards, there was a return to something more like normal politics, which was an opportunity for figures at the Treasury like Kingman, to create (and manage through) the new post-crisis agency of UKFI. The principle of non-interference by 'politics' in banking matters was at this point re-established by inserting old tropes and memes into UKFI's mission, and by recruiting senior City figures with non-executive experience of delivering shareholder value. From November 2008, UKFI was the holding company responsible for managing the government owned UK banks and government minority stakes in banks. UKFI thus became the single-most important institution in the public sector concerned with managing the aftermath of the crisis. The organization is marked by three particularly striking features: its view of its relationship with the state, its sociology, and its own definition of its mission.

The position of UKFI is ambiguous because it is a creature of the Treasury but claims to operate at arms length from the government. It began life by occupying a small number of offices in the Treasury building, and its operational budget was negotiated with the Treasury. But, from the very beginning, Kingman's message as chief executive was that UKFI operates at 'arm's-length' from the government. That was the theme of an op ed in the *Financial Times* placed by Kingman and Philip Hampton, UKFI's chairman, early in its life, and again in Kingman's own account to the Treasury Select Committee of the relationship between the government and UKFI (Hampton and Kingman 2008; Treasury Select Committee 2008). The new agency is thus inserted into an old pattern of institutional arrangements between agencies and the democratic state in Britain. As Flinders' study shows (2008), the doctrine of the 'arm's-length' relationship has been a central feature of constitutional rhetoric in Britain and a key device insulating the workings of agencies with delegated functions from accountability pressures of the democratic state.

The 'arm's-length' position of UKFI is thus not a constitutional oddity; it fits an established constitutional tradition designed to separate key social and economic functions from the direct control of democratic institutions. And it has proved very capable of maintaining that distance. In 2010, the new coalition government ignited a highly publicized 'bonfire of the quangos' whose public rationale was to bring control over a range of functions back within the reach of Ministers accountable to Parliament. UKFI conspicuously escaped that bonfire; indeed, as we shall see later, it has increased the length of the arm distancing it from ministerial control. Thus, from its foundation, UKFI has sought to reassert the established undemocratic pattern of financial government which was characteristic of the longer history of the City, and which was reinforced by the post-1979 settlement.

The constitutional cliché about arm's-length control was performed sociologically by the way UKFI was from the beginning closely integrated with elite networks and institutions in the City. The way in which the organization was put together meant that established mechanisms of search, advertisement, and selection were sidestepped. The first two chairmen of UKFI were both retired City grandees who had subsequently made reputations as City-friendly non-executives of major public companies. Before he departed to chair RBS (one of the banks under partial state ownership), the first chair of UKFI was Sir Philip Hampton, an ex-finance director of Lloyds Bank turned non-executive chair of Sainsbury. He was succeeded by Glen Moreno, an investment banker who had later become chief executive of Fidelity International and then retired to become non-executive chair of Pearson, the publishing conglomerate. The opening quote of this chapter gives Moreno's own account of his recruitment and that account illustrates well how, in the press of crisis, the Treasury turned instinctively to the tiny elite networks of the City with which it had established connections.

Moreno's seat was subsequently taken by Sir David Cooksey, appointed in August 2009 at the same time as John Kingman announced his intended departure. The Oxford graduate engineer, considered an outsider in banking circles, is nevertheless a well-known name in the City: his Advent Venture Partners, established back in 1981 and a strong investor in life sciences and technology, is one of the first private equity houses in Europe. The UKFI board serving under him, on the other hand, consists mainly of insiders: with the exception of the Treasury representative, the four remaining members have spent together 110 years of employment in blue chip banks and fund management corporations from both sides of the Atlantic, with CVs that include stints at Citigroup, Merrill Lynch, Barclays, and Warburg.

The doctrine of the arm's-length relationship and the close integration into City networks then fused with the tropes of shareholder value to close-off the possibility of any radical answer to the question of what should be done with the holdings acquired in the crisis of 2007–8, and how they should be managed in the meantime. The nationalization of the banks created a situation that could be operated by Kingman and Moreno, provided nationalization was conceived as an interim stage governed by one simple principle: the taxpayer is a shareholder in failed banks which must be first managed and then sold off in a way that maximizes shareholder value. As UKFI elaborated its role and mandate, it increasingly offered, not so much the nationalization of the banks but the privatization of the Treasury as a new kind of fund manager. The Framework Document, which sets out the rules of engagement for the organization, is crystal clear:

> the Company should . . . develop and execute an investment strategy for disposing of the investments in an orderly and active way through sale, redemption, buy-back or other means within the context of an overarching objective of protecting and creating value for the taxpayer as shareholder. (UKFI 2009: 13)

UKFI thus acquired the identity of an engaged, responsible, large institutional investor whose relations with company management are governed by its investment objectives. There was to be no interference with day-by-day management decisions or second-guessing of business strategy. But UKFI, as engaged investor, does monitor pay for performance and meets with senior management to check on progress with value creation. The way this works is well illustrated by the controversy in the summer of 2009 over the remuneration package of Stephen Hester, chief executive of Royal Bank of Scotland, a package that attracted widespread critical comment because it offered huge rewards. But, for UKFI, this was acceptable because the long-term incentive in the form of a £6.9 million payout was conditional upon a doubling of share price. More generally, to check on progress, UKFI organizes a round of meetings with the management of the companies in which it holds investments: in the months between March and July 2009, for instance, it held over fifty investor meetings. UKFI is thus an active institutional investor which has the banks by the scruff of the neck and has the opportunity to energetically shake them to extract every last copper of value for the taxpayer as shareholder.

The creation of UKFI has thus solved the problem of managing the state's ownership of large parts of the banking system in a way that insulates ownership from democratic politics and allows the doctrine of shareholder value to remain supreme (without, of course, any recognition that shareholder value is partly what got us into this mess). Protecting the wider banking system from the disturbances of democratic political debate has, nevertheless, continued to be a tricky business, as developments in 2009–10 showed. In a prolonged general election campaign lasting for a year before the actual election in May 2010, issues of reward and control in the banking system were appropriated as instruments in the partisan battle. And just as the democratic scrutiny of the conditions that had given rise to the collapse largely focused on substantively marginal but symbolically powerful issues (for instance, Sir Fred Goodwin's severance package at Royal Bank of Scotland), so the attentions of politicians now largely focused on marginal but symbolically useful issues again, especially those around staff bonuses and profits.

Although bonuses go to the heart of some structural aspects of the way the banking markets operated in the run up to the crisis, in the party political struggle they performed an essentially symbolic function: that is, bonuses left the structural conditions of the industry untouched but provided material for populist banker bashing, while having the incidental advantage of raising attractive headline sums for the exchequer. Chancellor Darling's one-off levy on bonuses had by September 2010 raised over £3.5billion, five times more than originally estimated (Jetuah 2010). In his June emergency budget, the new coalition chancellor George Osborne attempted to sugar the pill of spending cuts with a new levy on bank balance sheets – a levy that was confirmed as a permanent feature in the announcements accompanying the historically unprecedented cuts in the Comprehensive Spending Review (Hoban 2010).

These measures view the banking industry opportunistically, as a resource to be raided to provide populist headlines, to drum up support for difficult spending decisions, and as a source of some supplementary funds to (marginally) moderate the depth of cuts. But they do little to tackle the structural issues behind the crash. The reforms of the regulatory system announced by the new coalition government are fundamentally a product of a process which we have described in earlier chapters: the battles over turf between, notably, the Bank of England and the FSA – a battle decisively won by the former.

The wider question of the structural reform of banking has, meanwhile, become entangled with the politics of coalition formation in the wake of the May 2010 general election which resulted in a Conservative–Liberal Democratic partnership that includes senior politicians who had earlier used very different rhetoric about bankers and banking. The most outspoken critic of the banks in the new Cabinet was Vince Cable, the Liberal Democrats' economic spokesman, who became business secretary in the coalition government; significantly, George Osborne, the Conservatives' Treasury spokesman, is now Chancellor and effectively the minister for economics and finance. It is clear the Treasury, the original institutional author of the view that banking policy needs to be protected from democratic politics, and the organization that did so much to shape the philosophy and operating principles of UKFI, is the dominant institution. The cabinet committee concerned with banking is chaired by Osborne, not the more radically inclined Cable. Moreover, the question of separating retail and investment banking – a key Liberal Democrat manifesto proposal – has, as outlined in Chapter 6, been delegated to an independent commission, chaired by Sir John Vickers, former head of the Office of Fair Trading, with instructions not to report until September 2011. In short, the issue of structural reform of the banking system has been buried.

Meanwhile, UKFI pursues with even more determination a strategy shaped by the desire to minimize democratic control over its workings and maximize its capacity to deliver value for the shareholder (HM Government) out of the banks whose ownership it inherited. Symbolically, UKFI has now moved physically out of the Treasury into the City to emphasize the original 'arm's length' operating philosophy. UKFI's second Annual Report repeats emphatically the ownership philosophy which animated it at foundation. In its chairman's words:

> We have also worked with all our companies in the active, engaged shareholder role which we were created to fulfill. Our interactions include work to help

improve governance, and to help ensure the banks are devising and implementing strategies that build shareholder value for the taxpayer. We have emphasised the importance of a robust approach to risk, and we have agreed pay structures and levels which are fair and appropriate whilst allowing the companies to attract and retain staff of the calibre necessary to protect and build the value of the taxpayer's investment. (UKFI 2010: 7)

The remit of UKFI thus continues to be, in its own words:

to manage these shareholdings commercially to create and protect value for the taxpayer as shareholder and provider of financial support, with due regard to financial stability and competition, and to devise and execute a strategy for disposing of the Government's investments in an orderly and active way over time. (UKFI 2010: 10)

The Treasury through UKFI has thus solved a major potential problem created for financial elites by the crisis: how to manage the huge state holdings in the banking system in a way that protected management from democratic oversight. The problem has been solved by weaving together two stories – one about the constitution, the other about shareholder value. UKFI is the institutional incarnation of this success in storytelling. Managing a second potential problem – the possibility that the crisis might provoke major public intervention in bank regulation and in refashioning the structure of the industry – has proved trickier. But this possibility too has been dissipated in populist banker bashing. Indeed, populist language has provided a cover for retreat: when the business secretary denounced 'spivs and gamblers' (Stratton 2010), in the banking sector to the annual conference of his party in September 2010, he had already lost the key battles to control the terms of banking reform. At the same time, another elite group has simultaneously been struggling to assert – or more accurately to reassert – control over policy. We next examine the interventions of the radical technocrats from the Bank of England and the FSA.

7.2 Technocrats fight back: the policy intelligentsia

If the twentieth century had reinvented capitalism as rule of experts, the first major crisis of the twenty-first century was profoundly threatening for the technocrats in the regulatory agencies – the FSA and the Bank of England. They had dominated financial matters in the era of the Great Moderation, after previously redefining central banking as a matter for those with economics PhDs, but now their credibility was threatened by unforeseen events. Just as in the case of the City PR men, their sunk capital provided the basis for a fight back which aimed to put financial reform on the agenda after Bischoff, Wigley, and others had tried to close it down, as discussed in

Chapter 5. Put simply, rather than come to terms with their role in an elite debacle, the technocratic policy intelligentsia preferred to represent the crisis as a kind of accident where, as we argued at the beginning of this book, 'arrow points to defective part'. Faced with any kind of disaster, technocrats tend to default onto explanations in terms of the intellectual failure to understand systems and fixes which involve identification of malfunctioning parts and their redesign. In short, the technocratic response to problems about knowledge limits and failure is more or better forms of knowledge.

This was all nicely ironic because, as we showed in our account of the crash in the first half of this book, the dominant – though not unanimous – pre-crash view of the system propagated by technocrats, and accepted by elected policymakers, was that the system of deregulated financial markets had no 'defective part'; or at least if there were defects, such as potentially risky instruments, the system was sufficiently intelligent to recognize these and devise robust methods of risk management. That view predominated because the government of financial markets was in the hands not just of a technocracy, but of an *econocracy*. An econocrat can be considered as a particular kind of technocrat, one whose background is in (mainstream) economics rather than in health, engineering, or other scientific expertise. Although the specific field of expertise is different, like other technocrats, the econocrat has an underlying belief in finding technical solutions to often complex policy problems. Given their specific expertise, econocrats can be found both in places where economic policy is debated, developed, and implemented (such as the Treasury or Bank of England) and also at other policy sites where an economists' toolkit might assist with decision-making. The rise of the econocrat in central government has been charted by, for example, Self (1976) and Parry et al. (1997), and was associated with the rise of cost–benefit analysis and new techniques for public expenditure control. However, the domain of the econocrat is much broader as their reach has extended into macro-economic issues, with positions held not only in central banks but also in the economic research departments of the largest private financial institutions and in the most prestigious university departments of economics, some of whose members enjoyed increasing authority as public intellectuals. Increasingly, authority lay with networks of individuals who rested those authority claims on the 'scientific' status of the knowledge which they derived from sub-disciplines such as financial economics, which are closely linked to the practice of finance.

The crash, we know, was immediately very damaging for this econocracy. By discrediting their pre-crisis claims that deregulated financial markets were mechanisms uniquely equipped to minimize and manage risk, it destroyed much of their intellectual capital. Moreover, the force of the crisis was so great that that authority of the econocrats was simply not equal to the task of rescuing the stricken system. The lesson of the story outlined earlier in this chapter about the rescue of failing banks was that only the institutions of the democratic state had the authority, and the fiscal resources, to prevent system collapse and fund a longer term recovery operation. Politicians were forced to improvise intervention in the vortex of the crisis, and they commanded the political and fiscal resources successfully to improvise. That 'democratic moment' did not last long, as we saw in the preceding section. The City and its Treasury allies hijacked rescue management and financial reform: they despatched control of the newly rescued institutions to the 'arm's-length' security of UKFI and ensured that proposals for regulatory reform minimized any disturbance to either institutional arrangements or corporate interests.

Had our analysis of the crisis and its aftermath terminated early in 2009, we would have concluded that, as a group, econocrats had been fully marginalized by the destruction of their intellectual capital and the revelation of the narrow and fragile foundations of their authority claims. But, from summer 2009, this technocratic elite responded to the challenge by forcibly reopening the argument about the regulation of finance which appeared to have been closed down. In the next phase, the econocrats took the leading role in troublemaking. But, as we show below, they have failed to form an alliance with senior politicians and democratic forces.

The most important source of econocratic dissent has predictably been the Bank of England. The Bank played its part before the crisis in propagating technocratic fantasies about the intelligence and flexibility of markets in the minimization and management of risk. But its long-term development as a central banking institution has endowed it with two crucial features: it is neither hostage to City interests nor is it any longer an institution of 'practical men' (sic) of the kind originally envisaged by its great shaping governor, Montagu Norman. Econocracy has its limits, but it also has strengths: a commitment to evidence and debate as a foundation of policy prescription, and a reflexive capacity – some ability to reflect on the experience of crisis, to try to determine what went wrong. We do not know enough about the Bank's inner workings in the months immediately after the crash to know how far this reflexiveness involved individuals actually revising their own view of the world, and how far it involved the ascendancy of some econocrats who had long been privately sceptical of the virtues of free markets and risk management systems. But we do know from the public evidence that the Bank's relative autonomy from City interests was culturally shaped by a group of econocrats like Governor Mervyn King and his financial stability director, Andrew Haldane, whose intellectual capital comes from academic economics rather than market experience.

Papers and speeches by senior Bank of England officials are never the result of individual reflection; they are the result of continuing internal debate within a small group of elite technocrats. In 2009, a series of related papers by Andrew Haldane and speeches by Mervyn King together mounted a radical critique of pre-2007 policies and the subsequent piecemeal reform. They argued that: the benefits of financial innovation had been greatly exaggerated; the UK economy was distorted and over-dependent on a large financial sector and the City; and structural reforms were needed to segregate retail banking from banking that rested on proprietary trading, and probably also to dismantle 'banking on the state', where serious moral hazard problems were created by banks that were 'too big to fail' in a system that was guaranteed by the taxpayer (Haldane 2009*b*, 2010*b*; King 2009*b*).

But the most striking feature of this attempt to regain the intellectual initiative in policy debates – and the core of any case for econocratic authority has to be that it is capable of supplying the intellectual firepower for reform – is just how limited has been its success. We earlier analysed the fate of the radical proposals to reform the structure of the banking system: we have seen that the strategy of the coalition has amounted to ensuring the Treasury's continuing control of the issue in the core executive, and a familiar bureaucratic strategy of delay by handing the tricky issues of structural reform to a Commission under orders not to report until September 2011, providing quite an extended period of time for deliberation and procrastination.

Why has the technocratic counteroffensive been so limited in its success? There are several overlapping reasons. The voice of the econocrats has been far from united and has been focused on making positions known through promotion of (sometimes competing) ideas. Limited success is in part because econocratic debates are institutionally entangled with struggles about 'turf', and paradigm choice is disconnected from broader political choices. Consider the case of Haldane's extended critique of both the practice of regulation and the existing intellectual framework within which it operates. If all this was certainly brave and independent, it also represented a narrowing of the expert imagination. Andrew Haldane is not J.M. Keynes or William Beveridge because he has no discernible political values beyond hostility to socialization of private banking losses, and his world view is marked by a naïve puritan scientism. Take as an example Haldane's major attempt to rebuild technocratic capital by 'rethinking the financial network' in ways which would give the econocrats a new role in both explaining the financial crisis and making the world safe. In doing so, he boldly proposed a paradigm shift into epidemiology and ecology as ways of relating financial crisis to other kinds of system failure and disaster (Haldane 2009*a*: 3). This gambit is intellectually radical because it focuses potential solutions on whole system mapping and reconstruction; but it is also politically ambiguous because Haldane's gambit involves replacing one failed mathematization with another in a way that would insulate expert-led banking reform from democratic politics, and do this long before the experts have developed a workable new practice of macro-prudential regulation based on any fresh paradigm.

If we consider these Bank econocrats as a group, they are a breakaway elite splinter whose radicalism is driven by their disruptive commitment to empirics (which had not figured much except as ornament in other, earlier stories about the economic and social value of finance). The elite currency of debate is – in a way that Montagu Norman would have found incomprehensible – systematically assembled economic data. It is their shared commitment to economic arithmetic (rather than a specific theoretical problematic or algebraic method) which ties them together. Thus, Haldane has explained ballooning bank balance sheets before 2007 by producing elegant, forensic analysis of how the banks spoiled return on assets so as to maintain return on equity which was a more important measure for the stock market (Alessandrini and Haldane 2009).

But consider now a different version of the technocratic counteroffensive, one that superficially looks like that which emerged from the Bank but which in its analysis and motivations is strikingly different. On his assumption as new chair of the FSA in 2008, Adair Turner rapidly began to use language critical of the preceding regime in a manner that aligned him with the intelligentsia in the Bank. He began his attack with a calculated and incendiary interview aside about 'socially useless' financial innovation (Turner 2009a), and backed his views up with a very academic lecture at Cass Business School, which took the long view of changes in bank lending and bank balance sheets that led them far from any role of intermediation between saving households and borrowing firms (Turner 2010a). But, both by career experience and institutional location in the summer of 2009, Turner (a self-described 'technocrat') was a very different animal from the kind of econocrat so influential in the Bank, and so ably typified by Haldane. The authority of figures like Haldane rests on their claim to scientifically derived expertise; their training is in economic theory and their stock in trade is the analysis of data. Turner, by contrast, rests only very lightly on his original academic training and, in line with his early career in consulting, is more the master of the new assignment which involves creating a narrative with confirming evidence.

In many ways, Adair Turner's career has been that of a well-networked fixer who parlayed his first career at McKinsey into a series of elite positions in banking and public life before joining the House of Lords. He has authored publicly commissioned reports, like that on pensions (Turner 2004), that draw on the management consultant's facility, and has also occupied positions like that of Director General of the Confederation of British Industry which draw on the good networker's capacity for elite diplomacy. During his more public later career, he retained a connection with investment banking via his role as vice chair of Merrill Lynch Europe up to 2006. His qualities are exemplified in the FSA-sponsored *Turner Review* (2009b) (note the 'calling card' personalization which connects the document with its author) which, with the skill of a good management consultant, Turner produced within a few months of being appointed as chair of the FSA. By contrast with Haldane's subtle exploration of past and future imaginings of financial systems, Turner's report exhibits the management consultant's intellectual assurance about the evident causes of a practical problem combined with a politically adroit deflection of direct blame from the bankers, who are the equivalent of incumbent management in a McKinsey report.

In all of this, Turner is so much more worldly and less threatening than the academically puritan Haldane. His report's opening problem definition puts the emphasis on how global trade imbalances ensured more money than good assets in all markets. Fundamentally, he claims, the problem then was lack of full understanding of the way the machinery of markets worked and regulators who diverted onto procedure and lost sight of the big picture. His prescriptions follow from this diagnosis: more investment in properly skilled regulatory personnel by the FSA, and more intensive surveillance of markets and institutions by these personnel. The new approach must be 'more intrusive and more systematic' (Turner 2009*b*: 88). In short, if Haldane's analysis could be summed up as 'arrow points to the defective system', Turner's is a less challenging 'arrow points to the defective part'.

There were very good institutional reasons for Turner's stress on equipping the FSA with more personnel and with more intrusive powers: after the comprehensive failure to spot and prevent the crash, it was fighting for its life. In the original reforms that created the now-discredited system in 1997, the Bank had been the big loser when it was obliged to surrender its jurisdiction over bank supervision to the newly created FSA. The post-2007 Bank agenda for reform now offered the possibility of reclaiming some of that lost 'turf' at the expense of the FSA. Because the Authority was the kingpin of the regulatory system after 1997, it suffered correspondingly from the crisis which discredited light-touch regulation and the Turner analysis was part of an attempt to reinvent it as a more adversarial, intrusive regulator (Turner 2009*b*: 88–9). And indeed, while the 2009 White Paper and the 2010 Banking Act disappointed many, they were, from the point of view of the FSA, a highly effective damage-limitation exercise: the FSA would retain responsibility for regulating financial services, despite the effect of the crisis on its reputation.

We now know that this was a Pyrrhic victory for the FSA, which was effectively served with a timetable of abolition by the incoming Coalition government in 2010. But the broader lesson of the 2010 general election campaign was about the disconnect between any econocrat or technocrat arguments and the democratic debates. The general election campaign of 2010 was conducted almost as though Haldane, King, and Turner did not exist and had never intervened. Labour offered continuity: its manifesto commended the marginal reshaping of the regulatory system in the White Paper and the Banking Act, and even repeated, virtually verbatim, the UKFI commitment to sell off the public holdings in banks at a price that would maximize return to the taxpayer. In the adversarial politics of a general election, it was the third and smallest of the main British parties which, under the influence of one man (Vince Cable), advocated the structural reform of breaking up the banks. But it was the Conservative Party which, as we have seen in Chapter 6, proposed to abolish the FSA and transfer jurisdiction over banking regulation to the Bank – a proposal faithfully implemented after the election, despite Turner's attempt to reinvent the Authority as an adversarial regulator, and even though it was the Bank's original incompetence that brought the FSA into existence. The Bank thus decisively won the struggle in bureaucratic politics for 'turf' but little else changed: the opportunism of Turner's conversion proved fruitless, while the more radical econocrats in the Bank failed to make a connection to mainstream democratic politics.

The Bank's manoeuvring in the wake of the crash, and then in the wake of the 2010 general election, represents, therefore, a master class in bureaucratic politics about turf combined with (so far) practically irrelevant fundamental reflections on the deficiencies of banking. The Bank has re-emerged as the dominant regulator, despite a history of incompetence and despite being tainted with the failings of the post-1997 regime. But the attempt by its most influential econocrats to define a new reform agenda is more intellectually interesting than politically relevant. Haldane's new imagery, and the associated arguments for structural change in banking, are obviously a matter for continuing debate amongst the intelligentsia but have not so far connected with democratic politics. The position in late 2010 is that both Haldane and Turner have (in the idiom of the 1940s officer class) had a good crisis, but reform of finance is no closer. Indeed, apart from making finance 'safer', nobody has given much thought to what the objectives of financial reform should be. And if we raise this question in the United Kingdom, it is necessary to ask specific questions both about what banking and credit has done for the economy and what it should do. The latter set of questions is very important in the UK case given our difficulty in finding a sustainable national business model and a place in the international division of labour amongst high- and low-income countries. These questions about the *is* and *ought* of banking in the United Kingdom are answered in Sections 7.3 and 7.4 of this chapter.

7.3 The wrong kind of credit: inflating asset prices

It is useful to begin with an analysis of the role of credit in the British economy before the crash. This is relatively uncontroversial because it overlaps with the technocratic analysis of bank activity and lending patterns in Turner's Cass Lecture (2010a). The observations are nevertheless radical in their implications because they suggest that Britain has a finance system that generates the wrong kind of credit which diverts funds into (unsustainably) inflating asset prices through overfunding of home purchase by households and coupon trading by financial firms. In this section, we present some empirics on these points and set them in context by drawing a simple distinction between sustainable and unsustainable circuits between credit and debt. Our argument is that too little credit went to the right place for generating sustainable claims on more resources and too much went into circuits predicated on asset price inflation which was unsustainable. In developing these arguments, we will first consider some generalities about the nature of these circuits in financialized capitalist economies before turning to present some empirics on the British case.

Since 2007, many have said that households and firms all took on too much debt before the crisis and we are now living through a period of private sector deleveraging. But that observation is not very helpful because the key questions concern not the amount of debt but the sustainability of the circuits around debt or credit which are, after all, two sides of the same thing. Debt is not a problem when put to productive use to create credit which facilitates physical investment and material transformation via infrastructure, care services, or manufacturing, as the basis for economic advancement and social improvement. The connection to sustainable growth is crucial because all debt is effectively a claim on the economy's ability to generate resources in the future and the right kind of debt is both proportionate and (via credit-funded material investment) resource increasing. Sustainability is about establishing a virtuous stable circuit between debt and the trajectory of the economy going forward, which is underwritten by public and private investment in people, machines and infrastructure combined in material transformations with physical and financial returns (improved productivity, increased employment, profits, and lower carbon footprint). With this argument, we are offering a post-Minskian general analysis of financialized capitalism which focuses not only on what the banking system does by way of extended lending but also on how those funds are applied to hasten or postpone the Minskian moment.

From this point of view, if all debt is a claim on future resources, the sustainability of debt is linked to the amount of resources that an economy can create, and this depends partly on how credit is applied. Thus, the financial crisis of 2007–8 was also a crisis of the 'real economy' because on the one hand the markets were unable to sustain the belief that debt would not be repudiated at some point in the future and on the other hand the real economy was increasingly unable to generate the resource growth required to pay down liabilities (on rising asset prices). However, much economic discussion of these issues since 2007 has diverted from this basic point; paid too much attention to the secondary issues of psychology, behaviour, and belief inside the financial markets; and neglected the circuits between financial markets and the rest of the economy and related questions of material transformation. The emphasis on belief is of course understandable when financialized capitalism is prone to asset price bubbles inflated by irrational exuberance and deflated by loss of confidence. Think only of the UK economy busts after 1989 or 2007, or the US economy after the new economy boom and the tech stock crash in 2000. Each cycle ends in a bust after pulling asset prices away from their normal reference points such as price/earnings on the stock market, yield in commercial property, or affordability in housing.

As Robert Boyer (2000) presciently observed, in financialized capitalism the new problem of asset price bubbles has replaced the old problem of commodity price inflation which nonetheless still preoccupies some central bankers who are, like elderly generals, fighting the last war. If we have a new object, there are still questions about how to comprehend it: for example, there are limits in understanding the new cyclicality in the kind of psychological frame proposed by Akerlof and Shiller (2010). These authors use the term 'animal spirits' to cover everything (from confidence to stories) which suppresses economic rationality and promotes 'excesses'. The phrase is taken from Keynes, but Akerlof and Shiller's appropriation of 'animal spirits' both generalizes and simplifies Keynes' (1936) original and subtle analysis in *The General Theory*, which distinguished between the motives for productive investment and the dynamics of speculation in liquid financial markets. In many ways, an emphasis on material transformation does no more than apply the Keynesian insight in a different and Minskian context. Hence, we wish to tell a different story about credit and debt circuits as the material context of exuberance, first by generalizing about financialized economies before considering the specifics of the British economy.

Generically, in capitalist economic systems, asset price increases can be an unsustainable source of gains without material transformation because the possibility of such gains is inscribed in the dual character of capitalist assets, which have both use value and exchange value. For example, the factory and its productive machines can be operated or sold on, just as the owner occupied house can be lived in or traded. But this possibility of gain is hypothetical in many kinds of capitalism because the market in assets is limited and the practices of debt and credit provision do not encourage mass indebtedness or active asset trading. Financialized capitalism removes these inhibitions and facilitates asset trading by ordinary consumers and businesses along with old and new financial actors, from investment banks to private equity. All become increasingly preoccupied with value crystallization and extraction from asset trading rather than realizing value streams from material transformation.

In stylized terms, financialization undermines the biblical injunction against neither lending nor borrowing. The banks are already in the business of lending and are attracted to lending more against assets if, as Minsky argued, bankers always like to do the conventional thing (see also Chapter 4). What could be easier for bankers than lending against commercial or residential property which offers an apparently steady stream of returns? But then households also find it attractive to borrow to fund consumption and realize gains on house property; while businesses find it attractive to borrow to financially re-engineer the corporation for acquisition or for loading up balance sheets with debt. Old and new financiers gear up to trade in existing markets and create new markets in coupons and bundles of assets. Most assets do not change hands and many owners resist easy money, but enough assets change hands to shift reference prices which rise unsteadily. If asset prices are rising, why not buy coupons, companies, or property and then make a turn by selling on into a rising market?

Dealing into rising asset markets makes dealers look clever and everybody else feel rich through wealth effects. But it does so in what is otherwise a world of difficulty, where the financial returns from building and operating a business in competitive product markets will always be uncertain, and limited household earnings will always make capital gains very attractive because most current income goes on necessities. This will, of course, end badly for anyone with poor timing who does not get back into cash or resilient assets before asset prices crash, and the immediate cause of the crash will usually be a psychological failure of confidence which leads to crises of illiquidity and insolvency. But the underlying and fundamental cause is the growth of financialized circuits of credit and debt which have nothing to do with material transformation. As debt accumulates – without any commensurate increase in the economy's capacity to generate material resources – only (increasingly unjustified) confidence prevents a collapse.

If that is the general story of (mass) financialized capitalism, the United Kingdom in the 2000s or the late 1980s provides case history of how credit can lubricate everything except sustainable growth. Our analysis below shows how unregulated credit and indiscriminate lending in the 2000s ensured that funds were diverted onto the wrong objects and circulated into the wrong parts of the UK economy so that accumulating debt created longer term problems. The two key aspects of this problem are the gross overfunding of house purchases which started after credit deregulation in the mid-1980s and the stagnation of bank lending for any productive purpose which dates from the mid-1990s when lending for other purposes took off. As Figure 7.1 shows, by 2007, some 79 per cent of all British bank lending was accounted for by lending on property assets (residential and commercial) and by lending to other financial institutions trading in coupons increasingly derived from these assets.

Indiscriminate lending for consumers loaded revolving debt onto the household balance sheet and caused a housing bubble in the decade before the crisis. The empirics here are quite striking. Non-secured consumer debt more or less doubled to £4,000 per head of UK population between 2000 and 2007 and much of that went on consumption with a high import content (Ertürk et al. 2008: 10). House prices doubled in real terms which pushed up the debt burden on new entrants and on low-income households, who could spend up to 40 per cent of disposable income on mortgages; for those already 'on the ladder' of home ownership, it also produced euphoria through equity withdrawals which turned into new kitchens and cars.

While it now suits some popular commentators to blame consumers for this credit binge, there is a more useful academic literature about the emergence of new forms of Anglo-American subjectivity around financialized behaviours in the 2000s (Aitken 2007; Langley 2009). Housing was increasingly seen as investment through house flipping and buy to let, but it was the banks and regulators who made such behaviours possible by offering 100 per cent mortgages, interest-only repayments, and indifference to borrower's income or job security. All this changed after 2009 as mortgage lenders insisted on 25 per cent deposits from first-time buyers: on the long view, it is supply-side lending practices not subjectivities which determine what happens inside the world of consumer credit.

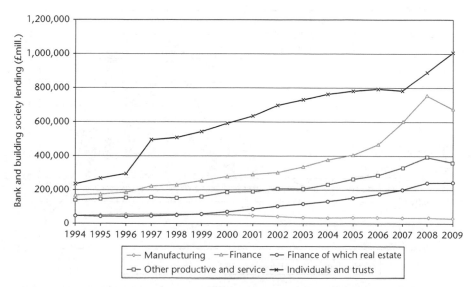

Figure 7.1. UK bank and building society total stock of lending 1994–2009
Notes: Sterling amounts outstanding, nominal data.
Source: Bank of England.

But in the broader capitalist context, subjectivity does matter because the so-called 'feel good' about the economy wins and loses elections, influences consumption and savings decisions, and much else. Most commentators fix on employment and unemployment as indicators of feel good but, for most political and economic subjects, unearned income is just as useful as earned income (and maybe better if capital gains are taxed at lower rates and the unearned gains are broadly spread via the institution of home ownership). The economic feel good in the New Labour years, partly the result of house prices increasing faster than other prices, enabled consumption demand funded by housing equity withdrawal; both of these unsustainable developments were driven by a finance system which lent extravagantly for house purchase and remortgage.

As Figure 7.2 shows, in the years of the Blair premiership (1997–2007), the real value of equity withdrawals was larger than the real increase in gross domestic product (GDP) and in every year from 2002 to 2007 the value of housing equity withdrawal was at or above 4 per cent of GDP. Table 7.1 demonstrates that this simply repeated an earlier pattern of unsustainability on a larger scale. After the initial deregulation of credit creation, in Mrs Thatcher's premiership, the value of housing equity withdrawal was greater than the increase in value. The difference was that the Thatcher boom ended abruptly in a housing bust as real prices fell by 30 per cent, while New Labour

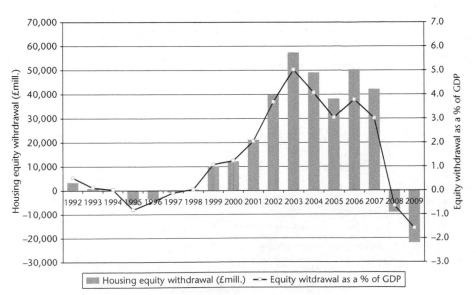

Figure 7.2. Value of UK housing equity withdrawal and equity withdrawal as a percentage of UK GDP

Source: Bank of England and ONS.

Table 7.1. A comparison of housing equity withdrawals and growth in gross domestic product (GDP)

	Prime minister	Real 2009 prices		Equity withdrawal as a share of GDP growth (%)
		Housing equity withdrawal (£ million)	Change in real GDP (£ million)	
1970–4	Edward Heath	22,168	60,569	36.6
1975–8	James Callaghan	24,790	68,523	36.2
1979–90	Margaret Thatcher	251,179	241,066	104.2
1991–6	John Major	10,829	127,664	8.5
1997–2007	Tony Blair	364,645	352,922	103.3
2008–9	Gordon Brown	−29,451	−51,691	57.0

Notes: All money data is in 2009 prices, and equity and GDP totals are seasonally adjusted. Averages are calculated by summating annual changes and dividing by the GDP in the year prior to entering government. In the year that tenure ends, the last full year is used for the calculations.

Sources: Derived from Bank of England and ONS.

postponed this outcome as house price rises stalled on much lower volumes in 2009 and 2010.

Under Mrs Thatcher and Mr Blair, the barometer of feel good was house prices (not full employment as in the post-war long boom). The positives were accentuated during the Brown Chancellorship by an adventitious conjuncture of low inflation in labour and product markets. The result was steady increases in real incomes for those in work, especially those working in the expanding public sector professions. The process was 'adventitious' because at root it had little to do with the Chancellor's domestic policies: it had more to do with an overvalued currency; mass inward migration which kept downward pressure on labour costs in the private sector; and the flood of cheap manufactured imports, especially from China – imports that in turn helped weaken British manufacturing for which finance was doing nothing. Figure 7.3 presents aggregate data on the central economic paradox of the bubble in the United Kingdom before 2007: credit was cheap and everybody was over borrowing except non-financial companies, which drew very little credit for any useful productive end connected with material transformation.

The total of investment in (and bank lending to) productive business was calculated by adding subtotals for three sectors: manufacturing and other production; construction and distribution; plus public and other services. Productive business investment and bank lending to productive business therefore includes everything except investment by (and bank lending to) other finance businesses and property businesses in real estate or commercial property. The graphs show that right through the bubble productive business investment was completely flat at 10 per cent of GDP, while bank lending to productive business declined sharply from 30 per cent towards 10 per cent,

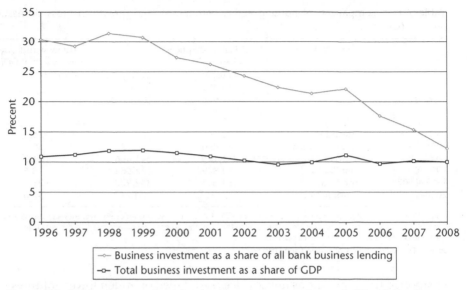

Figure 7.3. UK business and productive investment as a share of all bank lending to businesses and as a share of GDP

Notes: The data is the net of acquisitions less disposals and expenditure on leased asset and new building work. It excludes spending on land and existing buildings. All data is in current prices and not seasonally adjusted. Portfolio investment is excluded.

Source: ONS.

mainly because bank lending to other financial firms and property developers ballooned in the bubble.

If bank lending did nothing for production, the production and finance sectors were increasingly intertwined because larger productive firms were increasingly streams of income and bundles of assets in a financialized game driven by finance-led changes in ownership. This was most obvious in the 2000s with the advance of leveraged private equity using cheap bank finance to capture ever larger corporate targets, as outlined in Chapter 3. The formula of buying to hold and sell on for a higher price with gains for the equity holders attracted increasing public criticism in the United Kingdom (Ertürk et al. 2010), which was ironic because the private equity chiefs at the Treasury Select Committee were no better and no worse than the house flippers in the property TV programmes; and both were symptoms of an unsustainable asset price bubble. Equally insidious was the way in which the pursuit of short-term financial goals in a shareholder value frame distracted the whole non-financial corporate sector. An anaemic UK corporate sector chose to use cash to build reserves, engage in M&A activity, and bolster its share price through share buybacks and debt/equity swaps (IMF 2006). These moves were of course part of a general attempt to improve shareholder value ratios and bolster the share price and market value of firms. If we remember that in the long run giant firms find it difficult to grow earnings faster than GDP (Froud et al. 2006), this could be represented as just another way of indexing earnings to unsustainability.

Since the bubble burst, politicians and journalists have shown a kind of confused buyer's remorse about such results and their remorse has increasingly taken the form of demands that the banks lend more to SME business. There is some justification for this demand in that, before and after the crash, SMEs have been meanly treated by the banks which lend cautiously. But the banks can also with some justice claim that there is limited large and small business demand for loans, rooted in long-standing attitudes and behaviours which preceded the present forms of financialization. In particular, non-financial businesses often choose independence from finance by funding investment from retained earnings. While corporate business is often cautious about burdensome shareholder value expectations, and about gearing up for higher interest payments, much non-corporate business is about sustaining a lifestyle, not growing a business. For any business, dependence on bank borrowing is risky in a cyclical economy where bank lending criteria change. Demand and supply have long intersected to create a kind of permanent stand-off between finance suppliers and those running productive business; whether effort should be put into changing this secular outcome depends on a broader macro view of the trajectory of the national economy over the last thirty years. This is the task which the next section takes up.

7.4 The United Kingdom after Thatcherism: where do the jobs come from?

Even radical critics of finance can ground their critiques in mainstream economic theory because they start from a textbook list of the (invariant) functions of finance in a capitalist economy (Nissan and Spratt 2009). Technocrats with respect for empirics, like Haldane or Turner, are smart enough to see that any effective critique of finance must be empirically grounded in data about what the banking system is doing and its immediate effects (with other macro data excluded as irrelevant). We favour a different approach to defining what finance and banking should be doing, which ranges across a much broader field of data. In our view, the question about what role finance should play can only be answered at national level by considering the present condition and the past macro-economic trajectory of the national economy. This does connect with general issues because we will usually be interested in the question of whether and how the national economy can generate the jobs to employ its citizenry and distribute welfare, as well as in newer questions about sustainability. But it is only after taking a historical and specific view of the (variable) national performance record on these issues, can we decide whether and how finance should be directed or redirected so as to underwrite different processes of material transformation. Put another way, the restriction of the problem definition by the current generation of UK technocrats is unjustifiable.

It is difficult to answer the questions about national trajectory in the British case for two related sets of reasons: confusions about the variable gap between promise and outcome, engendered by the rhetoric of neo-liberalism. Those who use neo-liberalism as a concept generally fail to register a variable gap: on the one hand, there is the political promise of the programme which is about liberating enterprise and freeing the private sector to create jobs; on the other hand, there are the programme's economic results which involve growing clientism from tax breaks for the rich and state expenditures on health education and defence. Following Joan Robinson (1962) on 'bastard Keynesianism', we introduce the concept of bastard neo-liberalism to describe the variable outcomes of the neo-liberal project in countries like the United Kingdom, the United States, and Australia. British discussion of results is peculiarly confused by the myth of Thatcherite renewal: if we read former Labour government minister Peter Mandelson (2010*b*) or his Tory successors, the elite political classes agree that flexibilized labour markets, privatization, and all the rest rescued the country from the 1970s chaos (so poignantly captured in newsreel footage of the three-day week), as well as ending secular decline. The mainstream political imaginary cannot conceive that Thatcherism inaugurated an unsustainable business model which combined feel good from housing equity withdrawal and jobs from state expenditure.

The political myth can be countered by some revisionist economic history where we can begin with narrative before turning to empirics. The end of the first long boom in the 1970s saw the ascendancy of a diagnosis of Britain's problems: a weak and constrained private sector was being 'crowded out' by an over-large public sector, over-regulated labour markets inhibited managerial initiative, and over-protected trade unions obstructed innovation and challenged state authority. Thatcherism's prescription was a new economic order designed to liberate the private sector to create jobs and wealth. From the early 1990s, Labour came to accept the original diagnosis and remedy so that Tony Blair and Gordon Brown did not undo the Thatcher revolution. The British after 1979 thus embarked on a thirty-year-long experiment to halt decline by constraining union power in the private sector, enhancing managerial authority in flexible labour markets, and creating a tax and corporate reward system to match. The national background to financial crisis in 2007–8 was this economic experiment in enterprise, which was formative for the whole political class.

There has been very little empirical analysis of whether and how the private sector responded to Mrs Thatcher's new framework. The diagnosis established a presumption that the prescription should work. Quite fortuitously, North Sea oil came on stream and prevented balance of payments crises – the old index of failure. And the complexities of official statistics obscured the record of private sector job creation, which was the new index of success. Privatization and outsourcing were a kind of bookkeeping adjustment, which effectively reclassified many public workers, and in the Thatcher years steadily inflated measured private sector employment. On our calculations, based on numbers employed in the year of privatization, some 750,000 workers were transferred into the private sector. Strikingly, this number accounts for some 71 per cent of the apparent overall increase in private sector employment from 1979 to 1997.[1]

Closer examination of employment trends in the years from 1979 to 1997 discloses an economy with continuing problems about private sector job creation, and this set a pattern for New Labour. Manufacturing employment fell from 7 million in 1979 towards 4 million by the mid-1990s, as shown in Table 7.2. The 1979–82 recession permanently destroyed 20 per cent of manufacturing employment; subsequently, the Conservatives abandoned British manufacturing to global competition while welcoming inward investment by the Japanese – a development that brought few compensating jobs. The government gambled on the capacity of the service sector to create jobs, especially on the expansion of financial services after City deregulation in the 'Big Bang' of 1986. As Table 7.2 reveals, financial services did indeed show increased numbers employed from a very small base of around 620,000 in the early 1970s; but the increase in financial service employment was all over by the time the effects of deregulation kicked in at the end of the 1980s. In terms of job creation, the most substantial and durable achievement of the Conservative years was a 1 million plus rise in state employment sustained by Mrs Thatcher's pragmatic acceptance of increasing public expenditure regardless of her rhetoric about rolling back the state.

All this set the scene for New Labour after 1997. It inherited the historically engrained economic problems that had defeated Thatcherism: a palsied manufacturing sector, a bias towards finance, and a reliance on the state for employment creation. Once the utilities had been privatized, New Labour leant more heavily on the state to fill in for a private sector, which was incapable of significant job creation. Economic outcomes were again obscured by the categories of official employment statistics, which identified state employees as those working for public agencies. But this failed to register how privatization and outsourcing had expanded *para-state* activities: this is where private employment is sustained by state funding and concessions, as

---

[1] Our calculations of numbers transferred are based on numbers employed by privatized firms in the year of privatization as disclosed in organization's report and accounts.

Table 7.2. British manufacturing, finance, and state employees, and total jobs, 1971–2008

		Manufacturing (Great Britain)	Finance (Great Britain)	State employment (UK)	Total workforce jobs (UK)
		No.	No.	No.	No.
Pre-Thatcher governments	1971	7,886,059	620,324		
	1978	7,123,476	730,294	5,598,000	26,861,000
	Change	−762,583	109,970		
Pre-Thatcher government – immediate post-'Big Bang'	1978	7,123,476	730,294	5,598,000	26,861,000
	1987	5,107,180	939,824	6,248,000	27,052,000
	Change	−2,016,296	209,530	650,000	191,000
Post-'Big Bang' to New Labour government	1987	5,107,180	939,824	6,248,000	27,052,000
	1997	4,059,561	978,415	6,676,000	28,697,000
	Change	−1,047,619	38,591	428,000	1,645,000
Post-New Labour	1997	4,059,561	978,415	6,676,000	28,697,000
	2008	2,709,080	1,062,977	8,009,000	31,661,000
	Change	−1,350,481	84,562	1,333,000	2,964,000

Notes: Breaks in series end 1981, 1991, and 1997 related to changes in SIC classifications. The employment data for manufacturing and finance relate only to employees and excludes N. Ireland. 1978 is used as the full year prior to the Conservatives winning the general election on 4 May 1979. 'Big Bang' reforms were enacted on 26 October 1986. New Labour won the general election on 2 May 1997. Total jobs and state employment relates to the United Kingdom and the latter is the summation of jobs in public administration, education, and health.

Source: Nomis, ONS.

with nursery education and services for the elderly. State influence on job creation is now best measured by adding together the number of state employees working in the public sector and the number of para-state employees working in the private sector. On calculations by the Centre for Research on Socio-Cultural Change (CRESC), the para-state employed 1.7 million in 2007, or roughly one-third of the 5.7 million total employed directly by the state (Buchanan et al. 2009).

Many of those who are used to categories like 'knowledge economy' and 'creative industries' identified new poles of job creation in the economy. But this was largely part of what Atkinson and Elliott (2007) labelled 'Fantasy Island'. With low wage imports from China and elsewhere rising, the number employed in British manufacturing continued to decline every year after 1997: indeed, over the whole period it fell from 4 million to 2.7 million in 2008. Chapter 5 discussed and explained the disappointing trend of employment in finance over this period. Here, we can simply remind readers that, in the fifteen years after 1992, the numbers employed in finance did not increase at all from a base of 1 million (which, by 2008, accounted for less than 4 per cent of the total British workforce); over the same period, finance increased its share of output to 9.1 per cent and its share of profits to 12.8 per cent just before the bubble burst (Buchanan et al. 2009: 13–14). Meanwhile, there was a large increase in (non-financial) service sector private employment which actually includes many para-state jobs. Overall, state plus para-state employment increased by nearly 1.3 million between 1998 and 2007. This accounts for no less than 57 per cent of the total increase in the number of employees.[2]

By 2007, therefore, state and para-state became leading sectors and together employed 7.5 million, or 28 per cent of the workforce (excluding self-employed). This was not a deliberate economic strategy but an unintended effect of New Labour's political strategy of spending on health and education. After an initial period of 'prudence' within Tory expenditure limits, Mr Brown as Chancellor sanctioned an unprecedented expansion of state expenditure. After 2000, real public expenditure increased sharply, by nearly 50 per cent to £606 billion by 2007. The public sector deficit pushed towards 3 per cent, which was the formal limit under the fiscal rules imposed on the United Kingdom by membership of the EU. Further expansion of state and para-state employment was plainly unsustainable even in advance of the financial crash. But the question of what would come next had not even been posed in advance of the 2007–8 crisis. Uncompetitive manufacturing had made the British economy one of the weakest of the big capitalist economies at the end of the first 'long boom' in the 1970s. As the post-2007 recession began, the

---

[2] This calculation is based on the Annual Business Inquiry (ABI) measure of employment, which excludes the self-employed, defence, and Northern Ireland.

narrative about Thatcher's revolution and Brown's management licensed claims that the UK economy was now especially well prepared to weather the new storm. Then in a kind of ghostly return, overexposure to property and financial markets ensured that Britain was among the first major economies into recession and among the last to emerge, falteringly, from it.

The immediate problem was the fiscal damage consequent upon financial crisis because (with differences about extent and timing) all mainstream politicians agreed on the necessity for public expenditure cuts. But these would undermine the use of state expenditure to sustain the former industrial regions and bolster women's employment. Under Gordon Brown, as under his Conservative predecessors, long-standing problems about regional imbalance between the southeast and the rest of the United Kingdom worsened. However, New Labour's increased expenditure on health and education did operate as a kind of undisclosed regional policy. State and para-state (S&PS) employment expanded right across the national economy, but was particularly critical where private sector job creation was weak or failing. Table 7.3 shows that, in London and the South, state and para-state accounted for no more than 23 to 32 per cent of employment growth between 1998 and 2007; while in the Midlands, the North, Wales, and Scotland, it accounted for between 38 and 61 per cent of the employment growth over the same period, with most of the rest induced by public expenditure multiplier effects. Increasing state and para-state employment was crucially important in former industrial areas like the West Midlands and the North East, where declining manufacturing was not replaced by any other autonomous private sector activity.

The dispersed expenditures on health and education were equally important in meeting a new requirement for gendered employment. Policy rhetoric about increased labour market participation and household calculations about the benefits of two wage earners, both worked to push the female participation rate to 70 per cent. At this point, S&PS employment becomes crucial because nearly 70 per cent of the S&PS workforce is female and half of all female S&PS jobs are part-time. Thus, right across the United Kingdom, the state in the New Labour years worked to put the second (female) wage earner into the average household. Over the period 1998–2007, the S&PS sectors accounted for 904,000 new female jobs, or 81 per cent of the total increase in female employment over these years. Postponing public expenditure cuts – as Labour in its closing days in office proposed to do – averted the threat to the mixed economy of those many households that now combine one private and one state-funded job.

Thus, developments after the 2008 bail out of the banks undermined the (undisclosed) national business model and challenged the narrative of national economic transformation, a narrative that had been shared by the

Table 7.3. Change in UK employment by region and source of change by major sector, 1998–2007

	Total change in employment, 1998–2007		Sectoral contribution to change, 1998–2007	
	Private sector	Public and para-state sector	Private sector	Public and para-state sector
	No.	No.	%	%
North East	54,718	65,952	45.3	54.7
North West	230,105	142,177	61.8	38.2
Yorks and Humber	146,915	129,671	53.1	46.9
East Midlands	142,483	88,430	61.7	38.3
West Midlands	67,410	104,768	39.2	60.8
East	187,196	110,826	62.8	37.2
London	392,358	120,155	76.6	23.4
South East	396,231	135,696	74.5	25.5
South West	263,365	124,625	67.9	32.1
Wales	106,685	81,936	56.6	43.4
Scotland	192,738	168,266	53.4	46.6
Total	2,180,204	1,272,502	63.1	36.9

Note: Data refers only to employees and Great Britain. Public sector refers to traditional public sector activities undertaken directly by the state, and para-state refers to activities that depend on the state for revenue.

Source: Annual Business Inquiry, ONS.

political classes and their allied metropolitan elites. The question of how finance could be mobilized to fix a broken national business model should have been the number one issue in the 2010 general election, not least because the United Kingdom had a high carbon economy which was unsustainable in other ways and required massive investment in infrastructure. The high carbon economy was being discussed but not by politicians. The non-mainstream radicals imagined a 'green new deal' (New Economics Foundation 2008) and were somewhat unexpectedly abetted by the finance sector which saw infrastructural investment and green technologies as a business opportunity. As Wyn Bischoff argued in his report for the Treasury, 'society continues to face significant unmet needs which we believe are likely to remain unresolved without significant and continuing development of new financial products and markets' (Bischoff 2009: 45). However, mainstream politicians in the 2010 election avoided such issues about long-run choices. Indeed, as we saw earlier in this chapter, they barely discussed banking reform, leaving it to technocrats and econocrats.

Meanwhile the problems of the broken business model were discussed in a coded way starting from Peter Mandelson's comments early in 2010: 'Britain needs to build a new growth model for the future .... The recovery can only be driven by private enterprise and investment. Much more real engineering and

217

less financial engineering' (2010*a*). The incoming coalition prime minister and chancellor made speeches on the need for 'rebalancing the economy' (see e.g. Cameron 2010*a*, 2010*b*), but without specifying adequate policy instruments, or more fundamentally coming to terms with the failure of the thirty-year supply-side experiment. The incoming coalition's economic policy included more incentives for enterprise and optimistic faith in an Office for Budget Responsibility forecast that the private sector would be able to create 2 million jobs within four years. Precisely, how 'private enterprise and investment' can create employment when it has signally failed to do so up to now is not explained and cannot be explained if financial reform is left to technocrats who pursue safer banking.

In conclusion, the theme of this chapter has been the end (and the failure) of a thirty-year experiment in a national system that was in the epicentre of the financial crisis. That experiment privileged key interests, especially in financial markets, and insulated those interests from the influences of democratic politics. The crisis briefly created an opportunity for a re-examination of the failed strategy that began with Thatcherism, and equally briefly created an opportunity to open the financial system to stronger democratic control. These opportunities have been wasted. In the final chapter, we describe how those lost opportunities might be recouped.

8

Reform? Hubristic Intervention or Effective Democracy

And there fell out the map of an island, with latitude and longitude, soundings, names of hills, and bays and inlets, and every particular that would be needed to bring a ship to safe anchorage upon its shores. (Robert Louis Stevenson (1883), *Treasure Island*)

Any technical practice is defined by its ends; such and such effects to be produced in such and such an object in such and such a situation. The means depend on the ends.... Left to itself, a spontaneous (technical) practice produces only the theory it needs as a means to produce the ends assigned to it. (Louis Althusser (1969), *For Marx*)

Either democracy will extend its authority from the political to the economic system, and be established more firmly, because on broader foundations; or it will cease to exist, save in form, as a political institution. (R.H. Tawney (1940), *Why the British People Fight*)

We do not end this book by proposing ten steps to better banking. Our book has highlighted the frustration of our hopes for security in the debacle that has played out, given the current division of labour between technocracy and politics, and given the current division of power between finance and democracy. The only credible response is not a list of technical fixes but an intellectual project for making the politics of finance explicit which could lead towards a political plan for putting banking and finance under democratic control. If this seems wild or nonsensical to our readers, that is because most of those who did not see it coming before 2008 still do not get it afterwards. The underlying problem is a reliance on monological knowledge and master conceptualization when present-day capitalism can only be understood by holding different knowledges together in a relation of dialogue, as we have tried to do throughout this book and in our opening quotations for this conclusion.

The cultural tropes which console and rule our imagination were our starting point, in Chapter 1 about Bernanke's story before the crisis, but they are not our destination. That is the point we make by the quotation from Stevenson's novel (1883) about the map and the dream of adequate technical knowledge. In *Treasure Island*, the quest is for a map 'with every particular' of topographic and marine detail which will indicate where Flint's treasure is buried and (just as important) bring a ship to safe anchorage regardless of the storm. In the early chapters, Blind Pew's search for the map of the island has entranced generations of children, just as, in the papers on the Bank of England's web site, Haldane's paper (2009*a*) about a 'remapping' of the financial network on epidemiological coordinates now enthrals the intelligentsia. The quest for a map and safe anchorage is a powerful cultural trope, because a world without maps and cartography would not be navigable. However, maybe we need to think again about the kinds of maps and pilots which are most useful.

Put another way, one of the key messages of this book is that technocrats are good servants but bad masters. If the thirty-year experiment after Thatcher and Reagan demonstrates that point, Althusser (1969) on technical practice explains why this is so. Many kinds of engineering and the social scientific discourses of governance, performance measurement, and economic management are instrumental knowledges, with given ends and a limited capacity for reflecting on their own presuppositions because theory and conceptualization are deployed only to measure the relation between means and ends. Such practices appear to work well enough in routine circumstances but are ill-adapted to extreme situations. As in the case of 1980s monetarism, the social logic of technical practice in extreme situations is not measured proportionality but it is hubristic intervention in line with crude a priori about causality, as well as an inability to think through roundabout repercussions. The first two sections of this conclusion, Sections 8.1 and 8.2, develop this perception by arguing that financial crisis management and bank bailouts after 2008 represented hubristic intervention by technocratic elites, which consolidated the subordination of politics to finance which was in any case the logic of the inhibited practice of elected politicians.

In the concluding pages of some reports on the financial crisis, a list of technical fixes promises to take us to a safe harbour but instead demonstrates only that we are all adrift without a compass. This book has attempted to find some bearings which could lead towards a much more political analysis of, and intervention against, finance. The introduction to this book reframes the crisis as an elite political debacle rather than some kind of socio-technical accident, and Chapters 1 to 7 have developed this argument. The front half of the book describes the aggrandizement of finance through business model, war machine, and bricolage, under cover of a dubious alibi about financial innovation which was good enough to convince detached technocratic elites. The back half of the book analyses the collapse of public regulation before the crisis and the frustration of financial reform after the crisis across several different jurisdictions representing variations on the fusion of finance and political power outside the processes of accountability.

In this conclusion, we draw the political corollary by envisaging a reassertion of democratic control which is easy to ask for but difficult to think through, leave alone implement. Thus, Section 8.3 criticizes technical fixes for safer finance through higher capital adequacy and such like and instead starts discussion of how business models and bricolage might be limited through a package of measures. Section 8.4 follows on with an examination of the difficulty and possibility of more democratic control. From a reformist point of view, financial crisis is not the antithesis of normalcy, and the subsequent failure of reform is thus not an aberration: the financial crisis and subsequent non-reform are simply the concentrated expression of the everyday experience and values of a hobbled democracy. As successive chapters of this book have demonstrated, many important aspects of this dilemma are novel. Post-1979 developments include: the rise of a new kind of technocracy aligned with political elites, the rise of business lobbying in story-driven capitalism, the atrophy of class-based party systems in the old jurisdictions, and the rise of the EU as a new jurisdiction.

But our current problems are also a ghostly return insofar as this book builds up an indictment of finance which echoes the classical liberal collectivist critique of business power from social democrats and left liberals in the interwar period. In Tawney's liberal collectivism, as Terrill has (1973) argued, the effective precondition of functioning mass democracy is the dispersion of power as a volatile capacity amongst multiple sources and transmuted into various forms. Tawney (1940) in the opening quotation underlines this point by arguing that the fusion of economic and politico-social power is always profoundly threatening because the danger is that democracy then survives only as an empty form. Substitute the finance sector in 2010 for economic system in Tawney's quote from 1940 and we have a fair enough statement of the present dilemma.

8.1 Inhibited politicians

The introduction and first chapter of this book began by observing the detachment of our regulators and central bankers in the period of the great complacence in the mid-2000s, and this section of the conclusion looks at their behaviour change after 2008 and what came after pre-crisis hubristic detachment. Extreme intervention with bailouts for banks and markets after

2008 postponed the reckoning but did not work to solve any major problem. The central bankers and politicians were not saving the world but spending public money so that, in the next phase, taxpayers and service consumers must foot the bill for keeping banks and markets going, while policymakers have not dealt with rotten banks or made finance safe by limiting the sector's capacity to socialize losses. This section considers the politicians who have, by 2010, become increasingly inhibited for a variety of reasons described in the European case where the sectional interests of finance are increasingly elided with the national interest. By way of contrast, the next section considers the continuing appetite for hubristic intervention amongst technocratic elites.

The story of policy in and after the crisis is about how extreme policy intervention initially tracked the changing form of banking and financial crisis in a responsive mode; it thereby created a fiscal crisis of the state and fed a sovereign debt crisis in the eurozone, amidst growing fears of a municipal and local debt crisis in the United States and elsewhere. What started as a local US housing market problem in sub-prime lending in 2006, morphed into a liquidity crisis, initially through a run on banks that were overly dependent on the interbank money market, and then into a global credit crisis after the fall of Lehman in autumn 2008, when few counterparties could be trusted. Throwing liquidity at banks did not solve the problem for insolvent banks which needed capital injections to shore up their equity base in response to declining asset values. This did not prevent a banking-led downturn, with the loss of output equal to 10 per cent or more of global GDP. The IMF (2010) estimated that finance-led recession had resulted in more than 30 million job losses, most of them in the developed economies. The immediate policy counter was fiscal stimulus packages at national level so that, by late 2009, governments from the United States and China to Spain, France, and Germany had committed themselves to extra public expenditure of approximately $3 trillion on infrastructure, temporary relief measures, and the extension of unemployment benefits.

This policy stance was then reversed as European political elites in 2010 rediscovered their belief in fiscal prudence and began to plan public expenditure cuts. Their increasing public debts were subject to the judgement of the bond markets which decided the terms on which national governments could refinance their debt, given that European governments could not make the US assumption that the rest of the world would keep their bond markets going. The UK and other North European governments were under no immediate pressure from the bond markets but Gordon Brown's UK government was already planning public expenditure cuts of £50 billion before the May 2010 general election. The Coalition government which was formed after the election developed firm plans for £80 billion of cuts by the autumn of 2010. In the election campaigns of 2010 in the United Kingdom, Germany, Sweden, and the Netherlands, responsible parties disagreed only about the timing and scale of sweeping cuts. The expected consequences for the weak, vulnerable, and less organized included cutbacks in public services, higher fees for tertiary education, and lower benefits for the unemployed, the ill, and the old. The only discretion was about which areas (like health or education) might be spared by imposing deeper cuts elsewhere.

Meanwhile, although the aggregate ratio of debt to GDP across the whole EU was manageable, from early 2010 the bond markets had started picking off weak, small South European countries with short-dated debt that needed refinancing, large holdings by foreign professional investors, and limited prospects of economic growth. Europe's political leaders then managed symptoms without addressing any of the underlying problems about structural imbalance and banking interconnectedness which were leading to threat of sovereign government default and panic about contagion. Their quixotic defence of the indefensible in the financial markets rewarded hedge funds which had wagered against weak national governments that could, in any case, only sell bonds at interest rates of up to 10 per cent, which already covered the purchasers for default risk. By May 2010, the situation had deteriorated so that the EU, together with the IMF, had to throw $110 billion at Greece and pledge $640 billion more, in the form of a Luxembourg-based special purpose vehicle (SPV) called the ESFS, to placate bond markets and ensure Greek access to liquidity up to 2013. By November 2010, further capital injections of some $85 billion were required for Ireland and the markets were focusing on the weakness of Portugal and Spain. The German government meanwhile vetoed plans for issuing a Europe-wide bond and resisted an enlargement of the bailout fund before conceding a new permanent bailout fund which would not operate before 2013 (Pratley 2010; Traynor 2010).

At this point, two debacles collided as financial crisis crashed into European Monetary Union, a policy debacle in an elite-run institution with a democratic deficit whose successive encounters with European electors show the indifference of low turnouts mutating into euro-scepticism led by populist nationalists. Monetary union was initiated in the early 1990s in an attempt to press the project of European integration further, but without addressing underlying macroeconomic imbalances arising from German domination of European manufacturing and the commitment to free trade with low-wage Asia. It was not clear how Greece or Spain or indeed Italy could maintain their precarious position in the international division of labour if they could no longer depreciate their national currencies. Equally culpable, there was one loosely enforced rule about the maximum size of national government deficits but no other prescription for managing adjustment. The long-term logic of monetary union was economic adjustment via fiscal austerity on the Southern and Eastern periphery. Expenditure cuts plus low growth rates will most likely further erode the legitimacy of the European project on the periphery. Meanwhile, the bond markets are not placated and it is not clear whether and how EU governments can save the existing monetary union.

Just as in the case of financial innovation, technocratic elites were centrally involved in legitimizing European monetary union and they entirely dominated the newly created European Central Bank (ECB) after 1998. But what European central bankers and bureaucrats were performing by 2010 was the subordination of political calculation to the short-term interests of the financial sector. These financial interests were at every stage being represented and enforced by elected politicians in national governments defending the interests of 'their' banks. The broad position currently is that national politicians will support their national banking sector on all technical matters. The crucial caveat is that such support is qualified when specific issues like bankers' pay or bailouts for sovereign governments have resonance in mass politics; in this case, political calculations about popularity and electoral advantage take precedence.

The European 'stress tests' of July 2010 provide a nice example of national governments supporting their bankers on a technical issue. The ECB head, Jean Claude Trichet, and others were encouraged by US bank stress tests which had in 2009 reassured the markets; the idea of such tests was thoroughly congenial for technocrats because of the association with engineering and accident prevention. In the July 2010 tests, eighty-one of eighty-four banks tested passed the test, including rotten Irish banks, like Allied Irish and Bank of Ireland, whose subsequent restructuring in November aimed to deal with their continuing heavy dependence on ECB funding (Brown and Jenkins 2010). At every stage, the possibility of meaningful stress tests was undermined by the political lobbying of national governments concerned that 'their' banks should not fail. Thus, as critics observed (Kay 2010), the stress test was not of balance sheet soundness but of requirements for regulatory capital. This requirement was irrelevant in many of the 2008 failures and was now set low at 1 per cent below the new Basel requirements for 2019 (Harding and Rappeport 2010). Each country stress tested its own banks in a worst case 'adverse scenario' which was initially made undemanding by an ECB ruling that default on holdings of sovereign debt should be excluded as a possibility. Other parameters could then be set in an optimistic way, as in the case of Irish 'adverse scenario' stress projections of a 17 per cent fall in property prices in one year, made after Irish house prices had on one index fallen by 19 per cent in the first quarter of 2010 (Harding and Rappeport 2010).

There was more political intrigue in the sovereign debt bailouts for South European governments, triggered by bond market pressure but then shaped by conflicted North European governments. The overriding importance of electoral considerations is manifest in the attitude of the German government which wants to reduce costs to the German taxpayer by insisting that bond holders should, in EU parlance, make a 'private sector contribution' to resolving debt crises. 'Haircuts' for bond holders would in any case equalize the post-crisis sacrifice between creditors/borrowers and debtors/lenders who failed to enact prudential pre-crisis oversight over the follies of banks and governments. However, on the advice of the ECB, this is still only a possibility in the post-2013 bailout arrangements; and when Angela Merkel initially raised the issue of future bond holder losses in late 2010, it 'spooked the markets' (Fidler 2010). So the position in early 2011 is that European governments have so far protected not only retail bank depositors but also holders of sovereign debt and bank bonds; for example, holders of senior bonds in failing Irish banks are being paid in full.

The explanation for such consideration is that the bond holders in South European banks and governments are other (mainly North) European banks which had, pre-crisis, embarked upon an extensive buying spree of financialized assets in other eurozone countries. According to the imperfect Bank for International Settlements (BIS) data, European banks account for three-quarters of all banks lending to peripheral European economies, with German, French, and British banks having the largest exposure (Jenkins et al. 2010). Table 8.1 shows the resulting pattern of cross-holdings in government debt: in a majority of European countries, 25 per cent or more of public debt is now externally held, while in Ireland, Italy, Portugal, and Greece between 50 and 90 per cent of public debt is externally held. Large cross-border exposures within the banking system further complicate matters: according to BIS calculations, UK banks have – largely through property loans – a £82.5 billion exposure to the Irish private sector, which in Mervyn King's understated

Table 8.1. Externally held public debt

	Externally held debt as a per cent of GDP (%)
Estonia	6.3
Bulgaria	8.6
The United Kingdom	18.4
Poland	20.4
Latvia	25.8
The United States	26.0
Spain	29.4
Germany	38.7
Ireland	47.6
Hungary	48.5
France	49.5
Italy	53.8
Portugal	61.8
Greece	93.5

Source: Financial Stability Report, June 2010, Bank of England.

phrase, is 'by no means trivial' (Hamilton 2010). In effect, the rights of the foreign bond holder in peripheral countries are defended so as to postpone another round of capital injections into banks in the central economies.

After observing such behaviour, we can ask a more general question about why governments are so considerate of the perceived interests of their national financial sector. In our view, mainland Europe has adopted British-style deference to finance due to the pre-crisis ballooning of bank balance sheets. There has been much discussion of size, focused on whether individual banks are 'too big to fail'; whether banking systems are 'too interconnected to fail'; and whether the banking sector is 'too big to save' in small European countries like Iceland and Ireland. But the broader and more fundamental political problem is of dependence because the banking sector is too big to be subordinated as a sectional interest which elected politicians can ignore or override.

Of course, relative size is not the only relevant factor and there is considerable variation, with a large and diverse country like the United States having a relatively low ratio of bank assets to GDP. However, size does matter across a range of medium-sized European countries (including the United Kingdom, Denmark, France, Germany, the Netherlands, and Switzerland). Figure 8.1 shows that, if we add together the assets in the six largest banks in France, Germany, and the United Kingdom, the top six banks in each country have total assets equal to two to five-times national GDP. European national

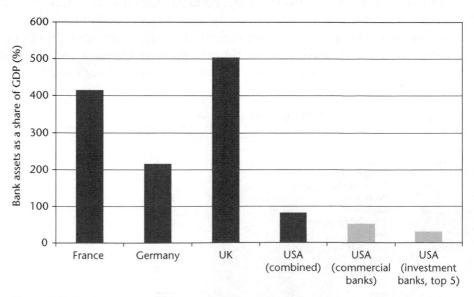

Figure 8.1. Bank assets as a per cent of GDP

Note: The average asset per bank is the summation of six banks in France, Germany, UK, and US commercial banks, and five banks for US investment banks.

Source: Bankscope.

governments with very large and sickly financial systems are unable to make a political distinction between the short-term interests of their finance sector and the national interests of their electorates; in such cases, the major distress or failure of any significant element in an interconnected national finance system would be a national disaster for taxpayers and citizens.

Consequently, elected politicians broker a series of devils' bargains with finance and other governments to keep things going. In return for not-so-cheap liquidity, the Irish and Greek governments are forced to cut public expenditure while guaranteeing that French, German, Dutch, and British holders of bank and sovereign debt will be paid. In North European countries, governments are effectively subsidizing their banks to grow their way out of their bad assets problem and offset the need for further provisions against their earlier mistakes. Part of the deal is ECB policies providing cheap liquidity; another element is lenient national policies towards banks which borrow cheaply and charge retail customers much higher rates. There is still some way to go because, according to IMF calculations, banks globally need to take $2.3 trillion of write-downs on coupons and loans but, as of 2010, they have so far made no more than $1.5 trillion of provisions; in particular, European banks need to make further provisions of around $500 billion on bad assets (IMF 2010: 11–12).

Before turning to consider technocratic intervention, we can note that in the United States, as in the EU, political action has been inhibited, albeit in a rather different kind of way. Reform of finance in the United States is structurally obstructed by the decline of party under an electoral system of *sauve qui peut* – let every person save themselves. Here, individual elected politicians act under populist pressure and are subject to intense finance lobbying: after mid-term elections in 2010, a Republican-controlled Congress and a divided Senate will most likely block or dilute the Democratic president's proposals for reforming finance and/or fiscally stimulating the economy. Some of the proposals of the Dodd Frank Act will be considered in Section 8.3 but immediately we can note that political paralysis throws into relief the continuing freedom of action for technocrats, hubristically exercised but, under freedom of information rules, subject to disclosure in the United States.

8.2 Hubristic technocrats

The response of technocrats is different because their hubris survives untrammelled, as we can demonstrate by considering the US case with some cross reference to UK and European central bank policy. Crisis in the United States immediately licensed technocrats to carry out costly interventions which supported privately owned banks and such like with limited disclosure and accountability through any political process. After the initial paroxysm in autumn 2008, technocrats were also increasingly prepared to experiment with major interventions like quantitative easing (QE), whose economic consequences and social benefits are highly uncertain. And, while political action for reform was thoroughly inhibited by mid-2010, the technocrats planned further large-scale intervention with further QE. We do not doubt the good intentions of Ben Bernanke or Mervyn King, but their actions only serve to consolidate the unhealthy subordination of political calculation to financial power which we observed in the previous section.

The first indicator of technocratic hubris in the US case is the Federal Reserve's reluctance to identify the firms that were recipients of $3.3 trillion in emergency loans and assistance through a variety of programmes after the late-2008 collapse of Lehman. After resisting a freedom of information law suit by Bloomberg, the Fed was finally forced to disclose under pressure for greater accountability from both the left and right of Congress, led by Bernie Sanders, the maverick independent senator from Vermont (Braithwaite 2010). The publication of details of 21,000 transactions under half a dozen programmes in December 2010 caused a furore because emergency credit had been provided to many firms which manifestly were neither failing nor distressed US banks or insurers. Consider, for example, the Term Auction Facility (TAF) which provided one to three-month loans at low rates against poor quality collateral when the overnight market had dried up. The biggest cumulative borrower from TAF was Barclays, which borrowed $232 billion after buying Lehman's US operations out of bankruptcy; the largest TAF user at any one point in time was Bank of America, followed by Wachovia, Wells Fargo, JP Morgan Chase, and Barclays (Harding and Braithwaite 2010). Major beneficiaries of TAF also included Rabobank and Toronto–Dominion, which are among the select few international banks with triple A credit ratings (Harding and Braithwaite 2010).

The Fed's generosity also extended to firms like Caterpillar, Dell, General Electric, and Toyota which are 'non-financial' in that they all had substantial and secure manufacturing businesses (Rushe 2010). Senator Sanders who had forced these disclosures understandably could not see the social benefits of transactions which benefited private firms, especially banks which could make a gain after borrowing cheaply from the government: 'these secret Fed loans, in some cases turned out to be direct corporate welfare to big banks that used these loans not to reinvest in the economy but rather to lend back to the federal government at a higher rate of interest by purchasing treasury securities' (Rushe 2010).

The prospect of such disclosure and condemnation did not inhibit the Fed in late 2010 from further large-scale intervention by a new round of quantitative easing, which in non-technical terms could be described as creating money so the central bank can buy financial assets from commercial banks. This performs the Bernanke doctrine of 2002, as noted in Chapter 1, that a central bank retains expansionary monetary policy options after it has reduced the short-term interest rate to zero. The adoption of a second round of quantitative easing (QE2) in November 2010 also meets the criteria of hubristic intervention in three ways. First it is a technocratic back-door monetary policy adopted because democratic politics blocks fiscal reflation which would otherwise be the US administration's first choice. Second, it is a heroically large-scale operation: the QE2 announcement has committed the Fed to purchasing $600 billion or more of Treasuries between November 2010 and June 2011. This injection of cash to the financial markets follows the previous QE, which involved the purchase of $1.75 trillion of bonds in one year between early 2009 and early 2010. Given the total size of the US Treasury market of about $9 trillion, the first round of QE was a huge operation in macro-economic terms; the follow up QE2 is equivalent to monetizing about 55 per cent of the US government's expected 2011 fiscal deficit. Moreover, this excludes the Fed's role as the underwriter and holder of mortgage-backed securities in the United States, replacing the traditional functions of failed Fannie Mae and Freddie Mac.

Thirdly, QE2 is also hubristic because there is no theoretically clear and empirically defensible view of how QE works. In the United States, in late 2010, this is being undertaken without any 2008-style excuse that 'there will be no economy on Monday' if such intervention is not immediately introduced. The domestic policy rationale for QE is that the central bank asset purchases expand commercial bank reserves and therefore encourage more lending; such purchases also raise security prices, which drives down long-term interest rates. But the catch is that liquid banks are not then obliged to lend to US domestic customers who may not want to borrow, and long-term interest rates are in any case already low (Federal Reserve Statistical Release, H15) when the nominal return on US ten-year Treasuries is currently around 3.5 per cent. What is certain is that US QE causes turmoil in foreign exchange markets and world capital markets: low-cost liquidity provided by the Fed becomes a source of profit from the carry trade between the cheap and weak US dollar borrowings and higher return investments in emerging economy financial instruments. Both China and Brazil have blamed QE in the United States for the recent destabilizing volatility in their foreign exchange markets, while other countries, like India and Australia, also complain 'that QE is merely bringing them overvalued currencies and bubbly asset markets by pushing investors to seek higher returns elsewhere' (*Economist* 2010: 89).

QE is not just American arrogance. Just as the econocracy in the high-income capitalist countries were thinking much the same thing about financial innovation before the crisis, they are now doing much the same thing with expansionary monetary policy. The Bank of England has been a much bigger user of QE in relative terms because, since March 2009, it has bought almost £200 billion of government bonds, or gilts, equivalent to 14 per cent of GDP, though the Bank of England has been much tougher than the Fed about purchase terms, which include a haircut for private sellers. The ECB formally denies it is doing QE but obtains much the same effect through twelve-month long-term refinancing, which expands the assets that banks can use as collateral at the ECB. The result is a ballooning of central bank balance sheets in the case of the Fed, the Bank of England, and the ECB. Thanks to bailouts, liquidity provision, and asset purchases, the Fed's balance sheet has more or less trebled in size from well under $1 trillion before the crisis to $2.4 trillion (Reuters 2010); the quality of assets is also lower due to loans to banks and purchase of assets from Fannie Mae and Feddie Mac.

Increasingly, the central banks start to look like investment banks in 2006 as they are booking profits on spread and volume which take no account of balance sheet risks. The Fed paid a record $35 billion in profits to the US Treasury in the first half of 2010 because it earns more on the long-term bonds it buys as part of its QE programme than it pays to banks on their reserves held at the Fed (Harding and Rappeport 2010). The downside risk is in the central bank balance sheet if the value of purchased securities falls and loans go bad, and this is a problem in Europe as much as the United States. The ECB and the national central banks of the eurozone collectively have liabilities of €1,886 billion, which is twenty-four times their capital as a result of propping up the fiscally weak eurozone countries and their troubled banks (Plender 2010). It is striking that a 4.3 per cent fall in the value of assets held – some of which are collateral from other banks and weak sovereigns – would wipe out all their capital.

These developments are of conjunctural importance and certainly mark some kind of break with earlier forms of financialized capitalism. The capitalism created by the combined inhibitions of the politicians and the hubris of the technocrats is neither a bank-based nor a capital market-based one. In Chapter 4, we argued that banks reinvented themselves so that the traditional financial intermediation theories about banks, households, and firms no longer accurately represented the relationship between the finance and the rest of the economy. Post-crisis we have another reinvention of the financial system in the industrialized world which might now be called central bank-based capitalism because the balance sheets of central banks are the (drivers of) financial markets where an uncertain intermediation takes place. Central banks sustain both banks and bond markets and, indirectly, control stock markets. This is a financial revolution of a new and undemocratic kind because rights are exercised and risks are incurred by a few central bankers for the many. And, while social welfare for the masses is being deliberately cut by politicians, corporate welfare for the banks is being expanded in an undisclosed way by the technocrats.

8.3 Technical fixes?

Official reports on crisis usually end with a section which lists the fixes that will deliver safer finance through intervention in banking practice. In this section, we take a rather different approach which starts from an argument about how re-regulation of banking practice will fail to deliver safer finance under present conditions *when there is extensive bricolage inside finance* and also *an over-mighty finance sector which sets limits on regulatory action* by technocrats and dependent politicians. This point is a crucial implication of our earlier arguments in this book; this argument is briefly developed here by considering the case of increased capital requirements in Europe and the Dodd Frank prohibition on proprietary trading by banks in the United States. After considering the difficulties in using such interventions to change practice, we sketch the principles of an alternative kind of 'rat catcher' intervention which would diminish the sector by spoiling its business models. On banking practice it is often futile to simply try and complicate regulation so as to deal with finance as it is; our alternative policy would be to simplify finance so as to make it more amenable to regulation and limit the scope for bricolage.

If banks were over-levered before the crisis, why not change practice by raising the amount of capital they are required to hold? From this point of view, the increase in capital adequacy now required by the 2010 Basel III regulations is not very demanding. The minimum ratio of 'tier one capital' to 'risk weighted assets' was set at 7 per cent when some academic critics of finance were asking for ratios as high as 15 per cent, and Bank of England Governor Mervyn King publicly envisaged asking for 'capital levels many times higher than the level set out in Basel III' (Guerrera and Pimlott 2010). There was some tightening of the definition of core capital but the denominator remained 'risk weighted assets' not total assets. The new Basel III formula retained a variable capital allowance for different classes of assets according to their perceived risk of default, measured by credit ratings and value at risk calculations, even though such variable allowances – before 2007 – had been a driver of securitization designed to take regulatory capital-intensive assets off bank balance sheets. Meanwhile, non-compliant banks did not face full implementation of the new code until January 2019. When the provisions of Basel III were published in autumn 2010, they were cynically summed up by Lex in the *Financial Times* as 'a widely expected relative leniency' (Lex 2010c).

Expectations were low because Basel III like its predecessors was shaped by lobbying and provided a new opportunity for bricolage. The eight-year lead-in to full implementation of Basel III was a concession to under-capitalized banks in Germany and France. National politicians insist on technical regulation which meets their own sector's needs and so the German government, in the late stages of negotiation on Basel III, insisted on either a low adequacy ratio and/or a long lead-in (Masters 2010). Successive Basel regulations have become an input for bricolage within the finance sector and the main result of Basel I and Basel II was an unintended change in bank behaviour which increased riskiness in banking. Basel I allocated zero default risk to government bonds, ignoring their market risk and maturity mismatching in their funding, and unintentionally encouraged emerging economy banks to invest in government bonds. It contributed significantly to the banking disasters in the emerging economies from the Far East in 1997 to Russia in 1998 and to Turkey in 2001.

As already noted, Basel II was the basis for bricolage via securitization, which moved high capital requirement assets like mortgages off bank balance sheets and sustained the levered banking project of maximizing return on equity, while simultaneously minimizing capital adequacy requirements. Basel III retains the risk weighting of assets, which is an invitation to create new forms of securities whose weight as capital is determined by regulatory risk weightings rather than underlying asset quality, and an invitation furthermore to try out novel accounting treatments of SPV, derivative netting, and repos. As Lex in the *Financial Times* cynically inquired about Basel III, 'what tricks will banks perform to reduce RWAs in order to boost capital ratios?' (Lex 2010*d*).

If the crisis was caused by trading in derivative products, why not change practice by banning proprietary trading by banks? *Inter alia*, this was taken up in the Dodd Frank Wall Street Reform and Consumer Protection Act, which was signed into law by President Obama in July 2010. This was quite unlike the technical fiddling of Basel III because Dodd Frank covered a broad range of issues including consumer protection and aimed to deliver the most comprehensive and radical overhaul of US financial regulation since the New Deal. Instead of forcing structural change by breaking up the big banks and conglomerates, the Dodd Frank Act aimed to prohibit old practices and require new behaviours in ways that recalled the spirit of the Glass–Steagall Act of 1933 which separated wholesale trading and retail deposit taking in US banks. The two Dodd Frank provisions which attracted most attention were the new requirements to put (standard) derivatives trading onto exchanges and the so-called 'Volcker rule' which prohibited a bank both from engaging in own-account proprietary trading and from owning or investing in a hedge fund or private equity fund; this was backed up by other injunctions on practice. As Haldane (2010*a*: 14) has noted, Glass Steagall was 'simple in its objectives and execution' and the 1933 Act itself is 'just 17 pages long'. If Dodd Frank's objectives are simple, the execution is hugely complicated because the Act, which is only a preliminary to further detailed rule writing by agencies, already has 1,603 sections, a table of contents which is fifteen-pages long, and then an opening section on definitions which takes up another ten pages (Dodd Frank 2010). Such complication delivers less, not more, control.

Dodd Frank was like Basel III in that it was shaped by lobbying (albeit within a national frame) and provided a new opportunity for bricolage within finance. On the Volcker rule, the bricolage has focused around the definition of categories and what constitutes proprietary trading. By autumn 2010, the banks were arguing that, if Dodd Frank prohibited own-account trading activity, the banks had very little of that activity in-house. According to the banks, the issue was not whether buy, sell, and hedging activities used balance sheet capital but whether the bank was serving clients by various activities including market making. In September 2010, Jamie Dimon, CEO of JP Morgan Chase, explained that JP Morgan would continue to serve 16,000 clients at 100 trading desks and the new rules would not substantially reduce the volume of 'trading' which had accounted for 22 per cent of the bank's revenue in the previous year (LaCapra 2010). The backup for such positions is provided by finance sector lobbying which, after the mid-term elections, is focused on the sympathetic Republican-dominated House of Representatives.

The implementation of Dodd Frank requires the drafting of more than 200 rules by regulatory agencies like the Securities and Exchange Commission; significantly, the drafting of these rules is subject to legislative oversight by Republican Representatives prepared to use resolutions, budget measures, and investigative hearings 'to ensure the final language meets their expectations' (Mattingly 2010). As for the curbs on bank-owned in-house hedge funds and private equity units, after last-minute amendments to the Dodd Frank bill, banks like Goldman and Citigroup have seven to twelve years to comply (Keoun 2010). The long lead-in is, of course, reminiscent of Basel III and very different from Glass Steagall, which gave banks just one year to get out of underwriting with revocation of banking licenses for any banks which were still non-compliant after eighteen months.

Capital adequacy in Europe and the Volcker rule in the United States, both illustrate the practical difficulties of writing regulations that constrain financial practice in a world where regulatory proposals are a starting point for political lobbying and where regulatory provisions are an input for finance sector bricolage. But these attempts at re-regulation also raise more fundamental questions about whether the objectives of the regulators are well chosen. For example, would the world be a safer and better place if tough rules on banking capital adequacy could be enforced? Many different kinds of banks failed after 2008 for various reasons of illiquidity and/or insolvency: some of them like Northern Rock had risky business models of reliance on wholesale funding but respectable Basel II adequacy ratios, which is perhaps not surprising in a world of lobbying and bricolage.

If these conditions were removed, higher capital ratios on a broader denominator would tie up large amounts of extra capital inside the banking sector as a kind of insurance provision against exceptional 2008-style disaster. This would ordinarily – and in other years – depress return on capital in banking. Barclays Capital estimates that the top thirty-five US banks will need between $100 billion and $150 billion in equity capital under Basel III (Masters 2010). A pessimist like former investment banker, Bill Winters, anticipate a halving of the 20–25 per cent pre-crisis banking return on equity, while the BIS anticipates a target 15 per cent banking return on equity (Guerrera et al. 2010). Meanwhile, the technical discussion of capital adequacy and risk weightings completely disconnects banking from any consideration of social purpose. Under Basel regulations, banks now need to hold five times as much capital when lending to a small business or an entrepreneur than when investing in a triple A-rated investment vehicle. Interestingly, this point has been raised by bloggers but not by the mainstream finance media (see e.g. http://www.subprimeregulations.blogspot.com).

The discussion of capital adequacy regulations illustrates the limits of technical practice as a form of knowledge which takes its ends as given. However, in technical practice, there is some discussion of means/ends relation which is often completely absent in many other areas of intervention, such as bankers' pay. Here, politicians in all jurisdictions feel they must be seen to be doing something for electoral reasons given the now-settled public hostility to high pay for bankers. In early 2010, a *You Gov* poll in the United Kingdom found that 76 per cent of respondents wanted bonuses capped, 59 per cent supported windfall taxes on bankers' bonuses, and 60 per cent wanted the tax extended to hedge fund and private equity partners (Asthana 2010). The position is broadly similar in the United States: in late 2010, a poll of 1,000 adults by Selzer for *Bloomberg* found that 71 per cent favoured banning big bonuses at Wall Street firms and a further 17 per cent favoured a 50 per cent tax on bonuses exceeding $400,000 (Dodge 2010). Interestingly, this is not an issue where US opinion divides on predictable left vs right lines about the merits of business regulation and high taxes. Some 76 per cent of Republicans support a ban on bonuses, which is actually higher than backing among Democrats or independents.

But, if we consider the British and European policy response, discussion of what to do about pay has been bogged down in governance provisions on the issue of disclosure and the main result so far is new regulations about withholding bonus payments for several years so as to relate bonuses more closely to long-term performance, which chimes with the tenor of earlier recommendations on best practice. The British Walker report originally proposed disclosure not of named individuals but of the number of bankers in high-end earnings bands above £1 million; but this modest result is unlikely if, as Sir David Walker now argues, the United Kingdom should wait until similar measures are adopted within the EU, the United States, and the G20 (Walker 2010). On withholding bonuses, the FSA in December 2010 proposed new requirements for deferring bonus payment for three to five years, limiting the cash component to as little as 20 per cent and outlawing guaranteed (nonperformance-related) bonuses to retain staff (Murphy et al. 2010). Similar proposals are being made by the Committee of European Banking Supervisors (Murphy et al. 2010).

These proposals on bankers' pay reflect not only some timidity but also an inability to think through the problem and solution because the proposals to change the form in which high rewards are paid does not engage with practice or address underlying problems. Much official discussion of pay presupposes an incentivized banker who knowingly takes risks when the more serious problem is collective bricolage. Furthermore, changing the form of pay systems does not tackle volume-based business models and the comp (compensation) ratio system which sets up a kind of joint venture between shareholders and senior investment bankers, as discussed in Chapter 4. The comp ratio survives completely unreformed as a driver of pay levels. The present UK coalition government is divided on whether (and how) to restrain bonuses and whether bonuses should be taxed. Meanwhile, London bonuses will most likely be down by around 20 per cent in 2011 because turnover is temporarily reduced (Jenkins et al. 2010), which may mitigate the immediate political pressure, though not the underlying problem. Recent experience on pay disclosure – one of the remedies widely discussed – in non-financial companies and on bonus withholding in US investment banking is not encouraging. Corporate governance rules in the United Kingdom and the United States, which require ever greater disclosure of individual CEO pay in large public companies, have not slowed the rise of chief executive pay; while failed investment banks like Lehman or Bear Stearns effectively deferred compensation by paying staff in equity, which made no difference to their corporate appetite for risk even though 30 per cent or more of equity was employee owned in the mid-2000s.

If the policy response on pay is superficial, one response might be that we need some fundamental intellectual analysis of what is wrong with banking and finance practice. But the results of fundamentalism are no more encouraging because academics and technocrats are caught between the intellectual conservatism of endorsing old paradigms for understanding capitalism which are all too familiar and the intellectual radicalism of recommending new paradigms which are underdeveloped and do not yet exist.

In many accounts of financial crisis, the starting point is a reified account of capitalism or the generic functions of banking, so that analysis of problem and solution treats the case of finance as an illustration of a general a priori about how capitalism is and should be. Consider, for example, the pro-market, pro-competition economics-based commentariat in the United Kingdom. When it comes to problem definition, the *Economist*, for example, was predictably censorious about the role of government-sponsored Fannie Mae and Freddie Mac in 'America's deeply flawed system of housing finance' where their guarantees were 'a solution to a non-existent problem' (*Economist* 2008). When it comes to solutions, the invariant prescription is more competition: this position is clearly represented in the membership of the UK's Banking Commission, which includes Sir John Vickers and Claire Spottiswoode (see also Chapter 7), or in John Kay's report (2009) on *Narrow Banking*, which recommends the separation of utility banking and the creation of a 'competitive market place' with 'a restructured retail sector focussed on the needs of consumers' (Kay 2009). The banking sector is explicitly to be remodelled so that it is more like the supermarket sector.

The intellectually radical technocrats and academics are altogether more interesting because figures like Haldane, Lo, and Shiller cannot be accused of predictably repeating themselves. However, as Haldane demonstrates with his proposals for a new epidemiological understanding of financial networks (2009a), any new paradigm will be work in progress for some time as its supporters struggle with multiple and intersecting issues about measurement, mapping, and devising new practices of intervention. If the shift is radical, we could also expect an early phase of learning by doing where part of the learning comes from what are afterwards identified as policy mistakes. There is also the prior question of what fundamentals are called into question and what assumptions are carried over into the new paradigm. With Haldane, the shift from physics-based to biology-based understandings leaves mathematization and scientism unexamined and unquestioned. Haldane's new paradigm is just like the old one insofar as both rest on the dream of an adequate technical knowledge of the complexity of finance and markets which will allow technocratic mastery. The political effect is to reproduce the current depoliticization of finance and shore up the position of the econocracy and the technocratic elites, and their hold over financial market regulation. From this point of view, it is not Haldane's proposal for paradigm change but his carefully evidenced political arithmetic on issues like leverage and banking profits (2010a and c) which is impressive because that does engage with the activity specifics of the financial sector.

After briefly discussing the limits of intellectualism about banking practice, it is possible to sketch an alternative regulatory approach which focuses on changing the business model and diminishing the finance sector by altering the conditions around practice. The technical interventions we propose stem from our specific analysis in this book of the finance sector and from a broader historical perspective on major reform projects. Our alternative approach to future banking reform has parallels with Thomas Carlyle's retrospect (1840) on the Poor Law reform of 1834. For Carlyle, the precondition for reforming assistance to the workless poor was not a 'stretch of heroic faculty' by the policy intellectuals of utilitarianism like Edwin Chadwick, but 'toughness of bowels' by the political classes under Lord Melbourne. After all, the premise of reform was only that 'if paupers are made miserable' their numbers will decline, and this is 'a principle known to all rat catchers' whose aim is always to make the granary less attractive by stopping holes, introducing cats, setting traps, and poison (Carlyle 1840: 17). The same 'rat catcher's' principle can be the starting point for dealing with the working rich in banking, provided we remember that the chief aim of reform is not to reduce the population but to frustrate their business models in ways which will incidentally deliver a smaller and more modestly paid cadre of working rich.

The principle is important because it directs us towards the objective of changing the habitat, which in this case means the conditions around finance sector practice (rather than directly mandating changes in banking practices as in the capital adequacy or the Volcker rule earlier considered). The principle also directs us towards a package of measures – the equivalent of cats, traps, poison, and stopping holes – which would be varied in the light of prior discussion and subsequent results. We would add that many of these proposals for finance are quasi-political and aligned with popular sentiment in ways that will usefully make life more difficult for political elites who have no stomach for reform.

If business models are the object of intervention, then investment banking is the first and most obvious target for a national level tax which could immediately take a large 50 per cent top slice from each investment banking firm (or division's) compensation fund (calculated on the basis of the rolling average ratio of compensation to turnover over the previous five years). The internal wages fund could therefore be reduced through taxation without engaging any of the detail about how wages are internally distributed amongst groups inside the firm or how it is paid out through bonuses or other means. This is an advantage because the form of payment would quickly become an object of bricolage if, for example, the one-off 50 per cent tax on 'bonuses' above £25,000 in the United Kingdom imposed by the previous UK government was to be renewed. The banks will not year after year pay a bonus tax on behalf of their employees as they did in the United Kingdom in 2010 but will instead devise other forms of pay (Vina 2009).

A comp tax would probably strain the joint-venture relationship between bankers and shareholders, particularly if shareholders returns are affected by any attempt to minimize the effect on the post-tax compensation pool. As part of a package of measures to restrain banking, active shareholders would be needed to ensure that the burden of any comp tax was not partly transferred to other stakeholders; any wrangling about distribution between bankers and shareholders will, in the context of lower returns on equity, usefully stress the business model. The finance sector is of course adept at tax avoidance and evasion but that is less of a problem with comp tax than with many others because the comp tax bears on individual incomes and the wages fund. The benefits of avoidance will in due course show up in the income tax returns of individual residents; and the US or British tax authorities are meanwhile technically capable of deciding whether new wages fund arrangements at firm level are being entered into solely for tax purposes.

A tax on compensation could also be pressed more aggressively than taxes on bank profits or their balance sheet and capital base: it is much easier to halve wages than to halve returns on capital. Taxes on capital usually have to be softened so that they do not harm bank ability to lend to retail customers or sustain wholesale market liquidity. For example, the Obama proposals in the United States for a bank levy to recover costs of bailout bizarrely included provision for the levy charges on banks to be tax deductible so that the net costs to the banks and the net revenue gains of the US Treasury may be modest (Guha 2010). The revenue from the comp fund tax could also be hypothecated for practical and political benefit. The revenue from a halving of pay levels in investment banking could be applied via a kind of sovereign wealth fund which invested in a range of projects like transport infrastructure, alternative energy, or social housing in pursuit of a modest return of no more than 5 per cent.

The war machines of private equity and hedge funds are more difficult to tackle because they change tactics opportunistically and have no one standard business model. But if a comp tax were levied on investment banks, in-house banking activity will simply move two blocks down the road so that big banks contract as risky activity moves into small firms which are less regulated and less visible. One general line of attack on war machines is to withdraw the tax privileges and change the tax rules which boost the profits of financial engineering and the pay of the working rich partners. In the case of private equity, the starting point here is a willingness to consider the withdrawal of the tax privileges traditionally enjoyed by debt financing in high-income countries, where corporations can deduct interest payments before a profits figure is struck and tax liability and dividends are then calculated. The earlier debates on private equity explored in Chapter 3 also point to a much stricter treatment of private equity 'carried interest', which can be treated as income not capital gains and taxed in the usual way.

The tax concessions on debt were designed for a different era so that non-financial companies could operate with some prudent mix of equity and debt coupons which would offer different profiles of risk and reward for investors. This reasonable arrangement has been bricolaged into a source of profit for private equity and generally encourages leverage. When we are considering a package of business model changing measures, this tax concession on debt should be revisited, which is likely to require some public inquiry to explore the possibility of differentiated arrangements for companies of different sizes, for financial and non-financial companies, or other ways of reducing the tax advantages of debt for financiers. The matter is urgent because the unintended consequence of the existing tax concession has been to encourage the levered business models of the financier who benefits privately by hanging debt around operating businesses; this will resume cyclically as soon as borrowing is easy and asset prices are rising. These changes should be accompanied by a broader public inquiry into the institutionalization of tax avoidance in alternative investment activities through the use of offshore tax havens and such like.

There are a variety of other policies which change the conditions around finance sector practice and they would need to be considered as a package along with the measures suggested above. The best-known proposal is for a general financial transactions tax (FTT). This was originally advocated by James Tobin in the early 1970s as a tax on currency transactions at a rate of maybe 0.5 per cent on the value of transactions, and it has since been advocated in various forms as a way of throwing sand into the machine of finance as a transaction-generating machine. The United Kingdom has long had a stamp duty on private share purchases and the Swedes experimented in the late 1980s with a more general tax on purchase and sale of many different kinds of securities, including derivatives.

An FTT may therefore be a useful revenue-raising device, or it may have a more interesting role as part of a national package of measures designed to make financial activities in a specific centre less profitable. It is unlikely to be effective on its own to reduce the international volume of trading under present conditions, especially if bricoleurs within finance can sustain volumes by redesigning their activities so as to reduce the number of *taxable* transactions using many current possibilities of process redesign or geographic re-routing. Banking and investment firms which cannot avoid tax costs will seek to pass them on to investors and consumers who are often ignorant, locked-in, or price-insensitive so that margins are maintained and the end user pays. All these objections have been publicly rehearsed, yet there is some international backing for such a tax: in November 2009, EU leaders indicated their support, encouraging a more hostile IMF to consider such a development (Barber and Parker 2009). Other countries have meanwhile introduced unilateral measures to deal with specific problems: for example, Brazil introduced a 2 per cent charge on foreign portfolio investments in October 2009 to reduce inflows of 'hot money', and even the cynical Lex column commented that the whole notion of taxes on capital flows 'deserves a wider airing' (Lex 2010*a*).

Such rat-catcher interventions to change the habitat avoid many of the problems arising from intervention in finance practice which is either ineffectual and/or an input for further bricolage; they also avoid any need to wait for concerted international action which is unlikely to come in any timely or meaningful way. Consider, instead, what happens after one country goes first with rat-catcher intervention. Mobile investment banking or alternative investment activity will shift elsewhere outside the boundaries of the nation which taxes the comp ratio, withdraws the privileges on interest, or introduces transaction tax. But if the national prime mover has a banking sector which is four or five times GDP, shrinking the relative size of the banking sector may be a policy objective. The migration may just shift the problem elsewhere and will not deliver a global solution, but nothing else delivers coordinated global reform. Meanwhile, the first high-income country, or group of countries, to act resolutely against the business models of finance may encourage others to follow. We have in Chapter 5 argued that the benefits of an expanding finance sector are exaggerated in the finance sector's own narrative; in the UK case, employment in finance did not increase after the early 1990s and in Chapter 1 we showed that the bailout costs after the crisis were greater than the tax revenues in the five years before crisis. On this basis, a prudent government should not spend any of the tax revenues from finance but set them aside as provision for the costs of the inevitable, next crisis. This is the mad logic of the UK case where an otherwise unexceptional national economy is attached to an over-large and internationally competitive finance sector. It is perhaps time to call the bluff of the bankers, hedge fund managers, and others who are always threatening to leave unless they are given favoured treatment.

At the same time, after the finance sector has been diminished in a variety of ways by the rat-catcher intervention, it is necessary to consider whether and how regulation can be used more positively and the question of practice cannot be completely ignored not least because of the need for rules. It is nevertheless difficult to discuss these rules because finance intersects with many of the other things that national governments will want to do, and that requires new institutions and a redesign of fund flows. The specifics of redesign would vary according to national circumstances because, as analysis of job creation in the United Kingdom in Chapter 7 showed, the problems of national economies and therefore the tasks of finance are specific to time and place. There is a clear need for a general shift towards a modestly profitable and sustainable low-carbon and high-employment economy, and that would, for example, in most national cases, probably require some new kind of socially managed physical investment and productive enterprise loan fund which is continuously fed by long-term savings diverted from the orthodox channels of fund management and investment in the markets.

If the ecology and objectives of finance change radically, and then vary, in different ways according to national circumstance, it is hard to be specific about rules on finance sector practice. We can, however, be clear about the general principle of action which should be not to complicate regulation but to simplify finance. This principle is important because, whatever the changes, finance will need to service the established large demand for credit and insurance transactions. For example, in many economies, half or more of households will expect to take out mortgages as owner-occupiers, just as most manufacturing exporters will want to fix exchange rates.

Some thought therefore needs to be given to making financial activities, as described in Chapter 2 of this book, both simpler and more legible, thereby limiting the scope for bricolage and making effective regulation easier. The general aim here should be to turn the complex circuits of Chapter 2 involving many steps, SPVs, and shadowy players into short, direct chains with ascertainable beginnings and ends. This should not be misunderstood as a call for a rejection of innovation and a demand for a return to earlier technologies of banking. There is nothing intrinsically wrong or bad about securitization or derivatives. Short-chain securitization in the Danish style does deliver on some of the promises about democratization of finance made by Bernanke and others before the crash without creating complex circuits and 'originate and distribute' excesses as in the United States. The much simpler system of securitization that has evolved in Denmark works through covered bonds for which the originating banks retain full responsibility; while bond sales do free up sufficient capital for banks to finance a next round of mortgages and SME loans. A simpler system of this kind could be encouraged by regulators over that currently in widespread use (see Frankel et al. 2004; Boyce 2008).

If we doubt the possibility of simple technical fixes, we do accept the need for technical knowledge and analysis of roundabout repercussions through public debate about a package of proposals and old-fashioned open inquiries where many views are represented. Meanwhile, a package of proposals (including a comp ratio tax and other measures) to change habitat conditions and undermine finance business models is itself a way of taking the political initiative. The response to such proposals would highlight the problem of elites (especially political elites) who are against bad bankers but have little stomach for serious reform that is in line with majority opinion, which would endorse a halving of excessive wages and other measures. Then, if there is an alternative approach and those outside the metropolitan elites have specific proposals, the next question is how do the outsiders acquire the political leverage to follow through? That is the theme of our next section.

8.4 Democratizing finance: possibilities and dangers

This book tells a story about the hobbling of democratic politics which led to an elite political debacle set up by abdicating politicians, implicitly blessed by hubristic technocrats and driven by largely unreflective finance practitioners. Democracy was hobbled in the age of market triumphalism that guided so much policy in financial markets from the beginning of the Thatcher and Reagan revolutions. The new languages of deregulation and of rule by regulators drawn from an econocratic clerisy, all told the same story: politics, especially democratic politics, was to have only a marginal place in financial life. Symptomatically, the phrase 'democratization of finance' was widely used especially in the United States in the 1990s and 2000s to denote the inclusion of more citizens in market processes of credit provision. After outlining this problem definition and criticizing the misrule of experts, we draw the conclusion that the only antidote to elite misrule is a revitalization of mass democracy through a variety of non-market institutions.

In taking this position, we are returning to classical centre-left objectives and updating Tawney's project, which was to make the mass franchise meaningful by bringing economic power under popular control; the challenge now is to envisage a twenty-first century democratization of finance which brings banks and markets under democratic control and directs finance for some social purpose. The possibilities are different in the various jurisdictions considered in this book, so we will, in this section, separately consider Britain, the EU, and the United States while trying to draw some general lessons.

The marginalization of democratic politics was particularly complete in the United Kingdom because, as Chapter 5 argues, it drew on a long history of weak democratic engagement with the control of financial institutions, especially of those institutions at the heart of the City of London. That history emphasizes the magnitude of the task we now face. There is only the thinnest strain of scepticism in British political culture in the face of the stories told by financial elites – a feature that explains why, despite the opening of a window of opportunity for democratization at the height of the crisis, the window slammed shut very quickly. It explains why the doctrine of 'arm's-length' management of the institutions that came into public ownership in 2008 – arm's length from the democratic state, not from the City elite – was accepted so readily. It also explains why the *chutzpah* of the Bischoff and Wigley reports was accepted with a straight face.

There are, moreover, reasons for pessimism about the chances of extending democratic control over finance that are not directly connected with the immediate politics of finance. The age of Thatcherism was also an age when some of the historically radical centres of opposition to capitalist economic power continued their long decline: trade union organization weakened, especially in the private sector; the Labour Party further marginalized its already half-hearted commitment to economic radicalism by reinventing as 'New Labour'; class-based popular organization in the wider society was increasingly supplanted by newer identity based movements – based on, variously, gender, ethnicity, and environmentalism. These developments constrain the possibilities of mobilization for democratic control of finance, but they also create opportunities. The political parties themselves are, over the long term, literally dying as popular institutions, with small and ageing memberships. As their popular roots wither away, they are shrinking into a set of tiny metropolitan caucuses obsessed with the game of high politics in Westminster and Whitehall. Their huge appetite for money in an age of advertising and survey-led campaigning makes them prey to powerful financial interests and their allies in the corporate media.

But the very decay of the metropolitan elites has created gaps within which a new politics of popular mobilization has grown. It is fragmented, sometimes anomic, often blazing up as short-lived campaigns: the new style is epitomized by UK Uncut which turned corporate tax avoidance into a high-profile public issue in the winter of 2010 by using new social media to organize direct action against Arcadia and Vodafone stores (Taylor et al. 2010). This is a world of ferment, miles away from the ritualized confrontations of the metropolitan party elites, or the somnolent world of local party meetings dominated by a few stalwarts. The metropolitan elites believe they live in a world of 'apathy' that needs the attention of a metropolitan agency like the Electoral Commission to probe the causes of 'low' participation. But, as the extensive surveys of the new world of participation by Pattie et al. (2003, 2004) show, there is no 'apathy': popular engagement is alive and kicking, but it has moved away from official channels and the institutions of the metropolitan elite like parties. It ranges from the most parochial – an uncountable variety of local campaigns on almost every conceivable issue – to the most global: a surge of popular engagement with groups concerned with global poverty, global human rights, and the global physical environment. What is more, this is a world of ferment because it has learnt to use the new social technologies of mass mobilization, and to exploit new hard technologies to make those social technologies more effective.

There is a *substantive* agenda for reform of the financial system, and it is dealt with elsewhere in this book. But that substantive agenda has no hope of being realized if it is promoted through the established institutional world of political, regulatory, and financial market elites – that is the lesson of the lost opportunity of 2008–9 described in earlier pages of this book. Any alternative must engage with the opportunities created by the new worlds of popular mobilization and that engagement is only possible if we have a story because effective political action often comes about by trumping a bad story with a better story that is clearly characterized and well evidenced. Some elements of this new story are already in place. High pay and tax avoidance lack legitimacy in a country like the United Kingdom where median average earnings are no more than £22,000 and the opinion poll evidence suggests that rat-catcher interventions would be hugely popular. But this hostility needs to be channelled and developed by telling a broader story about how the overpaid bankers delivered the wrong kind of finance because too much credit went into circuits predicated on asset price inflation that was unsustainable. And that needs to be balanced with a positive story about what finance could do going forward to serve unmet social needs. In that respect, our story here can overlap with that of the Bischoff report. However, in developing the story about what finance could do, the generics about ageing populations and inadequate infrastructure in high-income countries needs to be balanced with attention to national specifics of time and place. This has to be so because what we want from finance in the United States or Australia would be different from that in the United Kingdom.

If it is possible to tell a new story, there are at least three areas where rich possibilities of mobilization exist. First, there is now a very well informed population of groups – mostly communicating virtually – that are concerned with challenging the claims of the financial and regulatory elite, and systematically exposing the interests and deals that lie underneath the vast lobbying operations of corporate finance. That population is much larger and more vigorous in the United States and, surprisingly, in the analysis of the lobbying world of Brussels; it is also growing in the United Kingdom and it is an important source countering the kinds of mystification promoted by reports like those by Bischoff and Wigley.

Second, there is a rapidly growing world of NGOs that are critical in general of the business practices of shareholder value maximization, but which have yet done comparatively little to engage with the financial practices that brought the system to crisis in 2008. Such organizations span a wide spectrum of positions and include powerful development charities convinced that financial institutions are fundamentally implicated in global poverty, as well as domestic campaigning groups responding to the social consequences of the age of austerity precipitated by the financial crash and Christian denominations that are now packed with activists critical of the market order. While only about 6 per cent of the population are regular churchgoers, even at that level they vastly outnumber regular attendees at meetings of political parties – and include a disproportionate number of active and engaged citizens. This diverse world is unlikely to be anything more than a source of contingent alliances on particular issues – but its very diversity, energy, and (often) popular roots make it a potentially critical source of such alliances.

Third, there is the old world of trade unions which retain a membership in millions and are beginning to show some interest in broader issues beyond the wage bargain. This is perhaps their way of editing themselves back into the political script as players with serious views about what is to be done. For example, the Trades Union Congress under Brendan Barber has focused on issues like inequality and corporate tax avoidance, drawing on the expertise of figures like Richard Murphy, and individual trade unions, Unite and the GMB, had some success in highlighting the excesses of debt-fuelled private equity before the crash. While trade union membership has been in decline for more than thirty years, it is still the case that 25 per cent of the UK workforce is unionized and the unions have more than 6 million individual members. While their main strength is in the public sector, Unite organizes around 30 per cent of all workers in finance, mainly in retail banking and insurance. This base makes unionists a major potential force for change.

The question is whether and how these three worlds of dissent can be brought together in popular campaigns. Banking after the crisis could be the rallying point for a coalition of losers because taxpayers, customers, and the retail workforce are all now losers from shareholder value-driven banking. Many local communities are losers as they contemplate the abandoned, half-built development projects despoiling their town centres; local businesses are losers as retail banks centralize and shrink their local business services in the name of efficiency. Unite could join forces with NGOs on issues like the high street banks' pay incentives for retail advisers to 'sell to' consumers, which may have some force as the high street banks brands are vulnerable to direct action. A new kind of politics of leafleting and boycotts outside high street branches would not directly address the problems about wholesale banking, but it would threaten the flow of savings and loan feedstock from the retail branches of conglomerates.

Real possibilities therefore exist to expose financial oligarchies to democratic influences in campaigns that would be formative, but these are currently only possibilities. If we look at the two other important jurisdictions examined in this book – the European Union and the United States – we can see some of the limits to those possibilities. They amount to cautionary stories for anyone with democratizing ambitions in the United Kingdom.

The possibilities for democratizing finance in the European Union are slight. It is true that some of the forces making for potential empowerment in the British case can also be detected across the Union. Across Western Europe, old political parties are in decline, and are challenged by vigorous forces from civil society. In Europe, more generally, the *financial* crisis caused an *intellectual* crisis for the econocrats embedded in financial institutions. But in the Union itself, the institutional shape of policymaking, especially the regulation of financial markets, is both oligarchical in structure and arranged to maximize the influence of corporate elites. The ECB exhibits a highly developed form of domination by an econocracy, insulated from popular political forces: the appointment of its leading personnel; the arrangements for oversight by the European Parliament; and the internal culture of the institution itself – which maximizes econocratic influence – all help ensure this.

Moreover, as we saw in Chapter 5, the practice of policymaking in Brussels – notably the Commission's 'comitology', with its reliance on co-opting affected interests – imparts a powerful bias in the system favouring the corporate sector. The bias is reinforced by the evidence, also summarized in Chapter 5, that the complexity of the Brussels policymaking system, coupled with a culture that gives a special place in policymaking to affected interests, has encouraged a hyper-professionalization of lobbying: expensive professional lobbyists and expensively assembled lobbying operations by corporate interests are two of the most distinctive features of the Brussels system. In short, any realistic efforts to democratize finance in the EU are going to have come through the route of influence from democratically influenced national systems.

The evidence from the United States is even more cautionary for those interested in democratizing financial regulation in the United Kingdom. Here is a political culture which historically has possessed what has been conspicuously lacking in the United Kingdom: a well-entrenched tradition of populism which viewed financial elites on Wall Street, and their allies in Washington, with deep suspicion. This provides a remarkable contrast with the demeanour of subjection exhibited by democratic politicians in the United Kingdom to the City for decades. Moreover, institutional arrangements in the US system have been designed to give that populist suspicion space for expression. There is a vigorous network of corporate critics in civil society, often able to access the considerable resources of the US university system and of charitable foundations; in short, there exists already in the United States in a highly developed form precisely those civil society institutions whose nascence in the United Kingdom we cited above as a source of hope.

What is more, the culture and the institutional structures of American democracy increase further the possibilities of democratic control: since the 1930s, there has been a vigorous regulatory state presence in the financial arena. The institutions of the regulatory state are subject to a system of legislative oversight in Washington alongside which the activities of Parliamentary select committees in the United Kingdom look amateurish. As we have shown in earlier pages, this more vigorous democratic environment has indeed had some effects: in the range and intellectual coherence of post-crisis critiques of the system; and even in the ability of the policymaking system to produce, albeit in a restricted fashion, some legislative reform of regulation.

But the United States does not provide any straightforward kind of model to follow. This is a system where corporate finance rode in the saddle during the years of the Great Complacency; where there was an almost unparalleled capacity to shape regulatory policy, and where key parts of the financial elite enriched themselves on a scale not seen since the age of the Robber Barons who, unlike the financial engineers of Wall Street, actually built important parts of the infrastructure of the American economy. And, in the US system, two conditions that allowed corporate finance to exercise power still exist in the post-crisis world. These two forces are particularly important for they point also to problematic features that persist in the United Kingdom.

First, the policymaking elite and the corporate financial elite in the United States remain entangled in symbiotic relations. The path from the leading institutions of Wall Street to the leading positions in the Federal Executive and in the regulatory agencies remains well trodden in both directions. That is a condition which, we have seen, also exists in the United Kingdom: in the sociology of a key institution like UKFI, and in the dense networks that link City corporate elites and those in key parts of the core executive, notably the Treasury. Moreover, the American symbiosis of corporate and governmental elites feeds, and is fed by, a well-resourced and highly professional lobbying industry, to which the limited character of US reforms is a striking testimony, and this sophisticated lobbying industry is also now increasingly in evidence in the United Kingdom.

Second, the formally important systems of democratic control and oversight in Congress are seriously compromised by the role of corporate interests in political finance. It is a well-documented feature of the American system that, despite decades of campaign finance reform, democratic politicians retain a huge appetite for corporate financial support, and corporate interests stand ready and willing to provide that support. The weaknesses of party institutions and the rise of hugely expensive advertising-led campaigns, moreover, mean that the critical relations are now between individual politicians and corporate interests. That helps explain why the Congressional system was well designed to provide 'show trials' of individual culprits from Wall Street that made good television box office, while at the same time Congress was easily suborned to restrict the impact of regulatory reform.

In the UK system, there is no great danger of individual politicians being 'bought' by corporate interests. There is little point in trying to suborn members of parliamentary select committees because their policy influence is slight, and there is little point in individual Members of Parliament (MPs) canvassing corporate donations because their ability to use such resources in individual campaigns is highly restricted. But nevertheless, the importance of corporate finance in shaping policymaking behaviour in the United Kingdom matches the American pattern. In the United Kingdom, however, the key connection is not between the individual politicians and corporate interests but between the national parties and those interests. The very condition identified earlier as creating a space for mobilization in civil society – the death of the parties as mass movements – has also made national party leaderships desperate for money, and corporate interests are by far the most important sources of that money.

As far as the United Kingdom is concerned, this suggests that the democratization of finance has to rest on more than the hope that a new world of civil society can be mobilized. It must also rest on institutional reforms which open up the enclosed networks linking the core executive and City interests to new social forces, and it must rest on a reconfiguration of the system of party finance in a way that reduces the appetite of the party leaderships for corporate money. Thus the problem of reforming finance is both in itself distinctively different and also like so many others. If there are to be democratic remedies to elite-dominated and unaccountable processes, which bring debacle in finance and other areas, it is necessary to capture existing positions and create new fora where other stories and other values can be pressed by non-elite actors who live outside the metropolitan bubble. In doing so, this book's argument about finance as elite debacle is a contribution to that political struggle by provincial radicals who, like Wright Mills (1962), 'do not claim to be detached'.

References

Acharya, V. and Johnson, T. (2005). *Insider Trading in Credit Derivatives*. http://faculty. london.edu/vacharya/assets/documents/acharya-johnson.pdf accessed 10 June 2010.

Aitken, R. (2007). *Performing Capital: Toward a Cultural Economy of Popular and Global Finance*. New York: Palgrave Macmillan.

Akerlof, G.A. and Shiller, R.J. (2010). *Animal Spirits: How Human Psychology Drives the Economy, and Why It Matters for Global Capitalism*. Princeton, NJ: Princeton University Press.

Alessandrini, P. and Haldane, A. (2009). Banking on the State. Speech Given at the Federal Reserve Bank of Chicago Twelfth Annual International Banking Conference on 'The International Financial Crisis: Have the Rules of Finance Changed?' 25 September 2009. London: Bank of England. http://www.bankofengland.co.uk/publications/speeches/ 2009/speech409.pdf accessed August 2010.

Allen, K. (2009). Campaigners Blast Walker Reform on Banks. *Guardian*, 26 November.

Allen, F. and Gale, D. (1994). *Financial Innovation and Risk Sharing*. Cambridge, MA: MIT Press.

—— Santomero, A.M. (1997). The Theory of Financial Intermediation. *Journal of Banking and Finance*, 21: 1461–85.

—— —— (2001). What Do Financial Intermediaries Do? *Journal of Banking & Finance*, 25: 271–94.

Alter-EU (2009). *A Captive Commission: The Role of the Financial Industry in Shaping EU Regulation*. http://www.greenpeace.org/raw/content/eu-unit/press-centre/reports/a-captive-commission-5-11-09.pdf accessed 15 August 2010.

Althusser, L. (1969). *For Marx*. London: Verso.

Amable, B. (2003). *The Diversity of Modern Capitalism*. Oxford: Oxford University Press.

Anon (2005). Moody's Assigns (P)B3 Rating to Proposed GBP100 Million Mezzanine Notes Issued by Focus (Finance) Plc. *Moody's Investor Service*, 22 February.

—— (2007a). Moody's Downgrades Focus's Debt as Sale Starts. *Reuters*, 5 March.

—— (2007b). Focus DIY Sold for £1 to Private Equity Firm. *Guardian*, 19 June.

Arnold, M. (2007). Buy-Out Tax Rate is 'Lower Than a Cleaner's'. *Financial Times*, 4 June.

—— (2009). Candover Abandons €3bn Buy-Out Fund. *Financial Times*, 3 December.

Asthana, A. (2010). New Poll Reveals Depth of Outrage at Bankers' Bonuses. *Observer*, 21 February.

Atkinson, D. and Elliott, L. (2007). *Fantasy Island: Waking up to the Incredible Economic, Political and Social Illusions of the Blair Legacy*. London: Constable.

References

Augar, P. (2005). *The Greed Merchants: How the Investment Banks Played the Free Market Game*. London: Penguin.

Bachelor, L. (2009). Watchdog Investigates NatWest Ads. *Observer*, 10 May.

Barber, T. (2007). EU Adopts Flexible Stance on Bank Crises. *Financial Times*, 16 September.

—— Parker, G. (2009). EU Leaders Urge IMF to Consider Global Tobin Tax. *Financial Times*, 11 December.

Barclays Capital. (2009). *Gilts Outperforming. Equity Gilt Study*. London: Barclays Capital.

Barthes, R. (1970). Interview. *L'Express*, 31 May.

Bawden, T. and Waller, M. (2009). Gordon Brown Lambasts RBS for 'Irresponsible' Action. *The Sunday Times*, 19 January.

Benston, G.J. (1994). Universal Banking. *Journal of Economic Perspectives*, 8: 121–43.

—— Smith C.W. (1976). A Transactions Cost Approach to the Theory of Financial Intermediation. *Journal of Finance*, 31: 215–31.

Bernanke, B.S. (2002). *Deflation: Making Sure 'It' Doesn't Happen Here*. Remarks by Ben S, Bernanke Before the National Economists Club, Washington, DC, 21 November. http://www.federalreserve.gov/boarddocs/speeches/2002/20021121/default.htm accessed 10 June 2010.

—— (2004). *The Great Moderation*. Remarks by Governor Ben S. Bernanke at the Meetings of Eastern Economic Association, Washington, DC, 20 February. http://www.federalreserve.gov/boarddocs/speeches/2004/20040220/default.htm, accessed 10 June 2010.

—— (2007*a*). Regulation and Financial Innovation. *Federal Reserve Bank of Atlanta's 2007 Financial Markets Conference*. Sea Island, 15 May. http://www.federalreserve.gov/newsevents/speech/bernanke20070515a.htm, accessed 8 November 2008.

—— (2007*b*). *The Subprime Mortgage Market*. Speech Given at the Federal Reserve Bank of Chicago's 43rd Annual Conference on Bank Structure and Competition, Chicago, 17 May. http://www.federalreserve.gov/newsevents/speech/bernanke20070517a.htm accessed 10 January 2009.

Bernstein, P.L. (1992). *Capital Ideas: The Improbable Origins of Modern Wall Street*. New York: The Free Press.

Bezemer, D. (2009). No One Saw This Coming: Understanding Financial Crisis Through Accounting Models. *MPRA Paper No. 15892*. http://mpra.ub.uni-muenchen.de/15892/ accessed 27 September 2010.

Bhattacharya, S. and Thakor, A.V. (1993). Contemporary Banking Theory. *Journal of Financial Intermediation*, 3: 2–50.

Biggs, B. (2008). *Hedgehogging*. London: Wiley.

BIS (1986). *Recent Innovations in International Banking*. Basel: Bank for International Settlements.

—— (2004). *BIS 74th Annual Report*. Basel: Bank for International Settlements.

Bischoff, W. (2009). *UK International Financial Services – The Future*. London: HM Treasury.

Blair, T. (2010). *Oral Evidence to the Iraq Inquiry*, 29 January. http://www.iraqinquiry.org.uk/transcripts/oralevidence-bydate/100129.aspx accessed 10 October 2010.

Blundell-Wignall, A. (2007). *Structured Products: Implications for Financial Markets*. Paris: OECD.

Bollen, J. (2010). Secondary Buyouts Rise as Private Equity Spends Cash Pile. *efinancial News*, 26 July. http://www.efinancialnews.com/story/2010-07-26/secondary-buy-outs-soar accessed 20 August 2010.

Bourdieu, P. (1984). *Distinction: A Social Critique of the Judgement of Taste*. Cambridge, MA: Harvard University Press.

Bovens, M. and 't Hart, P. (1996). *Understanding Policy Fiascos*. New Brunswick, NJ: Transaction.

—— —— Peters, B. Guy (2001). *Success and Failure in Public Governance: A Comparative Analysis*. Cheltenham: Edward Elgar.

Boyce, A.L. (2008). Covered Bonds vs Securitization, Transparency vs Opacity: Which is the Right Question. Washington, DC: American Enterprise Institute. http://www.aei.org/docLib/Boyce%20-%20Covered%20Bonds%20vs.%20Securitization.pdf accessed 1 December 2010.

Boyd, J. and Gertler, M. (1995). Are Banks Dead? Or Are the Reports Greatly Exaggerated? *NBER (National Bureau of Economic Research) Working Paper No. W5045*. Washington, DC: NBER.

Boyer, R. (2000). Is Finance-led Growth Regime a Viable Alternative to Fordism? A Preliminary Analysis. *Economy and Society*, 29: 111–45.

Braithwaite, T. (2010). Fed to Face Probe of Actions During Crisis. *Financial Times*, 12 May.

Braudel, F. (1982). History and Time Spans. *Essays by Braudel* (trans. Sarah Matthews). Chicago: University of Chicago.

Bream, R. (2001). Yell Buy-Out Highlights LBO Revival. *Financial Times*, 30 May.

British Bankers' Association (2006). *Banking Business – The Annual Abstract of Banking Statistics*. London: BBA.

British Private Equity and Venture Capital Association (BVCA) (2006). *Private Equity & Venture Capital: Performance Measurement Survey*. London: BVCA.

—— (2007). *A Guide to Private Equity*. London: BVCA.

—— (2010). *A Short Response to the CSFI Report 'Private Equity, Public Loss?* 27 July. London: BVCA.

Brown, G. (2004). Speech by the Chancellor of the Exchequer. *Mansion House*. http://webarchive.nationalarchives.gov.uk/20100407010852/ http://www.hm-treasury.gov.uk/speech_chex_160604.htm accessed 10 August 2010.

—— (2006). Speech by the Chancellor of the Exchequer. *Mansion House*. http://webarchive.nationalarchives.gov.uk/20100407010852/ http://www.hm-treasury.gov.uk/speech_chex_210606.htm, accessed 10 August 2010.

—— (2008). Speech by the Prime Minister at Reuters, London. 13 October. http://webarchive.nationalarchives.gov.uk/+/number10.gov.uk/news/speeches-and-transcripts/2008/10/speech-on-global-economy-17161 accessed 10 August 2010.

Brown, J.M. and Jenkins, P. (2010). Irish Banks Need for Liquidity Support Grows. *Financial Times*, 10 December.

Brummer, A. (2007a). Taxing Time for Locusts. *Daily Mail*, 5 June.

—— (2007b). The New Robber Barons. *Daily Mail*, 6 June.

Brussels Sunshine (2010). *MEPs Ring Alarm Bells over Financial Industry's Excessive Lobbying Power*. http://blog.brusselssunshine.eu/2010_06_01_archive.html accessed 29 June.

Buchanan, J., Froud, J., Johal, S., Leaver, A. and Williams, K. (2009). Undisclosed and Unsustainable: Problems of the UK National Business Model. *CRESC Working Paper Series 75*. University of Manchester.

Buckingham, L. (2007). Striking a Blow at the Private Equity Pillagers. *Mail on Sunday*, 10 June.

Budden, R. (2004). Apax and Hicks Sell Yell Stake: Private Equity Groups Complete Profitable Exit from Telephone Directories Business with £700m Placing. *Financial Times*, 7 January.

Buffett, W.E. (2006). *To the Shareholders of Berkshire Hathaway Inc.*, 28 February. Omaha, NE: Berkshire Hathaway Inc.

Buiter, W. (2009). *The Unfortunate Uselessness of Most 'State of the Art' Academic Monetary Economics*, 3 March. http://blogs.ft.com/maverecon/2009/03/the-unfortunate-uselessness-of-most-state-of-the-art-academic-monetary-economics/ accessed 5 June 2010.

Bukharin, M. (1927). *Economic Theory of the Leisure Class*. New York: International Publishers.

Burnham, P. (2010). Class, Capital and Crisis: A Return to Fundamentals. *Political Studies Review*, 8: 27–39.

Butler, Lord (2004). *Review of Intelligence on Weapons of Mass Destruction*. Report of a Committee of Privy Counsellors (Chairman: The Rt Hon The Lord Butler of Brockwell KG GCB CVO). *House of Commons Paper HC 898*. London: The Stationery Office.

Cadbury, A. (1992). *Financial Aspects of Corporate Governance*. London: Gee.

Cain, P. and Hopkins, T. (1986). Gentlemanly Capitalism and British Expansionism Overseas, 1688–1850. *Economic History Review*, 39: 501–25.

Cameron, D. (2010a). *Creating a New Economic Dynamism*. 25 October. http://www.conservatives.com/News/Speeches/2010/10/David_Cameron_Creating_a_new_economic_dynamism.aspx accessed 15 November 2010.

—— (2010b). *Transforming the British Economy*. 28 May. http://www.conservatives.com/News/Speeches/2010/05/David_Cameron_Transforming_the_British_economy.aspx accessed 15 November 2010.

Cameron, D. R. (1988). Distributional Coalitions and other Sources of Economic Stagnation: On Olson's 'Rise and Decline of Nations'. *International Organization*, 42: 561–603.

Campa, J.M. and Hernando, I. (2006). M&As Performance in the European Financial Industry. *Journal of Banking & Finance*, 30: 3367–92.

Cannadine, D. (2002). *Ornamentalism. How the British Saw Their Empire*. Oxford: Oxford University Press.

Carlyle, T. (1840). *Chartism*. London: J. Fraser.

Caselli, S. and Gatti, S. (2005). *Banking for Family Business: A New Challenge for Wealth Management*. Berlin: Springer.

Cassidy, J. (2008). The Minsky Moment. *The New Yorker*, 4 February.

Casu, B. and Girardone, C. (2004). Financial Conglomeration: Efficiency, Productivity and Strategic Drive. *Applied Financial Economics*, 14: 687–96.

CEBR (2005). *The City's Importance to the EU Economy*. London: Centre for Economics and Business Research/City of London Corporation.

Cecchetti, S. (2009). IFC Bulletin No 31 Measuring Financial Innovation and its Impact. *Proceedings of the IFC Conference*, 26–27 August 2008. Basel: Bank for International Settlements.

Celent (2005). *Collateralized Debt Obligations Market*, Report, 31 October. Paris: Celent.

Centre for the Study of Financial Innovation (CSFI) (2003). *Sizing Up the City – London's Ranking as a Financial Centre*. London: City of London Corporation.

Chapman, J. (2010). The Real Losers in the Battle for Alpha. *Financial Times*, 22 August.

Chassany, A-S. and Alesci, C. (2010). Golden Era May Elude Private-Equity Investors as Prices Rise. *Bloomberg*, 28 February. http://www.bloomberg.com/apps/news?pid=newsarchive&sid=agin57fZ6ARo accessed 1 August 2010.

Citigroup (2010). *Citi Perspectives/Prime Finance: The Liquidity Crisis & Its Impact on the Hedge Fund Industry*. London: Prime Finance.

City of London Corporation (2000). *London–New York Study*. London: Corporation of London.

Coen, D. (2007). *Lobbying in the European Union. PE 393.266*. Brussels: European Parliament.

Cohen, N. and Arnold, M. (2008). Focus DIY Puts Private Equity in Pension Spotlight. *Financial Times*, 4 September.

Colley, L. (1992). *Britons: Forging the Nation 1707–1832*. New Haven: Yale University Press.

Comptroller of the Currency Administrator of National Banks (2010). *OCC's Quarterly Report on Bank Trading and Derivatives Activities. First Quarter 2010*. Washington, DC: Treasury. http://www.occ.treas.gov/topics/capital-markets/financial-markets/trading/derivatives/dq110.pdf accessed 16 July 2010.

Connor, K. (2010). *Big Bank Takeover: How Too-Big-To-Fail's Army of Lobbyists has Captured Washington*. Washington, DC: Institute for America's Future.

Corbett, J. and Jenkinson, T. (1996). The Financing of Industry, 1970–89: An International Comparison. *Journal of the Japanese and International Economies*, 10: 71–96.

Cutler, T., Williams, K. and Williams, J. (1986). *Keynes, Beveridge, and Beyond*. London: Routledge & Kegan Paul Books.

Datamonitor (2008). *UK Current Accounts 2008: A Comprehensive Survey*. London: Datamonitor.

—— (2009). *Rebuilding Consumer Trust in Day-to-Day Banking*. London: Datamonitor.

Davey, J. (2002). Archer Set to Make £78m From Sale of Focus Wickes. *The Times*, 30 November.

Davidson, P. (2008). Is the Current Financial Distress Caused by the Subprime Mortgage Crisis a Minsky Moment? Or Is It The Result of Attempting to Securitize Illiquid Noncommercial Mortgage Loans? *Journal of Post Keynesian Economics*, 30: 669–76.

Dawkins, R. (1976). *The Selfish Gene*. New York: Oxford University Press.

de La Dehasa, G. ed. (2008). *How to Avoid Further Credit and Liquidity Confidence Crises*. London: Centre for Economic Policy Research.

de Larosière, J. (2009). *The High-level Group on Financial Supervision in the EU*. Brussels: European Commission.

Deleuze, G. and Guattari, F. (1988). *A Thousand Plateaus: Capitalism and Schizophrenia* (trans. B. Massum). London: Athlone.

Diamond, J. (2005). *Guns, Germs and Steel: A Short History of Everybody for the Last 13,000 years*. London: Vintage [1997].

Dodd-Frank Wall Street Reform and Consumer Protection Act. http://docs.house.gov/rules/finserv/111_hr4173_finsrvcr.pdf

Dodge, C. (2010). Banning Big Wall Street Bonus. *Bloomberg News*, 13 December. http://www.bloomberg.com/news/print/2010-12-13/banning-big-wall-street-bonus-favored-by-70-of-americans-in-national-poll.html accessed 15 December 2010.

Dorn, N. (2010). The Governance of Securities: Ponzi Finance, Regulatory Convergence, Credit Crunch. *British Journal of Criminology*, 50: 23–45.

Duarte, J., Longstaff, F., and Yu, F. (2005). Risk and Return in Fixed-Income Arbitrage: Nickels in Front of a Steamroller? *Anderson School of Management Working Paper UCLA*.

Dunleavy, P. (1995). Policy Disasters: Explaining the UK's Record. *Public Policy and Administration*, 10: 52–70.

Dymski, G.A. (2009). Why the Subprime Crisis is Different: A Minskyian Approach. *Cambridge Journal of Economics*, 34: 239–55.

Dyson, K. and Marcussen, M. eds. (2009). *Central Banks in the Age of the Euro: Europeanization, Convergence, and Power*. Oxford: Oxford University Press.

Economist (2005). Locusts, Pocus. *Economist*, 5 May.

—— (2008). Fannie Mae and Freddie Mac: End of Illusions. *Economist*, 17 July.

—— (2010). The Fed's Big Announcement: Down the Slipway. *Economist*, 4 November.

Edwards, J. and Fischer, K. (1994). *Banks, Finance and Investment in Germany*. Cambridge: Cambridge University Press.

Eichengreen, B. (2009). Out of the Box Thoughts about Global Financial Archtiecture. *IMF Working Paper, WP/09/116*. Washington, DC: International Monetary Fund.

El-Elrian, M.A. (2010). Navigating the New Normal in Industrial Countries. *Per Jacobsson Foundation Lecture*, 10 October. Washington, DC: IMF.

Engelen, E., Ertürk, I., Froud, J., Leaver, A. and Williams, K. (2010). Reconceptualizing Financial Innovation: Frame, Conjuncture and Bricolage. *Economy and Society*, 39: 33–42.

Ertürk, I. and Solari, S. (2007). Banks as Continuous Reinvention. *New Political Economy*, 12: 369–88.

—— Froud, J., Johal, S., Leaver, A. and Williams, K. (2008). *Financialization at Work: Key Texts and Commentary*. London: Routledge.

—— —— —— —— —— (2010). Ownership Matters: Private Equity and the Political Division of Ownership. *Organization*, 17: 543.

—— —— —— —— Shammai, D. and Williams, K. (2008*a*). Corporate Governance and Impossibilism. *Journal of Cultural Economy*, 1: 109–27.

Ethical Corporation (2006). Special Reports: Finance – Hedge Funds and Private Equity – Trading Down Corporate Responsibility. *Ethical Corporation*. http://www.ethicalcorp.com/content.asp?ContentID¼4681 accessed 10 January 2010.

European Central Bank (2006). *Financial Stability Review*. Frankfurt: ECB.

—— (2007). *Financial Stability Review*. Frankfurt: ECB.

European Private Equity and Venture Capital Association (EVCA) (2005). *Employment Contribution of Private Equity and Venture Capital in Europe*. Brussels: EVCA.

Evans, P.B. and Wurster, T.S. (1997). Strategy and the New Economics of Information. *Harvard Business Review*, 75: 71–82.

Fabozzi, F.J. and Kothari, V. (2007). Securitization: The Tool of Financial Transformation. *Yale ICF Working Paper No. 07-07*. http://ssrn.com/abstract=997079, accessed 20 March 2010.

Fama, E.F. (1980). Agency Problems and the Theory of the Firm. *The Journal of Political Economy*, 88: 288–307.

Federal Reserve Statisical Release, H 15 Selected Interest Rates, release date 23 December 2010 (http://www.federalreserve.gov/releases/h15/update/).

Feenstra, F. (2007). In U.S. Fixed Income, Hedge Funds Are The Biggest Game In Town. *Greenwich Associates*, 20 August.

Feldman, R. and Lueck, M. (2007). *Are Banks Really Dying this Time? The Region*. Minneapolis: Federal Reserve Bank of Minneapolis.

Fidler, S. (2010). The Audacity of the Euro: A Look at a Tense 2010. *Wall Street Journal*, 24–28 December.

Financial Services Authority (2006). *Private Equity: A Discussion of Risk and Regulatory Engagement. Discussion Paper 06/6*. London: FSA.

—— (2008). The Supervision of Northern Rock: A Lessons Learned Review. *FSA Internal Audit Division*. London: FSA.

Financial Stability Forum (2007). *Update of FSF Report on Highly Leveraged Institutions*. Basel: Financial Stability Forum, 19 May.

Financial Times (2010). Hedge Rows. Editorial. *Financial Times*, 14 April.

Fleming, S. (2007). City Fat Cats 'Paying Less Tax Than Cleaners'. *Daily Mail*, 5 June.

Flinders, M.V. (2008). *Delegated Governance and the British State: Walking Without Order*. Oxford: Oxford University Press.

Folkman, P., Froud, J., Johal, S. and Williams, K. (2007). Working for Themselves? Capital Market Intermediaries and Present Day Capitalism. *Business History*, 49: 552–72.

Frank, T. (2002). *One Market Under God*. London: Vintage.

—— (2004). *What's the Matter with Kansas?* New York: Henry Holt & Co.

Frankel, A., Gyntelberg, J., Kjeldsen, K., and Persson, M. (2004). The Danish Mortgage Market. *BIS Quarterly Review*, March.

Froud, J., Johal, S., Leaver, A., and Williams, K. (2006). *Financialization and Strategy: Narrative and Numbers*. London: Routledge.

—— Leaver, A., McAndrew, S., Shammai, D., and Williams, K. (2008). Rethinking Top Management Pay: From Pay for Performance to Pay as Fee, *CRESC Working Paper Series No. 56*.

—— —— Nilsson, A. and Williams, K. (2009). Narratives and the Financialised Firm. *Kölner Zeitschrift für Soziologie und Sozialpsychologie*, 64: 288–304.

—— Moran, M., Nilsson, A., and Williams, K. (2010a). Opportunity Lost: Mystification, Elite Politics and Financial Reform in the UK. *Socialist Register*, 47: 98–119.

—— —— —— —— (2010b). Wasting a Crisis? Democracy and Markets in Britain after 2007. *The Political Quarterly*, 81: 25–38.

Galbraith, J.K. (1994). *A Short History of Finance*. London: Penguin Books.

Gangahar, A. and Brewster, D. (2008). Hedging Industry Resents Taking Blame for Turmoil. *Financial Times*, 20 September.

Gapper, J. (2008). Short Selling Reveals Corporate Realities. *Financial Times*, 18 July.

—— (2010). A Short Story of a Star Hedge Fund. *Financial Times*, 15 April.

Gibson, M.S. (2004). Understanding the Risk of Synthetic CDOs. *Finance and Economics Discussion Series 2004–36*. Board of Governors of the Federal Reserve System.

Giddens, A. (1991). *Modernity and Self-identity: Self and Society in the Late Modern Age*: Stanford, CA: Stanford University Press.

—— (1993). *New Rules of Sociological Method: A Positive Critique of Interpretative Sociologies*. Stanford, CA: Stanford University Press.

Gordon, M. (2007). Am I Alone in Struggling to Make Sense of Private Equity's Appeal? Letter to the *Financial Times*, 30 January.

Gorton, G., and Metrick, A. (2010). *Slapped in the Face by the Invisible Hand: Banking and the Panic of 2007*. http://papers.ssrn.com/sol3/papers.cfm?abstract_id=1676947 accessed 10 August 2010.

Greenbury, R. (1995). *Directors' Remuneration*. London: CBI.

Greenhill, S. (2008). 'It's Awful – Why did Nobody see it Coming?': The Queen Gives her Verdict on Global Credit Crunch. *Daily Mail*, 6 November.

Greenspan, A. (2002). *Speech by Dr Alan Greenspan on World Finance and Risk Management*. Lancaster House, London, 25 September.

—— (2004). Economic Flexibility. *HM Treasury Enterprise Conference*. London, 26 January.

—— (2005). Remarks by Chairman Alan Greenspan – Consumer Finance. *Federal Reserve System's Fourth Annual Community Affairs Research Conference*. Washington, DC, 8 April.

Grunwald, M. (2009). Person of the Year: Ben Bernanke. *Time*, 16 December 2009. http://www.time.com/time/specials/packages/article/0,28804,1946375_1947251,00.html accessed 10 October 2010.

Guerrera, F. and Pimlott, D. (2010). Pandit and King Clash over Basel III. *Financial Times*, 25 October.

—— Baer, J., and Jenkins, P. (2010). A Sparser Future. *Financial Times*, 20 December.

—— Sender, H., and Baer, J. (2010). Goldman Sachs Settles with SEC. *Financial Times*, 15 July.

Guha, K. (2010). US Bank Levy Will be Tax Deductible. *Financial Times*, 14 January.

Gurley, J.G. and Shaw, E.S. (1955). Financial Aspects of Economic Development. *The American Economic Review*, 45: 515–38.

Hacker, J. (2006). *The Great Risk Shift: The Assault on American Jobs, Families, Health Care, and Retirement – and How You Can Fight Back*. Oxford: Oxford University Press.

Hackethal, A. and Schmidt, R.H. (2003). Financing Patterns: Measurement Concepts and Empirical Results. *Working Paper Series: Finance and Accounting*, 33, University of Frankfurt.

Haldane, A. (2009*a*). Rethinking the Financial Network. *Financial Student Association.* Amsterdam, 28 April.

—— (2009*b*). Small Lessons from a Big Crisis. *Federal Reserve Bank of Chicago 45th Annual Conference.* 8 May.

—— (2010*a*). *The $100 Billion Question.* Speech at the Institution of Regulation and Risk, Hong Kong, 30 March.

—— (2010*b*). The Debt Hangover. *Professional Liverpool dinner.* 27 January.

—— (2010*c*). What is the Contribution of the Financial Sector: Miracle or Mirage. In A. Turner et al. (eds.), *The Future of Finance.* London: London School of Economics and Political Sciences.

Hall, D. (2008). *Private Equity: Financial Investors, Public Services, and Employment.* London: Public Services International Research Unit, University of Greenwich.

Hall, P.A. and Soskice, D. (2001). An Introduction to Varieties of Capitalism. In P.A. Hall and D. Soskice (eds.), *Varieties of Capitalism.* New York: Oxford University Press, pp. 1–68.

Hamilton, S. (2010). King Says UK Exposure to Ireland is 'By No Means Trivial'. *Bloomberg News,* 16 November. http://www.bloomberg.com/news/2010-11-16/king-says-u-k-banks-exposure-to-irish-economy-is-by-no-means-trivial-.html accessed 3 December 2010.

Hamilton, R., Jenkinson, N. and Penalver, A. (2007). Innovation and Integration in Financial Markets and the Implications for Financial Stability. In C. Kent and J. Lawson (eds.), *The Structure and Resilience of the Financial System.* Canberra: Reserve Bank of Australia.

Hampel, R. (1998). *Committee on Corporate Governance.* London: Gee.

Hampton, P. and Kingman, J. (2008). A Precise Mandate to Protect Taxpayers' Interests. *Financial Times,* 14 November.

Harding, R. and Braithwaite, T. (2010). European Banks Took Big Slice of Fed Aid. *Financial Times,* 1 December.

—— Rappeport, A. (2010). US Economy Shows Faster Growth. *Financial Times,* 23 November.

Harrod, R. (1951). *The Life of John Maynard Keynes.* New York: Harcourt Brace & Co.

Hawkes, S. and Pascoe-Watson, G. (2009). Bank Bosses Under Pressure. *Sun,* 11 February.

Hilferding, R. (1910 [1981]). *Finance Capital.* London: Routledge and Kegan Paul.

HM Treasury (2005). *The UK Financial Services Sector: Rising to the Challenges and Opportunities of Globalisation.* London: The Stationery Office.

—— (2009a). *Reforming Financial Markets.* CM7667 London: The Stationary Office.

—— (2009b). Report Sets Out Vision for UK Financial Services Sector. Press Release 47/09: 07 May.

—— (2010). Sir John Vickers to Chair the Independent Commission on Banking. Press Release 16 June. http://www.hm-treasury.gov.uk/press_11_10.htm accessed 10 August 2010.

Hoban, M. (2010). *Bank Levy: Draft Legislation, Written Ministerial Statement.* 21 October. London: HM Treasury. http://www.hm-treasury.gov.uk/d/banklevy_wms211010.pdf accessed 15 November 2010.

References

Hobson, J.A. (2006 [1902]). *Imperialism: A Study*. New York: Cosimo Publishing.

Holmes, C. (2009). Seeking Alpha or Creating Beta? Charting the Rise of Hedge Fund-Based Financial Ecosystems. *New Political Economy*, 14: 431–50.

Horton, M., Kumar, M. and Mauro, P. (2009). *The State of Public Finances: A Cross-Country Fiscal Monitor*. SPN/09/ Washington, DC: International Monetary Fund.

House of Commons Treasury Committee (2008a). Banking Crisis – Volume 1, HC 144–1, Session 2007–08. *Oral Evidence*. London: House of Commons.

—— (2008b). The Run on the Rock, HC 56-1. *Fifth Report of Session 2007–08*. London: House of Commons.

Hughes, J. (2009). Completion of SIV Asset Disposal Near. *Financial Times*, 7 July.

—— (2010). FSA Plays Down Prop Trading Impact. *Financial Times*, 2 March.

Hutton, W. (2008). As We Suffer, City Speculators are Moving in for the Kill. *The Observer*, 29 June.

IMF (2006a). *Global Financial Stability Report, April*. Washington, DC: International Monetary Fund.

—— (2006b). *Global Financial Stability Report, September*. Washington, DC: International Monetary Fund.

—— (2006c). *World Economic Outlook. Globalization and Inflation, April 2006*. Washington, DC: IMF.

—— (2010). *Global Financial Stability Report, April 2010*. Washington, DC: IMF.

Institute of International Finance (2009). *Reform in the Financial Services Industry: Strengthening Practices for a More Stable System*. December. Washington, DC: Institute of International Finance.

International Corporate Governance Network (ICGN). (2008). *Statement on the Global Financial Crisis. 10 November 2008*. http://www.iasplus.com/resource/0811icgn.pdf accessed 17 November 2008.

Ipsos MORI (2008). Datamonitor Consumer Survey.

Ishikawa, T. (2009). *How I Caused the Credit Crunch*. London: Icon Books.

Jenkins, P. (2009). RBS Chief in £6.9m Pay Deal. *Financial Times*, 21 June.

—— Guerrera, F. (2010). Goldman Versus the Regulators. *Financial Times*, 19 April.

—— Parker, G. (2009). Bankers Hit Back at Walker Review. *Financial Times*, 15 July.

—— Goff, S. and Mathurin, P. (2010). Bank Ties Across EU Carry Risk Concerns. *Financial Times*, 1 December.

—— Rigby, E. and Parker, G. (2010). Leading Bankers Fight to Rescue Bonus Truce. *Financial Times*, 14 December.

Jensen, M.C. (1989). Eclipse of the Public Corporation. *Harvard Business Review*, September–October.

—— Meckling, W.H. (1976). Theory of the Firm: Managerial Behaviour, Agency Costs and Ownership Structure. *Journal of Financial Economics*, 3: 305–60.

Jetuah, D. (2010). HMRC Collects £3.4bn in Bankers' Bonus Tax Raid. *Accountancy Age*. http://www.accountancyage.com/accountancyage/news/2270213/hmrc-collects-4bn-bankers-bonus#ixzz12zFpO7ux accessed 22 September 2010.

Johnson, S. (2009). The Quiet Coup. *The Atlantic* May.

—— Kwak, J. (2010). *Thirteen Bankers: The Wall Street Takeover and the Next Finacial Meltdown*. New York: Pantheon Books.

Jones, E. (1999). Is Competitive Corporatism an Adequate Response to Globalisation? Evidence from the Low Countries. *West European Politics*, 22: 159–81.

Jones, D. (2008). *Cameron on Cameron*. London: Fourth Estate.

Jones, S. (2010). Funds Left Struggling for Gains Amid Volatility. *Financial Times*, 16 August.

JP Morgan (2001). *Global Structured Finance Research: CDO Handbook*, 29 May. New York: JP Morgan.

Kagan, R. (2001). *Adversarial Legalism: The American Way of Law*. Cambridge, MA: Harvard University Press.

Kay, J. (2009). *Narrow Banking: The Reform of Banking Regulation*. London: Centre for the Study of Financial Innovation.

—— (2010). Banking Needs More Robust Stress Tests Than These. *Financial Times*, 27 July.

Keen, S. (2009). Bailing Out the Titanic with a Thimble. *Economic Analysis and Policy*, 39: 3–24.

Keoun, B. (2010). Volcker Rule May Give Goldman, Citigroup Until 2022 to Comply. *Business Week*, 29 June.

Kerpen, P. (2010). Goldman Hearing—A Political Show Trial. *Fox News*, 27 April.

Keynes, J.M. (1936). *The General Theory*. London: Macmillan.

Kiff, J. and Mills, P. (2007). Money for Nothing and Checks for Free: Recent Developments in U.S. Subprime Mortgage Markets, *IMF Working Paper 07/188*, July. Washington, DC: IMF.

King, M. (2003). Speech by Mervyn King. *East Midlands Development Agency/Bank of England Dinner*. Leicester, 14 October.

—— (2007). Speech by Mervyn King. *Lord Mayor's Banquet for Bankers and Merchants of the City of London*. The Mansion House, London, 20 June.

—— (2009a). Speech by Mervyn King. *Lord Mayor's Banquet for Bankers and Merchants of the City of London*. The Mansion House, London, 17 June.

—— (2009b). Speech by Mervyn King, Governor of the Bank of England to Scottish Business Organisations, Edinburgh, 20 October.

Klein, M.A. (1971). A Theory of the Banking Firm. *Journal of Money, Credit and Banking*, 3: 205–18.

Kolade, W. (2007). Interview. *Radio 5 Live*, 9 October.

Kosman, J. (2009). *The Buyout of America: How Private Equity Will Cause the Next Great Credit Crisis*. New York: Portfolio.

Kregel, J. (2008). Using Minsky's Cushions of Safety to Analyze the Crisis in the US Subprime Mortgage Market. *International Journal of Political Economy*, 37: 3–23.

Kynaston, D. (1995). *The City of London, A World of Its Own 1815–1890 Vol1*. London: Pimlico.

LaCapra, L.T. (2010). B of A Says Volcker Rule Won't Be Too Tough. thestreet.com 14 September.

Lahart, J. (2007). In Time of Tumult, Obscure Economist Gains Currency. *Wall Street Journal*, 18 August.

Lakoff, G. (1993). The Contemporary Theory of Metaphor. In A. Ortony (ed.), *Metaphor and Thought*. Cambridge: Cambridge University Press.

References

Lane, J.E. (1995). The Decline of the Swedish Model. *Governance*, 8: 579–90.

Langley, P. (2009). Debt, Discipline, and Government: Foreclosure and Forbearance in the Subprime Mortgage Crisis. *Environment and Planning A*, 41: 1404–19.

Leland, H.E. and Pyle, D.H. (1977). Informational Asymmetries, Financial Structure, and Financial Intermediation. *Journal of Finance*, 32: 371–87.

Lemke, T. (2001). The Birth of Bio-Politics – Michel Foucault's Lecture at the Collège de France on Neo-Liberal Governmentality. *Economy and Society*, 30: 190–207.

Lenin, V.I. (1917 [1966]). *Imperialism: The Highest Stages of Capitalism*. Moscow: Progress Publishers.

Levine, M.E. and Forrence, J.L. (1990). Regulatory Capture, Public Interest, and the Public Agenda: Toward a Synthesis. *Journal of Law, Economics, and Organization*, 6: 167–98.

Levi-Strauss, C. (1966). *The Savage Mind*. Chicago: University of Chicago Press.

Lewis, M. (2009). *The Big Short. Inside the Doomsday Machine*. London: Allen Lane.

Lex (2006). Goldman Sachs. *Financial Times*, 15 March.

—— (2010*a*). Tobin Tax. *Financial Times*, 17 February.

—— (2010*b*). Private Equity. *Financial Times*, 22 August.

—— (2010*c*). New Bank Capital Rules. *Financial Times*, 13 Sept.

—— (2010*d*). Basel III. *Financial Times*, 23 September.

Leyshon, A. and Thrift, N. (2007). The Capitalisation of Almost Everything: The Future of Finance and Capitalism. *IWGF Workshop on Financialization*. London, 12–13 February.

Lipper (2007). *Lipper HedgeWorld Prime Brokerage League Table*. New York: Lipper/ThompsonReuters.

Lisle-Williams, M. (1984). Merchant Banking Dynasties in the English Class Structure: Ownership, Solidarity and Kinship in the City of London, 1850–90. *British Journal of Sociology*, 35: 333–62.

Litan, R.E. (2010). In Defense of Much, But Not All, Financial Innovation. *Regulation 2.0 Working Paper*, 37.

Llewellyn, D.T. (1999). *The New Economics of Banking*. Manchester: Manchester Statistical Society.

Lucas, D.J., Goodman, L., and Fabozzi, F.J. (2007). Collateralized Debt Obligations and Credit Risk Transfer. *Yale ICF Working Paper No. 07-06*. http://papers.ssrn.com/sol3/papers.cfm?abstract_id=997276 accessed 20 June 2010.

Macartney, H. (2010). *Variegated Neoliberalism*. London: Routledge.

—— Moran, M. (2008). Banking and Financial Market Regulation and Supervision. In K. Dyson (ed.), *The Euro at 10: Europeanization, Power, and Convergence*. Oxford: Oxford University Press, pp. 325–40.

MacKenzie, D. (2006). *An Engine, Not a Camera: How Financial Models Shape Markets*. Cambridge, MA: MIT Press.

—— (2010). The Credit Crisis as a Problem in the Sociology of Knowledge. Unpublished paper. September. Edinburgh: University of Edinburgh UK, School of Social & Political Science.

Mackintosh, J. (2008). Call to End Ban on Short Selling. *Financial Times*, 6 October.

Macmillan Committee (1931). *The Report of the Committee on Finance and Industry.* Cmnd 3897, London.

Mandelson, P. (2010*a*). Address by Lord Mandelson. *Federation of Small Business.* Aberdeen Exhibition and Conference Centre. http://www.fsb.org.uk/conference2010/address-by-lord-mandelson accessed 26 May.

—— (2010*b*). *The Third Man.* London: Harper Press.

Manning, R.D. (2000). *Credit Card Nation.* New York: Basic Books.

Marcussen, M. (2006). The Fifth Age of Central Banking in the Global Economy. *Frontiers of Regulation.* University of Bath: 7–8 September.

—— (2009). 'Scientization' of Central Banking: The Politics of A-Politicization. In M. Marcussen and K. Dyson (eds.), *Central Banks in the Age of the Euro Europeanization, Convergence, and Power.* Oxford: Oxford University Press.

Marglin, S.A. (1974). What Do Bosses Do? *Review of Radical Political Economics,* 6: 60–112.

Mason, P. (2008). Pretty Big Steps. Does the Real Minsky Moment Lie Ahead? *BBC News. Paul Mason's Blog,* 5 October.

Masters, B. (2010). Bankers Poised for Basel III Accord. *Financial Times,* 9 September.

—— Baer, J. (2010). Leading US Banks Face $150bn Basel III Shortfall. *Financial Times,* 22 November.

—— Murphy, M. (2010). Banking Reform: Suspense Over. *Financial Times,* 18 August.

Mattingly, P. (2010). Derivatives, 'Volcker' Rules May Be House Republican Targets. *Bloomberg.com,* 20 December. http://www.bloomberg.com/news/2010-11-19/derivatives-volcker-rules-may-be-house-republican-targets.html accessed 15 December.

Mayer, C. (1998). Financial Systems and Corporate Governance: A Review of the International Evidence. *Journal of Institutional and Theoretical Economics,* 154: 144–65.

Mayor of London (2008). Mayor Acts to Protect the Global Capital of Finance. Press Release, 12 December. London: Mayor of London. http://www.london.gov.uk/media/press_releases_mayoral/mayor-acts-protect-global-capital-finance accessed 15 August 2010.

McCann, K. (2010). MEPs: Banking Lobby Is A 'Danger To Democracy'. *Public Affairs News,* Brussels, 30 July.

McDonald, L.S. and Robinson, P. (2009). *Colossal Failure of Common Sense: The Incredible Inside Story of the Collapse of Lehman Brothers.* New York: Crown Business.

McKinsey Global Institute (2008). *Mapping Global Capital Markets.* Fifth Annual Report. http://www.mckinsey.com/mgi/publications/third_annual_report/index.asp accessed 20 May 2010.

Meerkatt, H. and Liechtenstein, H. (2008). Get Ready for the Private-Equity Shakeout. Boston Consulting Group and IESE Business School. http://www.iese.edu/en/files/PrivateEquityWhitePaper.pdf, accessed 5 April 2010.

Merton, R. and Bodie, Z. (1995). A Conceptual Framework for Analyzing the Financial Environment. In D.B. Crane (ed.) *The Global Financial System:A Functional Perspective.* Boston, MA: Harvard Business School Press, pp. 3–32.

Metrick, A. and Yasuda, A. (2007). Economics of Private Equity Funds. *Working Paper.* Pennsylvania: Wharton Business School.

Milbourn, T.T., Boot, A.W.A., and Thakor, A.V. (1999). Megamergers and Expanded Scope: Theories of Bank Size and Activity Diversity. *Journal of Banking & Finance*, 23: 195–214.

Miller, M.H. (1986). Financial Innovation: The Last Twenty Years and the Next. *The Journal of Financial and Quantitative Analysis*, 21: 459–71.

Miller, G.P. (1998). On the Obsolescence of Commercial Banking. *Journal of Institutional and Theoretical Economics*, 154: 61–73.

Miller, P. and Rose, N. (1990). Governing Economic Life. *Economy and Society*, 19: 1–31.

Mills, C.W. (1940). Situated Actions and Vocabularies of Motive. *American Sociological Review*, 5: 904–13.

—— (1956). *The Power Elite*. New York: Oxford University Press.

—— (1962). *The Marxists*. New York: Dell Publishing Company.

Milne, R. (2008). Hedge Funds Hit as Porsche Moves on VW. *Financial Times*, 27 October.

—— (2009). *The Fall of the House of Credit: What Went Wrong in Banking and What can be Done to Repair the Damage?* Cambridge: Cambridge University Press.

Minford, P. (2010). The Banking Crisis: A Rational Interpretation. *Political Studies Review*, 8: 40–54.

Minsky, H.P. (1986). *Stabilizing an Unstable Economy*. New Haven and London: Yale University Press.

—— (1996). Uncertainty and the Institutional Structure of Capitalist Economies: Remarks upon Receiving the Veblen-Commons Award. *Journal of Economic Issues*, 30: 357–68.

Mitchell, T. (2002). *Rule of Experts: Egypt, Techno-Politics, Modernity*. Berkeley, CA: University of California Press.

Mizen, P. (2008). The Credit Crunch of 2007–2008: A Discussion of the Background, Market Reactions, and Policy Responses. *Federal Reserve Bank of St. Louis Review*, 90: 531–67.

Mokyr, J. and Nye, J.V.C. (2007). Distributional Coalitions, the Industrial Revolution, and the Origins of Economic Growth in Britain. *Southern Economic Journal*, 74: 50–70.

Montgomerie, J., Leaver, A., and Nilsson, A. (2008). Losing the Battles but Winning the War: The Case of UK Private Equity Industry and Mediated Scandal of Summer 2007. *CRESC Working Paper Series, no. 57*.

Moran, M. (1986). *The Politics of Banking: The Strange Case of Competition and Credit Control*, 2nd ed. London: Macmillan.

—— (1991). *The Politics of the Financial Services Revolution: The USA, The UK and Japan*. London: Macmillan.

—— (2001). Not Steering but Drowning: Policy Catastrophes and the Regulatory State. *The Political Quarterly*, 72: 414–27.

—— (2006). The Company of Strangers: Defending the Power of Business in Britain, 1975–2005. *New Political Economy*, 11: 453–78.

—— (2007). *The British Regulatory State: High Modernism and Hyper-Innovation*. Oxford: Oxford University Press.

—— (2009). *Business, Politics, and Society: An Anglo-American Comparison*. Oxford: Oxford University Press.

Morris, P. (2010). *Private Equity, Public Loss?* London: Centre for the Study of Financial Innovation (CSFI).

Moran, M. (2011). *Politics and Governance in the UK*, 2nd ed. Basingstoke: Palgrave Macmillan.

Murphy, M. and Parker, G. (2010). Bankers Braced for Tough Pay Rules. *Financial Times*, 8 December.

—— Goff, S., and Jenkins, P. (2010). PM Joins in as Tide Turns Against Bankers. *Financial Times*, 17 December.

Naik, N. (2007). *Hedge Funds: Transparency and Conflict of Interest. IP/A/ECON/IC/2007-24*. Brussels: European Parliament.

Nakamoto, M. and Wighton, D. (2007). Citigroup Chief Stays Bullish on Buy-outs. *Financial Times*, 9 July.

National Venture Capital Association (NVCA) (2006). The Venture Capital Industry – an Overview. www.nvca.org/def.html accessed 16 January 2006.

New Economics Foundation (2008). *A Green New Deal. Joined Up Policies to Solve the Triple Crisis of the Credit Crisis, Climate Change and High Oil Prices*. London: Green New Deal Group.

Newmark, E. (2010). Mean Street: Goldman's Senate Hearings–Let the Show Trial Begin! *Wall Street Journal Blog*, 26 April. http://blogs.wsj.com/deals/2010/04/26/mean-street-goldmans-senate-hearings-let-the-show-trial-begin/ accessed 3 June 2010.

Ng, S. and Hudson, M. (2007). Mortgage Shakeout May Roil CDO Market–Subprime Defaults Lead to Wavering at Big Street Firms. *The Wall Street Journal*, 13 March.

—— Mollenkamp, C. (2008). A Fund Behind Astronomical Losses. *Wall Street Journal*, 14 January.

Nissan, S. and Spratt, S. (2009). *The Ecology of Finance*. London: New Economics Foundation.

Northern Rock Plc (2006). *Annual Report and Accounts 2006*. Newcastle upon Tyne: Northern Rock plc.

Nyberg, L. (2008). Hedge Funds and the Recent Financial Turmoil. In *Nordic Hedge Fund Investment Forum*. Stockholm, 28 January.

Nye, J.S. (2004). *Soft Power. The Means to Success in World Politics*. Washington, DC: Public Affairs.

O'Connell, D. (2007). Can Confidence Check this Minsky Moment? *The Sunday Times*, 12 August.

Oakeshott, M. (1962). *Rationalism in Politics and Other Essays*. London: Methuen.

Olson, M. (1982). *The Rise and Decline of Nations: Economic Growth, Stagflation and Social Rigidities*. New Haven: Yale University Press.

Organisation for Economic Co-operation and Development (OECD) (2007). *Economic Outlook No. 81*. Paris: OECD.

Ormerod, P. (2010). The Current Crisis and the Culpability of Economic Theory. *Journal of the Academy of Social Sciences*, 5: 5–18.

Orwell, G. (1941). *The Lion and the Unicorn: Socialism and the English Genius*. London: Secker & Warburg.

Owen, D. (2007). *The Hubris Syndrome: Bush, Blair and the Intoxication of Power*. London: Politico's.

References

Paletta, D. (2009). Agencies in a Brawl for Control of Banks. *Wall Street Journal*, 22 December.

——— (2010). Obama, Dodd to Meet on Financial Regulatory Overhaul Bill. *Wall Street Journal*, 19 January.

——— Solomon, D. (2009). Geithner Vents at Regulators as Overhaul Stumbles. *Wall Street Journal*, 4 August.

Parry, R., Hood, C., and Oliver, J. (1997). Reinventing the Treasury: Economic Rationalism or an Econocrat's Fallacy of Control? *Public Administration*, 75: 395–415.

Pattie, C., Seyd, P., and Whiteley, P. (2003). Citizenship and Civic Engagement: Attitudes and Behaviour in Britain. *Political Studies*, 51: 443–68.

——— ——— ——— (2004). *Citizenship in Britain: Values, Participation and Democracy*. Cambridge: Cambridge University Press.

Paulson, H. (2010). *On the Brink: Inside the Race to Stop the Collapse of the Global Financial System*. New York: Business Plus.

Pauly, L. (2009). The Old and New Politics of International Financial Stability. *Journal of Common Market Studies*, 47: 955–75.

Perrow, C. (1984). *Normal Accidents: Living with High-risk Technologies*. New York: Basic Books.

——— (2010). The Meltdown Was Not an Accident. In M. Lounsbury and Paul M. Hirsch (eds.) *Markets on Trial: The Economic Sociology of the U.S. Financial Crisis: Part A, Research in the Sociology of Organizations*, 30(a): 309–30.

Philippon, T. (2008). The Evolution of the US Financial Industry from 1860 to 2007: Theory and Evidence. *Working Paper*, NYU, November.

Plender, J. (2010). Too Much Firefighting Could be Bad for the ECB. *Financial Times*, 17 November.

Plungis, J. and Snyder, J. (2010). BP Chief to Apologize for `Complex' Accident in Gulf. *Bloomberg News*, 17 June. http://www.bloomberg.com/news/2010-06-16/hayward-says-unprecedented-combination-of-failures-led-to-well-explosion.html accessed 26 October 2010.

Power Base (2010). *Power Base*. New Labour: Donors. http://www.powerbase.info/index.php?title=New_Labour:_Donors accessed 30 August 2010.

Pratley, N. (2010). Merkel Leaves Questions Hanging Over Germany's Attitude to Crisis. *Guardian*, 6 December.

Prosser, D. (2007). Angela Knight: A Telling Advocate For the Big Banks. *Independent*, 24 February.

Public Citizen (2010). *Eleven to One. Pro-Reform Derivatives Lobbyists Vastly Outnumbered by Opposition*. Washington, DC: Public Citizen.

Quaglia, L. (2007). The Politics of Financial Services Regulation and Supervision Reform in the European Union. *European Journal of Political Research*, 46: 269–90.

——— (2010). Completing the Single Market in Financial Services: The Politics of Competing Advocacy Coalitions. *Journal of European Public Policy*, 17: 1007–23.

Radcliffe Committtee (1959). *Report of the Committee on the Working of the Monetary System*. Cmnd 827, London: Stationery Office.

Reinhart, C.M. and Rogoff, K.S. (2009a). The Aftermath of Financial Crises *NBER Working Paper Series*. http://ssrn.com/abstract=1329274 accessed 20 February 2010.

—— —— (2009b). *This Time is Different. Eight Centuries of Financial Folly*. Princeton: Princeton University Press.

Renick Mayer, L., Beckel, M., and Levinthal, D. (2009). Crossing Wall Street. *Open Secrets Blog*, 16 November. http://www.opensecrets.org/news/2009/11/crossing-wall-street-1.html accessed 25 May 2010.

Reuters (2010). Update 1 – US Fed's Balance Sheet Grows to Record Size. *Reuters*, 9 December. http://www.reuters.com/article/idUSN0926838320101209 accessed 14 December 2010.

Rhoades, S.A. (1993). Efficiency Effects of Horizontal (in-market) Bank Mergers. *Journal of Banking & Finance*, 17: 411–22.

Robbins, M. (2009). 'Half of Private Equity Firms' Are Ignoring Transparency Guidelines. *Independent*, 13 January.

Roberts, A. (2010). *The Logic of Discipline: Global Capitalism and the Architecture of Government*. New York: Oxford University Press.

Robinson, J. (1962). *Essays in the Theory of Economic Growth*. London: Macmillan.

Rose, N.S. and Miller, P. (2008). *Governing the Present: Administering Economic, Social and Personal Life*. Cambridge: Polity Press.

Roxburgh, C. (2006). Industry Comment: The Outlook for European Corporate and Investment Banking. *McKinsey Quarterly*, August.

Rushe, D. (2010). US Fed Lent $3.3tn to Multinationals, Billionaires and Foreign Banks. *Guardian*, 2 December.

Salas, C. and Hassler, D. (2007). CDOs May Bring Subprime-like Bust for LBOs, Junk Debt, *Bloomberg News*, 13 March. http://www.bloomberg.com/apps/news?pid=newsarchive&sid=a0uS8xp4v2CE accessed 13 May 2010.

Sarangi, A. (2006). *Northern Rock: This Train Has Left the Station*, Equity Markets. ING Equity Markets report, 19 September. London: ING.

Schaff, P. (1951). *The New Schaff-Herzog Encyclopedia of Religious Knowledge, Vol. 1. Aachen – Basilians*. Grand Rapids: Christian Classics Etheral Library.

Schapiro, M. (2010). Testimony Before the Subcommittee on Financial Services and General Government, 28 April. *U.S. Securities and Exchange Commission*. http://www.sec.gov/news/testimony/2010/ts042810mls.htm accessed 7 May 2010.

Scheer, D. (2007). Insider Trading Concerns Rise as Stock Options Surge. *Bloomberg*, 7 May.

Schmidt, R. and Tyrell, M. (2003). What Constitutes a Financial System in General and the German Financial System in Particular? *Working Paper Series: Finance and Accounting, No. 111*. Frankfurt on Main: Johann Wolfgang Goethe University.

Schmidt, R.H., Hackethal, A., and Tyrell, M. (1999). Disintermediation and the Role of Banks in Europe: An International Comparison. *Journal of Financial Intermediation*, 8: 36–67.

Scholes, M. and Blaustein, P. (2005). Liquidity and the Fama-French Pricing Factors. Powerpoint Presentation, cited in J. Treussard (2004). Automatic for the People? Hedge Funds, Traditional and Clones. Working Paper. Boston University Department of Economics, Boston, MA.

Schor, J.B. (1998). *The Overspent American: Why We Want What We Don't Need*. New York: Basic Books.

Scott, J. (1997). *Corporate Business and Capitalist Classes*. Oxford: Oxford University Press.

—— (1998). *Seeing Like a State. How Certain Scheme to Improve the Human Condition Have Failed*. New Haven, CT: Yale University Press.

Securities and Exchange Commission (SEC) (2003). *Ten of Nation's Top Investment Firms Settle Enforcement Actions Involving Conflicts of Interest Between Research and Investment Banking*. http://www.sec.gov/news/press/2003-54.htm accessed 13 April 2010.

—— (2010*a*). *SEC Charges Goldman Sachs With Fraud in Structuring and Marketing of CDO Tied to Subprime Mortgages*. Press Release, 16 April. http://www.sec.gov/news/press/2010/2010-59.htm accessed 25 August 2010.

—— (2010*b*). *Goldman Sachs to Pay Record $550 Million to Settle SEC Charges Related to Subprime Mortgage CDO*. Press Release, 15 July. http://www.sec.gov/news/press/2010/2010-123.htm accessed 25 August 2010.

Self, P. (1976). *Econocrats and the Policy Process: The Politics and Philosophy of Cost–Benefit Analysis*. London: Macmillan.

Senate Permanent Investigation Subcommittee (2010). Senate Subcommittee Launches Series of Hearing on Wall Street and the Financial Crisis. *Press Release*, 12 April.

Sender, H. (2008*a*). Apollo Unit Suspends Cash Payments on Debt. *Financial Times*, 3 June.

—— (2008*b*). Goldman Sachs to Reduce Hedge Fund Client Numbers. *Financial Times*, 6 November.

Shadab, H.B. (2009). The Law and Economics of Hedge Funds: Financial Innovation and Investor Protection. *Berkeley Business Law Journal*, 6: 240–97.

Sherwood, B. and Gemson, S.-C. (2008). Capital Falls Out of Love with the City. *Financial Times*, 10 October.

Shiller, R., J. (2004). Radical Financial Innovation. *Cowles Foundation Lecture Discussion Paper No. 1461*, Yale University.

SIFMA (2007). *Global CDO Market Issuance Data*. http://archives1.sifma.org/assets/files/SIFMA_CDOIssuanceData2007q1.pdf accessed 26 April 2010.

Skidelsky, R. (2010). The Crisis of Capitalism: Keynes Versus Marx. *Indian Journal of Industrial Relations*, 45: 321–35.

Smith, P. (2002). Focus Founder Nets £75m Windfall From Sale. *Financial Times*, 30 November.

Stalmann, S. and Knipps, S. (2007). *How Important are Hedge Funds for the Investment Banking Industry?* Dresdner Kleinwort, 6 February.

Stevenson, R.L. (1883). *Treasure Island*. London: Cassell and Company.

Stigler, G.J. (1971). The Theory of Economic Regulation. *The Bell Journal of Economics and Management*, 2: 3–21.

Stiroh, K.J. and Rumble, A. (2006). The Dark Side of Diversification: The Case of US Financial Holding Companies. *Journal of Banking & Finance*, 30: 2131–61.

Stock, J.H. and Watson, M.W. (2002). Has the Business Cycle Changed and Why? *NBER Macroeconomics Annual*, 17: 159–218.

Stratton, A. (2010). Vince Cable Ploughs Ahead with Attack on City 'Spivs and Gamblers'. *Guardian*, 22 September.

Swagel, P. (2009). *The Financial Crisis: An Inside View*. Washington, DC: Brookings Papers on Economic Activity.

Taibbi, M. (2009). Goldman Sachs: The Great American Bubble Machine. *Rolling Stone*, 3 July: 1082–3.

Tait, N. (2010). EU Agrees Tougher Rules for Hedge Funds. *Financial Times*, 19 October.

Taleb, N.N. (2007). *The Black Swan. The Impact of the Highly Improbable*. London: Allen Lane.

—— (2009). Ten Principles for a Black Swan-proof World. *Financial Times*, 7 April.

Tavakoli, J.M. (2008). *Structured Finance and Collateralized Debt Obligations: New Developments in Cash and Synthetic Securitization (Wiley Finance)*. Hoboken, NJ: John Wiley & Sons.

Tawney, R.H. (1921 [1923]). *The Acquisitive Society*. London: G. Bell & Sons.

—— (1940). *Why the British People Fight*. New York: Workers Education Bureau Press.

Taylor, M., Lewis, P., and Gabbatt, A. (2010). Philip Green to be Target of Corporate Tax Avoidance Protest. *Guardian*, 29 November.

Tenorio, V. (2010). It Could Have Been Worse. *The Deal*, 8 January.

Terrill, R. (1973). *R. H. Tawney and his Times*. Harvard: Harvard University Press.

Tett, G. (2009). *Fool's Gold*. London: Little, Brown Book Group.

—— (2010). Silos and Silences. Why So Few People Spotted the Problems in Complex Credit and What That Implies For the Future. *Banque de France Financial Stability Review*, No. 14 Derivatives – Financial innovation and stability, July: 121–9.

Thomas, H. (2007). Economist Idol – Minsky's New Found Fame. *Financial Times Alphaville*, 20 August.

Thompson, H. (2009). The Political Origins of the Financial Crisis: The Domestic and International Politics of Fannie Mae and Freddie Mac. *Political Quarterly*, 80: 17–24.

Toynbee, P. (2007). Comment & Debate: This Wild West Capitalism is Born of Servility to the City: The Private Equity Sector, With its Attendant Risks to Employees, Pensioners and Tax Revenue, Should be Reined in and Regulated. *Guardian*, 5 June.

Traynor, I. (2010). David Cameron In Fresh Bid to Cap Brussels Budget. *Guardian*, 16 December.

Treanor, J. (2007). ABN Amro Shares Soar as Contest Hots Up. *Guardian*, 17 April.

—— (2010). Goldman Sachs Handed Record $550m Fine Over Abacus Transaction. *Guardian*, 16 July.

Treasury (2009). *Financial Regulatory Reform – A New Foundation: Rebuilding Financial Supervision and Regulation*. Washington, DC: Department of the Treasury.

Tufano, P. (2002). Financial Innovation. In G.M. Constantinides, M. Harris, and R.M. Stulz (eds.), *Handbook for the Economics of Finance. 1*, part 1, pp. 307–35.

Turner, A. (2004). Pensions: Challenges and Choices. First Report of the Pensions Commission. http://www.webarchive.org.uk/wayback/archive/20070801230000/ http://www.pensionscommission.org.uk/publications/2004/annrep/index.html accessed 13 July 2010.

—— (2009a). How to Tame Global Finance. *Prospect 162*, 27 August.

—— (2009b). *The Turner Review: A Regulatory Response to the Global Banking Crisis*. London: Financial Services Authority.

References

Turner, A. (2010a). *What Do Banks Do, What Should They Do and What Public Policies are Needed to Ensure Best Results for the Real Economy*. Cass Business School, London, 17 March.

—— (2010b). What Do Banks Do? Why Do Credit Booms and Busts Occur and What Can Public Policy Do About It?, *The Future of Finance: The LSE Report*. London: London School of Economics and Political Science.

UKFI (2009a). *Annual Report and Accounts 2008–9*. London: UK Financial Investments Ltd.

—— (2009b). *Shareholder Relationship Framework Document*. London: UK Financial Investments Ltd.

—— (2010). *Annual Report and Accounts 2009/10*. London: UK Financial Investments Ltd.

Valukas, A.R. (2010). Lehman Brothers Holdings Inc. Chapter 11 Proceedings Examiner's Report. http://lehmanreport.jenner.com/ accessed 14 May 2010.

Vennet, R.V. (2002). Cost and Profit Efficiency of Financial Conglomerates and Universal Banks in Europe. *Journal of Money, Credit, and Banking*, 34: 254–82.

Verdier, D. (2000). State and Finance in the OECD: Previous Trends and Current Change. *Politics and Society*, 28: 35–66.

Vilella Nilsson, A. (2010). Telling Stories About . . . Business Representation of Giant Corporations. Unpublished PhD Thesis submitted to the University of Manchester, School of Social Sciences.

Vina, G. (2009). Darling Levies 50% Tax on UK Bank Bonuses Above £25,000. *Bloomberg.com*, 9 December. http://www.bloomberg.com/apps/news?pid=newsarchive&sid=apBsS4lVEOM4 accessed 10 December 2010.

Vitols, S. (2005). German Corporate Governance in Transition: Implications of Bank Exit From Monitoring and Control. *International Journal of Disclosure and Governance*, 2: 357–67.

Volcker, P. (2009). Paul Volker: Think More Boldly. *Wall Street Journal*, 14 December.

von Clausewitz, C. (1873). *On War*, (trans. J. J. Graham). London: Truebner.

Walker, D. (2007). *Disclosure and Transparency in Private Equity: A Consultation Document*. July. London: BVCA.

Walker, S. (2007). Interview. *Radio 5 Live*, 9 October.

Walker, D. (2009). *A Review of Corporate Governance in UK Banks and Other Financial Industry Entities*. London: HM Treasury.

—— (2010). Britain Must Call For More Open Bank Pay Rules. *Financial Times*, 21 November.

Wallerstein, I. (1995). *Historical Capitalism with Capitalist Civilization*. London: Verso Books.

Warsh, K. (2007). Testimony of Mr Kevin M. Warsh, Member of the Board of Governors of the US Federal Reserve System. *Committee on Financial Services*, 11 July. Washington, DC: US House of Representatives.

White, L.J. (1996). Technological Change, Fiscal Innovation and Financial Regulation in the US: The Challenges for Public Policy. *Center for Financial Institutions Working Paper 97-33*, Wharton School Center for Financial Institutions, University of Pennsylvania.

White, M. and Saner, E. (2010). Dinner with David Cameron? How Parties are Bridging the Funding Gap. *Guardian*, 28 September.

Wigley, R. (2008). *London: Winning in a Changing World*. London: Merrill Lynch Europe.

Williams, K. and Williams, J. (1987). *A Beveridge Reader*. London: Allen & Unwin.

Wilson Committee (1980). *Report of the Committee to Review the Functioning of Financial Institutions*. Cmnd 7397, London: The Stationery Office.

Wilson, S. (2007). Have We Reached a Minsky Moment? *MoneyWeek*, 5 April.

Wyplosz, C. (2001). *The Fed and the ECB Briefing Notes. Committee for Economic and Monetary Affairs of the European Parliament*. Geneva: Graduate Institute of International Studies.

Index